# Why Do You Need This New Edition?

In today's complex society, succeeding in a business or professional setting requires that you work collaboratively with others, efficiently adapt to change (technical or otherwise), and communicate effectively. According to a report by the Center for Creative Leadership (2006), a successful leader must build relationships, collaborate, and effectively manage change. Each of these skills requires communication competence.

In an effort to help you meet the challenges and opportunities of the future and more easily transition from the academic setting to business and professional careers, we have revised our book for a fourth edition. The fourth edition of *Business and Professional Communication: Plans, Processes, and Performance* represents our most thorough revision to date. We scrutinized every paragraph of the manuscript and edited each for content, clarity, brevity, and readability. We condensed extended examples and explanations, and summarized even more information in figures and tables. Despite the addition of several new sections, the book is no longer than the previous edition. In addition to the numerous and detailed revisions throughout, what follows are some of the specific changes that are new to the fourth edition:

- Based on the suggestions of several reviewers, the order of some chapters has changed so the content in later chapters more clearly builds on the information covered in earlier ones. Interviewing (formerly covered in Chapter 2) is now covered in Chapter 5, and communicating in organizational groups and teams (formerly covered in Chapter 5) is now covered in Chapter 3.
- Technological innovations as they relate to the business world have been updated throughout the text while obsolete methods have been deleted.
- A new unit in the chapter on sales presentations describes methods of building customer trust in your company, products, marketing, and industry.
- Chapter 4 categorizes different kinds of sexual harassers and their behaviors, and new figures identify the four sources of power in interpersonal relationships as well as methods of overcoming informal network barriers for women and minorities.
- Chapter 5 includes new sections on the performance appraisal interview and goal planning.

- Chapter 7 explains database searches using EBSCO Information Services, to which many community college and university libraries subscribe.
- Chapter 8 uses new visuals and includes a new section explaining the most frequent problems of text visuals and how to correct them.
- Chapter 11 explains methods of building customer trust during sales meetings and presentations.
- Chapter 12 provides extensive new material on assessing some of the most common risks that people face.
- Chapter 13 updates some of the most recent crises that affected American business and government over the past few years, including JetBlue, the U.S. government during Hurricane Katrina, Major League Baseball's steroid scandal, *E-coli* in California spinach, and poisoned pet food from China.

# Business and Professional Communication

## Plans, Processes, and Performance

# Business and Professional Communication

## Plans, Processes, and Performance

### FOURTH EDITION

**James R. Disanza**

*Idaho State University*

**Nancy J. Legge**

*Idaho State University*

Boston · New York · San Francisco
Mexico City · Montreal · Toronto · London · Madrid · Munich · Paris
Hong Kong · Singapore · Tokyo · Cape Town · Sydney

**Acquisitions Editor:** Jeanne Zalesky
**Project Manager:** Lisa Sussman
**Marketing Manager:** Suzan Czajkowski
**Production Editor:** Beth Houston
**Editorial Production Service:** GGS Book Services
**Composition Buyer:** Linda Cox
**Manufacturing Buyer:** JoAnne Sweeney
**Electronic Composition:** GGS Book Services
**Cover Administrator:** Kristina Mose-Libon

For related titles and support materials, visit our online catalog at www.ablongman.com.

Between the time Website information is gathered and then published, it is not unusual for some sites to have closed. Also, the transcription of URLs can result in typographical errors. The publisher would appreciate notification where these errors occur so that they may be corrected in subsequent editions.

**Library of Congress Cataloging-in-Publication Data**

DiSanza, James R.
  Business and professional communication: plans, processes, and performance/James R. DiSanza, Nancy J. Legge.—4th ed.
    p. cm.
  Includes bibliographical references and index.
  ISBN-13: 978-0-205-58185-6
  ISBN-10: 0-205-58185-4
  1. Business communication.   2. Communication in organizations.   3. Communication in management.   4. Interpersonal communication.   I. Legge, Nancy J.   II. Title.

HF5718.D59  2009
658.4'5—dc22                                                                              2007048807

Printed in the United States of America

10  9  8  7  6  5  4  3  2          12  11  10  09  08

Credits appear on page 301, which constitutes an extension of the copyright page.

*For Alexis and Jacob*

# Contents

**5**   *Professional Interviews*    **72**

**PART TWO** • *Creating a Professional Presentation*    **99**

**6**   *Considering Audience Feedback*    **101**

**7**   *Preparing and Delivering Presentations*    **117**

# *Preface*

Given that many textbooks today never make it to a fourth edition, we're pleased to have had the opportunity to write this latest version of *Business and Professional Communication: Plans, Processes, and Performance*.

This textbook was originally designed as a radical departure from traditional B&P fare. We wanted to avoid repeating units covered in basic public speaking courses and avoid hashing theories from business management and social psychology. Instead, our focus remains on the basic *communication skills* required in any business or professional career. Like all previous editions, this book also introduces students to material that is largely ignored in other business and professional textbooks, including interpersonal politics, technical presentations, risk communication, and crisis communication.

In addition to a new emphasis on easy-to-read tables and charts and several new content units, every paragraph of this edition has been examined and edited for improved readability. The result is a tighter manuscript with a renewed emphasis on clarity and brevity. We hope that it meets the needs of both instructors and students in the business and professional course.

Writing a book is never an individual accomplishment. Without the help of a variety of people this project could not have been accomplished. The new edition has been enriched by the enthusiasm of and pedagogical suggestions made by our colleagues at Idaho State University, including Bruce Loebs, John Gribas, Jackie Czerepinski, Sharon Sowell, Monica Eckert, Tom Eckert, and KayLynn Broadhead.

We extend much gratitude to our editor, Lisa Sussman, and all the good people at Allyn and Bacon for their much-needed editorial assistance and support. We would also like to extend our thanks to the following reviewers who offered suggestions and provided feedback on this and prior editions of the book: Carol L. Adams-Means, University of Texas, San Antonio; Lauren Arnold, University of Pittsburgh–Johnstown; Timothy Ball, James Madison University; Eileen M. Berens, Villanova University; LeAnn M. Brazeal, Kansas State University; Edward C. Brewer, Murray State University; Patrice Buzzanell, Northern Illinois University; Judy H. Carter, Amarillo College; Russell Church, Middle Tennessee State University; Richard Crable, California State University–Sacramento; Lydia M. Daniels, Golden Gate University; Julie Davis, College of Charleston; Raymie McKerrow, Ohio University; Beverly Neville, Central New Mexico Community College; Susan Opt, University of Houston–Victoria; Collier Patton, Central Texas College; Tracy Russo, University of Kansas; Marilyn Shaw, University of Northern Iowa; and D. F. Treadwell, Westfield State Community College.

# 1

# *The Role of Communication in Business and the Professions*

The new millennium brought with it enormous changes in business and professional life. Globalization, international trade, the environmental movement, rising health-care costs, new technologies, reductions in the size and scope of government, international terrorism, and the constant pressure for increased productivity are just a few of the changes that accelerated during the early years of the new century. Despite these rapid changes, many people agree on one thing: A person's success in a business or professional career depends in large measure on the ability to communicate with others. Let's look at some of the contributions communication makes to employee motivation and productivity, organizational change, and individual career success.

Communication is crucial to employee motivation. There is a consensus among professionals that "truly effective communication does not occur until the employees understand how the 'big picture' affects them and their jobs. Changes in the economy, among competitors in the industry, or in the company as a whole must be translated into implications for each plant, job, and employee."[1] Even bad news can motivate employees. In a study of communication practices in business, researchers found that "the company with the highest bad-news to good-news ratio appeared to be performing very well, in terms of employee satisfaction and economic performance."[2] As the researcher explained, when bad news is candidly reported, problems can be solved or reduced before they are company threatening. In addition, reporting bad news makes good news more believable.

Whereas good communication provides a motivating work environment, ineffective communication often leads to a drop in the quality and quantity of work, higher absenteeism, and higher staff turnover.[3] According to Mike Greene and Mike Hollister, partners in Greene, Hollister, Inc., a Boca Raton, Florida, management consulting firm, "You can tell when communication is awry. Employees start leaving early . . . and behaving irresponsibly, even though you've done a good job of hiring."[4] A healthy communication environment means that employees enjoy going to work because it is satisfying and they like to share ideas with their coworkers and supervisors.

Effective communication is also important to managing organizational change. Faced with increased global competition, downsizing, restructuring, and the constant need to cut costs, U.S. corporations are making major changes to enhance productivity in every aspect of their business. Moreover, government agencies are not immune from these pressures. Because of various downsizing efforts, the federal government employed 62,000 fewer people in 1998 than in 1990.[5] Remaining employees face greater pressures for efficiency and productivity than ever. For example, in 2002 the Government Printing Office (GPO) was forced to bid against private contractors for the right to print the massive federal budget. The GPO submitted the lowest bid, winning the contract and saving taxpayers almost $120,000 over the cost of printing the previous year's budget, where no competing bids were taken.[6] Although these competitive pressures can be beneficial for companies and agencies, the changes can kill employee motivation and creativity.

Effective communication is one way to reconcile the competing needs of organizational change and employee security. A study of 10 leading U.S. companies revealed that "organizations can convert employees' concerns into support for major changes if they effectively address employees' fears about restructuring and reorganization. On the other hand, if communication is inadequate, employees will be more resistant to change."[7] To ensure creativity in a competitive environment, employees must be able to exchange mundane news. Innovativeness is spurred when people from different parts of an organization talk casually, compare notes on problems, and work together to create new solutions and opportunities.

Effective communication is also essential for individual career success. A study of job competencies showed that oral communication was more important than written communication for entry-level job seekers in business. The specific skills preferred by managers in this study include following instructions, listening skills, conversation skills, giving feedback, communicating with the public, meeting skills, presentation skills, handling customer complaints, and conflict resolution skills.[8] A 2004 study issued by the National Association of Colleges and Employers reports the top 10 qualities or skills employers look for in new hires.

1. Communication skills (verbal and written)
2. Honesty/integrity
3. Interpersonal skills (relates well to others)
4. Motivation/initiative
5. Strong work ethic
6. Teamwork skills (works well with others)
7. Analytical skills
8. Flexibility/adaptability
9. Computer skills
10. Detail oriented[9]

Although several of these skills relate to personality (e.g., honesty and motivation), many relate to communication, including verbal and written communication, interpersonal skills, teamwork skills, and analytic abilities. According to Annette Gregorich, a vice president of human resources for Multiple Zones International, "I've actually seen people lose promotions because they couldn't write a proposal or stand in front of the management team and make a presentation."[10]

Despite the emphasis on communication by many companies, employees often lack these skills. A survey of 470 human resource executives rated communication as the most critical employee shortcoming. Managers of training departments consistently cite communication as one of the most critical areas for additional employee development.[11]

One of the most pronounced threats to your career success is the outsourcing of jobs to other countries where labor is cheaper than it is in North America. Although this trend started in the early 1990s with manufacturing jobs, it is "moving quickly up the wage-skill chain from call-center employees to software engineers, medical specialists, lawyers, and financial analysts."[12] The growth of the Internet allows complex jobs from financial auditing to software development to be handled overseas, where the finished product is created and easily returned to the United States. The savings in labor can amount to as much as 60 percent over the same work performed in North America.[13] Rough estimates suggest that in addition to millions of manufacturing jobs, the United States has lost 400,000 to 500,000 information technology jobs to outsourcing in the past few years.[14] Jobs that can be easily routinized (broken down into discrete parts), even jobs in engineering, accounting, and financial analysis, are liable to move overseas in the coming years. For example, in 2000, Sab Maglione, a computer programmer living in New Jersey, was hired by an insurance company as an independent contractor, where he worked for very good money. But he soon found himself training the representatives of Tata Consulting, who eventually moved his work to India. His next contract in New York City paid half as much and ended when he was laid off in 2003 in favor of a foreign firm.[15]

Jobs that are not leaving the United States include management, sales, teaching, training, entrepreneurial, and consulting jobs that require directing and interacting with people, managing the work of others, and constant face-to-face consultation in work teams. Each of these jobs requires strong communication skills.

> No low wage worker in Shanghai, New Delhi, or Dublin will ever take Mark Ryan's job. No software will ever do what he does, either. That's because Ryan, 48, manages people—specifically, 100 technicians who serve half a million customers of Verizon Communications Inc. out of an office in Santa Fe Springs, Calif. A telephone lineman before moving up the corporate ladder, Ryan is earning a master's degree at Verizon's expense in organizational management, where he is studying topics like conflict resolution. That's heady stuff for a guy who used to climb poles.[16]

Strong communication skills play an important part in landing a good job that is safe from outsourcing. As we move further into the new century, communication skills will be the key to fulfilling your own professional aspirations.

But what exactly is communication, and how does it function? This chapter answers these questions by defining communication in two parts: First, we will define and explain the concept of meaning, and then we explain how messages flow between communicators. This leads us to the two overarching goals of most business and professional communication: shared meaning and ambiguity. We close the chapter with a discussion of strategic communication.

# *What Is Communication?*

The term *communication* has become an important one for people in business and industry. When pressed to define exactly what the term means, however, many managers are at a loss. What exactly is communication? For our purposes, **communication** is an exchange of messages between individuals for the purpose of creating or influencing the meaning that others assign to events. To fully understand our definition of communication, it is first necessary to understand our definition of *meaning;* then we will explain how communicators exchange messages.

## *Meaning*

**Meanings** are interpretations we develop for particular experiences. For example, going to a job interview is an experience that some relish and others despise. The difference is in the interpretation or meaning that each person associates with the activity.[17] The meaning that we give an event is not carried by the event itself; rather, events gain particular meanings as people converse about them. For example, most people hate the game playing and intrigue associated with organizational politics. Nevertheless, strategic thinking in organizational politics can be enjoyable. If you agree, your interpretation of organizational politics may change. As such, the meaning of any situation not only varies from person to person but also can change for individuals over time, based on their communication with others.

    **Shared meaning** occurs when two people share agreement in their interpretation of an experience or event.[18] Shared meaning may develop independently—for example, when two people learn that they both hate job interviews. More frequently, we attempt to negotiate shared meaning with others through communication. When businesspeople talk about effective communication, they usually mean communication that creates shared meaning between people. For example, salespeople work to persuade potential buyers to share their assessment of a product's value. On the other hand, **ambiguity** is the opposite of shared meaning. It occurs

*Communication is an exchange of messages for the purpose of creating or influencing meaning.*

Credit: Digital Vision/Getty Images

when a message sender's intent and the receiver's interpretation do not correspond.[19] Although businesspeople tend to emphasize the importance of shared meaning, ambiguity plays an important role in a variety of professional communication contexts, including organizational politics and organizational crises.

Communication creates or influences shared meaning through the use of signs and symbols. **Signs** are involuntary expressions of emotion and are usually nonverbal rather than verbal cues. Facial expressions, eye contact, posture, gesture, and vocal variations are all examples of nonverbal signs. Signs are involuntary because they are not normally under conscious control. When angry, you do not need to think about raising your voice, scowling, and slamming your fist. You exhibit these cues as a natural extension of your anger. As such, signs usually illustrate and emphasize the verbal portion of a message, although they can contradict a message, producing ambiguity and confusion for the listener.

**Symbols,** on the other hand, are voluntary expressions that stand for or represent something else. Symbols are voluntary because the choice of whether and how to express yourself symbolically is more conscious than is the case for signs. Letters are symbols because they stand for certain sounds. Words are symbols because they stand for objects, ideas, or states of mind. Symbols are necessary because my picture of a tree for example, cannot be transmitted to you directly. Instead, our culture has agreed that the word *tree* stands for objects with roots, a trunk, branches, and leaves or needles. If my use of the word *tree* creates a corresponding picture of a similar tree in your head, then this symbol has created shared meaning. If, however, when I use the word *tree* I am thinking of a Joshua tree, a variety common in the desert Southwest, but the word makes you think of a maple tree, the symbol has been only partly successful in helping us share meaning. However, sharing meaning is never as simple as selecting the one correct symbol to represent an idea. Effective communicators consider the logical and psychological meanings of their symbols.

To create shared meaning, the communicator must consider the logical relationship between a symbol and the thing it represents. This involves selecting the right words to stand for the objects, events, or states of mind to which the speaker refers. Although tools such as dictionaries aid this selection, the chore is complicated by the fact that almost every word has more than one definition. If I said, in response to the CEO's motivational presentation, "The boss's rhetoric is quite nice," this could be taken in two ways depending on my meaning for the term *rhetoric.* In one meaning, rhetoric is the art or science of using words effectively; thus my comment is a compliment. If, on the other hand, I meant rhetoric as artificial eloquence, showiness, and unnecessary elaboration of language and literary style, then my comment is an ironic insult. Multiple definitions increase the beauty and power of language but do so at the cost of precision.

In addition to the sheer number of definitions for each symbol, the fact that they are abstract (removed from the things they represent) further complicates the possibility of shared meaning. This abstraction is sometimes depicted as a ladder of possibilities.[20]

At the bottom of the ladder in Figure 1.1 is an event, an employee's lateness for work. The statements above the line are symbolic, meaning they represent the actual event. As we climb the ladder of abstraction, we increase the power of our description, moving from describing three events to describing the employee's general approach to work. But that increase in power also increases the ambiguity of the description. All language operates on a continuum that at one end may be highly precise but only minimally descriptive and at the other end is broader but more ambiguous.

In addition to the logical properties of language, psychological meanings must also be considered. Psychological meanings are the private associations that individuals have for a

**FIGURE 1.1**    *The Ladder of Abstraction*

| | |
|---|---|
| Symbols | You are a poor worker. |
| | You have a poor attitude toward your work. |
| | Your poor attitude is reflected in poor attendance. |
| | You have been late a variety of times this month. |
| | You have been late three times this month. |
| An Event | Late for work three times. |

symbol. For example, although the dictionary definition for the term *radiation* focuses exclusively on the emission of a wave or particle from an unstable substance such as plutonium, the psychological meanings some people have for *radiation* include accident, cancer, death, and so forth. These idiosyncratic meanings remind us that ambiguity lurks in the use of any symbol. If shared meaning is an important goal, then communicators must take account of psychological meanings through careful word choice and clear definitions.

Signs and symbols have enormous influence on the meanings people give events. (Remember that events do not have meanings.) People use symbols and signs to label or relabel events, thereby changing the meaning an event has for others.

Although automobile dealers still sell used cars, they don't often refer to them that way anymore. The label "used" lacks the class and cachet desired by car buyers, even those of us who can't afford a new vehicle. Thus the phrase "previously owned" has jumped into our language to remove the negative stigma (interpretation) associated with a "used car."

History is rife with moments when people change a label, hoping to persuade others to think differently about something.

Almost all persuasion is based on the ability of signs and symbols to label or relabel events for others. This persuasive function is vital for a variety of professional goals, including sales presentations and crisis communication. Through the use of signs and symbols people attempt to influence and manage meaning for others in organizations. Let's examine how signs and symbols are combined into messages.

## *The Flow of Messages*

The model depicted in Figure 1.2 illustrates the flow of messages between people.

The two large circles represent **source/receivers,** people who send and receive messages. Because communication is a circular process, we could begin anywhere in the model, but for convenience's sake we will begin with the left source/receiver. In the upper-left quadrant of the circle is **experience,** which is anything that happened to us in the past. Follow the arrow from experience to meaning. As stated earlier, meanings are the interpretations or attitudes we assign to our experiences. The subscript "1" after meanings emphasizes that these are unique to the individual and cannot be transmitted whole to another person.

For purposes of simplicity, meanings can be classified into two categories: cognitive and emotional. **Emotional meanings** are feelings such as sadness, surprise, and curiosity. Feelings are usually expressed directly in the form of signs, although it is also possible to put feelings into words, such as "I feel great about this project." On the other hand, **cognitions** are ideas, and before these can be sent they must be encoded into symbols. **Encoding** is the process of selecting symbols

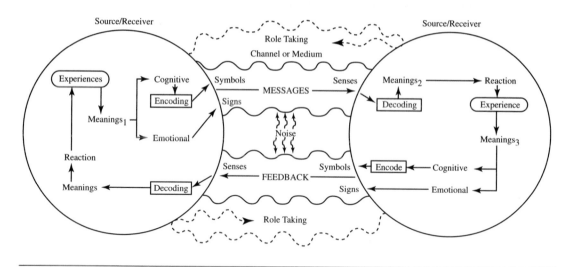

**FIGURE 1.2**   *A Model of Message Transmission*

*Source*: Adapted from a model by Christopher L. Johnstone, Pennsylvania State University. Reprinted with permission.

to stand for or represent cognitions. When trying to share meaning, we select symbols that we hope represent similar meanings in the receiver. We have covered some of the complexities of this selection process.

    **Messages** are composed of signs and symbols that travel along a **channel.** Common channels for oral communication include audio, visual, and tactile channels. **Noise** can interfere with the communication anywhere in the channel and tends to produce ambiguity. **Physical noise** is any concrete interference with the process of communication, such as the speaker's talking too fast, a construction crew working in the next room, or children crying in the audience. **Psychological noise** is any internal interference with listening, such as a bias against the speaker or a dislike for the subject.

    After the message completes its passage along the channel, it encounters the sense organs of the other source/receiver. The message is **decoded,** meaning that the receiver selects meanings to attach to the signs and symbols. It is important to emphasize that meanings are not sent; rather, the receiver selects meaning from within herself and attaches that meaning to the message. This is the reason for the subscript "2" behind meanings. The message then becomes part of the receiver's experience, which the receiver may further examine and interpret.

    Once a message is fully interpreted, this meaning becomes part of a new message, which includes both cognitive and emotional components. The cognitive components are encoded into symbols, and the emotional components are emitted as signs that travel along a channel. These are received by the first source/receiver through the senses, decoded, and then interpreted to create a new meaning.

    The return message is referred to as "feedback." **Feedback** includes information about how the first message was received. For example, a person who shakes his or her head no and frowns while you finish a proposal is indicating how the message was received. Feedback is valuable for sharing meaning because it allows us to estimate the degree of shared meaning that

**BOX 1.1 •** *Interview: Rick Phillips (Director of Public Relations and Government, J. R. Simplot Corporation, Boise, Idaho)*

(Simplot is a large, privately held agribusiness company with manufacturing and processing interests in food, livestock, and fertilizers.)

*In your opinion, how important are communication skills for young employees looking for their first job?*

The quality of your communication skills determines, in large measure, the quality of your life. For example, the communication you exchange with your spouse determines the quality of your marriage. The communication skills you display at work determine the quality of your career. Your communication abilities have far-reaching implications. Because everyone works in teams today, it doesn't matter if you are a manager, a mining engineer, or a welder. If you can't communicate effectively and persuasively, then you aren't going to make it.

*What are some of the common communication problems you encounter when dealing with internal and external audiences at Simplot?*

When dealing with external groups, one of our biggest problems is coming to understand the public's point of view. A large company like Simplot tends to hear from two groups: the people who love us and the people who hate us. Although we presume the general public fits somewhere between the extremes, figuring out exactly what that means is difficult. Sometimes the people who hate you are so loud it's hard to distinguish their concerns from the concerns of the average person. At one plant, which makes fertilizer, we started a community advisory panel of citizens to help us get a better handle on that vast middle area of public opinion. The group helps us understand the opinions of our audience, especially the vast, and usually silent, middle.

*I guess it's difficult to learn what an audience thinks and believes about an issue.*

Yes. One of my first experiences at Simplot drove this home. I was asked to meet with an environmental group in town that was concerned about pollution from the plant. I spoke a little, but tried, mainly, to listen to them and understand their point of view.

What I discovered was that they didn't have a single point of view, but a variety of issues and concerns that were dispersed unevenly throughout the group. At one point, one lady said the community would be better off without my chemical plant in town. Other members of the group disagreed. They wanted the jobs and economic benefits of the plant but wanted us to continue cutting pollution. While some members were mainly concerned with air pollution, others were interested in talking about water pollution. Although this group claimed to speak for a variety of environmentally active citizens in town, you couldn't categorize their concerns and issues in any simple way. I needed to talk with them to start to understand the variety and diversity involved. This wasn't a whole group of anti-Simplot people. Throughout the time I worked with them, I adapted my approach to various members, and I also learned that some members were exceptionally difficult to work with at all.

*What are some of the communication problems you deal with when addressing internal audiences?*

One of the things we are struggling with right now are new communication technologies like e-mail and other Web-based communication channels. There are a lot of technologies that can be used to send messages. But sending messages is not the same as achieving communication. New technologies present efficiency-versus-effectiveness dilemmas. Managers may put out a mass e-mail and think everyone will read it the same way they meant it, but it doesn't work that way. People often read things in an entirely different way, and sometimes that reading is based on the channel that's used. We had an incident in one of our offices that illustrates this. Like most companies, we must constantly evaluate every operation, every position in the company to make sure it's paying its own way and adding value to our products and services. One of our executives sent a letter home, as a courtesy, to all employees explaining the latest round of analysis and review the company would be going through and that no major layoffs or cuts were planned as a result of the review. Well, every spouse who opened that letter decided that their husband or wife would soon be out of work. The way they read it was the exact opposite of the manager's intent. Part of that was the channel through which the message was sent. I argue that face-to-face communication is still important in many, many instances. There are some times, some messages, where nothing can replace face-to-face interaction. The trick is being able to decipher which channel is appropriate for which message.

exists between speakers. Quizzical looks, for example, are a sign that the speaker has not succeeded in the quest to share meaning.

The wavy dashed lines from each source/receiver indicate the ability to view one's own communication from the point of view of the other person—to put yourself in the other person's shoes, so to speak. This form of **role taking** involves anticipating a reaction to a message rather than waiting for the person's feedback.[21] Thus, role taking can help a speaker anticipate difficulties or objections and develop ways to overcome these problems prior to actually speaking. As such, role taking also serves to reduce ambiguity and increases the chances of sharing meaning.

By representing the flow of messages, the model depicts the components and processes of communication. Encoding and decoding are complicated and, depending on how they are handled by communicators, serve to increase either shared meaning or ambiguity. Noise can interfere with message transmission, increasing the likelihood of ambiguity. Feedback and role taking facilitate the process of shared meaning. We will refer to elements of this model throughout the rest of the book. The interview in this chapter discusses a number of elements of the communication model.

## Goals of Communication

The model presented in this chapter suggests two overarching goals for communication in business and the professions. These goals are the foundation for the material in later chapters, and we will refer to them repeatedly throughout the book.

### Shared Meaning Is the Objective of Most Business and Professional Communication

As we have noted, shared meaning results when the intent of the sender and the receiver's interpretation correspond. When consultants, for example, talk about converting employee fears about restructuring into support for needed changes or discuss the importance of corporate values, they encourage managers to create shared meaning. Selling a product or service also requires shared meaning. Informing other people about safety or environmental procedures depends on the ability to share information accurately. In short, shared meaning is vital to a variety of organizational functions and goals.

However, shared meaning is not an "either–or" proposition; it exists on a continuum. At the low end of the continuum is **contractual shared meaning.**[22] In this form of sharing, two parties each give up something they would rather not part with to get something valuable from the other person. For example, salespeople might not want to put forth extra effort to exceed sales quotas but do so in order to receive a bonus at the end of the month. Similarly, organizations do not want to spend money on bonuses but do so to increase sales. Contractual shared meaning does not require that employees agree with the organization's sales goals or the choices of products it markets. All that is required is for each party to give up something in order to receive something else that cannot be achieved alone.

For example, despite their importance, safety regulations are notoriously difficult to enforce in manufacturing operations. Employees see regulations as excessive, and the demands of the job encourage drift away from anything that is not directly connected to productivity. However, rewarding safe workers and punishing unsafe workers will improve compliance regardless of whether the employee thinks the regulations are important. This minimal form of shared meaning is the basis of many professional interactions, and we will discuss it more fully in the chapters on interpersonal and group communication.

A second kind of shared meaning represents relatively greater correspondence between sender and receiver; we refer to this as **consensual shared meaning**.[23] When parties share consensus, they agree about basic objectives and values. If an employee follows safety precautions because she believes they protect both the employee and the organization, she expresses a point of view shared by the plant management. Consensual shared meaning is the basis for most persuasive communication and is covered in the chapters on persuasive proposals and sales communication. Although it is safe to say that shared meaning is an important goal for business and professional communicators, there are times when ambiguity is valuable.

### *Ambiguity Is the Objective of Some Business and Professional Communication*

As we indicated in our model, ambiguity is a constant presence in the communication process. Ambiguity occurs when there is little overlap between a sender's intent and a receiver's interpretation. It is a myth, however, to believe that effective communication must always be clear.

Ambiguity is useful to leaders developing group or organizational mission statements. Ambiguous mission statements provide a sense of shared direction while leaving room for individual interpretation.[24] Ford's "Quality Is Job 1" assertion clearly sets company direction but leaves employees free to develop their own means to achieve quality. We will discuss a leader's use of ambiguity as a motivational technique in the chapter on groups and teams.

Ambiguity also plays a vital role in organizational crisis communication. In circumstances in which a clear apology creates unacceptably high legal liabilities, an ambiguous apology may be warranted. We cover the methods and ethical implications of the ambiguous apology in the chapter on crisis communication. Although less vital than shared meaning, ambiguity serves important functions in professional settings.

## *Effective Communication is Audience Centered*

The audience is vital to the success of all communication. In the professions, people communicate to accomplish goals. If these goals could be achieved individually, people wouldn't bother with communication. Thus we communicate to get a desired response from an audience. What does the audience know about the topic? Do they have a positive or negative attitude toward it? How did they arrive at that attitude? Knowing the answers to such questions can help a communicator adjust the content and delivery of the message, increasing the likelihood of the desired response.

The communication model indicates two methods of adapting to the audience. By paying attention to feedback, a communicator can adapt to better suit the audience. Does the audience need you to slow down? Have you lost your supervisor during a complicated explanation? By paying attention to feedback, a communicator can answer such questions and make appropriate adjustments.

Role taking is another means of assessing the audience. While role taking, a communicator imagines how others will react to his message. Ling, for example, owns a small landscaping company and wants to get a contract at the new shopping mall. After sketching out his sales pitch to the mall's management team, he attempts to imagine the members' concerns about or objections to his proposal. Are they concerned about quality? Is cost a concern? Will they want to know about liability insurance? Are they concerned about the small size of the company? The answers to these questions will help Ling adjust his content to address relevant concerns. Effective role taking allows communicators to adapt to feedback prior to actual interaction, thereby increasing the chances that receivers will respond in the desired way. Another term for role taking is *audience analysis,* which we cover extensively in Chapter 6.

## Effective Communication Is Strategic

As we have noted, people communicate to accomplish individual, group, and organizational goals that they cannot accomplish alone. Achieving your own and others' goals during communication requires the ability to think strategically. **Strategic communication** is a conscious process wherein the communicator specifies the goals that he or she wants to accomplish, learns about the audience and its position regarding the goals, and then selects communication tactics that will move the audience closer to those goals. This process is depicted in Figure 1.3.

**Strategy** is a term that refers to the objectives or goals that you want to accomplish. Prior to delivering any important message, you should stop to consider the short- and long-range goals you have for that situation. Short-range goals are those that can be immediately obtained from a particular audience in a particular setting. For example, Lainey, the public relations director for a chemical manufacturing company, needs to conduct a public relations campaign to achieve the short-range goal of reducing the community's concern about her plant's safety record.

Long-range goals, however, can't be achieved with a single message or within a single setting, but may take years and many messages to accomplish. Lainey's long-range goals include creating a positive impression of the plant as an important economic asset and

**FIGURE 1.3**   *A Model of the Process of Strategic Communication*

contributor to community causes. Lainey aims most of her campaign at changing the community's impression of safety, but she also plans to include information about the firm's importance to the local economy and even mention its charitable contributions. Although these comments probably won't change a lot of opinions, they are at least a first step to achieving her long-range plan. A person's short- and long-range goals are referred to as the person's strategy, which is depicted by a targetlike circle on the right side of Figure 1.3.

Step two in the strategic communication process involves learning about the audience's position regarding your goal. As we stated in the previous section, role taking and its more formal counterpart, audience analysis, are two methods by which communicators can learn about the knowledge and attitudes of the audience. Like most risk communicators, for example, Lainey knows that she must learn about her audience prior to structuring messages for them. If she assumes that the plant's safety record makes the public fearful when they are not, or, worse yet, assumes people aren't concerned about the safety record when they really are, then her persuasive message is likely to backfire. In order to learn more about the audience, Lainey plans to conduct a brief phone survey of 100 community leaders to find out what they know about the chemical plant's safety record and their perceptions of that record. The results of this survey will provide Lainey with an understanding of what the audience knows and believes about the plant's safety record and will help her make decisions about message channels, structure, and content.

The third step in the strategic communication process involves selecting specific **communication tactics** (represented by the arrow in Figure 1.3) that are designed to move the audience toward the intended goal. After Lainey discovered that people believed the plant had a poor safety record and were disturbed about the risk of a chemical spill, she decided to develop a persuasive campaign to reassure the community that the risks were small, that the plant was ready for any spill, and that the plant's safety record had improved. Lainey decided to host regular plant tours for the general public because she knew that making an audience more familiar with a risky situation tends to reduce their fears (see Chapter 12). She also decided to hold several public meetings and explain the plant's safety record in an interview with the environmental writers at the local paper. Once she selected these channels Lainey needed to develop specific informative and persuasive appeals that would explain the plant's procedures and reassure the public about their safety. She also needed to prepare responses to potentially hostile questions from community members. And, because the interview with the newspaper was to be conducted with a knowledgeable expert in environmental reporting, her comments to this person had to be set up differently than her comments to the lay public. Lainey used her short- and long-range goals and her understanding of audience knowledge and perceptions.

Strategic communication is a complicated process of focusing your goals, anticipating the audience, and consciously making tactical choices. Fortunately, strategic communication abilities can be improved with practice. If you devote yourself to learning the material in this book, you will achieve significant progress in your ability to think and communicate strategically.

## *Summary*

Despite enormous changes in business and the professions, most people agree that effective communication is vital for both individual and organizational success. Communication is the exchange of messages between individuals for the purpose of creating or influencing the meaning that others assign to events. Meanings are interpretations or attitudes that we develop for particular experiences. Events do not have a particular meaning; rather, meaning is given to events by people, and meanings change through communication with others. Shared meaning occurs when two people agree in their interpretation of an event. Ambiguity occurs when a message sender's intent and the receiver's interpretation do not correspond.

The communication model depicts source/receivers who want to influence each other's interpretations. Interpretations are influenced through signs and symbols. Signs are involuntary (usually nonverbal) emotional expressions. Symbols are voluntary expressions that stand for or represent something else. Signs and symbols form messages that travel through a channel that can be affected by noise. Messages are decoded by the receiver when he or she selects meanings from within him or herself to attach to the signs and symbols. This meaning is always somewhat different from the meaning that the original person intended to communicate. The return message is referred to as feedback. Role taking is the ability of communicators to put themselves in the position of other people to anticipate their reaction to a message. Feedback and role taking can improve shared meaning.

Shared meaning is the goal of most business and professional communication. Ambiguity, on the other hand, is sometimes useful in professional settings. Effective communication is audience centered, meaning that a communicator must adapt to the receiver's needs and preferences for the greatest effect. Effective communication is strategic, meaning that communicators must adjust their tactics for different audiences and goals.

## Questions and Exercises

1. Can you think of an instance of communication in which a misunderstanding occurred because someone didn't take account of the logical or psychological meaning of a term or phrase? What were the consequences of this misunderstanding? What could have been done to prevent the misunderstanding?

2. In the communication model, what happens to individuals who do not pay attention to feedback? Can you provide an example of this kind of miscommunication? What were the consequences of this problem?

3. Have you ever had a job in which you shared consensus with most managerial decisions and actions? If so, how did your approach to this job differ from other jobs where you were merely fulfilling a contractual agreement?

4. Describe some of the things managers do to encourage consensual shared meaning among employees. Are these techniques effective? Why or why not?

5. Identify a skill that you have acquired by tracing its acquisition through the four stages of skill development cited in this chapter. What level of competence do you have now in this skill?

6. In this chapter we suggested that symbols are used to influence the meanings that people apply to events. The following quotes present two opinions about the safety of irradiated foods. Advocates of irradiation argue that exposing fruits, vegetables, and meats to doses of radiation kills harmful pests and bacteria more effectively and more safely than chemical-based pesticides. Dissenters claim the process is dangerous.

   The vault has concrete walls 12 to 20 feet thick. A door in the vault opens, and food enters on a conveyor belt. The door closes behind it. A shutter opens, and rods of radioactive cobalt 60, the waste products from nuclear reactors, or rods of cesium 137, the waste products of atomic bomb construction, rise out of a bed of water. The food is exposed to a radioactive dose of 100,000 rads. The rods go back down into the water, and the shutter closes. The door opens, the food leaves. Now it is ready for you to eat.[25]

   Now from a proponent of food irradiation:

   Not even the most ardent food irradiation opponent argues that the process makes food radioactive, but as radiation chemistry has shown, irradiation does create tiny numbers of molecules known as radiolytic products—formed when the ionizing energy from a radioactive isotope or a linear accelerator splits food molecules, creating new ones.[26]

How is the word choice and sentence structure in each quotation designed to influence your interpretation of food irradiation? Point to specific words or sentences and the effect they are designed to have on your attitude. Does either of these quotations influence your attitude toward food irradiation? Why or why not?

## *Notes*

1. Young, M., and J. E. Post, "Managing to Communicate, Communicating to Manage: How Leading Companies Communicate with Employees," *Organizational Dynamics* 22, 1 (1993): 41.
2. Ibid., 39.
3. Dennis, M. C., "Effective Communication Will Make Your Job Easier," *Business Credit* 97 (1995): 45.
4. Nelton, S., "Face to Face," *Nation's Business,* November 1995, 22.
5. Wessel, D., "In March to a Surplus, Government Changed in Many Small Ways," *Wall Street Journal,* 3 February 1998, A1, A11.
6. Will, G., "Spat Shows How a Little Competition Will Save Taxpayers," *Chicago Sun-Times,* 22 December 2002 (online: www.suntimes.com/output/will/cst-edt-geo22.html).
7. Young and Post, 31.
8. Maes, J. D., T. G. Weldy, and M. L. Icenogle, "A Managerial Perspective: Oral Communication Competency Is Most Important for Business Students in the Workplace," *Journal of Business Communication* 34 (1997): 67–80.
9. "Recreate Yourself: From Student to the Perfect Job Candidate," Special Report from the National Association of Colleges and Employers (www.uncwil.edu/stuaff/career/nacearticle.htm).
10. Lancaster, H., "Making the Break from Middle Manager to a Seat at the Top," *Wall Street Journal,* 7 July 1998, B1.
11. Brown, R. M., "Rethinking the Approach to Communication Training," *Technical Communication* 41, August 1994, 406–415.
12. Tyson, L. D., "Outsourcing: Who's Safe Anymore?" *BusinessWeek,* 23 February 2004, 26.
13. Ibid.
14. Ibid.
15. Coy, P., "The Future of Work," *BusinessWeek,* 22 March 2004, 50–52.
16. Ibid.
17. DiSanza, J. R., "Shared Meaning as a Sales Inducement Strategy: Bank Teller Responses to Frames, Reinforcements, and Quotas," *Journal of Business Communication* 30 (1993): 133–180.
18. Harris, L., and V. E. Cronen, "A Rules-Based Model for the Analysis and Evaluation of Organizational Communication," *Communication Quarterly* 27 (1979): 12–28.
19. Eisenberg, E. M., "Ambiguity as Strategy in Organizational Communication," *Communication Monographs* 51 (1984): 227–242.
20. Hayakawa, S. I., *Language in Action* (New York: Harcourt Brace, 1942).
21. Blumer, H., "Symbolic Interaction," in *Interdisciplinary Approaches to Human Communication,* ed. W. Budd and B. D. Ruben (Rochelle Park, CA: Hayden, 1979), 135–153.
22. DiSanza.
23. Ibid.
24. Eisenberg.
25. Gibbs, G., "Zap, Crackle, Pop. Irradiated Foods Aren't Coming; They're Here." *The Progressive,* September 1987, 22.
26. Leslie, J. "Food Irradiation," *Atlantic Monthly,* September 1990, 28.

# Part I

## Dyadic and Group Communication

# 2

# *Listening and Feedback in Organizational Relationships*

Listening is one of the most important communication activities in organizational settings. For example, a large engineering firm employed a team of 24 engineers and an expensive consultant on a military project. The team encountered a critical problem that threatened to delay the project and cost the firm heavily in penalties for lateness under its government contract. The project head phoned the consultant and assigned him to work out a solution. Later, the project head learned that the consultant had been working on a different phase of the problem than the one for which a solution was required. Although both men believed they understood each other, this listening error cost the company $150,000 in lost person hours and penalties paid to the government.[1] Effective listening is vital for shared meaning and may be one of the most straightforward, least expensive ways to increase organizational productivity.

There is ample evidence that listening errors are abundant. Studies done by University of Minnesota Professor of Rhetoric Ralph Nichols suggest that the listening efficiency of the average college graduate is quite low. Nichols measured short-term listening efficiency (the ability to recall major details of a 10-minute presentation) at only 50 percent. Long-term listening efficiency (the ability to recall major details after several months) sank to 25 percent.[2] According to Lyman K. Steil, head of Communication Consultants Associated, 80 percent of people surveyed rated their listening ability as average or below average.[3] Poor listening causes appointments to be rescheduled, necessitates shipments to be rerouted, and hurts employee morale. Despite their importance, our listening skills are woefully inadequate given the demands of the modern business environment.

Listening is also vital to personal success. A study of employees at a daily newspaper indicates that effective listening plays a pivotal role in how others evaluate your competence, and such perceptions play a large role in advancement within any organization.[4] A second study examined the relationship between communication skills and upward mobility in a large East Coast insurance company and found that the ability to view the world through others' eyes, a view partly learned through listening to others, was centrally related to a person's chance of promotion within the organization.[5] Writing for the *Wall Street Journal,* Hal Lancaster says, "To get what you want in your career, stop talking and start listening and observing. Instead of aggressively selling yourself, learn how others communicate, how they process information and what their needs are."[6] In this chapter, we discuss methods of improving two forms of listening

# *Recall Listening*

**Recall listening** involves a person's ability to correctly interpret and remember the content of another person's message. Recall listening includes four processes. **Receiving** the message means that you hear and process the message that another communicates. **Attending** to the message involves a listener's ability to focus on the message and direct his or her attention toward it without distraction. If you have ever been to a noisy party, but still heard your name mentioned across the room, you know the difference between merely hearing a message and focusing your attention on it. The act of focusing brings the message clearly into conscious attention and forces background noise to fade from awareness. **Assigning meaning** to the message means assigning an interpretation to it. In most situations (excluding the need for ambiguity, discussed in Chapter 1), the ideal interpretation is similar to the meaning the sender had in mind when encoding the message. Finally, **remembering** is the ability to store and recall the major themes of a conversation for use in later decision making.[7] Listening is not a genetically determined trait and can be improved by practicing the following techniques.[8]

## *Motivate Yourself to Listen*

People who lack motivation to listen are ineffective because, from the outset, they regard the content as dull, and listening appears unimportant.[9] Studies indicate that when subjects are promised a reward for remembering the content of a presentation, their listening improves over the listening of those not promised any reward.[10]

To combat the motivation problem, good listeners admit that a subject may sound dry or that a presentation or group meeting may not be directly related to their job, but they then decide that, being trapped anyway, they will use this situation to their advantage. They develop motivation by listening for something that benefits them.[11] Good listeners search the messages for information that will provide insight into the speaker's background that could help in later interactions. They search for an idea that can be turned into a profitable product or save the organization money. As you search the message for these qualities or ideas, your motivation increases, as does your focus and attention on the message.

### *Focus on Content Rather Than Delivery*

In the visual age in which we live—one dominated by images on movie, television, computer, and cell phone screens—we have come to expect that messages will include slick delivery. It is not surprising, then, that we are turned off by more traditional message forms.[12] If we spend our time judging and critiquing the delivery, however, we do not attend to the message, and recall listening is hindered.[13]

Effective listeners are able to make a quick judgment about a speaker's delivery or the production qualities of a video, but they return their attention to the message.[14]

### *Defer Judgment*

One of the most severe barriers to effective listening is the tendency to become emotionally excited when a speaker's views differ from our own or when a speaker uses emotional language. In such cases, poor listeners become preoccupied by trying to calculate a response to the disagreeable argument or language. At such times, they no longer focus on the message but concentrate on methods of embarrassing or humiliating the speaker when he or she finishes. This seriously compromises the listener's ability to assign the appropriate meaning.[15]

To solve this problem, listeners should defer judgment until they have heard and properly understand everything the speaker has to say. Deferring judgment is easier when the listener tries to empathize with the speaker or see the speaker's point of view. Maintain emotional control, and get back to the task of listening.

### *Take Advantage of Thought Speed*

Although studies show that humans can think at a speed of over 400 words per minute, most people, be they in groups or in public presentations, speak at approximately 125 words a minute.[16] According to Sara W. Lundsteen, a professor at the University of North Texas, leftover thinking time leads to four mental patterns, only one of which is indicative of good listening.[17] These patterns are illustrated in Figure 2.1.

Our ability to rapidly process information often leads to **small mental departures** from the line of conversation. When used as a means to focus on the message, these small departures can aid a listener's ability to interpret and understand the speaker. However, during some conversations we allow our thoughts to depart more radically from the line of conversation. Imagine, for instance, a manager talking with a group of her employees about Friday's product-testing session. One employee's thoughts, however, turn to his vacation, which also begins on Friday. The second diagram in Figure 2.1 illustrates the tendency to use extra thought time to focus exclusively on issues **tangential** to the line of conversation. In a third pattern, listeners carry on a **private argument** that is related to, but not directly connected with, the line of conversation. For example, when another employee hears about Friday's product testing, he rehearses all of the reasons he believes the product won't be successful, getting wrapped up in what he plans to say to help kill the product's eventual release. Finally, **large departures** represent letting one's mind play extensively with thoughts that are only minimally related to the conversation (see Figure 2.1). For example, a third employee in the meeting who is very committed to the new product thinks extensively about changes that might make the product more appealing, should the tests go poorly.

Effective listeners take only small departures from the line of conversation and apply that spare thinking time to the message. Spend your departure time identifying developmental,

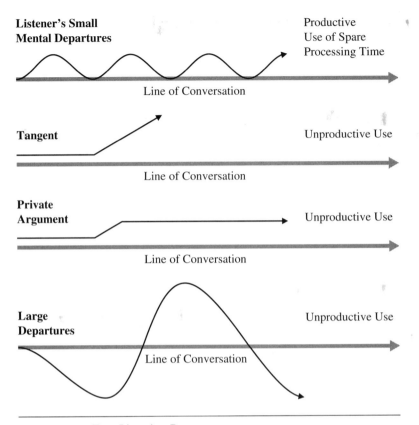

**FIGURE 2.1**    *Four Listening Patterns*

*Source*: Adapted from Lundsteen, S. W., "Metacognitive Listening," in *Perspectives on Listening,* ed. A. D. Wolven and C. G. Coakley (Norwood, NJ: Ablex, 1993), 106–123.

organizational, and argument tactics used by the speaker. How are the speaker's ideas structured? What kinds of evidence support the topic? How does the message fit together in a coherent unit (if it does cohere at all)? Review and summarize the speaker's points. Using thought speed appropriately will improve your recall listening.[18]

## *Listen for Meaning*

Listeners are often too focused on the words that speakers use. However, the meaning of a message comes not only from the words but also from the nonverbal cues. Nonverbal cues such as vocal qualities, facial expressions, and gestures constitute a large portion of the meaning of any message. According to some estimates, between 60 and 90 percent of the meaning of a message is nonverbal in nature.[19] Nonverbal cues comment on and help us interpret the words in the message. Imagine seeing this sign in a restaurant:

People who think the servers are rude should see the manager.

The message takes on two meanings depending on how it is read (with what nonverbal cues). One interpretation suggests that anyone who has a problem should take it to the manager. A second interpretation suggests that the manager might be even more rude than the servers.

Nonverbal cues help us assign meaning to messages. A simple response to a statement about whether people have a problem with the new proposal may elicit a "no" reply that suggests there is no problem, or "no" may be said in such a way that it clearly indicates a problem. Paying attention to nonverbal cues helps you interpret messages properly.

### Take Notes

Many managers do not like to take notes, perhaps because they view notes as secretarial work or believe they are unimportant to the larger process of communication and decision making. However, taking notes shows concern for what others have to say. In addition, experiments indicate that the behavioral involvement required for note taking increases our attention to the message. Note takers are better able to recall information than those who do not take notes.[20]

## Empathic Listening

Recall listening is not the only skill required in organizations. A survey of training managers at 106 Fortune 500 companies found that effective listening also includes active or empathic skills, such as building rapport and providing feedback. According to business communication researchers, good "workplace listening is interrelated with other communication behaviors and includes a good deal of 'empathy' in addition to recall."[21] According to Daniel Goleman, author of the book *Emotional Intelligence,* career success derives in large measure from the ability to skillfully listen to others' feelings. "To inspire people and move them in the right direction, you have to engage them emotionally."[22]

Some of the qualities of an empathic listener are attitudinal and involve your mind-set prior to listening, and others are communication related, including verbal and nonverbal feedback. Thus, empathic listening involves an **attitude of acceptance** for what others have to say, especially responding positively to emotions, and **providing feedback** that makes people feel as if their concerns have been addressed.

### Develop an Attitude of Acceptance

Whenever we communicate with another person we do more than present **content information;** we also present our individual **experiences** and **emotions.** These experiences are usually communicated nonverbally, with only minimal awareness by the sender. Messages such as these may communicate: "I am an excited person," "I am a serious person," "I am a self-disciplined person," "I am businesslike," and so forth. The next time you make a phone call to a business, notice the way the person responds. Some individuals answer the phone in an excited manner, suggesting they are interested in their job and care about your call. Others respond with vocal qualities that lack enthusiasm or suggest defensiveness. When we respond, we respond not only to the content, but also to the experience or emotion the other person communicates.[23]

Unfortunately, many organization members believe that business is a rational enterprise, and as such, no place for emotions. This attitude couldn't be more wrong. Emotion is a normal part of living and is reflected in communication.

Notice the manager's response to the employee's experience in the following hypothetical conversation:

*Larry:*    Melissa, can I talk with you for a moment?

*Melissa:*    Certainly, come on in.

*Larry:*    You've always said that your door is open for us if we have a problem. Well, for the first time I do have a concern I would like to discuss. First, I was turned down for a promotion in favor of someone outside the company, and today I was informed that I've been moved off the Smith Brothers account, one of the largest accounts in this agency. I can't believe this! Who in the company has it in for me? I'm mad as hell about this and want an explanation.

*Melissa:*    Larry, why are you still focused on this promotion thing? You know I favored you for the promotion, but sometimes we can't get everything we want.

*Larry:*    I don't need clichés, I want an explanation.

*Melissa:*    This isn't getting us anyplace. I thought we agreed that we won't talk about the promotion. It's in the past. Don't get emotional about it. As far as the reassignment . . .

*Larry:*    (very agitated) I didn't agree to do any such thing. I'm tired of slaving away for this company and never receiving any recognition. First the promotion, now the Smith Brothers account—that's one of our biggest accounts. Moving me off it signals that you don't have confidence in my work. It means I'll never have another shot at promotion. What are you doing to me?

*Melissa:*    I don't like your tone. You are rushing to judgment. Let's take an objective look at the shift in accounts. If you can't do that, then come back when you can control yourself.

In this excerpt, Melissa refuses to acknowledge or accept the experiences Larry communicates because she doesn't want to deal with distressing emotional content. Although Larry is obviously upset about the promotion, she dismisses it because "It's in the past." She also overrules his experience of frustration when she says they should take an "objective look" at the shift in accounts.

Developing an attitude of acceptance means learning to probe behind people's gut reactions. Melissa might have responded more positively if she had started by paraphrasing Larry's feelings and asking questions to probe the source of the response.

*Melissa:*    I thought after our last conversation about the promotion that you were over that, but apparently this is not the case. Am I right in sensing that you are still very frustrated that you didn't get the promotion?

*Larry:*    Well, I thought I was okay about it, but then this account shift came up, and it brought my original feelings back to the surface.

*Melissa:*    I see. Are you frustrated with me about the promotion? Do you feel that I could or should have done more to help secure it for you?

*Larry:*    No. But it would be nice to know if someone higher up prevented me from getting the promotion and if that same person is responsible for this account shift.

*Melissa:*    I don't know if someone higher up had anything against you personally. As far as the account shift, that was my idea. May I explain my reasoning?

In this response, Melissa paraphrases Larry's emotional response as frustration and asks questions to try to understand why this feeling has returned. She goes on to ask whether she is the source of Larry's frustrations and, in so doing, helps Larry probe beneath his response for its source. Larry will likely feel more positive about its conclusion because Melissa addresses rather than dismisses.

Developing an attitude of acceptance is difficult given certain thinking styles. Quick assumptions and inferences; simplistic evaluations; stereotyping the other's appearance, thoughts, or actions; or categorizing the other's personality are thought patterns that work against empathic listening.[24] Developing an attitude of acceptance means taking time to fully understand other points of view.

## Provide Feedback

Empathic listening includes feedback that indicates acceptance of the other person involved. Listeners should provide responses that confirm or reject others, rather than disconfirm them.

**Confirmation.** **Confirmation** is a response that does two things: It accepts the content level of the conversation, and it accepts the experience or emotion the person presents.[25] When your first author, Jim, called a national rental company to complain about waiting for over an hour to return a carpet steam cleaner, the customer service representative on the phone agreed with the content of the complaint, that an hour is too long to wait to return a small piece of equipment, and confirmed Jim's emotions by saying he understood why he was angry and that this was a perfectly legitimate response. The response is confirming because it agrees with the content of Jim's communication and the emotion behind it—the anger and frustration he felt. Confirmation contributes to a person's feelings of self-worth.

There are a variety of different confirming behaviors that indicate you are an empathic listener, and these are listed in Table 2.1. As you can see in the table, confirming messages offer **direct recognition** of the other person by looking at him or her, making frequent eye contact, and other nonverbal acknowledgment. **Agreeing with content** means the listener offers verbal agreement with or praise for the speaker's content. **Endorsing the emotions/ experiences** of the speaker accepts the other person's feelings as reasonable and legitimate.[26] However, you need not agree with another person to offer a positive, empathic response.

**TABLE 2.1**  *Definitions and Examples of Confirmation*

| | |
|---|---|
| Direct recognition | Nonverbal signals of interest, including looking straight, frequent eye contact, head nods, and other indications of attentive listening |
| Agreeing with content | Verbal agreement with or praise for the content communicated: "Yes, I think your assessment is accurate. Proceed as you see fit." |
| Endorsing emotions and feelings | Accepting the other's feelings as reasonable and legitimate: "I would feel the same way in your position." "You have every right to feel the way you do." |

*Source*: Adapted from Cissna, K. N. L., and E. Sieburg, "Patterns of Interactional Confirmation and Disconfirmation," in *Rigor and Imagination: Essays from the Legacy of Gregory Bateson*, ed. C. Wilder and J. H. Weakland (New York: Praeger, 1982), 253–282.

***Rejection.***    Despite its harsh-sounding label, **rejection** is a type of confirmation. In rejection, we validate another person's experience or emotional reactions but disagree with the content of the message.[27] For example, Janice and Satia are nurses in a hospital, and Janice is concerned about the way a particular doctor treats her. The doctor is abrasive and says things that make Janice feel incompetent. In talking to her friend Satia, Janice says she plans to take her problem to the hospital administrator. Satia responds by agreeing that her feelings are legitimate.

> *Satia:*    Yes, I agree. If he had done the same to me, I would feel like this too.

In saying this, Satia confirms Janice's feelings and gives them legitimacy; however, she disagrees with the proposed action.

> *Satia:*    However, taking this problem to the administrator without first talking to the doctor may make you look like you can't handle your own problems. In addition, the head nurse will look bad in the eyes of the administrator if you don't discuss this problem with her.

In this response, Satia disagrees with the content of the message—going to the hospital administrator to handle the problem. As such, rejection acknowledges the validity of the emotions expressed but denies the content of the communication, perhaps disagreeing with an assertion or suggesting an alternative course of action.

As you can see in Table 2.2, rejection includes a three-part message process. **Direct recognition** behaviors indicate active listening, **disagreement with content** signals disagreement with the message content, and **emotional/experiential qualifiers** indicate acceptance of the other person's feelings.

There are numerous events within organizations that call for the careful use of rejection. Organizational trainers, quality inspectors, line managers, human resource officers, and people who conduct performance appraisal interviews are frequently called on to teach, correct, and provide negative feedback to employees. Rejection represents one of the most beneficial methods of framing and communicating negative feedback. In our experience as teachers and corporate trainers, the best rejection messages—those that are most empathic—explicitly include all three elements cited in Table 2.2. For example, a teller trainer your first author knew at a bank

**TABLE 2.2**    *Definitions and Examples of Rejection Messages*

| | |
|---|---|
| Direct recognition | Nonverbal signals of interest, including looking straight, frequent eye contact, head nods, and other indications of attentive listening |
| Disagreement with content | Verbal disagreement with the content communicated: "I think you are wrong about how that event unfolded." |
| Emotional/experiential qualifiers | Verbal or nonverbal signals of understanding or acceptance for the feelings the other expresses: "You should feel proud; you earned that promotion." |

had a knack for teaching complicated procedures with minimal hurt feelings among her trainees. If a trainee continued to teller-stamp all incoming checks and documents rather than the few that required the stamp, she might say:

> Carol [looking directly at the person, making eye contact], I understand your desire to be sure about everything you are doing by teller-stamping every incoming check and document. After all, you are new at this; you're responsible for more money than you've ever seen in your life, and you're trying to be sure you're covered [an emotional/experiential qualifier]. But these two documents are the only ones that require a teller stamp [disagreement with content]. Anything more will only confuse people in the Proof Department.

In addition, rejection messages should be specific rather than general. To be told that one is "dominating" is less useful than to be told:

> I understand that you felt rushed to make a decision, but just now you did not allow several members of the group to make comments. I feel as if you are pushing the group faster than we should move.

Confirmation and rejection are an important foundation for effective empathic listening. Disconfirmation, on the other hand, should be avoided in all listening situations.

***Disconfirmation.*** Because it signals a lack of empathic listening, **disconfirmation** denies a person's experiences or feelings and, consequently, the other's feelings of self-worth.[28] For example, suppose an employee in a welding shop approaches his manager and says:

> ***Employee:*** I'm having trouble with this new procedure. Can I get some additional training before starting on this job?
>
> ***Manager:*** This procedure is nothing compared to the job we will be getting into in a few weeks. I thought you were qualified. (walking away) I guess we're going to have to do a better job of screening future applicants.

Disconfirmation is devastating to a person's view of self and destructive to productive relationships. In the previous example, the employee's request was met with an accusation that he is unqualified. It is doubtful the employee will ever openly speak of his concerns to the manager again. Table 2.3 lists and exemplifies several kinds of disconfirming remarks.

In Table 2.3 you can see that disconfirmation includes **avoiding involvement** through impersonal language and nonverbal distancing cues, such as avoiding eye contact, walking away while talking, failing to face the person directly, shuffling papers, or performing other tasks while listening. These make a person feel that what he or she has to say is not important. Note that, in the welding shop example, the manager distances himself when he begins to walk away in the middle of the conversation. Next, **tangential** or **irrelevant remarks** are not clearly connected to what the first person said and indicate a failure to listen. In the previous example, the manager's response is irrelevant to the request. **Imperviousness** indicates a lack of concern for or awareness of the other person's feelings. In the welding shop, the manager demonstrates imperviousness when he says, "This . . . is nothing compared to the job we will be getting into in a few weeks," denying the employee's right to feel troubled by the present job. Finally, **disqualification** occurs when

**TABLE 2.3**    *Definitions and Examples of Disconfirmation Messages*

| | |
|---|---|
| Avoiding involvement | Verbal or nonverbal distancing tactics, including avoiding eye contact, turning away, walking away, impersonal language |
| Tangential or irrelevant remarks | Verbal comments that are disconnected from or only minimally connected to the first person's remarks: "Let's discuss the production figures." "The next agenda item is the conference." |
| Imperviousness | Discrediting others' feelings: "You don't feel that way." (flat denial) "You're not angry at the decision: you're just a little miffed because you weren't told." (reinterpretation) "You can't possibly hold those feelings." (challenge the right to a feeling) |
| Disqualification | Direct disparagement of a speaker: "That wasn't a smart thing to do." |

*Source*: dapted from Cissna, K. N. L., and E. Sieburg, "Patterns of Interactional Confirmation and Disconfirmation," in *Rigor and Imagination: Essays from the Legacy of Gregory Bateson,* ed. C. Wilder and J. H. Weakland (New York: Praeger, 1982), 253–282.

someone disparages a speaker or the speaker's feelings.[29] The shop manager's statement "I thought you were qualified" is clearly an accusation that the employee is not qualified.

The disconfirming behaviors, whether they are expressed alone or in combination, indicate a lack of empathic listening because they disagree with the content another person expresses and the person's emotional experience. To improve your empathic listening abilities, develop an attitude of acceptance for the experience and emotions of the speaker, and practice confirmation and rejection. Eliminate disconfirming responses from your repertoire.

Because many organizational members spend entire days shuttling between interviews, meetings, presentations, and conversations with people, the vast majority of their time is spent listening. Effective employees are effective listeners. Devote yourself to improving your listening skills. The payoff could be huge.

## *Summary*

Advancement in many organizations depends on proficient listening skills. To improve recall listening, employees should motivate themselves, focus on content rather than delivery, defer judgment, take advantage of thought speed, listen for meaning, and take notes.

Whenever we communicate, our messages include both content and emotional/experiential information. Employees must develop the ability to accept emotional message elements and probe behind people's outward feelings for their source.

Empathic listeners respond with confirmation or rejection but avoid disconfirmation. Confirmation responses agree with the content of the message and accept the emotional content as well. Confirming responses include direct recognition, agreement, and endorsing the other person's feelings. Rejection is a type of confirmation in that it validates the person's feelings but disagrees with the message content. Rejection behaviors include direct recognition, disagreeing with the content, and an emotional/experiential qualifier. Finally, disconfirmation signals indifference to the speaker. Disconfirming behaviors include avoiding involvement, tangential or irrelevant remarks, imperviousness, and disqualification.

## Questions and Exercises

1. Consider the harm that inadequate recall listening can produce in an organization. Can you think of an incident in your work experience that was characterized by inadequate recall listening? What, if any, problems did this incident create? Which recall listening techniques could have solved this problem?

2. Can you think of additional techniques to improve recall listening? As a group or class, list the additional methods.

3. As a class or group, develop additional examples of confirming, rejecting, and disconfirming behaviors.

Are there any message examples that do not fit into one of the three categories?

4. As a class or group, develop a list of five errors you or your colleagues have made during your first few days on a new job. Now, come up with a way to talk to the person who committed the error using rejection. Follow the guidelines in Table 2.2 to construct your messages. Learn to use rejection to instruct and correct.

## Notes

1. Steil, L. K., L. L. Barker, and K. W. Watson, *Effective Listening* (Reading, MA: Addison-Wesley, 1983).
2. Nichols, R. G., "Do We Know How to Listen? Practical Helps in Modern Age," *The Speech Teacher* 10 (1961): 118–124.
3. "Secrets of Being a Better Listener," *U.S. News & World Report* 26, May 1980, 65–66.
4. Haas, J. W., and C. L. Arnold, "An Examination of the Role of Listening in Judgments of Communication Competence in Co-Workers," *Journal of Business Communication* 32 (1995): 123–139.
5. Sypher, B. D., and T. E. Zorn, "Communication-Related Abilities and Upward Mobility: A Longitudinal Investigation," *Human Communication Research* 12 (1986): 420–431.
6. Lancaster, H., "It's Time to Stop Promoting Yourself and Start Listening," *Wall Street Journal*, 10 June 1997, B1.
7. Brownell, J., "Perceptions of Effective Listeners: A Management Study," *Journal of Business Communication* 27 (1990): 401–415.
8. DiSanza, J. R., "The Role of Consciousness in Interpersonal Communication: Pedagogical Implications for the Introductory Course" (ERIC Document Reproduction Service No. ED 341098), February 1991.
9. Golen, S., "A Factor Analysis of Barriers to Effective Listening," *Journal of Business Communication* 27 (1990): 25–36.
10. Beatty, M. J., R. R. Behnke, and D. L. Froelich, "Effects of Achievement Incentive and Presentation Rate on Listening Comprehension," *Quarterly Journal of Speech* 66 (1980): 193–200.
11. Nichols.
12. Floyd, J. J., *Listening: A Practical Approach* (Glenview, IL: Scott, Foresman, 1985).
13. Harris, R. M. *The Listening Leader* (Westport, CN: Praeger, 2006).
14. Nichols.
15. Ibid.
16. Wolven, A. D., and C. G. Coakley, *Listening* (Dubuque, IA: Wm. C. Brown, 1992).
17. Lundsteen, S. W., "Metacognitive Listening," in *Perspectives on Listening,* ed. A. D. Wolven and C. G. Coakley (Norwood, NJ: Ablex, 1993), 106–123.
18. Harris.
19. Whalen, J. D., *I See What You Mean: Persuasive Business Communication* (Beverly Hills, CA: Sage, 1996).
20. Wolven and Coakley.
21. Lewis, M. H., and N. L. Reinsch, Jr., "Listening in Organizational Environments," *Journal of Business Communication* 25 (1988): 59.
22. Lancaster.
23. Watzlawick, P., J. H. Beavin, and D. D. Jackson, *Pragmatics of Human Communication* (New York: Norton, 1967)
24. Bruneau, T., "Empathy and Listening," in *Perspectives on Listening,* ed. A. D. Wolven and C. G. Coakley (Norwood, NJ: Ablex, 1993), 185–200.
25. Watzlawick, Beavin, and Jackson.
26. Cissna, K. N. L., and E. Sieburg, "Patterns of Interactional Confirmation and Disconfirmation," in *Rigor and Imagination: Essays from the Legacy of Gregory Bateson,* ed. C. Wilder and J. H. Weakland (New York: Praeger, 1982), 253–282.
27. Watzlawick, Beavin, and Jackson.
28. Cissna and Sieburg.
29. Ibid.

# 3

# *Communicating in Organizational Groups and Teams*

**The Leadership Role**
    Leaders Organize the Team's Work
    Leaders Define the Team's Focus

**Membership Competencies in Groups and Teams**

**Decision Making in Group and Team Meetings**
    Preparing and Conducting Meetings
    Decision-Making Agendas
    Discussion Techniques for Enhancing Creativity

*Brainstorming*
*Nominal Group Technique*
*Sen-sational Thinking*
*Morphological Analysis*
    Group Decision Support Systems

**Conflict in Groups and Teams**
    Too Little Conflict
    Too Much Conflict

**Summary**

Despite the portrayal of the organization as the home of rugged individualism, professional work is often done in groups and teams. Developing, marketing, and selling any product or service in a global market involves the coordinated efforts of many people.

    A **group** is a collection of three or more individuals who perceive themselves as a group, possess a common fate, and communicate with one another over time to accomplish both personal and group goals.[1] Therefore, people waiting in line for a ride at an amusement park are not a group, but several students who decide to study together do represent a group. Groups can take many forms, including the senior management group, regional sales groups, accounting groups, or engineering groups.

    In the past 10 years, however, the term *group* has gone out of favor, replaced by one of the newest management innovations, the **self-directed team.** Teams emerged as an explicit attempt to do more with less in an era of global competition and shrinking resources.[2] The self-directed team eliminates the job of supervisory managers on a production line, for instance, and places all authority for coordination, manufacturing, and delivering the product in the hands of the team. The team also hires, fires, and disciplines its own members, sets its own work goals, and completes jobs on its own with little or no supervision.[3] Because decisions are in the hands of a small number of teams, the company can react quickly to changing markets, producing a leaner, more flexible organization.

Teams differ from groups in several important ways. First, teams have more decision-making authority than do groups. Second, because of that authority, teams are more interdependent and communicate more frequently than do groups. Teams often meet several times a day to coordinate activity, avoid duplication, and make necessary decisions. Finally, teams emphasize constant training and assessment of progress toward clearly articulated performance goals.[4]

Although most of the concepts we discuss in this chapter apply equally to teams and groups, we will focus on team building. We begin with a discussion of the leadership role and team member competencies. We then cover the most frequently practiced team activity, the meeting, and close the chapter with a discussion of conflict management.

## The Leadership Role

Team members operate by taking a variety of roles. A **role** is an expectation about individual behavior patterns. Just as members of a family perform behaviors that distinguish them as parents, grandparents, and children, people in teams take on a limited set of repetitive behaviors that distinguish their membership roles. *Leader* is a term used to describe particular behaviors. Taken together, these behaviors are called a role.[5] The leadership role is crucial to team performance.

Leadership is a complex phenomenon that is sometimes confused with management. **Managers** guide members by explaining job requirements, setting performance criteria, and monitoring output; they provide compensation for successful work and punish failure. The authority to set goals and deliver rewards is conferred by the organization, and employees comply with the requirements to the degree that they desire the manager's rewards and want to avoid punishments. Referring to Chapter 1, management represents a contractual agreement whereby each person gives up something he or she would rather not part with or do in order to get something valuable from the other person. Supervisors in fast-food chains, retail stores, and other service industries usually function as managers rather than as leaders. Because of the part-time nature of employment, high turnover, and unskilled work, the simple employment contract provides adequate motivation for group members.

Self-directed teams, however, require more member commitment than managers can create using simple employment contracts. The increased authority and independence of the self-directed team requires that members be motivated and work hard without the benefit of direct supervision. Leadership provides a way to address these needs.

**Leaders** are able to specify issues of importance to members, raise employees' awareness of these issues, define how they should be interpreted or perceived, and then motivate members to transcend individual self-interest for the sake of the team.[6] Unlike simple management, where the authority is granted by the organization, the leader's authority comes from the members themselves, who voluntarily give up part of their right to specify goals and define issues to the leader. Members follow the leader not for rewards, but because they buy into the leader's vision. In Chapter 1 we referred to this kind of agreement as "consensual shared meaning," where people agree about basic objectives and values. Steven Jobs, cofounder of Apple Computers, is the classic example of a leader, a person who can drive individuals to innovate, create, and sacrifice for the company—not for financial rewards, but because the leader's vision is so compelling.

Although some managers do emerge as team leaders, it is equally likely that management and leadership roles are concentrated in different people. Although Jerry is the manager of his work group, he doesn't spend much time on the shop floor and doesn't know much about manufacturing details. He tries to hire good employees and protect the department's budget from cuts. Juan is the senior operator, and Jerry gives him wide latitude in deciding manufacturing priorities. Juan has no control over resources, but employees follow his lead because they like him and believe he knows what's best for the department.

What kind of person is likely to emerge as a team leader? Research indicates that emergent leaders are more communicatively flexible than nonleaders. In other words, leaders emerge by adapting their behavior to individual members of the group, to different tasks, and to different group priorities, depending on the circumstances.[7]

A study of several decision-making teams exemplifies leaders' adaptive behavior. In one meeting, the leader needed an open-ended, creative discussion of an agenda item. To facilitate this, he made few procedural comments, such as calling for votes, limiting discussion, making critical evaluations, or seeking critical evaluation. Instead, he encouraged people to talk and be creative, and used group identity comments to emphasize the creative and nonbureaucratic nature of this team. In a later meeting the same leader needed to reach resolution on three agenda items. His procedural comments increased from the first meeting, and his identity comments about the group's special role and creativity diminished. This leader adapted his performance to meet the different needs of the team in two different meetings.[8]

*Leaders are able to specify issues of importance to members, raise employees' awareness of these issues, and define how they should be interpreted or perceived.*

Credit: Bill Burke

---

**FIGURE 3.1** | *Leadership Communication Behaviors*

---

*Task Leadership Communication Behaviors*
    Contributing ideas
    Seeking ideas
    Evaluating ideas
    Seeking idea evaluation
    Stimulating creativity

*Procedural Leadership Communication Behaviors*
    Goal setting
    Agenda making
    Clarifying
    Summarizing
    Verbalizing consensus

*Interpersonal Leadership Communication Behaviors*
    Regulating participation
    Climate making
    Resolving conflict

---

*Source:* Adapted from Cragan, J. F., and D. W. Wright, *Communication in Small Groups: Theory, Process, Skills* (Minneapolis/St. Paul: West, 1995).

---

Team leaders are audience centered; they can assess member needs in context of the larger goal and enact behaviors that move the team forward. Despite the importance of flexibility, it is possible to describe two important categories of leader behavior: Leaders organize team efforts and define the team's context.

## *Leaders Organize the Team's Work*

Team activity is usually disorganized and messy, characterized by circular discussions, dead-end ideas, and conflicting solutions. Leaders use their communication skills to bring order to chaotic processes. Professors John F. Cragan and David W. Wright divide leadership communication behaviors into three categories: task, procedural, and interpersonal (see Figure 3.1). **Task communication** skills focus on accomplishing the team's performance goals. Therefore, **contributing ideas** and solutions is an important leadership function. If other members are hesitant to express their ideas, the leader can ease fears by laying out his or her own ideas. If members are still reluctant to contribute their ideas, it is up to the leaders to **seek ideas** from all group members through direct questions such as "Kim, do you have any ideas on this problem?" or "Gabrielle, we haven't heard from you for a while. What's your opinion?"

Effective teams must not only develop ideas, they must also cull poor ideas so that only the strongest solutions remain. The leader must **evaluate ideas** in such a way that members do not feel attacked. This means rejecting other people's ideas without disconfirming their experience or emotional reactions (see Chapter 2). The leader must also **seek idea evaluation** from other group members through such direct questions as "What do you think of our first solution?" "Are there ways to improve this concept, or should we set it aside for now?" Finally, under task communication behaviors, the group leader must **stimulate creativity,** allowing members to propose wild and offbeat ideas without criticism.

Leadership in the **procedural area** sets the agenda for the team's process. **Goal-setting** behaviors establish short- and long-range objectives. Leaders are also responsible for **agenda making** to keep meetings on track. Leaders must ask members to **clarify** their abstract ideas. This can be accomplished through specific questions, such as "What do you mean by that?" "Can you provide an example of how this idea would work in practice?" and "How will this help us reduce our costs?" When asked in a nonthreatening manner, these questions can encourage members to think more deeply about their ideas.

Good leaders also keep the team on track by **summarizing** the group's progress. Consistent summary statements help members understand where the group is going: "So, what I hear is that we have not one, but two problems. We don't deal adequately with members of the environmental community, and we are terrible with the press." Consistently summarizing members' ideas brings order to disorderly discussions. **Verbalizing consensus** involves finding the areas on which members agree. Such comments as "I believe we agree that in the future the press will not be invited to attend our meetings," made throughout the meeting (rather than at the end of a meeting), increase the chances of eventual agreement.[9]

Finally, **interpersonal communication** skills create a productive environment for members. First, the leader must **regulate participation.** Dominant members must be held in check, and less active members must be encouraged to participate. For instance, a comment such as "Larry, I know you're very concerned about this issue, but let's take the time to hear from people who haven't spoken" can open up a meeting to other opinions. **Climate making** means creating a nonthreatening atmosphere so that members feel comfortable contributing even their "crazy" ideas. Censuring members who make personal attacks and focusing criticism on ideas rather than on individuals helps create a positive climate. Finally, teamwork creates conflict, and good leaders are able to **resolve conflicts** and move the group forward. The last section of this chapter discusses a variety of conflict management skills. In addition to organizing group activity, good leaders must define important issues for members and motivate them to transcend individual self-interest.

## Leaders Define the Team's Focus

According to professors Carl E. Larson and Frank M. J. LaFasto, effective teams adopt elevating goals that inspire lofty and sincere aspirations.[10] *Charisma* is the word we use to describe leaders who can focus members' attention and devotion to a goal, and charismatic leadership is the effective use of symbols. As we said in Chapter 1, events do not have any particular meaning; we use symbols to give meanings to events. Charismatic leaders are exceptional at communicating their interpretations of an event, their vision or goals, in such a way that followers accept the interpretation as correct.

For example, in the early 1980s, Dale Daniels took over Lockheed's L1011 jumbo jet plant in Antelope Valley, California. Aircraft production at the plant was behind schedule and over budget. The previous management's fear tactics turned individuals and teams against one another. Daniels wanted to change the plant's culture to a more cooperative one. One of his first acts was to fire a supervisor from the previous management team who would not or could not stop using the fear tactics Daniels deplored. He also explained repeatedly that the firing was not "retaliation" but was a first step to creating a more "cooperative spirit" at the plant.[11] Daniels's explanations helped reinforce his vision for the plant and employees. Group leaders use a variety of strategies to communicate and gain commitment to their vision.

**Labels** are catchy symbols that categorize or describe a thing or event. A good label can help employees grasp the vision the leader wants to communicate.

As CEO of Maytag Corporation, Leonard A. Hadley inherited a company that was notoriously conservative when it came to investment in new products and technology. "For decades Maytag had a policy not to be the first to market with new technology, saying it would 'rather be right than be first.'"[12] In 1993 Hadley created the "Galaxy Initiative," a series of new products, each named after a planet in the solar system. The label was no doubt created to evoke feelings of cutting-edge technology and expansiveness, encouraging employees to think more innovatively than before.

Labels influence how we think about things, and leaders can focus and define member attention through catchy words or phrases that communicate their vision. If the leader repeats the phrase often and behaves in ways consistent with the spirit of the label (as Dale Daniels did), members may eventually come to accept the leader's definition.

Leaders can also communicate their vision by elevating **heroes** who exemplify that vision. Although it may be difficult for people to become attached or connected to abstract visions expressed in such words as *competitiveness, quality,* or *customer service,* it is easy to emulate someone who personifies an abstract vision. Heroes become symbols that stand for the leader's vision. By their recognition, heroes can set a high standard of performance that the leader wants from the team. The hero must, however, not be so superior that members view the standard as unattainable. Rather, the hero must set an achievable standard for other group members.[13]

A **ritual** is an event of passage that takes place when a milestone is achieved. Rituals include initiation ceremonies for new employees or parties celebrating individual accomplishment. Rituals often focus on praising heroes for important accomplishments. An officially sanctioned event at a publishing company is the annual meeting of the Ten-Year Club, otherwise known as the "Screw-In Ceremony." During the event, new members of the Ten-Year Club are initiated into the realm of long-term employees. A plaque with each new member's name is screwed into the mantel above the fireplace in the company's library. Newly "screwed-in" members are roasted, toasted, and presented gifts by other members. The event reinforces the importance of longevity in a company that encourages employees to become a part of the corporation, just as their names become a part of the building in which they are working.[14]

Leaders can specify important group values by encouraging rituals that reinforce those values. Rather than try to create new rituals from scratch, wise leaders capitalize on events the team has already developed, adjusting them to reinforce appropriate visions.

**Identification** occurs when members' interests and goals overlap.[15] Employees who identify with their team experience feelings of commitment, membership, and similarity with the group.[16] Members who identify with the team are devoted to its tasks and committed to success. Leaders can encourage team members to identify in a number of ways. The first method is **praise for the team's accomplishments,** which raises members' esteem and reminds them of the team's importance within the larger organization.[17] Another method of creating identification is by **espousing shared values.** For example, during a meeting, the team leader emphasizes, "We all believe that customer service is our number one priority." In essence, members are told that they all share the same interests and priorities.[18]

Constant references to a **presumed "we"** often go unnoticed but reinforce a taken-for-granted common bond among members. Statements such as "We must work together to solve this problem" or "We are going to improve quality in the next year" subtly suggest that all team members are committed to the same mission.[19]

---

**FIGURE 3.2** *Methods of Creating Identification*

---

*Praise for a Team's Accomplishments:* Raises members' esteem for the team.
"I want to congratulate the entire team on its efforts over the past six weeks. You've worked harder and accomplished more than any team I have ever led. Your efforts will play an important role in the coming product rollout."

*Espousing Shared Values:* Explicitly state that the team members share the same values.
"I know none of you would have come to this agency if community service were not your primary goal."

*The Presumed "We":* Subtly suggest that all members are committed to the same mission.
"*We* are going to move forward with this project despite the setback because *we* know how important it is to *our* company's future."

*The Common Enemy:* Portray outside interests that are trying to destroy the team.
"This is not a level playing field, because competitors in other countries have the benefit of government subsidies and low wages operating in their favor. To combat these unfair practices, we must become as efficient as possible in our own operation."

---

Finally, nothing unites a group like a **common enemy.** Companies often emphasize threats from "outsiders" as a way to stress togetherness and identification among employees.[20] Portrayals of powerful enemies bent on destroying the team can lead to an increased sense of unity and stronger collective acceptance of group values. Enemies should be chosen with care, however. Making an enemy of another unit in the company can poison relations between teams and prevent cooperation on important projects. A less destructive approach is to create a healthy sense of competition between teams to spur members to increased performance. Outside the company, portraying competitors as enemies creates a sense of commitment to team goals. The methods of encouraging identification with a team are summarized in Figure 3.2 Although leadership is vital, without committed followers, leaders can't accomplish much.

## Membership Competencies in Groups and Teams

A team's performance is partly determined by the competencies of the individuals involved. According to communication researchers LaFasto and Larson, members need two kinds of working knowledge and four kinds of teamwork skills for effective performance.[21] These competencies are depicted in Figure 3.3.

As you can see in the figure, working knowledge includes both a practical understanding of the task at hand (experience) and overall problem-solving skills. Although leaders should feel free to add new, inexperienced team members, the newcomers must be balanced by knowledgeable, competent members who thoroughly understand the task. The second knowledge factor is the member's problem-solving abilities. Problem solving includes the ability to clarify problems, contribute ideas, seek ideas from others, evaluate ideas, stimulate creativity, and clarify solutions.[22]

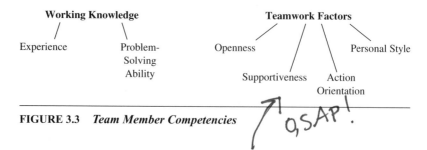

**FIGURE 3.3    *Team Member Competencies***

Aside from basic knowledge, four common teamwork factors are vital for effective member performance: openness, supportiveness, action orientation, and personal style. Openness is the willingness to surface ideas that need to be discussed and deal with those problems free of defensiveness, personal attacks, and hostility. Open members are straightforward without being insulting. Unfortunately, research by LaFasto and Larson suggests that most teams do not display open communication. On many teams, members don't trust each other, individuals pursue their own agendas, and one or more members display hostile or degrading behavior that alienates others. These problems must be avoided for successful team performance. The second teamwork factor is supportiveness, which includes a desire and willingness to help others succeed. Team members encourage each other, they defend members who are being attacked, they pitch in to help out on difficult projects, and they display an overall "we" approach to problems.

The third teamwork factor is action orientation. Being action oriented means a willingness to experiment, to take risks, to try new things to solve a problem. The opposite of action orientation is a belief that there is nothing that can be done to solve the problems a team faces. The fourth teamwork factor is a positive personal style. Team members may be either positive or negative toward their work and their colleagues. Members that are energetic, optimistic, engaging, confident, and fun are people we all want to work with. Poor members are cynical, defensive, hard-to-work-with whiners who constantly douse the creative fires of the group with flood tides of negativity. According to Lionel Tiger, Darwin professor of anthropology at Rutgers University, humans by their very nature are optimists, and Americans may be more optimistic than any other contemporary culture. Leaders who project optimism, such as Bill Clinton and Ronald Reagan, confound critics with their high approval ratings. Larry J. Kimbell, director of the Business Forecasting Project at UCLA's Anderson School, suggests that American optimism adds a half percentage point to the U.S. gross domestic product—which is worth approximately $38 billion a year.[23] Optimism provides significant inspiration for problem solvers and creative thinkers.

One of your authors realized the importance of optimism while providing leadership training for a large manufacturing concern. This team of senior managers included three women and two men. One of the three women, Sara, was consistently pessimistic and sarcastic about her work, the organization, and life in general. Although her teammates liked her personally and thought highly of her engineering skills, they and the upper management tried to isolate her from tasks that required teamwork and forward thinking. Consequently, her career had topped out, while the advancement potential of her teammates soared. Of course, this fact only fueled her cynicism and malaise.

What do you do when your team members lack either working knowledge or the teamwork factors? Training is the solution to skill deficiencies.

Research shows that high-performing teams make education and training easily accessible to members and that team members routinely take advantage of these opportunities.

**BOX 3.1 • *Interview: Laurie Jecha-Beard (Vice President, Agriculture, McCain Foods USA, Oakbrook, Illinois)***

(McCain Foods, headquartered in Florenceville, New Brunswick, Canada, is an international supplier of frozen potato products to restaurants and supermarkets.)

*What characteristics do you look for when hiring leaders for groups or teams at McCain?*

The characteristics of a leader include integrity, intelligence, dedication, trust, insight, strong initiative, effective communication skills, and, to some degree, charisma.

*What characteristics do you look for in team members?*

In many ways the characteristics for team members are the same as for team leaders. I often use the analogy of "the bus" when speaking about teams working together. Either a team member is "on the bus" or "not on the bus." If a team member is "not on the bus," that individual cannot or will not support the team when it tries to achieve its destination or goal. We want to ensure that all team members are "on the bus." We also need team members who know their business and take initiative.

*How important is creativity to the teams at McCain?*

Creativity is very important. New and innovative ideas are welcomed and nurtured at McCain. Often, experience and strong intellectual curiosity help provoke creativity. As a team leader, I try to recognize people who contribute ideas with a note, phone call, or other acknowledgment in front of their peers and superiors, as well as direct reports.

*How do teams at McCain manage conflict?*

In any business situation, conflict often results from stress or fear of the unknown. As a leader, it's my duty to avert stress/unknowns by working in a proactive format. It's a proactive rather than reactive stance toward conflict. I would rather prevent some conflicts from arising, exercising fire prevention rather than fighting fires after they start.

Low-performing teams, in contrast, often have training made accessible but are under so much pressure to improve productivity that they cannot afford to take time to train.[24] One of the best ways to handle training is to give each team a budget, mandate a certain number of hours of training per year per person (30 hours per year, for example), and allow the team to decide what kinds of training it needs. This method is consistent with the goals and processes of self-directed teams. The interview in this chapter discusses, among other things, the qualities necessary for effective team membership. Because teams are responsible for so much decision making, they spend an enormous amount of time in meetings.

## Decision Making in Group and Team Meetings

According to an article in *USA Today*, meetings have become the bane of American workers and an impediment to productivity. Roger Mosvick, a communication professor at Macalester College in St. Paul, Minnesota, says the number of meetings has jumped enormously, and many of these meeting are mind-numbing in their mundane content. Business professionals spend 25 to 60 percent of their time in meetings, and as much as half of that time is unproductive.[25] The length of most meetings also increased, inducing some companies to require attendees to stand as a way to shorten the proceeding.[26]

## *Preparing and Conducting Meetings*

The **agenda** is the map or guidebook for the meeting and, if it is thrown together thoughtlessly or not created at all, the meeting is very likely to spin off in unproductive directions.

Developing the agenda starts by soliciting topics from members. Team leaders should avoid scheduling oral reports during meetings. Reports are interesting only to a small subset of attending members and are better handled electronically. John E. Tropman, author and organizational consultant, recommends that each item for inclusion be sorted into one of three categories depending on the kind of activity it represents: announcements, discussions, or decisions.[27] **Announcements** are brief information items (not reports) that the entire group needs to hear. **Discussions** allow members to share information or examine a problem from a variety of different angles. **Decision items** require the group to vote or reach consensus on a topic. A sample agenda follows.

### AGENDA
Portneuf Valley Community Advisory Panel, Friday, May 16, 2008

1. Jeri Taylor from AGP will briefly explain why the company postponed plans for the liquefied gas plant in Michigan (announcement).
2. Teresa Martinez from the state Division of Environmental Quality will discuss the new proposals for hazardous waste cleanup (discussion).
3. Phillip Wilson wants the group to choose a date for the upcoming open house (decision item).

Notice also that this agenda is appropriately detailed. Many agendas do not include enough detail for members to know what is happening. Examine the following sample agenda.

### AGENDA
Portneuf Valley Community Advisory Panel, Friday, May 16, 2008

1. AGP on the postponement
2. The cleanup plan
3. Open house

This agenda is not detailed enough to let members know what will happen at the meeting.

When arranging the agenda items, Tropman recommends that announcements be placed early and controversial decision items be placed during the latter two-thirds of the meeting. Late arrivers are not harmed by missing the announcements but will arrive in time for important decision making. Early leavers will not have left prior to controversial decisions. Because controversy creates conflict, saving easier decisions for the last part of the meeting provides time to express support and reach agreement before adjourning. After the agenda is created and sent, a brief reminder may be appropriate.

Start the meeting on time; do not wait for late arrivers. Waiting gives the impression that lateness is fine and encourages future lateness from others. Do not admit any new business during the meeting. Although members may be unprepared to discuss new agenda items, this doesn't stop people from talking. At the end of a community advisory meeting, a panel member

*An effective team meeting requires extensive thought and preparation.*
Credit: Caryn Elliot

brought up rumors that one of the two companies sponsoring the group was using the panel's name on legal documents, to give the impression the panel endorsed the company. A 15-minute discussion ensued. Later investigation showed the rumor was false, but it wasted 15 minutes better spent elsewhere.

After the meeting, the team leader creates a record, usually in the form of minutes. However, normal minutes are too cursory to let outsiders know what happened. For example,

## MINUTES
### Staff Sales Meeting

1.  Members discussed falling sales in the southern region.

    Moved: Meet with advertising at the next opportunity and discuss changing ad agencies.

    Approved by 6 to 2 vote.

This review is too brief to fully explain the content of the meeting. On the other hand, transcribing the entire content of the meeting is not a viable option. Instead, team leaders should create **content minutes.** Each heading in the agenda should have a corresponding heading in the minutes. The recorder writes a summary of the discussion in one or two paragraphs and highlights the team's decision, if any, in bold or italics. Take a look at the following example:

**MINUTES**

Portneuf Valley Community Advisory Panel September 7, 2007

1. The group reviewed its early planning for a PM-10 study.

    Several people discussed concerns they had about the study, including the time it would take, the number of respondents that would have to be involved, and the kind of help needed to conduct it properly. The number one problem, of course, is money. Sue Wong reported that she might be able to come up with $15,000 to $18,000 to fund the project. The agency has some money set aside for such things. The only condition is that the study methods be approved by the agency prior to disbursement of the funds.

    ***Decisions: The group formed a subcommittee of Bill, Jean, and Bob to contact both the university and the agency in order to set up the study and procure the funds.***

Content minutes are superior to regular minutes because the summaries include relevant details and highlight decisions.

Finally, leaders must follow through on the team's decisions. Remind the team about the implementation of previous decisions in the announcement phase. Members are more likely to see meetings as productive when decisions are carried out and assessed for effectiveness.

## Decision-Making Agendas

Although the research is somewhat mixed, there is support for the notion that rational decision-making schemes produce more reasonable and intelligent results than teams that follow no particular procedure.[28] Most writers on decision making acknowledge the seminal influence of the philosopher John Dewey, who identified a set of mental operations for decision making referred to as the "Reflective Thinking Sequence." The basic steps of the Reflective Thinking Sequence are

   **I.** *Define the Problem:* A concise statement of the problem, its type, nature, and causes.
     **A.** What is the harm? What are the symptoms of the problem?
     **B.** How serious is the harm? Does the problem warrant a solution?
     **C.** Is there any way to look at the problem as a benefit?
     **D.** Who is affected by the harm?
     **E.** How widespread is the harm?
     **F.** What are the root causes of the harm?
     **G.** What, if any, obstacles are there to developing a solution?

   **II.** Develop Criteria: A set of standards against which to evaluate the worth of various solutions.
     **A.** What are the important standards that a solution must meet?
     **B.** Rank-order criteria in terms of importance.

   **III.** List Solutions: A list of possible solutions.

**IV.** Select a Single Solution: The solution that best meets the established criteria.
   **A.** Eliminate solutions that obviously fail to meet the criteria.
   **B.** What solution or combination of remaining solutions will solve the problem?
   **C.** Does the solution adequately meet the criteria previously elaborated?

**V.** Implement the Solution: The steps necessary to implement the solution.
   **A.** What must be done, and who will be responsible for implementing the solution?
   **B.** How will we know if the solution has been effective?

Unfortunately, defining the problem is the most misunderstood step in the process. Most teams rush past the problem on their way to solutions, leading to ineffective decisions. Imagine, for example, that you manage a large state recreation area. You want to address a recent drop in attendance at picnic and campground sites along the river. Several rangers believe the dropoff is the result of recent fee hikes at the park. An overzealous team will inappropriately define the problem as "visitor decline caused by increased user fees." By asking questions under "Define the Problem," the team can develop a more thorough understanding of the decline. For example, by inquiring about the harm and seriousness of the dropoff, the team can determine whether the problem is truly serious. Perhaps a decline might help the local environment recover. As such, fewer visitors becomes a benefit, and the problem is how to capitalize on the decline to help the environment recover. It is also important to ask whom is affected by the harm. If the state allocates money based on usage, then the reduction signifies less money for future improvements at the facility. This might be serious enough to warrant action. The group must also understand root causes: Are the fee hikes really the cause of this problem? Or is the new state-of-the-art swimming facility in town the source of the decline? Finally, it is important to inquire about the obstacles to developing a solution. If, for example, the state legislature sets fees for all state facilities, then reducing the fees is not an option.

The definition of the problem greatly influences the team's solution. As you can see in Figure 3.4, the solution depends on how the team defines the problem. If the team decides the decline is caused by the new pool, then one solution is better advertising to encourage customers to come to the park on weekends, the most crowded time at the pool. If, however,

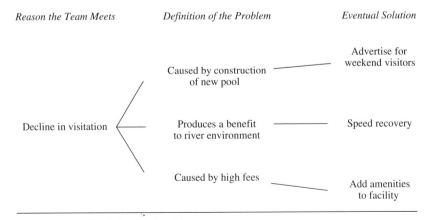

| *Reason the Team Meets* | *Definition of the Problem* | *Eventual Solution* |

Decline in visitation — Caused by construction of new pool — Advertise for weekend visitors

Produces a benefit to river environment — Speed recovery

Caused by high fees — Add amenities to facility

**FIGURE 3.4  *Defining the Problem***

the group defines the problem as a benefit to the environment, the solution is to invest in environmental recovery. Finally, if the group decides the problem is really related to fees, then one solution is to add amenities to the facility, making the fee increase seem less burdensome. As you can see, a thorough understanding of the problem is necessary for creative problem solving.

The next step is to develop criteria against which to evaluate solutions. Criteria must be specific and detailed, rather than general. When hiring a new employee, it is not enough to say, "We want the best candidate." The team needs to decide what standards it will use to determine the "best" candidate. The best candidate may have to meet the following criteria: a degree from a top-10 school according to industry rankings, a GPA above 3.2 in computer programming classes, and strong letters of recommendation. The park rangers developed the following criteria for their decision concerning the state recreation area:

1. The solution cannot change fees because these are set by the legislature.
2. The solution can cost no more than the $90,000 allocated for improvements to this area for the year.
3. It is preferable that the money be spent on capital improvements at the site rather than on noncapital expenses.
4. The solution should not increase environmental degradation to the recreation area.

Those criteria are rank-ordered from the most important to the least important.

Following the development of criteria, the team generates a list of possible solutions and then culls unworkable plans. Techniques such as brainstorming, morphological analysis, or computer decision support systems are useful methods for generating solutions.

The team selects a plan by eliminating plans that are obviously unworkable or fail to meet the specified criteria. For example, solutions that adjust fee structures are eliminated because they fail to meet the first criterion. Other ideas that cost more than $90,000 can also be dismissed. The remaining list represents solutions that are at least minimally appropriate. If one solution clearly meets all the criteria, then this is the appropriate choice. If, however, there are several competing solutions, each of which meets some, but not all, of the criteria, use the rank-ordering to help make the decision. The park rangers evaluated two competing solutions: creating an advertising and education program to encourage attendance or adding improved playground and parking facilities to make the fee increase less onerous to patrons. Although both solutions met the first two criteria, the advertising campaign did not meet the third criterion, that money should be spent on capital improvements. The team therefore decided to add playground and parking facilities to the sites. Finally, the team should spend time deciding who will implement the solution, and the team should meet again to evaluate the solution after its implementation. Although the procedural order presented here is not the only one available, it is serviceable for many kinds of decisions.

## Discussion Techniques for Enhancing Creativity

In Chapter 1 we briefly discussed the challenges that both organizations and individuals face in the new global environment. Globalization, the free movement of goods, services, people, and culture across national borders, creates intense competition, which leads to the everpresent possibility of losing customers to newer or more cheaply produced products and services. Government agencies must look for ways to reduce costs because taxpayers are reluctant to ante up more money, even for existing programs. As the rate of change increases, so does every organization's need for creative ideas. Most organizations justify the expense and time it takes to establish self-directed teams on the belief that they represent a more stimulating, creative environment than traditional, top-down bureaucracies. This section describes the basis of creative thinking and suggests several team-based discussion methods to enhance creativity.

According to communication researchers Johnson and Hackman, creative ideas reflect three qualities. First, a creative idea is innovative or novel. The goal of creativity is to produce a new product, ad campaign, manufacturing process, or service that hasn't been seen in the past. Rather than springing into existence out of nothing, most creative ideas combine existing elements into new and different combinations. For example, the company that created Post-it Notes, (3m), combined two already existing elements, minimally adhesive glue and paper, into a new product. Second, an idea is creative when it is relevant to the problem the team must address. Thus, in organizational teams the creative effort is made to solve some problem or take advantage of an opportunity. Third, creativity includes both lateral and horizontal thinking. **Lateral thinking** involves linking concepts that seem totally unrelated prior to the new idea. For example, the creator of the electric guitar combined a Hawaiian steel guitar with parts from a radio and telephone. **Horizontal thinking** is aimed at developing and evaluating ideas once they are proposed.[29] For example, the company that invented the Fruit Roll-Up, General Mills, needed to use lateral thinking to come up with a flat candy that could be rolled up and horizontal thinking to evaluate, develop, manufacture, and market the product. Creative thinking is different from mere problem solving, which involves adopting and implementing existing solutions to organizational problems.

People are often encumbered in their thinking about creativity—and their ability to be creative—by the myths that surround the process. Arguably, the most significant myth is the belief that creativity is limited to the small number of geniuses that a society produces each generation. We're tempted to believe that figures like Einstein, Mozart, Stephen Hawking, or Steve Jobs are endowed with something special in their genetic code that makes them creative, and the rest of us mere mortals are stuck in our noncreative ruts.[30] Although sudden insights and dramatic breakthroughs do occur during the creative process, most researchers see creativity as an extension of everyday problem solving.

According to many psychologists, creative thinking is the result of preparation and knowledge, diligent work, tolerance for ambiguity, and a willingness to take calculated risks. Obviously, extensive preparation and knowledge increase the probability of finding creative solutions. Creative problem solvers are able to tolerate messy, vague problems and resist settling on quick solutions. Creative thinkers take chances with new ideas. They apply their superior knowledge to take the most appropriate calculated risks, those most likely to succeed. They are not reckless because they have the experience and background to properly evaluate risks and accept only those most likely to pay off. These are traits that we can all cultivate in ourselves.

Most researchers also believe that the creative potential of any team can be increased by careful attention to the discussion process employed. Over the years, a variety of methods have been developed to improve team-based creative abilities. Some of these processes, like the Standard Agenda, encourage a clearer problem definition, whereas others are designed to encourage more horizontal thinking. We will describe and explain each of these creativity-enhancing discussion methods, starting with the most well-known method, brainstorming.

*Brainstorming.*   In his famous book on creative thinking, Alex Osborn invented the technique of brainstorming. Because **brainstorming** emphasizes creativity and innovation, it is useful when unconventional solutions are required. Brainstorming includes the following steps:

> **I.** Instruct members in the procedures and warm up.
> **II.** Brainstorm.
> **III.** Clarify ideas and eliminate redundancy.
> **IV.** Evaluate ideas and select the best solution.[31]

*warm-up B.C.E* (handwritten)

In step I, inform members of the rules and engage in a warmup session that brainstorms ideas to a nonsense problem ("Think of all the different ways to use an empty Coke can"). The warmup helps members get into the spontaneous, freewheeling frame of mind necessary to develop creative ideas. In step II, lead the group in an actual brainstorming session while recording ideas on a flip chart, overhead, or board. The rules for the brainstorming session are as follows: First, all evaluation or criticism of ideas is forbidden. The leader must interrupt criticism and discipline members to refocus their energies on generating ideas. Because putting limits on ideas dampens the creative process, wild and offbeat ideas are encouraged. Third, encourage members to make connections among ideas.

In step III, eliminate or combine redundant ideas. In step IV, evaluate and dismiss clearly unworkable solutions. After this, the team discusses and decides on the best solutions to the problem. Brainstorming is a frequently used and effective means of developing creative solutions to team problems.

*Nominal Group Technique.*   Sometimes organizations use ad hoc groups whose members do not know one another, do not meet regularly, but come together on a one-time basis to solve a problem. The **nominal group technique** equalizes participation among ad hoc group members who don't know one another and may be reluctant to speak.[32]

Most versions of the nominal group technique follow four steps:

> **I.** Silent generation of ideas
> **II.** Round-robin recording of those ideas
> **III.** Clarification of ideas through discussion
> **IV.** Preliminary vote or ranking of ideas

One of your authors facilitated a meeting for the U.S. Forest Service that used the nominal group technique. The agency wanted to protect migrating elk from off-road vehicles. After a presentation from Forest Service officials about elk habitat, twenty citizens were arranged into five groups and asked to silently generate solutions to the problem. In step II, each group facilitator recorded member ideas on a flip chart. The facilitator moved around the group recording ideas until all the solutions were represented on the chart.

In step III, members briefly clarify and discuss each idea. Members explain their ideas, and statements of agreement or disagreement are allowed, but this must not degenerate into open argumentation. Finally, in step IV, each group ranks its solutions. In the case of the Forest Service, each group's rankings were given to the Forest Supervisor, who made a final decision in consultation with his management team. In other cases, the entire assembly can come back together to discuss each group's ideas and craft a single solution. Nominal group procedures save time and ensure equal participation among members who have no history together.

***Sen-sational Thinking.***    The **Sen-sational Thinking** technique is an excellent way for a team to improve a product or service and reposition it in the market. The theme in this exercise is to look at the product or service from the perspective of the five senses: sight, sound, smell, touch, and, if relevant, taste.[33] If, for example, a team of consultants was asked to redesign an old Wal-Mart into a super center, they might proceed by using Sen-sational Thinking.

> *Sight:* Inside the store, the aisles are narrow. Center-aisle displays throughout the main aisles only serve to increase the crowding. People must constantly stop and turn around to avoid other shoppers and move through the store.
>
> *Sound:* The background music is audible, but not disturbing. You're never alone in the store, so you constantly hear parts of other people's conversations. Any privacy to stand and mull a particular product is interrupted by other people and their conversations.
>
> *Touch:* The major activity is maneuvering the cart: stopping, turning, pushing around other people to make space and continue to get where you need to go. On occasion, people bump into you from behind.
>
> *Smell:* The store smells musty, like a large, dusty warehouse.

Comments like these might give the redesign team ideas about how to improve the shopping experience in the new store.

***Morphological Analysis.***    The **morphological analysis** method encourages members to think laterally by "forcing" together elements that seem completely unrelated.[34] It's an ideal way to develop new products or services or create new solutions to existing problems. A morphological analysis breaks a problem into its major components and lists all the possible topics or subdivisions under each major heading. Then, by randomly combining those elements the team generates new ideas that might solve a problem or produce a new product or service. An example of morphological analysis is depicted in Figure 3.5.

In this example, a development team needs to create a new food product for quick, one- or two-person dinners. The team members break the problem into its major parts, including the kinds of food that might be included in the product, the various properties that a food product could possess, the various methods of cooking the product, and the kinds of packaging available. Then the team combines the elements from each category to come up with new product combinations. Although some combinations will not appeal to consumers, such as fish that comes in a can and is cooked on the stove, other combinations are more promising. For example, by combining

**FIGURE 3.5**   *Variables for New Food Products*

| Kinds | Properties | Heating Processes | Packages |
|---|---|---|---|
| Meat | Cost | Microwave | Pouch |
| Meat and vegetables | Convenience | Stove top | Can |
| Fish | Taste | Boil | Sealed tray |
| Bread | Texture | Grill | Box |
| Pasta | Odor | Bake | Cup |
| Salad | | | Sack |

elements from columns one, three, and four, this team came up with an idea for a pasta meal, spaghetti and marinara sauce, that comes in a waterproof pouch and is cooked by boiling the pouch, which is then opened onto a plate for a quick and convenient meal. Other products can be invented by combining different elements from different categories. Some form of morphological analysis may have been at work in the development of single-serving macaroni and cheese and Fruit Roll-Ups.

***Group Decision Support Systems.***     **Group decision support systems** (GDSSs) combine communication, computers, and discussion techniques to aid group or team decision making. As you can see in Figure 3.6, the typical group decision support center includes 20 individual computer terminals for group members around a semicircle. The terminals provide public and private message capabilities with other group members. A screen at the front of the room is controlled by a facilitator and displays information such as vote tallies and brainstorming lists. The software provides access to a variety of group functions, including analyzing and defining problems, brainstorming, and nominal group technique.

Research on the effectiveness and creativity of GDSS decisions is mixed, showing positive results for some meeting functions and poor results for others. For example, computers allow members to generate ideas simultaneously, whereas face-to-face groups are limited by the fact that only one person can talk at a time.[35] Thus, computers increase the flow of new ideas during brainstorming. Other research shows that members' feelings of identification and connection to their team and their organization are lower in computer-mediated groups than in face-to-face groups.[36] Lower identification means that members are less tied to the organization's culture and history of decision making, freeing them to think "outside the box" more frequently than members of traditional groups.

Although superior to face-to-face groups in brainstorming and other creative group functions, computer-mediated systems may not be adequate for other forms of decision making. A study by Susan Straus found that the lack of context cues and status markers prevented members from recognizing task-relevant experience from experts. In other words, the computer

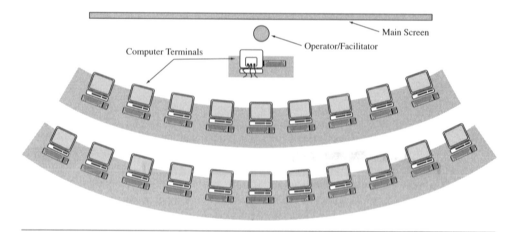

**FIGURE 3.6**   *A Typical Group Decision Support Center*

reduced the influence of the most knowledgeable members, which could lead to disaster in a real decision. Straus also noted that the computer groups were less satisfied with the process than were face-to-face groups.[37] Craig R. Scott, communication professor at the University of Texas, speculated that the repeated use of GDSS would reduce the benefit of equal participation and influence as members learn to recognize one another by identifying individual response habits.[38]

A study by Marshall Scott Poole and his associates at the University of Minnesota found that control groups exceeded the GDSS groups on a variety of critical and analytical thinking measures. Specifically, control groups showed more criteria definition statements, more solution statements, and more evaluation statements than GDSS groups. Overall, GDSS groups showed a lower level of critical discussion than normal groups.[39] Straus concluded:

Results of this and other studies discussed earlier paint a rather dismal picture of the use of [GDSS] for problem-solving tasks; performance outcomes are no better, or worse, than outcomes produced by [face-to-face] groups, satisfaction in [GDSS] groups is consistently lower, and [GDSS] groups invariably require more time to complete tasks.[40]

Despite these initial findings, researchers will continue to examine the costs and benefits of group decision support systems, and business will continue to experiment with the technology.

# Conflict in Groups and Teams

Conflict is an unavoidable part of human relationships. This is especially true in teams where contrary opinions are common. Conflict is defined as the interaction of interdependent people who perceive incompatible goals and interference from one another in achieving those goals.[41] The parties to a conflict are interdependent, in that the actions of any member affect the entire team. Although managers often attribute conflicts to differing personalities or faulty communication, the vast majority of conflicts would not exist without a real difference of interests or opinions. Each party to a conflict interferes with the other as they attempt to achieve their goals. The part of the team that wants to make concessions encounters interference from the side that does not, and vice versa. Despite the fact that most people prefer to avoid conflict, too little conflict can be as bad for a team as too much conflict.

## Too Little Conflict

Conflict is absolutely necessary for team performance. A healthy dose of conflict keeps a team from becoming complacent and forces members to constantly analyze and evaluate their decisions. In contrast, too little conflict leads to a phenomenon called "groupthink."

**Groupthink** occurs in teams that are so cohesive and lacking in conflict that members cease critical thinking, often leading to disastrous results. Irving Janis, the social psychologist who developed the groupthink hypothesis, believes several important U.S. policy failures, such as the Bay of Pigs in Cuba (1961), the Nixon Watergate scandal (1972), the destruction of the U.S. Pacific fleet at Pearl Harbor (1941), and the explosion of the space shuttle *Challenger* (1983), were the result of groupthink.

Some of the symptoms of groupthink include the **illusion of invulnerability,** whereby members believe nothing bad can happen to the team and that its decisions will always work out

*[handwritten: group-think — are heir of superiority]*

for the best. This illusion, especially common in highly successful groups, can lead to decisions that are not carefully evaluated. A second symptom is closed-mindedness, characterized by **rationalizations** to discount critics of any proposal. Group members also tend to **stereotype** outside critics as enemies who don't merit attention; thus, their opinion is ignored. Within the group, members work to enforce conformity to emerging decisions by putting **direct pressure** on dissenters ("You can't possibly believe that criticism is accurate") and using self-appointed **mind guards** to protect the group from contrary opinions.[42]

Leaders who want to avoid groupthink should assign every person the role of critical evaluator, encouraging every member to analyze and critique proposals. Leaders must also evaluate ideas if other members fail in this role and seek idea evaluation to ensure adequate decision making. Leaders should also insist on using the Reflective Thinking Sequence described earlier in this chapter. Despite the importance of conflict to decision making, it is possible to have too much conflict. In such cases, the conflict must be managed or resolved.

### Too Much Conflict

Although too little conflict can lead to groupthink, too much conflict tears at the fabric of group cooperativeness and hinders task accomplishment. It may surprise you to learn that people adopt certain strategies for handling conflict at the expense of other strategies. For example, Kim comes from a traditional Asian family that emphasizes deference to authority and resolving differences individually rather than in public. As such, he deemphasizes direct confrontation in favor of resolving issues in a one-on-one setting. Anthony comes from a loving but boisterous Italian family that is not hesitant about "having it out" when differences of opinion are apparent. Based on their different backgrounds, these two people developed different conflict styles. A **conflict style** is a person's orientation to conflict, which emphasizes certain strategies and tactics and ignores others. People have characteristic conflict styles that they use repeatedly, regardless of the situation.

Five traditional conflict styles are distinguished along two different dimensions: assertiveness and cooperativeness (see Figure 3.7).[43]

**Assertiveness** is the degree to which the participant attempts to satisfy personal needs in the conflict. **Cooperativeness** is the degree to which the person attempts to satisfy the other's concerns. Each style inside the matrix represents a different combination of assertiveness and cooperativeness.

*[handwritten: assert - personal]*

*[handwritten: cooperative - other's needs]*

*[handwritten: (collaborate)]*

| | **Cooperativeness** | |
|---|---|---|
| **Assertiveness** High | Competitive | Problem-Solving |
| | Compromising | |
| Low | Avoidance | Accommodating |
| | Low | High |

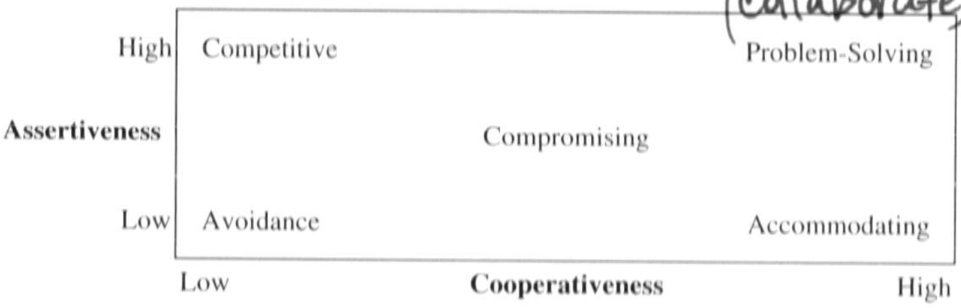

**FIGURE 3.7    *Conflict Styles***

In the top left corner, the **competitive style** is marked by high assertiveness and minimal cooperativeness. Forcing, threatening, and toughness are common tactics in the competitive conflict style. Although it may appear to be negative, the competitive style is useful when the issues involved are extremely important, time is short, you don't trust the other party, and you aren't interested in maintaining a long-term relationship with the other person.

At the bottom left corner is the **avoidance style,** marked by low assertiveness and low cooperativeness. Avoiders are apathetic and refuse to engage in conflict. This style is useful if preserving the relationship with the team member is more important than the issue. The **accommodating style** is characterized by high cooperativeness and low assertiveness. The accommodating person will engage in conflict but quickly cave in to the other person's demands. Accommodation is useful when the other person is more powerful and you will lose any competition.[44] It is also useful if preserving the relationship is more important than the issue.

In the middle of the figure is a style that emphasizes moderate levels of assertiveness and cooperativeness. The **compromising style** means that participants are willing to give in on some demands in return for concessions on others. Tradeoffs and tit-for-tat bargaining are common tactics for the compromiser. Compromising is superior to withdrawing or accommodating when both the issues and the relationship are important. If, however, the other person refuses to concede anything, the compromiser may feel betrayed. Even if the other party compromises, both sides often leave feeling they gave too much to the other person, which is why some people view compromising as a lose–lose proposition.

In the upper right corner of the matrix is the **problem-solving style,** characterized by high assertiveness and high cooperativeness. In problem solving, the team member works to create solutions that meet the important interests of both parties. An example of this kind of solution is found in the 1978 negotiations between Egypt and Israel over the Sinai Desert. The Sinai was Egyptian land before Israel won it during the Six Day War. Egypt's main interest was in the return of their ancestral lands without dividing them with Israel. Israel wanted to keep the Sinai as a buffer to give the country time to respond should Egypt ever mount an armed offensive. "Time and again, people drew maps showing possible boundary lines that would divide the Sinai between Egypt and Israel. Compromising in this way was wholly unacceptable to Egypt."[45] A solution was developed that forced neither side to compromise. Although the entire Sinai was given back to Egypt, it was not allowed to station any military forces near Israel. A problem-solving approach met the needs of both parties.

Which strategy is the most effective? It depends on the circumstance. Competing is best when there is one best solution and when conflicting values make the issue unresolvable through compromise. Problem-solving is more effective when parties have to work

**FIGURE 3.8    *A Four-Phase Model of Conflict Resolution***

| | |
|---|---|
| Introduction | Brief statement reviewing procedures for conflict resolution. |
| Explanation | Every party to the conflict discusses the source of the difficulty. |
| Clarifying | Develop a better understanding of all relevant positions and interests. |
| Problem-solving | Brainstorm solutions, eliminate solutions, and settle on a final solution. |

together in the future, they are open-minded, they show a willingness to ignore power differences and work together as equals, and problem-solving tactics are initiated before the conflict escalates.[46] Problem-solving is also a useful first approach in a conflict, whereas competing and compromising serve as useful backups. In general, competing, compromising, and problem-solving are superior to avoiding or accommodating because they encourage open discussion rather than deny the conflict. To help members resolve conflicts, we present a four-phase process that emphasizes problem-solving and compromising (see Figure 3.8).

The process in Figure 3.8 can be used to resolve conflicts between or within teams. In the **introduction phase,** the team leader or mediator opens with a brief review of the agenda for resolving conflict. The leader should remain neutral and emphasize the importance of understanding the source of the conflict before proceeding to solutions. In the **explanation phase,** each side of the conflict discusses the source of its disagreement. The leader can open by asking, "What is the problem we are confronting?" or "What is creating the discord in the team?" Each person should be allowed to speak his or her mind and explain concerns. The leader should use all the listening skills mentioned in Chapter 2 to understand each person's concerns. Don't interrupt or let others interrupt the speaker. Remind all participants that they, too, will have a turn to express themselves.

During the explanation session, the team leader should listen for both the positions people express as well as the interests behind those positions. A **position** defines what one person wants. For example, a property owner may want $100 per square foot for office space in her building, although property in that market usually rents for $80 per square foot. The rental price is the landlord's position. The landlord's **interests** are the needs, desires, fears, and concerns that motivate her to select the rental price.[47] Although that price may be high for the area, the landlord wants it so that she can, for example, upgrade the wiring for faster Internet access. Rewiring the building is one of the interests that motivates the price demand. It is easy to reach an impasse when parties negotiate over positions. Reconciling interests is much easier and more likely to lead to successful conflict resolution. Learn to listen for the motivations that drive people to adopt positions.

During the **clarifying phase,** the leader or mediator develops a better understanding of each person's positions and interests. Open questions that begin with such words as *how, what,* or *why* encourage people to clarify their interests. The leader can keep track of the issues by keeping a list of the positions of each party on a two-column sheet of paper. For each position, list the interests down the column. In the example in Figure 3.9, the landlord's position is $100 per square foot. She needs this for Internet wiring upgrades, electrical rewiring, and to meet new fire and earthquake codes. The potential tenant is the head of an engineering firm whose position is $75 per square foot, which he claims is the market rate

**FIGURE 3.9**   *Sample List of Positions and Interests*

| *Landlord* | *Potential Tenant* |
| --- | --- |
| *$100 per square foot* | *No more than $75 per square foot* |
| Needs the extra money to upgrade lines for the Internet. | Can't add costs to services and still compete. |
| Needs money to upgrade electrical wiring. | |
| Needs money to meet new fire and earthquake codes. | |

in that area of town. His interests are in keeping the cost of the services provided by his company as low as possible. To try to negotiate on the positions is very difficult. The best that could be hoped for is a compromise between $75 and $100. The interests, however, will prove useful in the resolution stage.

In the **problem-solving phase,** parties to the conflict develop a list of possible solutions using the brainstorming technique described earlier. Solutions that obviously do not meet the interests of either party are eliminated. Once the list is narrowed, parties take the remaining solutions and craft problem-solving ideas that meet the interests of both parties. For example, our hypothetical engineering team overcame their impasse by suggesting that the landlord drop the price to $80 per square foot, and in return the firm would draft the designs for the building improvements free of charge. The landlord said this was acceptable if the rent was set at $81. The minor increase was acceptable to the head of the engineering firm. If a solution that meets all parties needs cannot be developed, the leader or facilitator will have to suggest compromises that force each party to make concessions. The four-phase model is an efficient way to resolve many conflicts within and between groups.

## *Summary*

A group is a collection of three or more individuals who perceive themselves as a group, possess a common fate, and communicate with one another over time to accomplish personal and group goals. A self-directed team has full authority for coordination, manufacturing, and delivering a product or service.

A role is an expectation about individual patterns of behavior. The management role guides group activity by explaining job requirements, setting performance standards, and monitoring output. Leaders, on the other hand, specify issues of importance, raise employees' awareness of these issues, define how they should be interpreted, and motivate employees to transcend individual self-interests for the sake of the team. Leaders organize group activity through their communication behaviors in the task, procedural, and interpersonal areas. Leaders are also responsible for defining the team's focus through labels, recognizing heroes, enacting rituals, and encouraging identification. Membership competencies include working knowledge (experience and problem-solving ability) and teamwork factors, including openness, supportiveness, action orientation, and personal style.

Prior to team meetings, the leader should prepare an agenda of announcement, discussion, and decision items. After the meeting, the leader should create content minutes that summarize the group's discussion and highlight its decisions. The Reflective Thinking Sequences includes five basic steps: define the problems, develop criteria, list solutions, select a single solution, and implement the solution. Team creativity can be enhanced through several discussion techniques, including brainstorming, nominal group technique, Sen-sational Thinking, morphological analysis, and group decision support systems.

Too little conflict creates groupthink, which leads to poor critical thinking and ineffective decisions. People adopt one of five preferred styles for handling conflict: competition, avoidance, accommodation, compromising, and problem solving. The four-phase model of conflict resolution emphasizes problem solving and compromising. The phases include the introduction, where rules are explained, the explanation, where each party stakes out his or her position, clarifying, where the mediator attempts to understand interests behind positions, and the resolution phase.

## Questions and Exercises

1. Recall several successful team members you have encountered in classroom or work groups in the past. Which membership competencies did these teammates display? What were their effects on the group or team's performance?

2. Think of a supervisor you have worked for in the past. Was this person's supervision oriented toward leadership or management? What behavior did you see that supports your assessment?

3. Have any of your supervisors used the symbolic behaviors of leadership described in this chapter? Which strategies did they employ? How effective were these strategies, and why?

4. Write an agenda for one of your classes with enough detail that someone who did not attend can understand what happened. Show your agenda to someone who did not attend the class. Can this person understand the basic outline of that class period? If not, rewrite the agenda in the appropriate detail.

5. Recall your last creative or innovative idea. It could be an idea that you came up with for a class assignment or something new you proposed at work. Was this idea an example of lateral thinking, horizontal thinking, or some combination of the two?

6. List a conflict you have had with a classmate or coworker in the past month. List the positions people took. List the interests that motivated your positions. Put yourself in the shoes of the other person and attempt to list the major interests for each position he or she took. Compare the two lists of interests. Can you see any problem-solving solutions that meet the interests of both parties? If not, what compromises could be worked out to resolve this conflict?

## Notes

1. Baird, J., *The Dynamics of Organizational Communication* (New York: Harper & Row, 1977).
2. Eisenberg, E. M., and H. L. Goodall, Jr., *Organizational Communication: Balancing Creativity and Constraint* (New York: St. Martin's Press, 1993).
3. Barker, J. R., C. W. Melville, and M. E. Pacanowsky, "Self-Directed Teams at Xel: Changes in Communication Practices During a Program of Cultural Transformation," *Journal of Applied Communication Research* 21 (1993): 297–312.
4. Gribas, J., informal conversation, Pocatello, ID, 9 July 1998.
5. Wilson, G. L., and M. S. Hanna, *Groups in Context: Leadership and Participation in Small Groups* (New York: McGraw-Hill, 1993).
6. Bass, B. M., *Leadership and Performance Beyond Expectations* (New York: Free Press, 1985).
7. Fisher, B. A., "Leadership: When Does the Difference Make a Difference?" in *Communication and Group Decision-Making*, ed. R. Y. Hirokawa and M. S. Poole (Beverly Hills, CA: Sage, 1986), 197–215.
8. Wood, J. T., "Leading in Purposive Discussions: A Study of Adaptive Behavior," *Communication Monographs* 44 (1977): 152–165.
9. Gouran, D. S., "Variables Related to Consensus in Group Discussions of Questions of Policy," *Speech Monographs* 36 (1969): 387–391.
10. Larson, C. E., and F. M. J. LaFasto, *Teamwork: What Must Go Right/What Can Go Wrong* (Beverly Hills, CA: Sage, 1989).
11. Snyder, R. C., "New Frames for Old: Changing the Managerial Culture of an Aircraft Factory," in *Inside Organizations: Understanding the Human Dimension*, ed. M. O. Jones, M. D. Moore, and R. C. Snyder (Beverly Hills, CA: Sage, 1988), 191–208.
12. Quintanilla, C., "Maytag's Top Officer, Expected to Do Little, Surprises His Board," *Wall Street Journal*, 23 June 1998, A8.
13. DiSanza, J. R., "Shared Meaning as a Sales Inducement Strategy: Bank Teller Responses to Frames, Reinforcements, and Quotas," *Journal of Business Communication* 30 (1993): 133–160.
14. DiSanza, J. R., "The Wadsworth Publishing Company: An Ethnographic Analysis of Cultural Values" (master's thesis, San Francisco State University, 1985).
15. Cheney, G., "The Rhetoric of Identification and the Study of Organizational Communication," *Quarterly Journal of Speech* 69 (1983): 143–158.
16. DiSanza, J. R., and C. Bullis, " 'Everybody Identifies with Smokey the Bear': Employee Responses to Newsletter Identification Inducements at the U.S. Forest Service," *Management Communication Quarterly* 12 (1999): 347–399.
17. Ibid.

18. Cheney.

19. Ibid.

20. Ibid.

21. LaFasto, F., and C. Larson, *When Teams Work Best* (Thousand Oaks, CA: Sage, 2001).

22. Cragan, J. F., and D. W. Wright, *Communication in Small Groups: Theory, Process, Skills* (Minneapolis/ St. Paul: West, 1995).

23. Baley, J., "Joy to the World: Despite Everything, America Still Embraces a Culture of Optimism," *Wall Street Journal,* 22 December 1998, A1.

24. Yeatts, D. E., and C. Hyten, *High-Performing Self-Managed Work Teams: A Comparison of Theory to Practice* (Thousand Oaks, CA: Sage, 1998).

25. Armour, S., "Business' Black Hole: Spiraling Number of Meetings Consume Time and Productivity," *USA Today,* 8 December 1997, A1, A2.

26. Armour, S., "Some Companies Aim to Tame Meeting," *USA Today,* 7 May 2006 (online: http://www.ustaoday.com/money/companies/management/2006-07-05-meeting-usat_x.htm).

27. Tropman, J. E., *Making Meetings Work: Achieving High Quality Group Decisions* (Beverly Hills, CA: Sage, 1996).

28. Gouran, D. S., "Rational Approaches to Decision-Making and Problem-Solving Discussion," *Quarterly Journal of Speech* 77 (1991): 343–384.

29. Johnson, C. E., and M. Z. Hackman, *Creative Communication: Principles and Applications* (New York: Free Press, 1995).

30. Ibid.

31. Osborn, A. F., *Applied Imagination: Principles and Procedures of Creative Thinking* (New York: Scribner's, 1959).

32. Delbecq, A. L., A. H. Van De Ven, and D. H. Gustafson, *Group Techniques for Program Planning: A Guide to Nominal Group Techniques and Delphi Process* (Glenview, IL: Scott, Foresman, 1975).

33. DeVito, J. A., *Brainstorms* (New York: HarperCollins College Publishers, 1996).

34. Johnson and Hackman.

35. Poole, M. S., M. Holmes, R. Watson, and G. DeSanctis, "Group Decision Support Systems and Group Communication: A Comparison of Decision Making in Computer-Supported and Nonsupported Groups," *Communication Research* 20 (1993): 176–213.

36. Scott, C. R., and J. C. Fontsnot, "Multiple Identifications During Team Meetings: A Comparison of Conventional and Computer Supported Interactions," *Communication Reports* 13 (1999): 91–100.

37. Straus, S. G., "Getting a Clue: The Effects of Communication Media and Information Distribution on Participation and Performance in Computer-Mediated and Face-to-Face Groups," *Small Group Research* 27 (1996): 115–142.

38. Scott, C. R., "A Rationale for Declining Benefits Associated with Repeated Usage of Group Decision Support Systems for Organizational Decision Making" (paper presented at the annual meeting of the Western States Communication Association, San Jose, CA, February 1994).

39. Poole et al.

40. Straus, 138.

41. Hocker, J. L., and W. W. Wilmot, *Interpersonal Conflict* (New York: McGraw-Hill, 1998).

42. Janis, I. L., *Victims of Groupthink* (Boston: Houghton Mifflin, 1972).

43. Ruble, T. L., and K. W. Thomas, "Support for a Two-Dimensional Model of Conflict Behavior," *Organizational Behavior and Human Performance* 16 (1976): 143–155.

44. Folger, J. P., M. S. Poole, and R. K. Stutman, *Working Through Conflict: Strategies for Relationships, Groups, and Organizations* (New York: Longman, 1997).

45. Fisher, R., and W. Ury, *Getting to Yes: Negotiating Agreement Without Giving In* (New York: Penguin Books, 1983), 42.

46. Phillips, E., and R. Cheston, "Conflict Resolution: What Works?" *California Management Review* 21 (1979): 76–83.

47. Fisher and Ury.

# 4

# *Interpersonal Politics and Power in Communication*

Interpersonal relationships in organizations are unique. We interact with people at work because we must to achieve our strategic goals. As a result, most work relationships take place within a hierarchy of unequal power and authority.

Whenever hierarchies of authority, responsibility, and power develop they bring with them power imbalances and political maneuverings. Most people view power and politics as the least enjoyable aspect of the work experience. Unfortunately, the very nature of hierarchy guarantees that power will never be evenly distributed. When imbalances occur, political maneuvering is sure to follow. In this chapter, we familiarize readers with the most prevalent features of organizational life: power and politics. First, we explain the nature of organizational power and politics. Second, we discuss the experience of women and minorities as they struggle to attain their own powerful political connections within organizations. Finally, because sexual harassment represents a serious imbalance of power, we suggest strategies for managing it.

# Interpersonal Power and Politics

People are often disconcerted to learn that all interpersonal relationships involve some form of hierarchy. We define **hierarchy** as the relative position—above, below, beside—that people occupy vis-à-vis one another. The positions of a hierarchy are determined by who controls valuable resources in the relationship and who has power or influence to define the nature of the relationship (what will or will not take place).

However, in voluntary interpersonal relationships, such as friendship and marriage, the hierarchies of influence and control are fluid and change more freely than they do in involuntary organizational relationships. The more bureaucratic the organization, the more important and less fluid the hierarchy. Compared with voluntary relationships, people in organizations must learn to cope with an environment characterized by power and politics.

Unfortunately, most people believe organizational power and politics drain human potential and should be minimized or eliminated from organizational life. However, until the perfect human being is created, a human devoid of self-interest and therefore of passion, power, and politics will remain an important part of organizational life. This section covers three main issues: the nature of power in organizations, the nature of organizational politics, and methods of developing political power within a professional setting.

## The Nature of Organizational Power

Our culture typically defines **power** negatively, as the ability to dominate and control others. The ancient Greek Sophists, the entrepreneurial traveling teachers of Greece (entrepreneurial because they were the first to be paid for the knowledge they taught, a concept your authors are grateful for), believed that power was the ability to mobilize people and resources to accomplish a goal. Similarly, we define power as the ability to influence others. If you successfully influence tellers to handle customers more rapidly or salespeople to sell more cars, you have exerted influence over those individuals; you have exerted power.

However, leaders have no influence—and therefore no power—if followers do not act on their suggestions. Except when physical violence is used to coerce people, power is always partly exerted, as when people try to influence others and, partly given, as when others choose to be influenced. The amount of power someone has in a relationship could be expressed in a simple formula.

$$P_{ab} = D_{ba}$$ (The power of $a$ over $b$ is equal to the dependence that $b$ has on $a$.)[1]

The power ($P$) person $a$ has over person $b$ depends on the extent to which $b$ is dependent on $a$. If person $b$ desires the rewards $a$ controls, then $a$ has power over $b$. If, on the other hand, $b$ cares little for $a$'s rewards, then $a$ has little influence over $b$. For example, a bank we studied tried to convince tellers to sell more services to customers, and it offered the promise of full-time work in return. Because most of the tellers didn't want full-time work, the bank's offer had little influence, and sales did not increase.[2]

Figure 4.1 depicts the four different sources of power in interpersonal relationships.[3] Empowering yourself involves identifying what's needed in your organization and developing those resources for later use.

As a member of any organization, you have the ability to increase your power in each of these areas. You can increase your resource power by moving up the organizational ladder,

**FIGURE 4.1**   *Four Sources of Power in Interpersonal Relationships*

| Power Resource | Definition/Explanation |
|---|---|
| Resource control | Occupying a position that provides control over promotions, pay, or valuable assignments |
| Expertise power | Comes from having special skills or knowledge that someone else values |
| Communication skills | Possessed by people who listen well, persuade others, argue well in favor of their positions, or lead groups in an effective manner |
| Interpersonal network | Comes from a person's network of contacts, friends, and supporters |

wherein you will be granted greater control over budgets, attractive tasks, and raises. In terms of expertise power, it's important to identify the skills and knowledge that are valued by your organization. If an understanding of basic accounting is valued in your organization, acquiring this knowledge gives you expertise power.

Communication skills are the focus of this book, and your presence in this class testifies to your commitment to developing stronger communication-based power resources. Improving your ability to persuade, influence, and lead will improve your standing in the organization. Finally, cultivating an extensive personal network can provide the basis for powerful coalitions to help you get things done.

A career means, in part, a never-ending commitment to identifying and adapting to the needs of your organization. In so doing, you improve organizational productivity and gain personal power. And power is essential to effectively handling a second ubiquitous feature of organizational life—politics.

## The Nature of Organizational Politics

After interviewing over 100 executives from three large chemical firms, Robert Jackall, a business writer, argued that modern bureaucracy is a "moral maze" where slick talk, self-promotion, and sheer luck contribute more to success than effort or intelligence.[4] Further, most employees probably share the negative definition of politics put forward by Mayes and Allen:

> Politics is actions not officially sanctioned by an organization that [employees take] to influence others in order to meet [their] personal goals.[5]

In this view, politics consists of wheeling and dealing for personal rather than organizational gain.

However, the inventors of politics, the ancient Greeks, did not share this negative view. For the Greeks, any organized entity, be it a government or a business, is a conglomeration of divergent interests. Organizations need some way to reconcile interests through consultation and negotiation. Politics is a means of creating order out of diversity while avoiding forms of totalitarian rule. We agree with this point and define **politics** as the use of power to negotiate between and consolidate competing interests in an organization.

Our definition of politics clashes with modern preferences. Today, we criticize politicians and managers for failing to set aside personal interests and work only for the greater good of the nation or organization. Such protests, however, ignore two important principles. First, whether we are talking about professional politicians or organizational politics, most of us believe that our interests coincide with the larger interests of the organization. Thus asking us to sacrifice our interests for the organization doesn't make sense: Our interests are the organization's interests! Second, none of us would voluntarily sacrifice our individual interests for the sake of the organization. Ask yourself if you would voluntarily give up your job to help out the organization during an economic downturn. Given these two realities, it is unlikely that politics will ever disappear from the modern organization. Of course, this does not mean that all organization politics is ethical. See the Ethics Brief for an explanation of ethical principles to guide political activity.

## BOX 4.1 • *Ethics Brief*

Carlos, the chief operating officer of a small antenna design and manufacturing firm, is in a quandary. He has two competing proposals for new products, but his company can afford to pursue only one of the ideas. The first proposal is from Jenny, who believes that the company's existing CB antenna line is badly in need of retooling to take advantage of the newest technology. She believes this retrofit is vital if the product, an important source of company revenue, is going to remain competitive. The second proposal comes from Marcus, who wants to develop an entirely new line of marine antennas and thinks that, with the proper investment, the company's product will outclass the competition. Jenny is a personal friend of Carlos, the CEO. The two came to the company at about the same time and formed a quick friendship. In order to push her proposal for a revamped CB antenna, Jenny spent more time than normal with Carlos, playing golf, having lunch, and so forth. Whenever she could work it into the conversation, she discussed the advantages of retooling the CB antenna.

Marcus, on the other hand, is uncomfortable around people. He believes proposals should be accepted or rejected based only on their technical merit. Despite the fact that he has been with the company longer than either Carlos or Jenny, he never formed a personal relationship with either and is not interested in taking time away from his family to "hang out" with people from work. He is concerned that Carlos's decision will be based on

politics rather than on the merits of the case. The whole situation reminds him how much he hates organizational politics.

What are the ethical implications of Jenny's political behavior? How should she proceed while still meeting some standards of decent, ethical conduct? In this brief we outline three standards for the ethical conduct of organizational politics. These guidelines may help you engage in political activity that is both ethical and beneficial to you and your organization.

First, employees should balance self- and organizational interests. According to Nancie Fimbel, a professor at San Jose State University, almost all political activity is designed to bring about benefits to the organization and benefits to the self. Using political power to make a proposal, complete a job, acquire resources, or steer a team to a final decision benefits the organization because work is accomplished. However, these activities also benefit the individual, because the proposal or job brings increased credibility and esteem. As such, Fimbel suggests that ethical politics balances both organizational and individual interests. Unethical political activity benefits mainly the individual at the expense of the organization and its membership.*

For example, junkets to distant manufacturing operations for inspections and a day of skiing, hiring consultants who are friends, or favoring a proposal mainly because it benefits your unit are examples of politics where personal interests might outstrip organizational interests. As such, these activities should be carefully considered.

Because we aren't always aware of our own motives, you should carefully analyze your political activity to be sure that the organization and its members receive significant benefits from your activities. If these benefits are not apparent, then it may be necessary to reevaluate your goals. In other words, if Jenny truly believes that the retooled CB antenna is vital for organizational success, she can feel more comfortable politicking on its behalf.

Second, employees should maintain vigilant openness to change. Simply because it appears, in the early stages of a proposal, that your idea would benefit the organization doesn't mean that will always be true. Things change quickly in business. The ethical employee must be open to new information that might diminish the organizational value of his or her proposals. Jenny, for example, may learn that the CB antenna market is expected to decline in the coming years. As a result, the benefits of her proposal are diminished. If she disregards this new information and continues to push for her proposal, her actions are less ethical than before. The ethical employee seeks out counterarguments and tests the available evidence, remaining open to changing or withdrawing proposals that produce little or no organizational benefit.

Third, the ethical employee works to minimize harm to others. Despite attempts to politick for their ideas, employees must minimize the harm of their political activities throughout the organization. This can be done in several ways. (1) Attempt to maintain a positive, professional relationship with your rivals throughout the organization. Destroying collegial relationships is bad for morale. Besides, even if your proposal is accepted over others, you may need these people to make your ideas a reality. (2) Don't allow your success to be based purely on political maneuvering. If you also win the contest of ideas, your credibility will go up with both your superiors and your internal competitors. (See Chapter 10 for more information on making logical proposals.) (3) Be fair when arguing privately for your proposal. Admit the limits of your arguments and evidence. Acknowledge the strengths of competing proposals. Focus on the benefits of your ideas rather than the weaknesses of other people's ideas. Focusing on weaknesses when project supporters are not present to speak for themselves is unethical. In private, build up your ideas; don't tear down others' ideas. (4) Spread the benefits of your success to other organizational members. Distribute politically won resources to newcomers and allow them to prove themselves. Compliment opponents for the quality of their ideas and for forcing you to focus and sharpen your thinking. Publicly thank subordinates and other team members who had input into the ideas you presented. Be generous in your praise of other contributors.

Because almost all organizations are characterized by uncertainty and scarce resources, organizational politics is a fact of life. Remembering these three guidelines will help you practice politics in an ethical manner.

*Fimbel, N., "Communicating Realistically: Taking Account of Politics in Internal Business Communications," *Journal of Business Communication* 31 (1994): 7–26.

Generally speaking, there are two dimensions to organizational politics, both of which relate to communication. **Overt politics** involves a variety of communications, including threats, promises, negotiations, orders, coalition formation, and a host of other strategies to influence others and fulfill self- and/or organizational interests.[6] Any attempt to get a proposal accepted, sell an idea to other members, or convince a group that your interpretation is correct involves you in acts of overt politics. **Hidden politics** is the process by which employees decide which issues to raise in public, what arguments to present, which battles to fight, and how to fight them.[7] Let's look at two examples of politics in action.

Salt Lake City officials were devastated! In 1990 the International Olympic Committee selected Atlanta as the site of the 1996 Summer Olympic Games, and the decision likely meant that another U.S. city would not be considered for host duties for some time. Salt Lake officials were trying to land the 2002 Winter Olympic Games, but things looked grim. According to a report in the *Wall Street Journal,* Salt Lake City officials turned to a member of the International Olympic Committee for help. That person, Anita DeFrantz, had become an influential member of the American contingent to the committee. Salt Lake City officials held a banquet in Ms. DeFrantz's honor, gave her helicopter tours of the area, and taught her to ski. In return, Ms. DeFrantz helped the committee.

> She started tipping off the bid committee to the personal interests of each IOC member (upon learning from Ms. DeFrantz that one member was an avid gardener, the committee bought him a fancy book on horticulture). She talked Salt Lake boosters out of a planned statewide torch relay; locals thought the event would impress Olympic officials, but Ms. DeFrantz suspected they would consider it an inappropriate use of one of their most famous symbols.[8]

In this example we see both overt and hidden politics. Ms. DeFrantz is courted and asked to join a coalition of interests supporting the Salt Lake games. In addition, hidden politics is practiced as Ms. DeFrantz provides valuable advice designed to advance Salt Lake's bid. Of course, the world later learned that Salt Lake officials went well beyond small gifts to win the Games.

A more ethical example of overt and hidden politics is described as follows:

> James Johnson is the only African-American county manager in his southern state. He has been in his current position for six years, a remarkable achievement considering that the average tenure of county managers in his state is twenty-six months. He attributes his longevity to his ability to understand and adapt to organizational and local politics and still accomplish a great deal for the county's residents. Fortunately, he is also committed to teaching these skills to others. Two years ago he hired a bright young accountant. After completing an audit of all the county's operations, she came to him with a proposal to reallocate a substantial part of the budget.
>
> She had discovered that use of the county's workshop for disturbed youth (which I will label AT) had dropped steadily during the past five years, resulting in a costly and inefficient operation. Furthermore, the ratio of clinicians (psychiatrists, psychologists, and social workers) to clients was almost three times the state-required level. She also discovered that the Retired Citizens' Rehabilitation Center (labeled RCRC) had become seriously overloaded and understaffed. Since the population projections that she had obtained from the state indicated that the shift would continue at least through the year two thousand, she devised a plan to shift resources from the first program to the second. She developed a twelve-point presentation, complete with slide and videotape aids, to support her arguments that (1) the overall needs of the county's residents would best be served by the shift, (2) the county could save a great deal of money because the licensed psychologists and lawyers on retainer as consultants for the AT could be dismissed, and (3) the funds could be used more efficiently because the success rate of the RCRC was almost four times as great as that of the AT. Before going to the county board of commissioners with the proposal, however, she wanted Johnson to sit in on a rehearsal of her presentation.
>
> After the rehearsal he congratulated her for the quality of the presentation, but suggested that there were some details about which she might not be aware: (1) one of the board members had two children in the AT program and had saved thousands of dollars in

psychotherapy expenses because it was available, (2) another commissioner's spouse was a consultant for the AT program, (3) two other commissioners had been reelected primarily because they claimed to have done a great deal for the county's retired citizens (and almost certainly would be embarrassed by the funding comparison included in the slide presentation), and (4) in the past the commission had voted in favor of money-saving recommendations only in odd-numbered years, when a majority of them were up for reelection.

The young accountant was perceptive enough to understand that these were invaluable hints. She revised her presentation, making three major changes. First, instead of arguing that the county was inadequately meeting its obligations to retired citizens, she argued that the growth in the use-rate of the RCRC demonstrated how effective the existing programs had been under the leadership of the current board and suggested that their programs warranted continuation and expansion. Second, she argued that the plummeting use-rate of the AT program demonstrated the success of professionally designed and led treatment, and she proposed that the staff be professionalized further in two steps. As nonsupervisory personnel resigned (which happens quite often in programs with assaultive adolescents), their salaries would be frozen until a sufficiently large sum was available to hire the most senior consulting psychologist (who coincidentally was the commissioner's spouse) on a full-time basis. Because the AT staff's professional skills would be increased by the completion of step 1, the remaining consulting contracts could be shifted to the RCRC and the remaining nonsupervisory personnel could be transferred to that agency.

Finally, the accountant arranged to have Johnson present the proposal at the next commission meeting, which she would attend in order to provide "technical support." Thus, she was able to adapt to the existing power relationships, and to do so without the knowledge of anyone except her supportive, and quite satisfied, supervisor. (A postscript: While revising her presentation, she found two filed-away proposals much like her original one. Evidently, she was not the only accountant to notice this misallocation of funds. But the others had either chosen not to speak out or did so ineffectively).[*]

[*]*Excerpt from Strategic Organizational Communication, Third Edition by Charles Conrad, copyright, 1993 by Holt, Rinehart and Winston.*

As you can see, Mr. Johnson engages in overt politics by forming coalitions with his young staff. These exchanges work to the benefit of both parties, but especially for the young staff members, who acquire a valuable source of information. In addition, Mr. Johnson's advice represents hidden politics; Mr. Johnson helps his accountant decide on the most effective persuasive appeals for the county commission.

It's difficult to succeed in organizational politics without an adequate resource, expertise, communication, and interpersonal linkage power. In the next section we explain how to use interpersonal linkages to build a base of political support in an organization.

## *Creating a Power Base for Political Action: A Focus on Interpersonal Networking*

Interpersonal linkages can be the source of enormous political power. Increasing your interpersonal network power involves two abilities: impression management and aligning oneself with powerful others. We discuss each of these in the following text.

*Impression Management.*    **Impression management** means displaying traits that are rewarded by the organization. It involves conforming to organizational norms for dress and appearance, as well as such deeper norms as the organization's core values and decision premises. At the U.S. Forest Service, for example, natural resource conservation is a deeply held premise, forming the core of the organization's mission. Employees must reflect conservation values in their daily work if they hope to make a favorable impression on others. We group impression management skills into three categories: demonstrating emotional maturity, showing competence, and expressing confidence.

According to Joseph M. Fox, chair of Software A&E, and Donald G. Zauderer, at the American University in Washington, DC, many talented professionals find it difficult to advance within their organization because they fail to **demonstrate emotional maturity.**[9] Although people are rarely praised for being emotionally mature, immature behavior stands out and reduces peoples' perceptions of your competence. Even a single inappropriate outburst could destroy your credibility.

Emotionally mature people have a sense of perspective—the ability to tolerate and accept life's many setbacks without becoming overly frustrated or resentful.[10] One colleague we knew would express anger over the smallest perceived inequity. This person would explode with anger when she found out, for example, that the department wouldn't pay for faculty business cards. Such annoyances are part of life, and mature people handle them without complaint.

According to Nancie Fimbel at San Jose State University, **showing competence** means having the technical knowledge needed to efficiently solve routine problems. Competent people can handle their routine work without running to a superior to ask questions about every hiccup. However, they also know when the problems in a routine assignment have become so great that help is required.[11]

**Expressing confidence** is another way to cultivate a favorable impression. According to Fimbel, managers expect a sender to display the confidence warranted by their competence. "Sentences that state facts but that secondarily congratulate the message sender herself, as in 'I have completed the task,' sound confident. Phrases such as 'of course,' and 'clearly' add certainty to the content of the message by presenting assumptions as indubitable fact; 'as we decided' and 'as you know' assume the audience's agreement."[12] Nonverbally, confidence is communicated with high-immediacy behaviors such as voice modulation to express appropriate effect and suitable variation in pitch, rate, and volume, rather than monotone speech. Steady, sustained, substantial eye contact and affirmative body cues such as head nodding and hand gestures communicate high energy and a sense of confidence.[13]

Finally, confident people do not focus on failure. It isn't uncommon to think about the consequences of failure when working on a large or important project. Soon after she was named general manager of Hewlett-Packard's Medical Products Group, Cynthia Danaher told her 5,300 employees, "I want to do this job, but it's scary and I need your help." Three years later, she regrets those words. "People say they want a leader to be vulnerable just like them, but deep down they want to believe you have the skill to move and fix things they can't," says Ms. Danaher. "And while anyone who starts something new is bound to feel some anxiety, you don't need to bare your soul."[14] Instead, effective managers refocus their fears toward analyzing and correcting problems. At work, display an attitude of confidence to increase the confidence others have in you.

In summary, impression management involves demonstrating emotional maturity, showing competence, and expressing confidence. Good impressions mean that others are eager to associate with you, which improves your interpersonal linkage power.

***Aligning Oneself with Powerful Others.***     Finally, developing interpersonal linkages means forming coalitions with others to gain power and influence. For employees who are new to an organization, this is best accomplished by seeking out a **mentor,** "an individual with some tenure in the organization who is willing to serve as advisor, friend, observer, giver of feedback, helper, teacher, and sounding board, to a newer member."[15] The **mentee** or **protégé** is someone willing to be guided by the knowledge accumulated by the mentor. The benefits of a mentor include information, expertise, professional advice, political access, exposure to upper management, help in getting important assignments, and advocacy for promotion.

A study of more than 400 respondents conducted by researchers at Cleveland State University showed that mentors provide important strategic connections and enhance career success for protégés.[16] Although some organizations have formal mentoring programs in which a newcomer is assigned to learn from a more experienced employee, the newcomer is usually left on his or her own in such matters.

Developing a mentor involves several steps. First, the new employee must scout appropriate mentor possibilities in the organization. Research shows that both mentors and protégés choose partners who are of like identities, sharing similar interests and worldviews. Generally, you should search for someone who is somewhat similar to you in attitudes and interests, someone who is politically well connected in the organization, and someone who will serve as a mentor. Once you have selected several mentor possibilities, initiate a relationship with these people. Make an appointment to talk about your present assignment. Ask their advice about a decision you face. Seek their input about the organization's culture. Remember, it is the mentor, not the protégé, who decides whether a relationship is possible. If a person responds positively, take his or her advice and make it clear that you have acted on suggestions provided. Offer praise for his or her ideas and thanks for the help given. Share some of the credit if the mentor provided helpful advice on a successful assignment. Such comments increase your potential mentor's visibility in the organization and give him or her a reason to develop a closer working relationship with you. Offer to handle some of your mentor's workload or accept some of your mentor's less appealing tasks. All of these provide the potential mentor with incentive for building a stronger relationship.

## Building Interpersonal Networks: The Experience of Women and Minorities

Building interpersonal networks in organizations is vital for personal success and productivity. However, despite the growing presence of women and minorities in organizations, research shows that these employees are sometimes excluded from informal interpersonal networks. As a result, these employees suffer from restricted knowledge of the organization, have difficulty forming coalitions for political gain, have trouble finding powerful mentors, and may be less likely to move up the organizational hierarchy. The mobility limit is often referred to as the **"glass ceiling,"** an invisible barrier that prevents women and minorities from reaching the highest levels of management. Here, we address the reasons that women and minorities have difficulty gaining access to the informal communication network in organizations and suggest ways to overcome these obstacles.

## *Barriers to the Informal Network*

Although outright prejudice and exclusion against women and minorities is much less common, more subtle barriers exist. The first, and arguably most important, barrier to women and minorities in forming organizational networks and mentorship relationships is a universal **preference for similarity** in our organizational relationships. One study shows that the race of the mentor is the best predictor of the mentoring relationship.[17] As a result, white mentors tend to guide white employees, and black mentors tend to guide black employees. The problem is that there is a much smaller pool of politically well-connected minority managers in most organizations to adequately mentor the much larger pool of minority protégés.

A second obstacle to minority advancement is the **stereotype** that some white male managers may hold. Despite their advances into management ranks in the last 15 years, negative stereotypes of women and minorities persist in some organizations and industries. In some organizations, the presence of token female and minority employees leads some white male managers to exaggerate the differences between themselves and minority employees. They may inappropriately ascribe lower status and competence to all members of different gender, racial, or ethnic groups. For example, a 2005 report focusing on barriers to female advancement argues that men consider women less skilled at problem-solving, one of the qualities most associated with effective leadership. Because men far outnumber women in top management positions, this male-held stereotype dominates current corporate thinking.[18] These kinds of stereotypes create a barrier to developing mentors, and hinder advancement for women and minorities.

Finally, even if minority employees do accomplish cross-gender or cross-racial network relationships, these are likely to be weaker than same-gender, same-race contacts. Relationships based on similar gender and racial ties provide greater personal attraction, social support, and identification for both members than do relationships based on differences.[19] The Cleveland State study we cited earlier demonstrates that both men and women improve their career success outcomes through contact with well-connected male mentors.[20] However, cross-gender and cross-racial ties require more effort to maintain and may not create the same emotional, or social support benefits as do relationships based on similarity.

As you can see, even organizations that attempt to become more diverse can still present problems for minority employees. There are, however, solutions to these problems.

## *Overcoming Informal Network Barriers*

The problems just discussed leave women and minorities with a choice. First, they can pursue close, stable network contacts with similar individuals. Because these contacts are based on similarity, they are likely to provide enormous emotional benefits, but these ties may not provide visibility or political connection. On the other hand, women and minorities can forsake the emotional benefits of similarity-based ties and seek to network with different people. Although emotional benefits may not be met in these networks, organizational benefits are more likely. Faced with these choices, most women and minorities attempt to steer a middle course, maintaining two separate networks—one a network of like-minded individuals of similar gender and race that provides emotional and social benefits, and one a network of politically connected

**FIGURE 4.2**  *Overcoming Informal Network Barriers*

| | |
|---|---|
| Reach across the organization | Seek mentors in different hierarchical or geographical areas of the organization. |
| Seek out supportive nonminority managers | Look for those managers who demonstrate a desire to advance women and minorities. |
| | Don't limit your contacts to only those people who are similar to you and with whom you are comfortable. |
| Express and demonstrate a desire for advancement | Take on high-profile assignments. |
| | Express confidence in yourself, your work, and your eventual promotion. |
| | Seek constant evaluation and feedback from your superior and mentors. |
| | Take appropriate risks. |
| Become a member of your supervisor's in-group | Watch for opportunities to satisfy your supervisor's "tests." |

acquaintances and mentors who are committed to advancing minorities and provide access to organizational resources and information.[21] Properly managed, steering the middle course is a viable option for upwardly mobile women and minorities.

Figure 4.2 shows ways to help employees develop diverse contact with politically connected senior organizational members.

The fourth suggestion in Figure 4.2 requires explanation. Almost all supervisors are forced to distinguish between those subordinates who demonstrate higher commitment, trustworthiness, and competence than subordinates who, although not incompetent or untrustworthy, are less distinguished than the others. The **in-group** of employees may be a select association of protégés or a clique of the superior's most trusted employees. In-group members are given inside information, influence in decision making, attractive tasks, personal latitude, support, and attention from the superior in return for their commitment. According to researchers George Graen and Terri Scandura, the negotiation of in-group or **out-group** status usually takes place during a newcomer's first few weeks in the new organization. In stage 1, the leader "tests" the subordinate with requests or assignments and evaluates the subordinate's response for possible in-group membership. The superior is watching for greater-than-required expenditures of time and energy, the assumption of greater responsibility and commitment. This can be accomplished by staying after hours to complete a project, working hard to provide higher quality work, and completing the task in less than prescribed time limits.[22] In stage 2, the superior may propose a more collaborative relationship by offering resources in return for desired behaviors from the subordinate. The newcomer may respond positively, signaling an intention of becoming an in-group member.[23] Research confirms that achieving in-group status gives "the employee the opportunity for influence through role-making and negotiation leading to job growth and change."[24] The interview in this chapter reviews the importance of mentors for minority employees.

The Cleveland State study suggests that peer relationships that include both task and social support have a solid effect on accomplishing organizational work and achieving career advancement. "Since all employees cannot obtain a mentor, it is important to note that peers and colleagues can provide connection power which facilitates success."[25]

**BOX 4.2 • *Interview: Laverne Sheppard (Human Resources Manager, Astaris LLC, Headquartered in St. Louis, Missouri, Member of the Shoshone-Bannock Tribe, Fort Hall Reservation, Fort Hall, Idaho)***

(Astaris manufactures phosphates for various industrial and commercial applications.)

*Have the career and advancement possibilities for female and minority employees improved over the past two decades?*

I've seen improvement. There are now more women and people of color in top management positions within companies. In addition, most firms see things differently today. They know that there is a limited pool of qualified prospective employees available, and even if they wanted to, they can't further limit that talent pool by hiring only white males. Most managers know that being open to people of color, older people, and the disabled broadens their candidate pool considerably, making it easier to find the most gifted, qualified employees possible.

*So, being open to diversity improves one's ability to hire and recruit the most talented employees.*

Yes, but there is an added benefit to this kind of openness. North American companies now compete in global markets. To compete globally, they need diverse perspectives. And to get those diverse perspectives they need to hire employees from different backgrounds. Forward-thinking businesspeople recognize that having a diverse workforce actually strengthens the organization and makes it more competitive.

*Research suggests that one barrier to the advancement of women and minorities is that there is a much smaller pool of politically well-connected minority managers in most organizations to mentor the larger pool of minority protégés.*

Yes, despite the advances that women and minorities have made, this is still the case. It helps to know that someone who is like you is in a position to which you aspire. But for many women and minorities, there isn't anyone like them at the highest levels of the organizations. Many women

and minorities have to seek out people who are unlike them and try to identify these unlike people as mentors.

*How can companies encourage connections between mentors and minority protégés?*

One of the best ways is through the formation of a diversity council that includes people at all levels and from all groups—female and male, minority and nonminority—in the organization. This council can survey the organization's needs and decide whether a formal mentoring program is needed to advance the careers of women and people of color. If that's the case, which it often is, the council can meet with top managers and match them up with protégés throughout the organization. The new mentoring relationship is artificial in some ways, but we've seen it work because the minority employee does get some guidance and visibility in the organization.

*What advice would you give an employee whose organization doesn't have a formal mentoring program?*

I think that the first step is to identify managers, upper-level managers, who are in positions to which the employee aspires and try to establish some communication with that individual. Initially, that communication could be as simple as saying, "I'm trying to get a better understanding of your job so that I can prepare for advancement." Asking questions about what the person does is a way to open the door to a more encompassing relationship. It is also important for all employees, not just women and minorities, to express their career desires and job interests to their supervisor. People often make assumptions, such as "Well, the company knows I want to move into this area," but that is often not the case. At a minimum, your supervisor and the coworkers in your area should know your career goals and aspirations. Women in particular seem to assume that their work will speak for itself. In reality, it's up to everyone to promote themselves so that management knows what they've accomplished and what they want to accomplish. One of the most valuable things any employee can do is to schedule regular meetings with the supervisor. These meetings shouldn't be limited to narrow performance goals. The employee should also talk about what she has accomplished in the past several months and ask

whether she's on track for the goals she wants to accomplish in the future. Also, don't be afraid to speak up in meetings and tell people what you're working on. In a lot of cultures and subcultures, we're told not to brag, to defer to elders, to let them speak. These can be hard messages to overcome, but they must be overcome if one is to advance.

Although we have talked about organizational power and politics in positive terms, there are times when power imbalances lead to oppressive behavior, such as sexual harassment. The final section of this chapter defines sexual harassment and presents formal and informal solutions to this abuse of power.

## *Sexual Harassment: A Gross Imbalance of Power*

Since the 1991 Hill–Thomas hearings, workplace sexual harassment has received enormous attention. As a result, reports of sexual harassment have increased, and one of the professional world's dirtiest secrets has been forced into the light. Most survey results suggest that approximately 40 percent of all working women report being sexually harassed at some point in their career. Complaints about sexual harassment to the U.S. Equal Employment Opportunity Commission (EEOC) more than doubled between 1990 and 1995. In 1991 Congress amended Title VII of the Civil Rights Act to permit victims of sexual harassment to recover damages (including punitive damages) under federal law. Moreover, in 1993 the U.S. Supreme Court broadened the reach of this law by making it easier to prove injury from sexual harassment.

Except in cases of physical manhandling or assault, sexual harassment is based on communication. Lewd remarks, sexual jokes, or negotiations for sexual favors all involve some form of verbal and nonverbal communication. In addition, the methods of controlling and eliminating sexual harassment, such as formal grievances and lawsuits, or individual solutions, such as attempting to convince the harasser to cease and desist, are all based on communication.

Sexual harassment represents the abuse of organizational power. In this section we define sexual harassment and describe a variety of interpersonal communication solutions to the problem. Although sexual harassment has a variety of costs associated with it, including psychological and physical costs to the victims and direct and indirect costs to the organization, our position is that sexual harassment is discrimination against a particular gender and represents a gross abuse of power.[26]

The term *sexual harassment* was introduced into the English language by feminists to refer to behaviors whereby men humiliate women and treat them as "objects."[27] **Sexual harassment** was defined legally in 1980 when the EEOC established guidelines to interpret sexual harassment. The guidelines were established under Title VII of the 1964 Civil Rights Act. Sexual harassment includes unwelcome sexual advances, requests for sexual favors, and other verbal or physical conduct of a sexual nature that takes place under any of the following circumstances.

1. When submission to the sexual advance is a condition of keeping or getting a job, whether expressed in implicit or explicit terms.
2. When a supervisor or boss makes personal decisions based on an employee's submission to or rejection of sexual advances.
3. When conduct unreasonably interferes with a person's work performance or creates an intimidating, hostile, or offensive work environment.[28]

In practice, "sexual harassment has been characterized as an expression of **gender discrimination** coupled with the **abuse of organizational power.**" Most often, sexual harassment involves a range of unsolicited and unwelcome male attention that serves to emphasize a woman's sex role over her work skills and abilities. Although reports indicate that sexual harassment of women against men does occur, it is relatively infrequent (at most, in surveys 15 percent of men report being sexually harassed).[29]

Practically speaking, sexual harassment may include several general categories of behavior. **Verbal commentaries,** such as sexual jokes, lewd comments, and excessive comments about bodily appearance, are forms of harassment. For example, an anonymous communication professor reported the following incident of verbal commentary:

I was in class lecturing when I was writing something on the board and as I turned around a male voice from the back of the class said: "She's got nice looking tits." This was said loudly enough for the entire class to hear. I was so stunned and shocked that I said nothing. But when I told my mentor, who was then the dean of a law school, what had happened, he chuckled and said: "Well, you do have nice tits."[30]

**Verbal negotiation** includes propositions for sex, especially those that involve the promise of reward or threat of punishment if the person propositioned does not comply. **Physical manhandling** is unwanted groping, or inappropriate touching, and **physical assault** is the use of physical force.[31] Finally, in 1991 the courts ruled that a workplace permeated with sexual graffiti and pornography constituted a **hostile environment** that amounted to sexual harassment.[32]

According to the Sexual Harassment Support Web site, an information resource for victims, harassers can be classified into a number of categories. Although harassers may engage in more than one type of behavior, and thus these categories are not mutually exclusive, the classification scheme does represent a useful way to recognize different types of harassment behavior.[33] We summarize some of the categories in Figure 4.3.

There are a variety of solutions that individuals and groups can take to the problems of sexual harassment. **Formal solutions** include filing grievances or lawsuits to get the harasser to stop. **Informal solutions** involve face-to-face communication with the harasser.

According to Shereen G. Bingham, a communication researcher at the University of Nebraska at Omaha, whatever strategy one selects to stop harassment must address three goals: first, to **get the harassment stopped;** second, it must **maintain employment;** and third, it must help the victim **manage his or her own psychological and emotional well-being.** The primary obstacle to achieving these goals is the power imbalance that usually exists between the harasser (the high-power person) and the victim (usually a person of low power).[34] Because this imbalance makes it very difficult for a person to achieve all three interpersonal goals, responses should be made with appropriate thought to increase the likelihood of success.

**FIGURE 4.3**   *Categorizing Harassers and Harassment Behavior*

| | |
|---|---|
| The Power-Player | These harassers insist on sexual favors in exchange for raises, promotions, etc. Referred to legally as "quid pro quo" harassment. |
| The Mentor-Helper | These harassers try to create a mentorlike relationship with the target, while masking their sexual intentions. |
| One-of-the-Gang | Motivated by bravado or competition, groups of men embarrass women with lewd comments, physical evaluations, or other unwanted sexual attention. |
| The Serial Harasser | These harassers' outward credibility makes it difficult for others to believe they are harassers. They strike in private so that it's their word against the victim's. |
| The Groper | Whenever the opportunity presents itself (e.g., the elevator), these people's hands and eyes wander over the victim. |
| The Bully | These individuals use sexual harassment to punish their victims for some transgression and put them in their place. |
| The Great Gallant | Excessive compliments that focus on appearance or gender that are socially inappropriate and embarrassing to the victims. |
| The Pest | Hound victims for dates or attention. Usually their behavior is misguided rather than malicious. |

## Formal Strategies for Managing Sexual Harassment

The precise steps to filing a formal grievance—or larger still, a lawsuit—depend on the particular harassment situation, the organization's rules about sexual harassment, and its formal grievance procedures. Thus it is difficult to make specific recommendations. We can, however, offer several pieces of advice. First, our system of justice is based on the belief that a person (even a harasser) is innocent until proven guilty. The burden of proof in any harassment complaint rests with the victim of harassment. Most harassers commit their misdeeds in private, when only the perpetrator and the victim are present, making it difficult to corroborate harassment incidents. This disadvantage can be mitigated by following two rules.

First, many organizations encourage the victim to clearly say no to the harasser. This reduces the harasser's ability to claim his actions were all in fun or that the victim really wanted this kind of relationship.

Second, victims should document the incidents by keeping written records, which protects the victim from fallible memory and makes any case more convincing. Record exact words and language and try to describe the feelings produced by the harassment. Date the record and save it for future action. Without documentation, a victim's chances of redress are severely diminished.

## Informal Strategies for Managing Sexual Harassment

Despite the considerable evidence suggesting that direct, informal confrontations between victim and harasser are successful only half of the time, there are other benefits to be gained from confrontation, including personal empowerment. By taking matters into his or her own hands, a person may develop a stronger sense of personal power and control over his or her life.[35] As such, we have culled the following strategies from a larger list compiled by Bingham. We selected the strategies in Table 4.1 because research demonstrates these have the highest probability of success.

**TABLE 4.1   *Communication Strategies for Responding to Sexual Harassment***

*Nonassertive Message*

    a. *Description.* Hide or deny one's thoughts, feelings, beliefs, or wants.

    b. *Example.* Silence.

*Messages with a Face-Saving Component*

Assertive Message

    a. *Description.* Express thoughts, feelings, beliefs, and wants in direct, honest, and appropriate ways.

    b. *Example.* "I don't like it when you make sexual comments about my body, and I want you to stop doing it. This is a workplace; sexual jokes and comments are not appropriate."

Assertive-Empathic Message

    a. *Description.* Express thoughts, feelings, beliefs, and wants in direct, honest, and appropriate ways, and express special concern for the harasser's feelings and perspective.

    b. *Example.* "I don't mean to hurt your feelings but it bothers me when you make comments about my body. I enjoy working with you, but I'd appreciate it if you would stop making sexual jokes and comments."

Rhetorical Multifunctional Message

    a. *Description.* Redefine the situation in a way that precludes continuation of the sexual harassment, while also deflecting the implication that the harasser has a negative identity or that the harassing behavior has harmed the working relationship.

    b. *Example.* "I appreciate the fair treatment you've always given me on this job because I have something on my mind that relates to how well we work together. When you make sexual comments to me, I know you're just teasing, but deep down I end up feeling insulted anyway, and if we don't get this straightened out I'm afraid it might start to affect our work. I know you would never want to put me down or interfere with my job performance, and I would never want to do that to you. So I think the best solution here is for us to stop the sexual jokes and comments altogether. Sound fair to you?"

*Messages That Include Little or No Face-Saving Element*

Threat

    a. *Description.* Express intent to inflict injury or punishment on the harasser if the harassment does not stop.

    b. *Example.* "If you don't stop making sexual jokes about my body, I will file a complaint with your supervisor."

Aggressive Message

    a. *Description.* Express thoughts, feelings, beliefs, and wants directly and honestly in a way that coerces or attacks the harasser.

    b. *Example.* "You stepped over the line with that last comment, wise guy. Shut your big mouth and get away from my desk. I don't take abuse from you or anyone else."

Overt Manipulation

    a. *Description.* Provide information in a manner that influences the harasser to stop the harassment, reveals to the harasser that the influence was intended, but prevents the harasser from admitting awareness of the influence process (due to potential shame, embarrassment, or other negative consequences).

    b. *Example.* "I couldn't hear your last remark. Could you please repeat that comment a bit louder? Where did you say you wanted to touch me?" (said loudly in front of other workers)

*Source:* From Bingham, S., "Communication Strategies for Managing Sexual Harassment in Organizations: Understanding Message Options and Their Effects," *Journal of Applied Communication Research* 19 (1991): 88–115.

The first strategy in Table 4.1 is the **nonassertive message,** which represents avoidance. This strategy is useful if the victim views the harasser's motives as innocent or ignorant of the nature of the behavior and the damage it is doing. The nonassertive message is also useful if the risk to job or career is so high that the safest course of action is avoidance. Nonassertiveness may also serve as a temporary strategy while collecting information prior to a formal complaint.

After nonassertiveness, the remaining strategies are divided into two categories: strategies that help the perpetrator save face and strategies that include no such face-saving measures. The concept of **face** represents the desire of a person to present a positive and approved image to others.[36] Message strategies that preserve a person's face refuse the sexual harassment of the offender but do so in a way that minimizes damage to the person's image of self. Face-saving messages may minimize the harasser's desire to retaliate against the victim.

The first face-saving strategy is the simple **assertive message,** which allows the victim to stand up for personal rights in a clear and direct way without violating another person's rights. As such, the assertive message may be the best way to say no to the harasser in a way that would be approved of by other decision makers in the hierarchy.

According to Bingham, the **assertive-empathic message** attempts to "reconcile being assertive with being liked and maintaining rapport."[37] The message is assertive but includes an empathy component that may reduce the desire of the harasser to retaliate. The **rhetorical multifunctional message** includes features that protect the image of the harasser and express liking for the job or the present relationship, while refusing to accept harassment. These strategies aim at achieving all three goals for interpersonal messages.

The first non-face-saving strategy is a **threat,** which tells the harasser to cease the activity and states that the victim will proceed with a formal grievance if the harasser doesn't stop. Because the threat does nothing to protect the face of the harasser, it invites retaliation. However, with some harassers, a threat is the only form of persuasion that will be effective.

The second non-face-saving strategy is the **aggressive message**—a coercive message that ridicules or intimidates the harasser. This message is so blatant that it greatly increases the chances of retaliation. However, Bingham notes that some harassers may not take a person's objections seriously unless they are addressed in an aggressive fashion.[38] **Overt manipulation** turns the tables on the harasser in public, within earshot of family or coworkers, thereby embarrassing the harasser.

To decide on the appropriate strategy, it is necessary to evaluate the seriousness of the harassment; the organization you are in and its attitude toward this kind of abuse; the support you receive from colleagues, friends, and other organizational higher-ups; the likelihood that the harasser will retaliate; your relative power in the organization; the harasser's relative power in the organization; the likelihood of your submitting a formal complaint; and several other factors related to personal preference for conflict versus tolerance of the offending behavior.

## *Summary*

Politics is a central facet of communication within hierarchical organizations. We define power as the ability to influence or persuade. Organizational politics has two dimensions. Overt politics involves threats, promises, negotiations, coalitions, and a host of other strategies to influence organizational members. Hidden politics involves deciding what issues to raise and how to present them for greatest effect. One way to succeed politically is to create networks through impression management and aligning oneself with powerful others.

Building interpersonal networks can be more problematic for women and minorities. Preferences for similarity, subtle stereotyping, and the difficulty of creating strong ties across gender and racial boundaries often limit networking possibilities. To overcome these barriers, women and minorities should reach across organizational boundaries for contacts, seek out nonminority mentors, demonstrate a desire for advancement, become a member of the supervisor's in-group, and acquire task and social support from informed peers.

Sexual harassment is the result of gender discrimination and the abuse of organizational power. Sexual harassment can involve verbal commentary, verbal negotiation, physical manhandling, physical assault, or the creation of a hostile work environment.

Informal strategies fall into two categories: those that preserve the face needs of the harasser and those that do not preserve the harasser's face. Those that preserve the harasser's face reduce the possibility of retaliation but may not be strong enough to stop the harassment. Victims should carefully weigh the advantages and disadvantages of each strategy before confronting a harasser.

## Questions and Exercises

1. Describe your opinion about organizational politics before you read this chapter. What was the source of this opinion? Has reading this chapter changed your opinion about organizational politics in any way? Why or why not?

2. Why does human nature make organizational politics inevitable? What kinds of preferences and abilities would people need to make organizational politics a thing of the past? Would you want to live in a world where organizational politics no longer existed?

3. Discuss the advantages and disadvantages of the sexual harassment reduction strategies we discussed in this chapter. In what circumstances would you select formal over informal strategies? In what circumstances would you select informal

over formal strategies? How might the strategies be combined for greatest effect?

4. Review the story of James Johnson cited early in this chapter. Identify all the examples of overt and hidden politics in the story. Can you distinguish between the two kinds of organizational politics? Are there any political actions that do not fit into either category?

5. Apply the ethical standards outlined in the Ethics Brief to the story of James Johnson. Does the accountant in the story work to balance organizational and individual interests? What does she do to remain vigilant and open to change? What, if anything, does she do to minimize harm to others? In your opinion, is this an example of ethical or unethical political activity? Why?

## Notes

1. Emerson, R. M., "Power-Dependence Relations," *American Sociological Review* 27 (1962): 31–41.
2. DiSanza, J. R., "Shared Meaning as a Sales Inducement Strategy: Bank Teller Responses to Frames, Reinforcements, and Quotas," *Journal of Business Communication* 30 (1993): 133–160.
3. Hocker, J. L., and W. W. Wilmot, *Interpersonal Conflict* (Dubuque, IA: Wm. C. Brown, 1995).
4. Jackall, R., "Moral Mazes: Bureaucracy and Managerial Work," *Harvard Business Review,* September–October 1983, 118–130.
5. Mayes, B. T., and R. W. Allen, "Toward a Definition of Organizational Politics," *Academy of Management Review* 2 (1977): 420.
6. Conrad, C., *Strategic Organizational Communication* (Fort Worth, TX: Harcourt Brace, 1994).

7. Ibid.

8. Thomas, E., Jr., "Former U.S. Medalist Emerges as Quiet Force in the Olympic Arena," *Wall Street Journal,* 28 June 1996, A1.

9. Fox, J. M., and D. G. Zauderer, "Emotional Maturity—An Important Executive Quality," *Management Solutions,* September 1987, 41–45.

10. Blai, B., Jr., "Emotional Maturity at Work: Tips for the HR Executive," *Personnel,* December 1987, 56–58.

11. Fimbel, N., "Communicating Realistically: Taking Account of Politics in Internal Business Communications," *Journal of Business Communication* 31 (1994): 7–26.

12. Ibid., 13.

13. Leathers, D. G., *Successful Nonverbal Communication: Principles and Applications* (New York: Macmillan, 1986).

14. Hymowitz, C., "How Cynthia Danaher Learned to Stop Sharing and Start Leading," *Wall Street Journal,* 16 March 1999, B1.

15. Pepper, G. L., *Communicating in Organizations: A Cultural Approach* (New York: McGraw-Hill, 1995), 131.

16. Bahniuk, M. H., S. E. K. Hill, and H. J. Darus, "The Relationship of Power-Gaining Communication Strategies to Career Success," *Western Journal of Communication* 60 (1996): 358–378.

17. Kalbfleisch, P. J., and A. B. Davies, "Minorities and Mentoring: Managing the Multicultural Institution," *Communication Education* 40 (1991): 266–271.

18. Prime, J., "Women 'Take Care,' Men 'Take Charge:' Stereotyping of U.S. Business Leaders Exposed." (online http://www.catalystwomen.org/headlines/stereotype.html).

19. Ibarra, H., "Personal Networks of Women and Minorities in Management: A Conceptual Framework," *Academy of Management Review* 18 (1993): 56–87.

20. Bahniuk, Hill, and Darus.

21. Ibarra.

22. Dansereau, F., Jr., G. Graen, and W. J. Haga, "A Vertical Dyad Linkage Approach to Leadership within Formal Organizations," *Organizational Behavior and Human Performance* 13 (1975): 46–78.

23. Graen, G. B., and T. A. Scandura, "Toward a Psychology of Dyadic Organizing," in *Research in Organizational Behavior 9,* ed. L. L. Cummings and B. M. Staw (Greenwich, CT: JAI Press, 1987), 175–208.

24. Bahniuk, Hill, and Darus, 374.

25. Ibid., 374.

26. Albrecht, T. L., and B. W. Bach, *Communication in Complex Organizations* (Fort Worth, TX: Harcourt Brace, 1997).

27. Bingham, S. G., "Communication Strategies for Managing Sexual Harassment in Organizations: Understanding Message Options and Their Effects," *Journal of Applied Communication Research* 19 (1991): 88–115.

28. Sheffey, S., and R. S. Tindale, "Perceptions of Sexual Harassment in the Workplace," *Journal of Applied Social Psychology* 22 (1992): 1502–1520.

29. "Sexual Harassment," U.S. Equal Employment Opportunity Commission Web site, retrieved 2 February 2007 (www.eeoc.gov/types/sexual_harassment.html).

30. "'Our Stories': Communication Professionals' Narratives of Sexual Harassment," *Journal of Applied Communication Research* 20 (1992): 378.

31. Loy, P. H., and L. P. Stewart, "The Extent and Effects of the Sexual Harassment of Working Women," *Sociological Focus* 17 (1984): 31–43.

32. Swoboda, F., and K. D. Grimsley, "A Joke in the '60s, But Not Today," *Washington Post,* 27 January 1997, National Weekly Edition, 9.

33. "Sexual harassers: their patterns, personalities, and types of harassment," Sexual Harassment Support Web site, (www.sexualharassmentsupport.org/TypesOfHarassers.html).

34. Bingham.

35. Ibid.

36. Folger, J. P., M. S. Poole, and R. K. Stutman, *Working Through Conflict* (New York: Longman, 1997).

37. Bingham, 100.

38. Ibid.

# 5

# *Professional Interviews*

Manna nervously fidgeted with her briefcase strap for a moment. She couldn't stop thinking about how much was riding on the upcoming meeting. The door to the inner office opened, and a woman came out and introduced herself. Manna thought the woman was friendly but not overly so. She had probably held several similar discussions throughout the morning. Manna followed her into the office and took a seat at the table. She accepted the offer of hot coffee, but worried that it might only make her more nervous. The woman sat down and said, "So, tell me a little about yourself." So began Manna's job interview with a chemical manufacturing firm.

Interviews come in a variety of forms, including the employment interview—such as the one just described—and represent one of the most common forms of interpersonal communication in the modern organizational setting.

The secret to every stage of an interview is role taking. As you recall from Chapter 1, role taking is the ability to put yourself in the shoes of the interviewer or interviewee and understand his or her primary needs and concerns. Once these needs and concerns are understood, you are in a better position to adapt your responses and questions to the situation. This chapter covers two types of interview situations: the employment interview and the performance appraisal interview.

# The Employment Interview

Whether getting a first job with a business or getting a new job within the same organization, most people experience some form of employment interview. Although the world of job searches rapidly changes, the employment interview remains the primary tool for recruiting, hiring, and placing new employees in business, military, and government organizations. This section explains three phases of the employment interview: the pre-interview stage, the interview itself, and the post-interview stage.

## The Pre-Interview Stage

In the **pre-interview stage**, job candidates must secure an interview. This involves research, formulating a résumé, and writing a cover letter. Success depends on taking pre-interview preparation seriously.

***Research.*** One of the most frequent questions college students ask as they look toward graduation is: Where do I find a job? There are some obvious starting places for any job search, including such old stand-bys as classified advertisements in a local newspaper. But there is a wealth of other resources available to most college students. The career center at your university is an excellent starting point for finding field-specific job openings. In addition, one can find a variety of multipurpose job search resources on the Internet (see Figure 5.1). The growth of the Internet as a job resource was illustrated in a more recent survey. About 42 percent of laid-off managers landed interviews after posting résumés or retrieving job listings online; that's up from 20 percent in 1997.[1]

There are a number of resources you may use to help you find information about a specific organization. Consult company profiles in the College Placement Council's (CPC) *Job Choices, Standard and Poor's Register, Dun and Bradstreet Million Dollar Directory*, and *Moody's Directories*. Visit or call the Chamber of Commerce where the company is headquartered. You may also call the company directly and talk with someone in public relations or human resources. If appropriate, inquire with trade associations about the organization. Finally, many organizations and agencies have Web pages.

When researching an organization, the goal is to obtain basic information concerning the services or products offered, competitors, age and size, growth pattern, reputation, divisions and subsidiaries, locations, sales/assets/earnings, and new products or projects. This information will help you answer common interview questions such as "What do you know about us?" or "How do you feel about our company?" Figure 5.2 provides a form that you may adapt to compile information about the company. When you find a company with a suitable position that matches your goals, interests, and qualifications, you should to apply for the job.

The next step in the pre-interview stage is preparing a résumé and cover letter.

**FIGURE 5.1**    *Doing Job Research on the Internet*

| General Employment Sources | Types of Information Offered |
| --- | --- |
| America's Job Bank (www.jobbankinfo.org) | Over 1 million jobs posted, state-by-state search, post your résumé. Service of the U.S. Department of Labor and state agencies |
| Career Builder (www.careerbuilder.com) | Find jobs from 70 sites across the country, post résumés, search for jobs, career fairs, job search advice |
| Career Net (www.careernet.com) | A warehouse of links to job posting sites and employers, list your résumé, relocation tips |
| Employment Guide (www.employmentguide.com) | Job searches by location and employer, career advice and job fair articles, relocation services |
| Hot Jobs (www.hotjobs.yahoo.com) | Post your résumé, search specific fields for employment opportunities, résumé and job search tips |
| Job Search Engine (www.job-search-engine.com) | A meta job search engine, one-stop job bank, and career fair search |
| Job Web (www.jobweb.com) | Tailors advice to new college graduates, career planning advice, career fair searches by state, sample résumés and cover letters, interview tips |
| Monster Jobs (www.monster.com) | Career advice, résumé and interview tips, salary information, job search for all levels of job seekers, networking opportunities |
| Nation Job Network (www.nationjob.com) | Career assessment tests, salary wizard, search thousands of job postings, résumé advice, post résumés, links for job search information |
| Online Job Search Guide (www.job-hunt.org) | Award-winning Web site with 8,000+ job sites, resources for job seekers including postings, résumé and interview advice, Internet job advice, and a free newsletter |

***The Résumé.***    A **résumé** is a one-page (usually) description of your skills, education, and work experience. The biggest mistake most people make when preparing their résumé is to borrow a friend's résumé, an instructor's model, or a sample from a computer program or a placement office, then change the information on the form by inserting their own details. The problem with this all-too-typical approach is that the categories on the model résumé do not suit the individual's experiences, skills, or abilities. The best advice we can offer to those who are tempted to copy another form is: Don't do it! Rather than copying another's résumé, a candidate should begin with a blank sheet of paper and consider the three parts of a résumé: headings, leads, and descriptions.

*Headings.*    The **heading** is the category under which specific information is classified. Headings are the flags that signal individual areas of accomplishment. As such, the headings on your résumé should be different from headings on your friend's résumé. Typical headings for graduating seniors include "Career Objective," "Education," "Work Experience," "Honors and Awards," "Computer Skills," "Language Abilities," "Professional Memberships or Accreditations," and "Leadership Activities."

Headings should be concisely phrased and highlighted with boldfacing and/or capital letters, so that they are the first place an employer's eyes are drawn. You would be

**FIGURE 5.2   *Sample Form for Compiling Information When Researching an Organization***

Prospective Job Title: _____

Contact Person: _____

Contact Person's Title: _____

Company: _____

Address: _____

Telephone: _____

Research Source: _____

Size/Age of the Company: _____

Location(s): _____

Services/Products: _____

Growth Pattern: _____

Divisions/Subsidiaries: _____

Sales/Assets/Earnings: _____

New Products/Projects: _____

Reputation: _____

Compensation/Benefit Policies: _____

My Questions About the Company: _____

_____

_____

_____

surprised at how many résumés include categories that do not fit the individual. For example, creating an entire category called "Honors and Awards" to cover one award from high school only draws attention to one's weakness. On the other hand, the candidate who has language abilities or computer skills should create headings that draw attention to these desirable traits.

The candidate's name is the first heading on the résumé. Your name should be at the top of the résumé, either centered or left-justified. It should stand out from the address and phone numbers listed after your name.

If you are applying for a job in sales and have worked in retail sales for a number of years, you may consider a heading such as "Sales Experience" and make that the first heading after your name. If, on the other hand, you do not have much work experience, you may want to begin with "Education," demonstrating that you have completed a relevant degree.

Although the specific headings depend on your experiences and abilities, there are some headings that should not appear on a professional résumé. For instance, you should avoid including personal information such as race, gender, age, date of birth, health, height, weight, marital status, number and ages of children, and religious affiliation. It's unlawful for an employer to base a decision on personal information, and including it on a résumé gives the prospective employer more information than is needed. Finally, salary information should be omitted. If an application requires you to insert "Salary," you should write "negotiable."

*Leads.*   The next category of information on a résumé is the lead. **Leads** consist of the first information on each new line under the heading and should include the most important information for any individual entry. For example, under the heading "Education," it is generally more important to lead with your degree than with the institution from which you received the degree. The institution is usually less important than the fact and focus of the degree. For example, an ineffective lead appears below.

### Education

University of Montana, Missoula, Montana, May 2008. Bachelor of Business Administration, emphasis in marketing.   Instead of focusing on the person, this entry focuses on the school. A better lead should draw attention to the individual's assets.

### Education

**Bachelor of Business Administration**, emphasis in **Marketing**. Minor in **Computer Information Systems**. University of Montana, Missoula, Montana. May 2008.

Leads should include the most revealing information about you. For headings such as "Related Work Experience," lead with the title of the position you held rather than the name of the company (which does not emphasize your role). For instance, a poor lead may look like this:

### Work Experience

City of Tacoma, Chamber of Commerce, summer intern in Public Relations Department. Summer 2006.

Rather than emphasizing the individual, this lead focuses on the city. A better lead, using the same information, appears below.

### Work Experience

*Intern in Public Relations,* Chamber of Commerce, Tacoma, Washington. Summer 2006.

Many résumé models lead with the date, emphasizing the inclusive dates of employment rather than what the individual did during that time. This approach should be used only in those instances when the duration of employment is the most important aspect of the job, a very rare situation. To emphasize leads appropriately, use boldface or underlines. Finally, avoid using abbreviations. Don't write B.B.A. and force the reader to stop and decipher what it may mean. Tell the reader what it means to begin with.

*Descriptions.*    **Descriptions** include all the information that follows the lead. Read the following entry taken from a résumé:

> Yellowstone Natural Adventures. West Yellowstone, MT. Summers 2003–2006. Worked as a summer guide for white-water rafting trips in Yellowstone National Park. Duties included interacting with tourists, instructing them in proper safety guidelines and equipment use, giving presentations about the park, and overseeing proper campsite setup and breakdown.

Although this entry includes some interesting information, much of it is lost in the description because the emphasis is on the duties performed rather than on what the individual's experience brings to future work environments. Now read another description of the same job and note the differences.

> ***Instructor/Leader.*** Yellowstone Natural Adventures, West Yellowstone, Montana. Served as a white-water guide for five extended trips each summer into Yellowstone National Park area. Instructed fifteen to twenty participants on each trip in safety guidelines and proper use of marine and flotation equipment. Supervised three assistants to ensure that proper procedures were carried out in all areas of camping, rafting, and managing natural resources. Recognized by supervisors as outstanding with "Summer Employee of the Year" Award in both 2005 and 2006. Summer 2005–2006.

What is the difference between these two entries? Detail and action. The best descriptions use **action words** and specific **quantification** (when possible) to delineate what you did in the position. Whenever possible, omit phrases that promote listing—"Duties were" or "Responsibilities included"—and find active verbs that better describe what you did. Figure 5.3 provides a list of useful action words to describe your transferable skills and experiences. Good descriptions focus on transferable skills rather than merely relating job duties in laundry-list fashion. Your descriptions should demonstrate the skills, abilities, and experiences that employers seek.

Figure 5.4 includes a summary of "do" and "don't" advice for constructing résumés.

*Résumé Format.*    Reread the résumé several times and be sure to ask others to provide feedback and to proofread the résumé. Also make sure that your headings are consistently formatted, that the leads emphasize you rather than the institution or the date, and that the descriptions are accurate and reflect your skills and abilities. Phrasings should be consistent and parallel, and you should avoid using any abbreviations. Finally, try to keep your résumé to one page, because a brief scan doesn't allow the reader to get past the first page anyway.

Although it may be tempting to print your résumé on brightly colored paper to help it stand out from the others, remember that many readers dismiss résumés that are on different paper (such as fluorescent orange or neon blue) or have fancy borders, because they reflect an individual who is unprofessional or inexperienced. Select professional-looking, high-quality

**FIGURE 5.3**  *Action Words*

| | | | | | |
|---|---|---|---|---|---|
| accelerated | consolidated | established | launched | prioritized | streamlined |
| accomplished | contained | evaluated | led | processed | summarized |
| achieved | contributed | expanded | licensed | provided | supervised |
| administered | controlled | fabricated | logged | reconciled | supplied |
| advanced | converted | filed | maintained | recorded | supported |
| analyzed | coordinated | financed | managed | rehabilitated | surveyed |
| approved | corrected | finished | marketed | reinforced | systemized |
| arranged | corresponded | formulated | mediated | related | tallied |
| assigned | counseled | generated | moderated | relayed | taught |
| assisted | credited | guided | modified | reorganized | tested |
| authored | critiqued | headed | negotiated | reported | trained |
| billed | debated | hired | nominated | researched | transferred |
| budgeted | decided | increased | obtained | restored | translated |
| calculated | delegated | identified | opened | revised | transported |
| cataloged | delivered | implemented | organized | revitalized | trimmed |
| chaired | demonstrated | improved | originated | routed | tutored |
| changed | designed | informed | overhauled | saved | typed |
| classified | dispatched | initiated | participated | scheduled | upgraded |
| closed | displayed | inspected | performed | screened | used |
| collected | documented | instituted | persuaded | secured | validated |
| communicated | earned | integrated | pinpointed | selected | verified |
| completed | educated | inventoried | planned | serviced | won |
| conceived | encouraged | investigated | prescribed | simplified | worked |
| conducted | enlisted | issued | presented | solidified | wrote |

résumé paper that is white, off-white, light beige, ivory, or light blue. Paper should have at least a 25 percent cotton fiber content. Your résumé should be printed on an easy-to-read laser printer and copied by a professional. Employers want to hire people who understand the importance of professionalism. Figure 5.5 includes two sample résumés, one of which is good, the other poor. Examine these résumés for their strengths and weaknesses.

***The Cover Letter.***   Once your résumé is complete, you should compose your cover letter. A **cover letter** should be viewed as your chance to explain and highlight how your abilities, skills, and experiences listed on your résumé fit the job requirements. Each cover letter should be adapted to the specific job ad for which you are applying. Writing a persuasive cover letter involves identifying the needs of the potential employer (role taking) and then selecting relevant aspects of your résumé to demonstrate that you can fulfill those needs. Your cover letter should include three parts: an introduction, a body, and a conclusion.

The introduction of your cover letter should begin with a concise statement of the position for which you are applying. You might also state your immediate job objectives or your

**FIGURE 5.4**   *Résumé-Writing Tips*

| Do . . . | Don't . . . |
|---|---|
| Include information that is relevant to your experiences and abilities.<br>• Name (no need for middle)<br>• Address and phone numbers<br>• Job objective (optional)<br>• Education: degree, date, school, GPA optional (and only if over 3.0)<br>• Employment history: job title, company, location, dates, responsibilities<br>• Professional affiliations<br>• Honors and activities<br>• Computer/language skills | Include irrelevant information.<br>• "Résumé" or other document title<br>• Availability<br>• Personal information (age, birth date, marital status, height, pictures, religion, health, etc.)<br>• Salary desired<br>• References listed |
| Always use action verbs to describe what you did.<br>• Example: "Supervision" becomes "Supervised"<br>• Emphasize abilities and experiences<br>• Show how they are relevant and/or transferable | Offer a simple laundry list of duties or responsibilities. |
| Use consistency in writing structure and style. | Be inconsistent in structure or style. |
| Write out words in full. | Use contractions. |
| Make the document visually appealing.<br>• Be sure it is aesthetically balanced<br>• Use white space skillfully | Be concerned only with getting the information somewhere on the document. |
| Individualize your résumé.<br>• Consciously think about the form and content<br>• Be aware of headings and leads and their placement<br>• Consider what is most important and then prioritize and emphasize it | Copy a résumé format from someone else or a generic format. |
| Be specific about identifying and clarifying projects, successes, supervising experiences. | Offer only vague descriptions of jobs or activities. |
| Have a flawless résumé. | Make typographical errors or "correct" errors manually. |
| Use professional-looking, high-quality paper.<br>• At least 25% cotton<br>• Use neutral, classy résumé paper (off-white, ivory, etc.) | Use ordinary typing paper or use colored, flashy paper to be "different" and stand out. |

educational experience and then preview the traits you have that match the job requirements. The goal of the introduction is to attract attention and encourage the employer to continue reading.

The body of the letter should include two to three paragraphs. The first paragraph should show employers that you have the background, the training, and the qualifications they need. Let employers know that you want to work for their organization and why. Point out how your key assets are relevant to the position for which you want to be considered. In the second paragraph, stress your relevant accomplishments. Don't repeat what is on the

**Allison Lucas**
30682 Elmtree Lane
Phillipsburg, PA 16832
(814) 785-0964

## Retail Experience

**Sales Associate.**   Macy's Apparel, Pittsburgh, Pennsylvania. August 2005–Present.
- Work 20+ hours a week while going to school full-time.
- Assist customers with clothing purchases, make recommendations, and provide creative options in women's and children's clothing departments.
- Design and build displays for new items every week. Seek feedback and institute suggestions for displays.
- Manage inventory by tabulating stock and inventory control sheets in the two largest departments in the store.
- Train part-time workers during the season rush. Last year was promoted to train all incoming sales associates in a two-hour training session, "Assisting customers with selections and purchases."
- Commended by supervisor for "superior levels of customer service" in recent performance assessment.

**Grocery Supervisor.**   Buttrey Food & Drug, Phillipsburg, Pennsylvania.
December 2003–July 2005.
- Supervised stock clerks in the produce department. Oversaw 7 part-time employees and 1 full-time worker.
- Scheduled work assignments for 8 people.
- Ordered and received produce, oversaw pricing of produce items, and ensured products were high quality. Produce orders involved a $5,000 weekly budget.
- Designed and implemented displays of items. Christmas display of "produce stocking" won "Spirit of Christmas" award for the city in 2004.

**Cashier.**   Buttrey Food & Drug, Phillipsburg, Pennsylvania.
September 2002–December 2003.
- Engaged in positive customer relations with 100 customers per day.
- Balanced a cashier drawer of $3,000+ daily.

**Stocking Clerk.**   Buttrey Food & Drug, Phillipsburg, Pennsylvania.
August 2000–August 2002.
- Stocked shelves and inventory in frozen foods.
- Cited by management for efficiency.
- Asked to apply for promotion as cashier.

## Education

**Bachelor of Business Administration.**   Major in **marketing**. University of Pittsburgh.
December 2007.
- 3.6 Grade Point Average.
- Dean's List, College of Business: Fall 2005, Spring 2006, Fall 2006, Spring 2007.

**FIGURE 5.5**  *Sample Résumès*

**ALLISON LUCAS**
**30682 ELMTREE LANE**
**PHILLIPSBURG, PA 16832**
**(814) 785-0964**

**OBJECTIVE:**

To find an entry-level marketing position leading to sales or marketing management.

**EDUCATION:**

December 2007. University of Pittsburgh, Pittsburgh, Pennsylvania.
    B.B.A. Major in <u>marketing</u>
    <u>HONORS:</u> Member of Dean's List, College of Business
    Fall 2005, Spring 2006, Fall 2006, Spring 2007.
    3.6 GPA in major; 3.25 Cumulative GPA

**EXPERIENCE:**

Aug. 2005–Present. MACY'S APPAREL, Pittsburgh, Pennsylvania.
    Sales Associate.

    Learning the basic skills of salesmanship. Responsible for assisting customers, displays, and inventory control. Commended by supervisors for superior levels of customer service.

Dec. 2003–July 2005. BUTTREY FOOD & DRUG, Phillipsburg, Pennsylvania.
    Grocery Supervisor.

    Received management training in the areas of supervision, scheduling of work assignments, ordering stock, receiving merchandise, pricing, displays, bookkeeping, and customer relations. Reason for leaving: needed to reduce working hours to pursue a bachelor's degree to supplement work experience.

Sept. 2002–Dec. 2003. BUTTREY FOOD & DRUG, Phillipsburg, Pennsylvania.
    Cashier/Stocking Clerk.

    Learned the basics of stocking, ordering, and merchandising. Received cashier training and developed customer service skills. Reason for leaving: promoted to supervisor in produce department.

Aug. 2000–Aug. 2002. BUTTREY FOOD & DRUG, Phillipsburg, Pennsylvania.
    Stocking Clerk.

    Responsible for stocking, inventory control, and display in the frozen food department. Cited by management for efficiency. Reason for leaving: promotion to cashier clerk.

**REFERENCES:**

Confidential references available through Career Center, Box 8108, University of Pittsburgh, Pittsburgh, PA 17852, or by request.

**FIGURE 5.5** *Continued*

*Adapt your application materials to the particular organization to which you are applying.*

Credit: Bill Burke

résumé word for word, but show specific examples from your background, education, or work experience that demonstrate your ability to meet the requirements in the ad. Use the third paragraph to detail your interests and how they match the organization's needs. Again, emphasize how you can be an asset to the organization rather than how much you would like to work for them. Read the following excerpts from the body of a cover letter for a position in sales. Which is best?

### Letter 1

As you can see by my résumé, I have significant sales experience.

### Letter 2

For the last three years I have acquired significant sales experience working at Lamar's Apparel in Pocatello, Idaho.

### Letter 3

Your first job requirement emphasizes the need for sales experience. As my résumé indicates, I have spent the last three years acquiring significant sales experience at Lamar's Apparel. My position has taught me the basics of sales. I assist customers, display merchandise, and oversee inventory control. In the past six months I have been promoted twice because of my sales abilities. And I recently attended a weekend sales retreat to learn advanced sales techniques. I have already begun to implement some of these in my current job. As you can see, I have significant experience to offer your firm.

Letter 3 is best because it specifies why the applicant fulfills the job requirements. The reader is able to understand *how* the requirement is met by this applicant, and by being specific, the writer demonstrates that he or she has significant sales experience.

The final section of a cover letter is the close. You should articulate that you would like an interview. Convey the impression that you know the employer must do the inviting. Close the letter appropriately—"Sincerely" or "Yours Truly" are appropriate. Include your signature, your typed name, and a current address, phone number, and e-mail address where you can be reached. Examine the sample cover letter in Figure 5.6.

November 1, 2007


Mr. Luke Martin
Personnel Manager
Moondance Sales
26 Wall Street
Chicago, IL 60611


Dear Mr. Martin:

This letter is my application for the sales associate position advertised in the October 30 edition of the *Wall Street Journal*. I am currently a sales associate at Macy's, where I work part-time while I finish my degree, a Bachelor of Business Administration with a major in marketing. I will graduate with honors in December 2007. My career goal is to have a sales position that will lead to opportunities in training and management. My experience and enthusiasm make me an excellent candidate for your position.

Your job requires someone with sales experience. As you can tell from the enclosed rèsumè, I have been working as a sales associate for three years. During that time, I have had significant experience dealing with all types of customers—from very satisfied ones to very frustrated ones—and have been asked to help in selecting entire wardrobes for some people. My experiences in sales have taught me the importance of dealing with each customer on his or her own terms—and to avoid making blanket assumptions. My personal touch with customers has been successful. I was recently recognized by the store's manager as "superior in customer service." My approach to sales will be an asset to Moondance Sales, a company known for its one-on-one sales style.

In addition to being experienced in sales, I am highly motivated—your second job qualification. I began as a stock clerk in a local grocery store chain and learned the job so thoroughly that I was asked if I'd like to expand my skills to be cashier. Once I learned that job, I became supervisor of a whole department in the store. At each step, I enjoyed my job and worked to do it well and with great enthusiasm. My interests paid off, and my motivation became clear as I worked my way up in that organization to a managerial position.

In sum, I possess the traits that you require in a sales associate and believe that my experiences make me an excellent candidate for your position. I would be an asset to Moondance Sales because of my experience in the same sales techniques that Moondance is known for and because I have the initiative and the drive to be an effective sales associate.

**FIGURE 5.6** *Sample Cover Letter*

As you can see in the enclosed rèsumè, I have a number of other credentials that would be helpful to Moondance. I am genuinely interested in your company, because your creative and innovative approach to sales has always been a model that I have studied in developing my sales techniques. I appreciate your consideration for the position and hope to hear from you soon. Please contact me at (814) 785-0964 to arrange an interview. I look forward to hearing from you.

Sincerely,

*Allison Lucas*

Allison Lucas
30682 Elmtree Lane
Phillipsburg, PA 16832
(814) 785-0964

**FIGURE 5.6** *Continued*

## The Interview Stage

Ideally, your résumé and cover letter will lead to a phone call requesting an **interview**. Typically, candidates are not hired until they have at least one in-house interview—and usually several.

How will you distinguish yourself from the many other candidates for a position? Candidates must make a positive, lasting impression that communicates confidence, competence, and professionalism. Be aware that both your actions and your words help create that all-important impression.

***Presenting Yourself in an Employment Interview: Nonverbal Dimensions***.   Whether or not it is fair, you will be judged by how you present yourself in an interview. Your **nonverbal communication** is an important part of the interview process. This section discusses nonverbal self-presentation skills, including dress and body cues.

The interview is not the time to make a personal statement about the way you dress. Interviewees should respect and adapt to the interviewer's expectations. Although professional dress and appropriate style may vary slightly depending on the job, work environment, and geographic region, there are several commonalties to remember.

For men, a conservative business suit is almost always the rule. A well-tailored suit will go a long way in helping you present yourself professionally and confidently. The additional expense invested in a quality suit will pay tremendous dividends in making a positive first impression and will also make you feel good, enhancing confidence. Acceptable colors continue to be darker shades, including gray, navy blue, and black. Pattern designs may be worn only if they are subtle. In warmer climates, lighter shades of blue, gray, and even tan may be acceptable. A plain white or off-white shirt is never a bad choice. Other soft colors or designs may be acceptable if they look subtle and conservative rather than flashy. The same goes for neckties; think in terms of conservative, subtle patterns.

*Getting a job requires effective verbal and nonverbal communication.*
Credit: David Young-Wolff/PhotoEdit

For women, a conservative business suit is the best way to present a professional image. Studies show that women have a wider range of colors to select from when considering "professional dress." Although grays and blues are standard, women can often wear bright colors (red, bright blues, green) without appearing unprofessional. Women should wear blouses that are neither too revealing nor too frilly. Stockings should be flesh-toned. Finally, shoes should be sensible heels that are polished if not new.

Both men and women should be well groomed. Make sure your clothes are ironed and clean, hair trimmed and styled, and fingernails groomed. Avoid flashy and excessive jewelry and cologne or perfume that is too strong. In sum, moderation is almost always the key for the professional interview. You want to appear confident, professional, conscientious, and reliable.

Aside from your dress, nonverbal body cues can convey a positive or negative image. One of the first nonverbal traits that executives seek in prospective employees is punctuality. Candidates who do not arrive for the interview on time—and preferably five minutes early—rarely get a job offer. Greet office workers and interviewers with a firm handshake and direct eye contact. Get pen and paper out when you sit down and write down the name of the person interviewing you; have your interview questions within reach, ready to ask when given the opportunity. In addition, employers cited nonverbal qualities such as friendliness, appropriate eye contact, enthusiasm, and confidence as key to their extending a job offer to interviewees.[2] Now that you've made it this far, what should you say in an interview?

***Presenting Yourself in an Employment Interview: Verbal Dimensions***.  Although employers do consider nonverbal behaviors, studies indicate that the most important factor in receiving a second interview or the job offer involves the candidate's **answers** to questions.[3] This section will discuss typical questions and strategies for answering those questions.

The first thing to do is prepare for common interview questions. Figure 5.7 lists common questions interviewers like to ask. Answering questions is easier if you follow a four-step procedure: (1) state your answer briefly, (2) explain your statement with an additional two to three sentences, (3) provide some concrete example or testimony to support your claim, and

**FIGURE 5.7** *Typical Interview Questions*

1. Why don't you tell me about yourself?
2. What are your career goals? Where would you like to be in ten years?
3. Why did you decide to go into this field?
4. Why do you feel that you will be successful in this position?
5. What supervisory or leadership roles have you had?
6. How do you spend your spare time?
7. Which course did you like the best and why? the least and why?
8. Why are your grades low?
9. How does your previous experience relate to this position?
10. Why are you looking for this type of position—and why with us?
11. What are your strengths?
12. What are your weaknesses?
13. What will your references say about you?
14. What sort of pay do you expect to receive?
15. Why should I hire you?

(4) reconnect your answer to the original question. To see this four-step process in action, consider the following excerpt:

> *Interviewer:*   How does your previous experience relate to this position?
>
> *Candidate:*   I just completed an internship at a local television station that required skills similar to those for this position. As a production assistant, I worked closely with the producer to prepare every 6:00 news broadcast. Although I started out doing clerical work, in a few weeks I was making decisions about who should be interviewed, what questions should be included, and which news to prioritize. My experiences in the internship have taught me to be an effective communicator, and I have developed excellent oral and written communication skills. I learned to carry out and complete daily and monthly projects. And my position taught me to make good decisions under pressure. Good communication skills, project development, and experience with making tough decisions are precisely the traits required for this position.

This candidate followed the four-step procedure for answering an interview question. And although it is difficult for individuals to speak bluntly about themselves, it is precisely this sort of response that distinguishes the strongest candidates from the others.

Federal and state laws clearly regulate the kinds of questions that a person can and cannot ask during an employment interview. Although there are no limits on the kinds of information an interviewee can present, providing direct answers to illegal questions can create a problem for the candidate. See the Ethics Brief in this section for more information about illegal interview questions and how to respond to them.

Now that you know about questions and answers, we can talk about proven techniques for answering questions. Specifically, successful candidates make reference to the company, support their claims, actively participate in the process, exhibit natural but enthusiastic delivery, and ask good questions.[4] Each of these tips represents a way to adapt to the interviewer's expectations.

*Successful Candidates Refer to the Organization.*   Interviewees who make specific references to the company make a better impression than candidates who speak in vague and general terms about their goals or the company's objectives. For example, one study found that unsuccessful candidates admitted that they didn't know what they wanted to do for their careers and were "unable to find anything out" about the organization. One unsuccessful candidate said, "I really don't know what I want to do or where I'll be in five years. I thought I could give retail sales a try, though."[5]

Successful candidates, on the other hand, are specific in their career goals. They also make clear their desire to work for the organization. Thus, in a successful interview, a candidate suggested, "I really like how your company blends public relations techniques with marketing approaches in its sales division." Such answers require extensive research about the prospective employer.

*Successful Candidates Support Their Claims.*   Successful candidates support their claims with a variety of personal examples, illustrations, comparisons and contrasts, statistics, and testimonies from colleagues or employers.[6] A successful candidate may state, in response to the question "What would your references say about you?":

> My references would recommend me because I do quality work. I always give my best in my jobs and don't watch the clock. If a project requires me to put in more time than I'm scheduled for, I will put in the extra hours to ensure that it is done well. I don't want my

**BOX 5.1 •** *Ethics Brief*

Since the passage of the Civil Rights Act of 1964, employment screening interviews have been subject to federal and state equal opportunity employment laws. These laws are based on the belief that all persons—regardless of race, gender, national origin, religion, age, or marital status—should be able to compete equally for a job. Employers may refuse to hire candidates who are not qualified, but they may not base a hiring decision on factors other than skills, experience, and education. These are the only legal factors for selecting employees.

Although laws differ from state to state, it is illegal for employers to ask questions in the following areas: national origin or birthplace; age; race or ethnic background; religious affiliation; marital status; general physical condition; or voluntary affiliations such as clubs, fraternities, or sororities. Scrupulous interviewers avoid these areas and address questions directly to job qualifications.

What should a job candidate do if asked an illegal interview question? Unfortunately, there is no easy answer. Some people ask illegal interview questions out of malice. If you believe the question is malicious and you have decided that you wouldn't want to work for the employer, then simply refusing to answer the question is the best solution. This effectively ends the interview, which is what you wanted anyway. More often, interviewers ask illegal questions out of ignorance, which poses a problem for the interviewee. Refusing to answer the question will embarrass the interviewer and effectively end the interview. Answering the question puts the interviewee at risk, as the interviewer may use the information to discriminate against the candidate.

Fredric M. Jablin and Craig D. Tengler have developed a creative way to respond to illegal questions that keeps the interview and the chances of employment with the interviewer's organization

alive.* Rather than answering or refusing to answer the question, Jablin and Tengler suggest answering the concern behind the question rather than the question itself. According to Jablin and Tengler, *most illegal inquiries are related to gender and specifically discriminate against women.* Most such questions ask women about their marital or family plans, apparently trying to screen out candidates who might be too dedicated to their families to manage career responsibilities. Such questions as "Do you have plans for having children?" or "What happens if your husband gets transferred or needs to relocate?" are common. These questions clearly express the concern that the woman's family will come before her career. Creative responses address this concern, rather than directly answering the question: "I don't know at present. I plan on a career and believe my career will be successful with or without a family" or "My husband's career will not interfere with my career."† Or, when asked about working for someone younger than you, a candidate could respond, "My previous employer will tell you that I get along well with my coworkers and am able to subordinate my interests to the larger goals of the team."

Addressing the concern behind the question rather than the question itself is an ethical and personally advantageous way to manage the illegal interview question. Prepare yourself for an interview by thinking about answers to questions in each of the illegal areas. Be able to provide an answer that addresses the concern without destroying the interview. The job opening you save may be your own.

*Jablin, F. M., and C. D. Tengler, "Facing Discrimination in On-Campus Interviews," *Journal of College Placement,* Winter 1982, 58–61.

†Ibid.

name associated with things that aren't high quality. My summer employer for the last four years said that I was the best worker he's ever had—full time or summertime. And I think my work paid off for him; three of the accounts I got last summer are now loyal clientele at his firm. So, I think my references would say that I'm the kind of worker they would be happy to hire.

Aside from following the four-step procedure for answering, this candidate used concrete evidence, testimony, and statistics to support her claims. Compare that use of evidence with an unsuccessful candidate who spoke ambiguously in response to the same question.

> I think that, well, my references would say they liked me. I got along well with the people I worked with. I always enjoyed going to work.

If they support their claims at all, unsuccessful candidates use only personal experiences and do not elaborate on their brief answers.

*Successful Candidates Are Active Participants in the Process.*    Successful interviewees speak more, elaborate on their answers, and ask follow-up questions. In short, they are active participants in the interview process. At the end of the interview, successful candidates provide summaries of their relevant qualifications and how they relate to the employer's needs.[7] Unsuccessful candidates, in contrast, can be classified as passive participants; they need to be prodded to expand on their answers, they fail to have a dialogue with the interviewer, and they provide no summary statement at the end of the interview.

*Successful Candidates Have Natural but Enthusiastic Delivery.*    Unsuccessful candidates speak in monotone, are soft-spoken, and use few gestures. They display nervous habits such as playing with their hair, laughing at inappropriate times, scratching their nose, and avoiding eye contact by staring at the wall, the floor, or the desk. In short, unsuccessful candidates emphasize their nervousness rather than their interest, abilities, and enthusiasm. In sharp contrast, successful candidates speak quickly and use variety in their pitch, volume, and rate. They smile when discussing themselves and gesture naturally. They display good listening skills by looking at the interviewer and nodding when the interviewer talks. Successful candidates portray an image that is professional, competent, dynamic, and enthusiastic. The interview in this chapter illustrates the verbal and nonverbal elements of a successful interview.

*Successful Candidates Ask Good Questions.*    Most interviews include an opportunity for the candidate to ask questions about the position or the company. Many interviewers believe that the questions a candidate asks are more revealing than their answers to questions. And, although it's hard to list the kinds of questions one should ask, there are some questions that should not be asked. First, never ask a question that is answered in the materials supplied by the employer. Also, don't ask about salary or fringe benefits. Such questions communicate that you are more interested in pay than in the position or in vacation time than in working. Salary discussions should wait until a job offer is made.

Remember that a job interview is an information exchange, and you should find out as much about the organization as possible to determine if it is a good match with your goals and abilities. The most successful candidates ask questions about training and career expansion programs available at the company, about the kinds of clientele the organization handles, and first-person questions of the interviewer. For example, one question that impressed a recruiter was "What is the most rewarding thing you have experienced working for this company?" It is imperative that candidates develop several (four to five) questions tailored to specific company goals. Successful candidates also ask questions that place them in the position. Thus, rather than asking "What are the expectations for this position?" a successful candidate asks "What expectations would you have for me in my first year in this position?" Good questions communicate

**BOX 5.2** • *Interview: Tony Lapriori (Director of Employee Relations, Lord Corporation, Raleigh, North Carolina)*

(Lord is a supplier of adhesives; coatings; and shock, noise, and vibration control devices to aerospace, industrial, and commercial manufacturers.)

*How does Lord go about hiring new talent?*

For entry-level positions, we have a college recruiting program. We begin by asking our operating businesses if they have a need for entry-level employees for the coming year. Based on those requirements, we begin scheduling campus visits. We have one person who works full time as a university recruiter. If we go to, for example, Penn State to recruit, our recruiting manager will go and bring with him a recent Penn State graduate who now works at Lord. This is a very effective method of recruiting. It helps us establish an immediate connection with the recruit.

*What are some common errors you have seen in the cover letters and résumés of new college graduates?*

Of course, there shouldn't be any mistakes on either. You sometimes find résumés that are haphazardly put together. These certainly stick out. Even using a form, any form, is better than a disorganized, haphazard résumè. But I think people would do a better job if they took a look at the organization they are interested in and make specific changes to their letters based on this information. This greatly improves your chances of getting noticed.

*Should people personalize their résumès, too?*

We may get 100 résumès in a week, and many of them seem to follow the same format. The résumè is a statement of the individual, and I think it ought to display the candidate's individuality.

*What are some of the most important issues for candidates to think about in the interview?*

I think appearance is still a valuable thing. Often, it's the nonverbals that matter. If you bring a briefcase, it should look well organized. Better to show up with nothing than with a briefcase that's a complete mess. I can sense something about the person just by their level of organization. Organization skills aren't just appearance based. Organization, or lack thereof, is also demonstrated by how the candidate's answers are organized.

*Are there any other nonverbal cues you look for?*

Of course, people must be qualified for the job. A great interview can't overcome a lack of qualifications. Some people suggest that the company really owes them something. I think people need to display both self-assuredness and humility. A lack of balance turns me off. Some people spend their time boasting about themselves. It often sounds too good to be true. A young person shouldn't say, "I helped grow the company's sales by three million dollars." Another tip-off is constant, "I," "I," "I," instead of "we" accomplished these goals. I pick up on a lack of balance by the nouns and pronouns people use. Nobody works alone. Displaying teamwork values is one way to demonstrate humility. Also, thanking people or acknowledging other people for the help they provided along the way is another way to create a balanced interview.

*What's one of your favorite interviewing techniques?*

I'm always interested in learning about the candidate, but not from his or her perspective, from the perspective of people they've worked with. I really admire those people who can see themselves from another's point of view. Answers like "I think my last boss would say these are my strengths." Those that can't put themselves in another person's shoes . . . you can tell they're struggling. It also tells me whether the person ever sat down with a professor or former employee and discussed their performance. The candidate's response to such questions often determines how I think she did in the interview.

*Is there any other advice you would give?*

Honesty is still very important. People have to be honest. If you have flat spots, you have to be honest about those flat spots. We've received résumès where the person says they've got a master's degree, but after checking, it turns out that they don't. We check everything. I think honesty is still a key issue. Pick a job you think you can do, based on your qualifications, and be honest with yourself and your interviewer about your capabilities.

**FIGURE 5.8** *Sample Questions to Ask Interviewers*

1. Where are the people who formerly held the position for which I am applying?
2. Can you tell me about _____[a specific]_____ product line? or about specific clientele?
3. Can you tell me about training programs and opportunities for continued growth sponsored by the company?
4. What are the typical avenues of advancement in the organization?
5. Can you clarify what your expectations of me in this job are?
6. Tell me about evaluation procedures. How often am I evaluated and what form do the evaluations take?
7. What is the thing you enjoy the most about working for the organization?
8. What is the one thing you would change about the company if you were able?
9. Where do you think this organization will be in 10 years?
10. What is the atmosphere like in the office in which I will work?

that the candidate is thoughtful, prepared, and interested in the organization. Figure 5.8 presents a list of questions that one candidate prepared before an interview. Use the suggestions as a springboard for formulating your own questions.

*Successful Candidates Prepare for Objections.*    Although we would all like to believe that we're great candidates, most of us have flaws, and some of these are evident on our résumés. Astute interviewers will ask us about such flaws. Effective strategic communication (see Chapter 1) involves anticipating questions about our flaws (objections) and preparing responses ahead of time. The most common objections interviewers express involve one's employment record (e.g., the candidate has a history of "job hopping," has been fired from a position, or has a long employment gap) or job history (e.g., a lack of needed experience or too much experience).

We suggest a three-step format for phrasing responses:

1. Understand the objection
2. Acknowledge the objection
3. Neutralize the objection[8]

First, it is critical that you listen carefully to the interviewer. Make sure you understand what the interviewer is getting at. If you are not sure, ask for clarification using a phrase such as "Could you expand on that? I'm not sure what your hesitation [or objection] is." This request for more information demonstrates that you have actively listened and are earnestly trying to deal with the objection.

Next, acknowledge the objection by stating it in your own words. Make a statement like "In other words, you aren't sure that my qualifications fit the job requirements?" or "I hear that you're worried that, if hired, I may not stay on the job long enough to justify the expense of training me." Restatements such as these reflect that you grasp the concern and that you're willing to deal with the question in a nondefensive manner.

Finally, work on neutralizing the objection. Answer the objection fully, with no sign of defensiveness. This will require preparation prior to the interview. First, write down a brief statement of the objection, for example, "I don't have on-the-job experience." Next, develop your side of the story. Third, review it for negative, self-defeating, or defensive assumptions. Finally, reinterpret the event in a more positive way.[9] Chapter 10 offers a variety of methods of responding to objections, including offering evidence that denies the objection is real, accepting the objection but minimizing its effect, or turning the tables by suggesting what the interviewer thinks is bad is really positive.

## *The Post-Interview Stage*

The interview may be complete, but the interview process is not over. The first thing you should do after the interview is send a thank-you note to the organization, specifically the person who conducted the interview. This can be done with a card or via e-mail. About 42 percent of employers view candidates who send thank-you notes more favorably than those who do not send them.[10] In the note, refer to the interview, provide any additional information that was requested in the interview, summarize your qualifications, and reiterate your interest in the position. If you decide you don't want the job, thank the individual and the organization for their time and inform them of your decision. If you are still interested in the job, let them know.

***Getting the Job Offer***     Let's assume that the interview goes well and you receive a job offer from the company. It's time to determine if you still want the position and if the offer is desirable. Organizations usually give a candidate five to seven days to consider an offer. Consider the issues that are most critical to you both personally and professionally. If you have researched the company and asked the right questions during the interview, you have a head start on this assessment process. Consider the company's objectives, activities, professional and personal atmosphere, and location, including cost of living and cultural and recreational opportunities. Also ask yourself if you will be happy in the job itself. Finally, consider opportunities for continued learning and growth within the organization. If there are few opportunities for promotion, will you become bored with the job after a short time? Do your best to picture the real expectations of the job and compare those with your own desires and goals.

***Negotiating Salary***     **Salary negotiation** goes hand in hand with some job offers. Prepare for negotiation by learning about the industry's standard salaries for your position. You can learn about industry standards for compensation by talking with people in similar positions, consulting classified ads, or consulting sources such as *BusinessWeek's Guide to Careers, CPC Salary Survey*, and the *Wall Street Journal's Business Employment Weekly*.

Consider also the benefits the position offers, including health coverage, expense accounts, profit sharing and stock plans, bonuses, retirement funds, life insurance, and vacation time. Such benefits can distinguish great jobs from ordinary ones.

The organization usually opens negotiation with a written offer that the candidate can accept or reject. Requests for more than the original offer should be based on the candidate's advanced education or skills, or industry standards. Both sides usually trade offers until a mutually satisfactory figure is reached. A candidate's tenacity should be based on his or her options. If, for example, one candidate has been looking for work for six months, and the company's offer is the only one he has received, he ought to curb his tenacity and would probably be wise to accept something close to the organization's original offer. On the other hand, a candidate who has two or more offers is in a much stronger bargaining position. Such a candidate can press the organization harder than the first, knowing that, if the organization ceases negotiation, she can accept one of the other offers. A candidate who has higher offers from other organizations should mention them, which might induce the organization to up its offer. However, this kind of power play may also convince the organization that the candidate is unwinnable and cause it to cease negotiation.

If you accept the position, do so with a contact over the phone and follow up by signing the documents provided by the firm. If you decide to reject the job offer, it is a common courtesy to write a formal letter of rejection. Typically, your letter should let the employer know the reason for your rejection in a tactful and general way. If you do not want to live in the city where the company is located, avoid insult—for example, "I am turning down your offer to take a position working for a company near my hometown, where my family still resides." Be sure that your explanation is honest, but tactful. Thank the employer for considering you and for the courtesies extended. Letters of acceptance and rejection are vital aspects of professional life. They communicate that you are a quality individual.

***Dealing with Rejection***.   More often than not, candidates do not receive a job offer. Although it is hard to avoid viewing a **rejection** personally, try to keep the rejection of your candidacy separate from the rejection of you personally. There are several things candidates can do to keep rejections in perspective.

First, try to get feedback. There are a number of reasons for rejection: some are very good reasons, others are not. Be polite and diplomatic and suggest that you would like to learn from this experience. Ask if there is something that the employer could tell you that may help you in future interviews.

Second, send a thank-you note anyway. Don't ruin your future chances by acting angry or hurt. By displaying the professional attitude that employers seek, you keep your options open for the future.

Third, seek support. Don't keep your rejection "hidden" because you are embarrassed about it. Talk to family and friends who can lend an ear and keep you motivated. Talk about it for a few minutes and then move on. Don't dwell on the bad news for too long.

Finally, use the rejection as a learning experience. Consider that you attained valuable interview experience, that you were able to reevaluate your priorities and career options, and that you learned a great deal about yourself and your professional life. If you view the interview process as an opportunity to learn more about yourself and your career options, even a rejection can become a valuable learning opportunity.

## *Performance Appraisal Interviews*

Once you've obtained a job, a second kind of interview that all business and professional people encounter is the **performance appraisal interview**. This annual exercise is usually conducted by the employee's immediate supervisor for the purpose of evaluating the employee's previous performance and setting goals for the coming year. Many organizations will schedule at least one regular follow-up meeting at six months to make sure workers are on track and hitting targets.[11] Managers use performance appraisal interviews to reinforce existing positive behaviors and discuss negative behaviors or performance failures as a prelude to future development.[12]

Although the performance appraisal interview is rarely applied to part-time employees, it is frequently used in the supervision of professionals in the areas of production, marketing, sales, service delivery, and customer service. Government employees and not-for-profit corporations also subject their employees to annual performance reviews. And, almost everyone who enters management ranks will find themselves both giving performance appraisals to their employees and receiving them from their own supervisors. In keeping with our discussion of interviewing, we will discuss the performance appraisal interview from the point of view of the interviewee.

The performance appraisal interview is a vital part of the feedback process discussed in the communication model in Chapter 1. Employees who receive too little feedback do not know what positive behaviors they should continue performing, nor where they're coming up short of expectations. If done correctly, the performance evaluation process is a vital tool of effective feedback and communication. Ideally, the performance appraisal interview is two interviews: the performance planning or goal-setting meeting and the performance appraisal interview itself.

## *The Performance Planning Interview*

The **performance planning interview** is held annually, often at the beginning of the organization's fiscal year, so that both manager and employee can work together to establish performance goals for the upcoming year. Much of the work that needs to be done for the performance planning interview rests with your immediate supervisor, whose job it is to outline your job responsibilities and measurement criteria. To do this, he or she may review the organization's mission statement, your own department's goals, and your job description. Because not all organizations or managers take the performance appraisal process seriously, and because managers differ in their skills at the process, you should create your own performance goals and measurement criteria. Here is how the process works.

The best way to establish your goals for the coming year is to identify the key responsibilities of the job. The key responsibilities of the job are not the day-to-day tasks, chores, duties, and assignments that consume most of the hours that you spend on the job. Those things are activities, the key responsibilities are the reasons that we do all those mundane chores.[13]

For example, consider the position of secretary or administrative assistant. This person is involved in dozens of different tasks and projects during a day. But, if you narrowed these tasks to key responsibilities, they might include:

> Prepare documents
> Handle faxes, e-mails, and copies
> Manage the mail
> Make travel arrangements
> Keep track of daily budget expenditures
> Manage information
> Greet visitors[14]

Notice that this list is short. No matter how varied the job, there usually aren't too many major responsibilities—usually only five to seven key items. Second, each item should be stated succinctly. Finally, each item should be mutually exclusive.

Once you understand the key responsibilities of your job, it's time to determine methods of measuring each one. There are four methods of measuring output in each of the key responsibilities:

1. Quality
2. Quantity
3. Cost
4. Timeliness[15]

Apply the measurement criteria to each responsibility and determine which of the four measures of output are most important. Is this key responsibility best measured by the time in which it's completed? Is the cost of producing this output important? Or, is quantity the most important measurement criteria for this output? It's possible that for each key responsibility you will have more than one output measure. This is fine because the more measures you have of performance, the more accurate or valid the later assessment will be.

Quantity, cost, and timeliness criteria are the easiest to measure numerically. It may not be difficult to determine whether projects are turned in on time or if a particular production quota has been met. On a production line, quality can be measured by the number of defective parts produced, but in other areas—customer service, for example—determining quality is more difficult. It may be necessary to ask customers for some kind of quality evaluation of a person's work, or ask one's fellow employees to rate quality on some sort of measurement scale. Quality is usually the most difficult criterion to quantitatively measure.

Once the key objectives and quality measurements are selected, it's time to complete the preparation process by writing goal statements for the coming year. Goal statements should start with an action verb, identify a single key result for each objective, and state some verifiable criterion that clearly states whether the goal has been achieved. Some examples of goal statements that might be useful for a goal-setting meeting include:

> Reduce the number of customer complaints by 6 percent.
> Reduce the number of production defects by 4 percent.
> Expand the number of choices available on the dial-up program from 6 to 11.
> Establish two new workshop training programs, one in leadership, one in interviewing.

These statements are action oriented and easy to measure. For an example of a goal that's measured qualitatively, examine this one: "Design a waiting-room environment that creates a feeling in patients of professional excellence and personal concern." Although there are no easy-to-identify quantitative measures of this, it could be evaluated by talking with physicians about patient anxiety levels, or by talking to the receptionists about their interactions with the patients and whether the new room design has changed those in any way. Although this isn't quantifiable, such descriptive measures might serve as the only way to adequately measure whether some quality-based goals have been achieved.[16]

Once you have prepared for the performance planning interview, enter the meeting with the following objectives in mind. First, discuss your goal statements and see how they compare with those that your supervisor has prepared. Be ready to explain why your particular goal statements are appropriate and in keeping with your job description and your department's mission. Be prepared to admit and accept your supervisor's relevant goal statements that you had not thought of. Finally, discuss any mitigating contextual factors, such as the current economic factors in your industry, changes in your customer base, and so on, that could affect your ability to achieve the goals.[17] It is important for both you and your supervisor to catalog some of the possible changes (e.g., economic recession, government regulations) that could make goal achievement unrealistic or impossible. Having worked with your supervisor to set up your goals for the coming year, it's up to you to document the degree to which you have accomplished the goals set in the meeting. Solid documentation, even of instances in which you failed to achieve goals, is vital if you are to better understand and influence the outcome of the performance appraisal interview.

## *The Performance Appraisal Interview*

Some time after the goal-setting meeting, usually after six months or a year, your supervisor will conduct a performance appraisal interview. As we stated previously, this process involves a review of the employee's strengths and shortcomings and prepares the groundwork for future personal, job, and career development.

The interview may include any number of the following topics:

1. Review last year's appraisal (if applicable)
2. Measure the achievement of short- and long-term goals
3. Discuss employee's strengths
4. Discuss employee's weaknesses
5. Review employee's development needs
6. Discuss the employee's current level of job satisfaction
7. Explore talents that are not being utilized and discuss how to use them more productively
8. Examine whether current supervision is a fit for the employee
9. Set goals for the coming year (performance planning or goal setting)

Like the goal-setting interview, it's incumbent on the employee to do some preparation prior to this meeting. The first and most important thing to do is compare your actual performance against your goals by reviewing the data you have collected between the two meetings. If your goals were well developed and stated, it should be fairly easy for you to determine the level to which each has been achieved. By comparing your documentation against your goals, you will get a pretty good idea of how you'll be rated during the evaluation interview.

If you have failed to meet certain goals, try to ascertain whether the extenuating circumstances that you and your supervisor envisioned in the goal-setting meeting did affect your performance. This may provide you with an explanation for failing to meet certain goals.

The second area of preparation is to determine what, if any, development needs you have for the coming year. Are there any training courses or workshops that would enable you to better perform your job? Create a list of your development and training needs so that you can negotiate these with your supervisor.

Third, you should go through the procedure described in the previous section to create a new list of key requirements and goal statements for the coming year. This will prepare for the conclusion of the performance appraisal interview, or for a later performance planning interview.

During the interview, you have the following responsibilities as an employee. First, discuss what you have achieved against your development plan.[18] Compare your goal assessment with your manager. Most of the time, you'll come to similar conclusions about the quality of your performance. Be willing to discuss not only the areas where you agree, but also those about which you disagree. You'll probably be given the chance to explain areas of difference, but be certain that your manager is also allowed to explain his or her perceptions about these differences.

Although supervisors should be taught to reinforce both existing positive behavior and discuss negative behavior by backing it up with specific examples, not everyone does this.[19] Be sure to ask for both specific examples and clarification for any assessments that are unclear. It's appropriate for you to expect the supervisor to back up assessments with examples. Take an active role in the process by asking questions and seeking out information about areas that your supervisor has not focused on.

Try to be open and nondefensive. Don't use rationalizations to explain away criticisms. Approach the interview with the idea of giving serious consideration to all suggestions and taking whatever action may be necessary to make the evaluation a positive experience.

Be aware of possible nonverbal cues you present. A rigid posture and clenched fists may be read as defensive by your supervisor. Slouching and noncommittal grunts may be read as disrespectful or lacking interest. Sit upright, lean forward, and demonstrate interest with eye contact. Keep notes on the most significant areas of discussion and listen and respond appropriately.

The interview may close with an overall assessment of your performance or it may move on to goal setting for the coming year. In either case—planning your goals and documenting your performance—keeping an open mind and responding positively to your supervisor's suggestions are all part of making the performance appraisal interview a positive experience.

## Summary

The best interviewees are able to adapt their skills and experience to the employer's needs and concerns. Once positions are located, the candidate must research the company to understand its needs and concerns. Most job ads require that the candidate submit a résumé and cover letter. A heading is a category under which specific information is classified. Candidates should develop headings that relate to their specific skills, education, and experience. A lead consists of the first information on each line under the heading. Only the most important information should be included in the lead. Descriptions provide important detail about education or work experience.

The cover letter represents a chance to highlight specific skills and abilities that fit the organization's needs. The cover letter includes an introduction, body, and conclusion, and should specify why the applicant fulfills the organization's requirements.

In the interview stage, the candidate meets and talks with members of the prospective organization. The nonverbal dimensions of the interview consist of dress and body cues. Strong answers follow a four-step procedure: state an answer briefly, explain the answer, provide concrete examples, and reconnect the answer to the original question. In the post-interview stage, the candidate should send a thank-you letter to the contact in the organization.

The performance appraisal process is an annual exercise that evaluates the employee's previous performance and sets goals for the coming year. This process consists of the performance planning interview and the performance appraisal interview. Prior to the planning interview, employees should prepare a list of key responsibilities and measurement criteria. During the performance appraisal interview, candidates should avoid defensiveness and give serious consideration to their manager's suggestions.

## Questions and Exercises

1. Examine the list of tips for résumé writing in Figure 5.4. Given your experience in employment interviews, are there any tips you could add to this list? Are there other résumé-writing practices that you would clearly warn against?

2. Examine Allison Lucas's poor résumé in Figure 5.5. Identify the various features of that résumé that are inappropriate or unpersuasive. What content changes would you make to improve this résumé? What changes would you make in the

form and layout of the résumé to improve its appearance?

3. Look again at the suggestions for the nonverbal and verbal dimensions of an interview presented in this chapter. Are there any additional suggestions you would add to our list? Develop a list of additional nonverbal and body cues that candidates should be aware of during an interview. Develop a list of additional verbal cues that candidates should be aware of.

4. Take the list of typical interview questions in Figure 5.7 and prepare answers to five of the toughest questions on that list. Follow the four-step process for answering questions as outlined in this chapter. Review your answers with your instructor or colleagues in your class. What suggestions do they offer for improving your answers? Incorporate those suggestions into a revised response. Preparing answers prior to the interview will make you feel more confident and ready to handle even the toughest inquiry.

5. Using a job you currently or recently held, create a list of key responsibilities for that job as if you were preparing for a performance planning interview. Can you narrow the list of key responsibilities to five to seven items? Using the criteria of quality, quantity, cost, and timeliness, develop methods of measuring or assessing your yearly performance. How difficult was it to develop clear, measurable goals for your current job? Could you use these in a performance planning interview? Why or why not?

## Notes

1. Lublin, J. S., "As the Economy Cools, You'll Need to Rethink Some Job Strategies," *Wall Street Journal*, 2 January 2001, A9.
2. Enhorn, L. J., "An Inner View of the Job Interview: An Investigation of Successful Communicative Behaviors," *Communication Education* 30 (1981): 217–228.
3. Ugbah, S. D., and R. E. Majors, "Influential Communication Factors in Employment Interviews," *The Journal of Business Communication* 29 (1992): 145–159.
4. Enhorn.
5. Ibid.
6. Ibid.
7. Ugbah and Majors.
8. Wilson, R. F., and E. H. Rambusch, *Conquer Interview Objections: Triumph Over Barriers* (New York: Wiley, 1994).
9. Hyatt, C., and L. Gottlieb, *When Smart People Fail: Rebuilding Yourself for Success* (New York: Penguin USA, 1993).
10. Cox, J. A., D. W. Schlueter, K. K. Moore, and D. Sullivan, "A Look Behind Corporate Doors: Examining the Interview Process from the Organization's Point of View," *Personnel Administrator*, March 1989, 56–59.
11. Pratt, M. K., "No More Job Reviews," *ComputerWorld*, 2 April 2007, 29.
12. Fear, R. A., and R. J. Chiron, *The Evaluation Interview* (New York: McGraw-Hill, 2002).
13. Grote, D., *The Performance Appraisal Question and Answer Book: A Survival Guide for Managers* (New York: AMACOM, American Management Association, 2002).
14. Ibid.
15. Ibid.
16. Ibid.
17. Fear and Chiron.
18. Grote.
19. Chandra, A., "Employee Evaluation Strategies for Healthcare Organizations: A General Guide," *Hospital Topics* 84 (Spring 2006): 34–38.

# Part II

# Creating a Professional Presentation

# 6

## *Considering Audience Feedback*

Miguel and Jim had high hopes. The two sell advertising for an NBC affiliate, a station that is number one in overall ratings. They hoped their presentation to the largest home repair center in town would initiate a long and lucrative advertising campaign. They emphasized overall ratings, hit programming, and solid local news numbers. The center's managers listened attentively, but they bought only some spot ads during weekend sporting events. They made a much larger advertising deal with the local ABC affiliate.

What had Miguel and Jim done wrong? They spoke with their supervisor who, on learning the content of their presentation, was quick to find the flaw. "Who was your presentation designed for?" she asked. The two looked blank. "It sounded like your presentation was a simple rehash of our ratings. You didn't consider the center's concerns about the construction of the new Home Depot and that midweek traffic had dropped off. You didn't create an advertising package to solve these problems. The two of you didn't think about your audience."

Chapter 1 emphasized that effective communication is strategic and audience centered. Strategic communication is a process whereby the communicator specifies the goals he or she wants to accomplish and learns about the audience and its position regarding the goals. The speaker uses his or her understanding of the audience to select specific communication tactics that will move the audience toward the intended goal.

In dyadic and group encounters, we adapt to audiences by paying attention to immediate feedback or through role taking. Feedback is information about how our message was received. In role taking, we imagine how others will react to our message. Role taking and feedback are relatively efficient ways to adapt to interpersonal and group situations because feedback is immediate, audiences are small, and messages are more spontaneous.

It is possible to adapt spontaneously to feedback in public presentations, the same as in dyadic or group encounters. We know of salespeople who, seeing their prepared presentation draw negative reactions, ignore the text and develop a more interactive discussion of problems and solutions. Of course, adaptation "on the fly" requires enormous self-confidence, extensive speaking experience, and vast knowledge of the topic, and even then represents a significant gamble.

For public presentations, something more formal is required to fully account for and adapt to audience views. **Audience analysis** is a formal method of role taking that is useful for larger audiences. Through audience analysis, speakers can adjust the topic, presentation mode, and persuasive appeals prior to the presentation, eliminating or minimizing the need for adjustments on the fly. A careful audience analysis would have helped Jim and Miguel land the home center account. Although some people reject the entire notion of audience adaptation as a form of pandering, we maintain that it is the single most important key to effective communication. The Ethics Brief in this section defines the difference between legitimate audience adaptation and unethical pandering.

## BOX 6.1 • ETHICS BRIEF

One of the oldest raps against teaching communication or persuasion is that students are trained to pander to audiences. Some argue that, by teaching students to adapt to audiences, communication professors are telling students to change their message so that it caters to the audience's tastes and desires. As a result, communication classes teach an unethical form of flattery, rather than a real academic discipline. We agree that pandering is unethical. However, like most communication professionals, we also believe that it is possible to adapt to an audience without capitulating to it. Although we admit that the line between appropriate adaptation and inappropriate pandering can be difficult to draw, we can offer some advice in this regard.

First, most communication experts make a clear distinction between changing the means of presenting an idea to an audience so that the idea is easily understood or more acceptable and changing one's ideas to fit the audience. In the former, the speaker finds visual aids that can make a complicated concept clear or arguments that are persuasive to an audience. In the latter, the speaker changes his or her opinions to flatter the audience. Adapting to the audience does not force a speaker to develop inconsistent goals or philosophy. Rather, the outstanding communicator has a consistent philosophy but is inconsistent in how this philosophy is expressed. We are advocating inconsistency not in people's goals but in the strategies they use to explain those goals and the motivational strategies they use to encourage others to adopt those goals.[*]

Such inconsistency is needed in today's diverse work environment where no two individuals or groups respond similarly. If you find yourself changing your goals and philosophy frequently, you may have gone beyond simple adaptation and moved toward pandering. If, however, your goals are consistent, but your means of achieving them are flexible, then you are probably operating in the legitimate realm of audience adaptation. It is useful to talk with close friends in the organization, family members, or friends outside the organization if you are concerned about crossing the line between adapting and pandering. These individuals may be able to provide a healthy perspective to your decisions.

[*]Hart, R. P., and D. M. Burks, "Rhetorical Sensitivity and Social Interaction," *Speech Monographs* 39 (1972): 75–91.

This chapter develops and highlights key issues about the audience that need to be considered when preparing a presentation. Specifically, the chapter describes how to conduct a situational analysis and a listener characteristics analysis. We explain how to adapt to informed and uninformed audiences. We relate five different kinds of audiences and suggest content, structure, and delivery choices appropriate for each. We provide the Audience Analysis Checklist as a tool for analyzing the situational and listener characteristics prior to the presentation.

## Analyze the Situation

A first step in audience analysis involves **situational variables,** including occasion, audience size, organizational culture, environment, and time considerations.

### Occasion

Presentations are given on various occasions. The **occasion** is the purpose and context of the presentation. Occasions include an evening presentation to let the public know about a local Superfund site or a meeting of the city council to fund a community youth center.

To understand the occasion, the speaker must first consider the **purpose** for the presentation and adapt the message to fit that goal. A speaker who doesn't consider audience expectations about the purpose is likely to fail. For example, a person running for union president who uses an informative presentation on retirement planning to stump for election could well lose, rather than gain, votes. As listeners, we learn to expect certain activities at particular events and are disturbed if these expectations are violated. A speaker must therefore understand the reason for the presentation in order to meet audience expectations about the purpose.

Context is another important part of the occasion. **Context** involves what happens before and after your presentation. Are other presentations scheduled? If so, what will these speakers talk about? Is your topic related or not? Is there a common theme? If so, where does your speech fit? Generally, it is a good idea to make connections between your speech and the other speakers, the occasion, the theme, and the audience. This can be done by explicitly mentioning other speakers by name, referring to their topic, or explaining how your content fits into the larger theme.

### Size

Imagine walking into a large auditorium for a presentation to 150 people only to discover 7 people sitting in the auditorium. Or consider the opposite situation: You expect to speak before 10 people and you find that 100 have come to hear you. It is vital to know the approximate size of the audience so you can present with the appropriate **formality.** The general rule of thumb is that, as the size of the audience increases, so should the formality. It's easy to be conversational and make specific references to individual listeners when a few people are sitting around a table, but the same interaction is difficult for large audiences. Follow the guidelines in Figure 6.1 to adjust the formality of your presentation.

### Organizational Culture

When speaking in an organization that is not your own, it is important to have some information about its **culture.** Most organizations have implicit rules or conventions that are vital to the group's basic function.[1] Breaking the implied rules may damage the speaker's credibility and effectiveness.

**FIGURE 6.1**    *Methods of Adjusting Presentation Formality*

| *Methods to Increase Formality* | *Methods to Decrease Formality* |
|---|---|
| Formal attire | Informal attire |
| Manuscript delivery—read | Extemporaneous delivery—from notes |
| Questions held until after presentation is complete | Questions handled throughout the presentation |
| Deliver presentation from behind lectern | Deliver presentation from beside or in front of lectern |

Understanding the organization's culture requires knowing the conventions or norms for the specific group to whom you will speak. What status differences are there among audience members? Do those differences influence the way the people look at issues? Do the managers reserve decision making for themselves, do they consult with employees, or are decisions made by consensus? Will decision makers be present for your presentation? If not, should you arrange to meet them separately? Are you part of a regularly scheduled meeting? Can you visit the meeting of decision makers prior to the presentation? How long do presentations typically last? How are questions handled? Answers to these questions are vital because it is difficult to recover from violating organizational norms.

## Physical Environment

The **physical environment** also plays a critical role in successful presentations. Determine the seating arrangement and the availability of microphones and audiovisual equipment. If possible, visit the site ahead of time. Is there anything in the room that might confine movement during the speech? Will you be tied to a microphone and podium? Consider the noise that may interrupt the presentation. Many meeting rooms in hotels are adjacent to other rooms, and noise from other meetings can be distracting. Will caterers enter with dessert, ice water, or the like? Although it is impossible to anticipate all the environmental issues that could disrupt the presentation, the more prepared you are, the less likely such distractions will fluster you. Often, it is best to make light of obvious distractions because the audience has already taken note of them. If possible, pause until the distraction fades.

## Time

A final variable to consider when conducting a situational analysis is the amount of time allotted. A speaker is never told to "talk until you're done"; everyone is expected to speak for a given time limit. Whether you are a classroom teacher, a workshop leader, or the CEO of a company, if you run long past the allotted time, audiences will "tell" you (in various ways) that the time is up and their obligation to listen has ceased. Speaker credibility diminishes rapidly when a speech runs over time.

The situational factors of occasion, size, organizational culture, physical environment, and time are important issues to consider before you prepare to speak. Adapting to each of these situational constraints can play an important role in a successful presentation. In addition to considering elements of the situation, the speaker must consider various listener characteristics.

# Analyze Listener Characteristics

Before preparing the presentation, it is vital to understand various **listener characteristics.** These characteristics include relatively stable features—for example, demographics and captivity, and mutable interpretations, such as predisposition toward the speaker and topic.

## Demographics

An audience can be described according to its basic demographic characteristics. **Demographics** are the qualities over which an audience has relatively little control, such as age, gender, economic status, education, religion, sexual orientation, ethnic background, or cultural heritage.

Sometimes demographic information can help speakers tailor their message to specific audience interests. For example, if you were to speak at a monthly meeting of the AARP (Association for the Advancement of Retired Persons), it is relatively safe to assume that most of the audience are older Americans. A topic such as changes in the tax code should be adapted to the interests of AARP members by discussing the effects of these changes on retirement benefits, health care, and social security.

Demographic information can also help those who speak in foreign countries. Asian conceptions of decision making, for example, are different from those in North America, where individual responsibility is idealized. Asian cultures tend to avoid individual decision making in favor of consensus.[2] When traveling to Latin America, it is useful to know that people there prefer less interpersonal distance than people in North America. There are many similar recommendations that researchers and consulting firms can offer to international business travelers.

On the other hand, adapting to demographic characteristics, especially religious, cultural, and ethnic distinctions, can be deadly to a speaker in North America, Europe, or other diverse, capitalist societies. Cultural differences in thinking "are far from hard-wired: Asians living in the West and Westerners in Asia often find that their cognitive styles go native."[3] For example, while working for a firm in San Francisco, a consultant, seeing many "Asian faces," decides to apply her knowledge of Asian decision making. But, because the members of this audience were born and raised in America and share American approaches to decision making, they interpret the consultant's comments as patronizing and take offense.

Increased levels of interracial and interethnic marriage, the rapid rise of global travel, and the spread of culture through the mass media tend to blur racial and ethnic behavioral traits and preferences. According to G. Pascal Zachary, a writer for the *Wall Street Journal* and author of *The Global Me,*

> Nations and ethnic groups no longer impose a common identity on all their people. Now identity depends more on what they've studied; where they've traveled; with whom they are friends; what they do for a living; whom they marry; and perhaps even what music they enjoy, restaurants they eat in, style of dancing they prefer or books they read. The global spread of technology, trade, mobility and culture are revolutionizing individual identity.[4]

The freedom that people in capitalist democracies have to mold their identities makes predicting behavior based on racial or ethnic background virtually impossible.

Adapt to group or cultural differences only if you are absolutely sure that the members of your group share the relevant interpretations and meanings applicable to your topic.

## *Captivity*

After demographics, it's important to consider why the audience is at the speech. A **voluntary audience** is one that attends a presentation of its own free will. A **captive audience**, on the other hand, is required to attend.

Lively material will help hold the interest of captive audiences. Let the audience members know you understand their situation. Acknowledge their required attendance and provide some additional motivation. For example, Gina Marcelini, a human resources specialist, spoke to a group of new employees about the company's benefits package. In the beginning of the presentation, she acknowledged that her audience members were captive but offered additional incentive for them to pay attention.

> I know that the only reason you're here today is because you have to be and that you have sat through long sessions that cover the employee manual, job rules, etc. Everyone knows you have to attend this workshop before you can begin your job. But let me assure you that the information I have is critical to your future. If you listen closely, I can help you save money by choosing the right benefits package.

Captive audiences can become interested in the speaker and topic despite their captivity.

When you do not know if the audience is captive or voluntary, or cannot generalize about members' varied reasons for attending, it is best to assume that the audience is captive and provide motivation for listeners to pay attention. Volunteer audience members can hear reminders about the importance and relevance of your topic without it negatively affecting their perceptions of the speech.

## *Predisposition Toward the Speaker*

The audience's **predisposition toward the speaker** is a vital element of listener analysis. A speaker's ability to inform or persuade is based largely on how **credible** the person is to the audience. Typically, listeners will have a negative attitude if they believe the speaker is not a qualified expert on the subject or if they believe the speaker doesn't have their best interests in mind.

If the audience doesn't know much about the speaker and his or her credentials, it's important to do something to build credibility. If, on the other hand, the audience believes the speaker is credible, further credibility-building efforts may be unnecessary. In the worst case, the audience sees the speaker as inexperienced or unqualified on the topic, and in such situations it is vital to build credibility by touting qualifications or trustworthiness.

A good way to overcome skepticism about your qualifications is to have someone introduce the presentation and state your credentials, expertise, and experience on the subject. If this is impossible, you should establish credibility yourself in the speech introduction. We will discuss when and how to do this in the next chapter. Decisions about the speech introduction can be made more easily when you know the audience's predisposition toward you as the source.

## *Predisposition Toward the Topic*

Listeners' perceptions about the topic are based on two general issues: what they know about the topic and their meaning for the topic.

***Knowledge of the Topic.***   Determine what the audience already knows about the subject. Think of **knowledge of the topic** as a continuum. At one end listeners are unaware of the topic, and at the other end listeners are experts on the topic. It is vital to know where listeners are on the continuum, to avoid speaking over people's heads or being condescending. In order to determine what your audience knows, you need to ask members what they know about the topic. This information can make the difference between a powerful presentation and a boring one.

Understanding audience knowledge is vital for informative presentations, whereas persuasive presentations must also consider audience interpretation of the topic. Use the guidelines in Figure 6.2 to adapt informative presentations to audience knowledge. The left-hand column of Figure 6.2 provides tips for adapting to audiences with minimal or no knowledge of a topic, and the right-hand column includes strategies for audiences with extensive knowledge.

Some of the most challenging audiences include a mix of informed and uninformed listeners. Making the presentation too basic may bore informed members, but pitching the information at a higher level may confuse the uninformed. In these situations, publicly acknowledge the mixed nature of the audience.

> As many of you know, we have a difficult situation here, because several of you are already experts on this topic, but the rest of you are just starting out.

The acknowledgment makes the audience aware of the difficulty you face and makes them more likely to overlook periods of boredom (the informed listener) or confusion (the uninformed listener). The content for a mixed audience should err on the side of basic information, so that few are left behind. Do this even at the risk of alienating more expert listeners. The exception to the rules for mixed audiences is if the less informed members do not have decision-making authority. In this case, aiming the content at knowledgeable members might be most appropriate.

***Meaning for the Topic.***   Persuasive speakers must not only understand the audience's knowledge level, they must also know the meaning the audience assigns to the topic. An audience's **meaning for the topic** is their interpretation—positive, negative, or neutral—and the

**FIGURE 6.2**   *Strategies for Adapting to Differential Audience Knowledge*

| *Minimal or No Knowledge* | *Extensive Knowledge* |
| --- | --- |
| • Solid justification step required to tie topic to the audience's experience and concerns. | • Justification step may or may not be necessary. |
| • Provide extensive background material on the topic. | • Extensive background material is unnecessary. |
| • Define all relevant concepts and terms. | • Define only those terms for which conflicting definitions exist. |
| • Avoid jargon in favor of simple, everyday language. | • Use of jargon may be appropriate, depending on organizational norms. |
| • Use visual aids to picture difficult structures or processes. | • Visual aids may be unnecessary. |
| • Thoroughly explain all major parts of the visual aid. | • Explanations of visual aids, although still necessary, can be less thorough. |

*Speakers must understand the audience's perceptions of the topic in order to adapt the message accordingly.*

Credit: Bill Burke

reason they hold this interpretation. For example, after the dissolution of Robert's partnership in a firm that made antennas, he decided to start his own antenna company. He sought out old customers from the previous partnership and proposed that they purchase products from his new firm. Although they liked Robert personally, they expressed concern about contracting with Robert's fledgling company. When pressed for reasons, company representatives said they were concerned about whether Robert could deliver the desired specifications in the given time period. The representatives' concerns and the reasons for them are the meaning they assign to Robert's proposal. Robert must make these negative interpretations into positive ones if he is to get the contracts.

Once you know about the audience's interpretation of the topic, it is possible to choose specific adaptation strategies. Figure 6.3, categorizes audiences based on interpretation of the topic (positive or negative) and knowledge about the topic (minimal or extensive). Categorizing the audience aids in the selection of adaptation strategies for content, structure, and delivery. Each of the five audiences is discussed in the following text.

*Favorable Audience.*   As shown in Figure 6.3, a **favorable audience** has a positive attitude toward the topic yet has little specific knowledge. The speaker's task is to reinforce and strengthen favorable attitudes while supplying specific information the audience lacks. The content, structure, and delivery suggestions for favorable audiences can be found in Table 6.1.

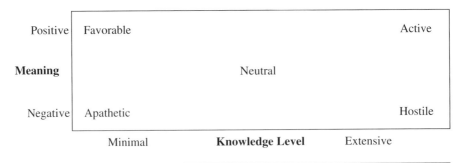

**FIGURE 6.3** *The Matrix of Audiences*

**TABLE 6.1** *Strategies for Adapting to Specific Audiences*

| Audience Type | Content | Structure | Delivery |
|---|---|---|---|
| *Favorable* | • Avoid abstract concepts.<br>• Use everyday language.<br>• Include visual aids to clarify content.<br>• Make content relevant with clear definitions and examples.<br>• Secure commitments through specific appeals to action.<br>• Be creative. | • Most patterns work well.<br>• Employ frequent connectives. | • Maintain eye contact.<br>• Vary pace, rate, and pitch.<br>• Use colorful, intense language. |
| *Apathetic* | • Use powerful attention getters in the introduction.<br>• State your personal interest in the topic in the introduction.<br>• Introduce a little information at a time and support it with vivid illustrations and examples.<br>• Keep language simple and clear.<br>• Use frequent, clear definitions.<br>• Focus on informative rather than persuasive content.<br>• Action steps should be incremental and simple. | • Use a pattern that is familiar: cause-effect, problem solution.<br>• Include clear connectives.<br>• Encourage audience participation and feedback. | • Enthusiastic, energetic, interactive delivery.<br>• Vary pace, rate, and pitch.<br>• Move around the room.<br>• Use colorful and interesting visual aids.<br>• Avoid handouts. |
| *Neutral* | • Explicitly state credibility.<br>• Emphasize the urgency and relevance of the topic to the audience.<br>• Develop examples that indicate the relevance of the topic to the audience.<br>• Demonstrate fairness to both sides of the issue.<br>• Support arguments with vivid examples and illustrations. | • Include counterarguments and refutations.<br>• Initiate a question-and-answer session.<br>• Close the speech by emphasizing the "pro" arguments. | • Be enthusiastic and energetic. |
| *Active* | • Focus on concrete actions the audience can take. | • Use a structure that emphasizes action.<br>• Use a structure that covers refutation strategies. | • Use a conversational, interactive style.<br>• Interactively work with audience to develop refutations. |
| *Hostile* | • Establish common ground.<br>• Don't alienate the audience with credentials.<br>• Cite the sources of statistics and testimony.<br>• Use sources the audience considers fair and credible.<br>• Use reluctant testimony. | • Move from areas of agreement to areas of disagreement.<br>• Use the balance structure.<br>• If possible, omit the question-and-answer session; if not, insist on a moderator. | • Exhibit calm confidence.<br>• Avoid overt enthusiasm for your position.<br>• Maintain eye contact. |

Because favorable audiences lack knowledge, the speaker should avoid confusing concepts and use common language whenever possible. Whenever new terms are introduced, include clear definitions and examples. Make the content relevant with examples that connect the topic to the audience's experience. Because favorable audiences will be predisposed to acting on persuasive appeals, encourage listeners to act on their beliefs.[5] For example, while speaking to a favorable audience about starting a charter school in his community, Terrell didn't simply end the speech with a general appeal for action. Because he knew the audience was already in favor of a charter school, he decided to create three committees to start the school. He circulated signup sheets at the end of his presentation, encouraging members to support the school by signing up for committee duties. In this way, Terrell helped the group members act on their positive interpretations.

In terms of structure, any of the patterns we discuss in Chapter 7 are appropriate. However, because the audience doesn't know much about this topic, the speech will require extensive use of the connective devices discussed in that Chapter.

Just because the audience is favorable does not mean that members should be taken for granted. Delivery for a favorable audience should include sustained eye contact, varied vocal pace and rate, and—most important—colorful, intense language. Maintain eye contact with the audience, vary your delivery style to keep their attention, and use humor and personal examples to make learning fun. Because a favorable audience already supports the topic, speakers are free to experiment by trying new ideas and urging specific action.[6]

*Apathetic Audience.*    Perhaps one of the toughest is the **apathetic audience**—a group that has little knowledge and a negative interpretation of the subject (Figure 6.3). Presentations for apathetic listeners need to inform and motivate favorable meanings. Thus the task is to grab the audience early and develop the speech in an interesting fashion to maintain interest.

Open the speech with strong attention devices and explain your interest in the topic.[7] In the speech body, emphasize clear explanations. Develop ideas slowly, provide a little information at a time, and support this information with vivid illustrations, examples, and stories, to capture the audience's imagination and aid learning. Keep language simple and make definitions frequent and clear. If at all possible, focus on informative rather than persuasive angles.[8] An audience is less likely to react negatively to straightforward information. If you must persuade an apathetic audience, focus on small, but specific, action steps that clearly explain what is needed, when it is needed, and where it is needed. Because apathetic audiences are likely to balk at action that is difficult, make the action as simple and easy to take as possible. For example, if you want the audience to purchase a product, fill out order forms in advance so members don't have to do it themselves. Finally, arrange for future contacts with audience members in order to follow up on your appeal to prevent backsliding.

Apathetic groups require familiar structures such as the cause–effect or problem solution patterns. Familiar patterns make information easy to understand and reduce the tendency to tune out. Motivate the apathetic audience by encouraging participation in a question-and-answer session after the presentation.

Delivery is the key to overcoming listener apathy. When speakers are energetic and demonstrate commitment to ideas, audiences are more likely to listen. Enthusiasm, if genuine, can be contagious. Vary your vocal pace, rate, and pitch. Move around the room to display energy. Avoid handouts, because they are an easy way for the audience to ignore you while they read (or stare at) your literature. Do not give the audience an excuse to tune out!

*Neutral Audience.*    A group that has a moderate amount of knowledge and is neither favorable nor unfavorable toward the topic is classified as a **neutral audience.** A speech before a neutral group should open with a statement of your credibility and experience on the topic. The audience must know that the speaker is qualified if they are to become more favorable. Neutral audiences can be won over by emphasizing the urgency and relevance of the topic. Develop a variety of specific examples to capture audience interest and help listeners see the various ways they are affected by the issue.

Demonstrating fairness is also critical. Neutral audiences are turned off by one-sided, ideologically biased arguments. Instead, speakers should demonstrate fairness to both sides of the issue but end by emphasizing that, after all the data are weighed, the speaker's position is the strongest.

When devising an organization strategy for the neutral audience, use a structure that addresses and refutes opposing points of view. Refutation is an argument that counters an objection to your proposal. For example, an audience may object to a sales pitch because they believe the product is too costly. Refutation rejects the objection by, for example, saying that the price is competitive with those of similar products on the market or by claiming that the price is a little higher but the quality makes the extra investment worthwhile. (Refutations are covered in Chapter 10.) Consider including a session that allows the audience to ask questions about the topic and your position. Once the question-and-answer period has concluded, offer a closing statement that summarizes the strengths of your position.

Delivery for a neutral audience should exhibit energy and enthusiasm. Communicate the interest you have for the topic. Enthusiasm can move listeners to make a commitment.

*Active Audience.*　An **active audience** is an informed audience that is favorable toward speaker and subject. Active audiences are enjoyable because the speaker fulfills a "pep talk" function that reinforces audience beliefs and actions. The key is to capitalize on listeners' favorable interpretations by encouraging specific action. One of your authors was asked to speak to a student rally on campus about a state initiative to cut property taxes. Students were generally against the initiative because the resulting budget cuts would force fee increases. Nancy knew this was an active audience, so she emphasized two specific actions. First, she encouraged students to vote against the initiative, and second, she asked every member of the audience to convince a friend or family member to vote against the initiative. Nancy's action step specified what her audience needed to do to act on their beliefs.

The structure for an active audience should emphasize specific action (these structures are covered in Chapter 10). It is also useful to provide the audience with refutations (counterarguments) that they can use against objections they might hear from others. When listeners use these refutations in other situations, it further reinforces their own commitment.[9]

Presentation style should reflect more interactive approaches than with previous audiences. Be conversational with the active audience. Build refutation strategies with them in the question-and-answer session. Provide written materials that reinforce belief or action.

*Hostile Audience.*　In contrast to the active audience, the **hostile audience** is knowledgeable about the topic, but members disagree with the specific viewpoint the speaker advocates. The audience's knowledge about the topic makes them difficult to persuade.

The first task in dealing with a hostile audience is to establish goodwill.[10] The introduction should establish common ground with them. Remind them that you share basic values or that everyone shares a desire to resolve the problem. Common ground helps the audience view you more favorably. Be especially careful in the introduction not to highlight credentials that might alienate the audience. For example, a member of the Sierra Club speaking to a community where jobs are threatened by environmental regulations should not focus on her Sierra Club attachments. She should instead emphasize the importance of both a healthy economy and a healthy environment.

As you develop your position, cite the sources of your statistics and testimony at every turn. Use sources that the audience considers fair and credible. Reluctant testimony—evidence that speaks against the self-interest of the source—is especially powerful to hostile audiences. In the case of the Sierra Club speaker, testimony from labor leaders who support environmental proposals is the strongest kind of evidence available.

The organizational structure should emphasize common ground and build from similarities before articulating differences. If possible, make your speech a two-step process: Build rapport and goodwill in the first part, and address the specific differences in the second step. The balance structure, covered in Chapter 10, in which the speaker eliminates possible solutions, ending with his or her solution, can be persuasive for hostile audiences. Be sure to acknowledge the downside of your solution, but suggest that it is the best alternative given the constraints. Depending on audience hostility, a question-and-answer session may be inadvisable. Avoid it if you fear ideologically motivated attacks. If it can't be avoided, insist on a neutral moderator to ensure that the discussion is respectful. Andrew was making a presentation to a local religious group against the statewide anti–gay marriage initiative. He expected harsh comments from a few members of the audience and asked for a moderator to lead the question-and-answer session. The moderator cooled hot tempers by directing the discussion to Andrew's argument that support of the initiative would hurt the tourist industry.

Delivery to a hostile audience should exude calm and confidence. Avoid overt enthusiasm for your position, because it may alienate those who believe you're wrong. Rather, exhibit confidence in your viewpoint. Don't be afraid to look directly at the audience. Eye contact communicates confidence and conviction.

*Mixed Audience.*    Many speaking situations include various combinations of the five audiences just discussed. **Mixed audiences** come in two different varieties. In the first, it is nearly impossible to find any clear pattern to the audience's beliefs. In such groups, every one of the five kinds of audiences depicted in Figure 6.3 is represented. The problem, of course, is that any approach is bound to alienate some members of this kind of mixed audience.

One researcher suggests that "the way to deal with a mixed audience is with delivery, not content."[11] Specifically, prepare the content of the speech as if the audience were impartial, and stick to the prepared text and supporting material throughout, adding nothing but cutting material if it appears that the audience does not need or want elaboration, or if they appear bored. Then adapt your delivery as the speech progresses. Begin with a tone of voice that is controlled and calm.[12] Monitor audience feedback and adjust the nonverbal language and delivery style according to audience response. For instance, if listeners "nod, smile, lean forward and watch you—typical signs of interest—shift to a more energetic and involved delivery."[13] But, if the response seems somewhat hostile, tone down the delivery to reflect a more neutral style. If the audience seems bored, pump up your enthusiasm. Tailor the style to the specific audience reaction, but do not change your content. It is more difficult to make impromptu changes in what you are saying than in how you are saying it.

The second variety of mixed audience is divided into two or three of the audience types cited in Figure 6.3. For example, Jenny's audience for her pitch to the city council includes an equal number of favorable, neutral, and hostile members. Adapting to this second kind of mixed audience is both challenging and fun. Because it is probably impossible to make an equally persuasive presentation to all of the elements of the mixed audience, the speaker must choose a

**target audience,** one or two of the audience types represented, as the focus of one's persuasive appeals.

Jenny must convince the city council members in her community to fund a youth recreation facility. Her audience is composed of three favorable members, three neutral members, and three hostile members. Because she only needs the votes of a simple majority, Jenny decides that her target audience will include the favorable and neutral council members. Jenny believes that the hostile members' strong opposition to raising property taxes means this group cannot be persuaded to her point of view. Instead, she focuses on acquiring the votes of the target audience but carefully avoids agitating or insulting the hostile members. Jenny decides to include basic information to improve the knowledge of the favorable and neutral groups. She demonstrates fairness to both sides of the issue, which works for the neutral audience members, and has the added benefit of acknowledging the concerns expressed by the hostile members. Jenny's goal is to move the neutral and favorable members closer to an active audience.

There are no absolute guidelines that we can provide for adapting to the second kind of mixed audience. Each circumstance forces the speaker to balance her personal goals against the kinds of audiences represented in the group and whether and how far each of those audiences can be moved by the presentation. Inevitably, attention to some portions of the audience must be minimized so that effective appeals can be developed for that part of the audience most able and likely to help the speaker achieve his or her goals.

Knowing all the adaptation strategies we presented, the key question is: How do I determine what kind of audience I am facing?

## Techniques for Analyzing the Audience

Figure 6.4 presents the Audience Analysis Checklist, a list of useful questions for analyzing situational and listener characteristics. These questions can be used in a variety of ways to better understand the audience prior to the presentation.

One way to use the checklist is to take it whole, and find answers to each and every question. In other cases, it is best to select the questions that are most relevant to your specific presentation. For example, when speaking to people from a variety of organizations, the questions about organizational culture become irrelevant and can be eliminated. If your presentation has an informative goal, as in a technical presentation, there is no need to go beyond the questions about audience knowledge. If, however, the presentation is persuasive, the speaker should include meaning questions and go on to use the matrix in Figure 6.3 to determine the type of audience he or she faces.

Once you have developed a list of specific questions, it is time to get answers. Some questions can be answered by the speaker, using his or her prior knowledge. For example, if you have seen presentations in the same room, you are well aware of its size, layout, visual aid possibilities, and potential for noise and distractions. The answers to other questions, however, aren't within the speaker's experience and must be obtained from the audience. Interview audience members to get answers to the most pressing questions on your list. If it's impossible to interview audience members, contact the representatives of the audience and speak with them. Representatives are usually the people who lead the group or set up the speaking schedule. As such, they are usually in a good position to answer questions about situational and listener characteristics.

If representatives of the audience are not available, try to interview people who are similar to the audience in most critical traits. It is also possible to get information about the audience by reading audience materials such as newsletters, or newspaper or magazine articles, or finding the

**FIGURE 6.4** *Audience Analysis Checklist*

(Use this list to stimulate appropriate questions for audience members or their representatives.)

## SITUATION ANALYSIS

*Occasion*
   Why has the audience gathered to hear this speech? What expectations does the audience have?
   What level of formality is expected?
   Are other speakers making presentations that must be acknowledged? Is there a common theme to the presentation?
      Should you connect your presentation to previous speakers or a common theme?

*Organizational Culture*
   Are there any informal conventions or norms for speakers in this organization?
   How will questions be handled?
   Who makes decisions? Will decision makers be present at the presentation? If not, should a separate meeting be
      scheduled?

*Environment*
   How large is the room? What is the layout of the room? What visual aids can be used in this room? How many people
      will be in the audience? What is the potential for noise and distraction?

*Time*
   How long should the speech last?

## LISTENER ANALYSIS

*Demographics*
   Are there any relevant demographic features you need to adapt to?

*Captivity*
   Is the audience voluntary or captive?

*Predisposition Toward the Speaker*
   Is your credibility high, low, or neutral? Does the audience believe the speaker is trustworthy? Does the audience
      believe the speaker displays goodwill?

*Predisposition Toward the Topic* (written in the form of survey questions that can be submitted to an audience)

*Knowledge*
   Have you heard about this topic before? On a scale of 1 to 10, how much information do you have about this topic?
      If you had to rate your knowledge of this topic, how much would you say you have: a little, a moderate amount,
      a lot of information?
   Briefly describe what you know about this topic.
   Describe any previous experience with this topic. On a scale of 1 to 10, what level describes your interest in this
      topic? Would you take time out to watch a television show about this topic? Would you volunteer to hear a speech
      about this topic? On a scale of 1 to 10, how concerned are you about this topic?

*Meaning*
   Describe your basic attitude toward this topic. Do you agree with the following claim? What is your opinion
      of this topic and why? On a scale from 1 to 10, with 1 being strongly against and 10 being strongly in favor,
      rate your support for this claim. In what, if any, ways do you support this claim? In what, if any, ways do you
      not support this claim? Describe your objections to the following argument. Write the top three reasons
      you have for supporting this proposal. Write the top three objections you have to this proposal. If you have had
      experience with a similar proposal, was that experience positive or negative? Why?

Based on answers to a series of predisposition questions, decide whether your audience is favorable, apathetic, neutral,
   active, hostile, or mixed.

group's page on the Web. These materials may reveal implicit group norms and provide insight into audience predispositions toward a variety of topics. If none of these options are available, the speaker must make educated guesses about the audience characteristics and hope these are adequate. Write the answers to the questions from the checklist and save them for speech preparation, which is the subject of the next chapter.

## Summary

Audience analysis begins with situational variables. Speakers should match their speech goals with audience expectations about the occasion and purpose. Speakers should adapt the formality to the anticipated size of the audience. Speakers also should be aware of the limitations of the physical environment and remain within prescribed time limits.

Audience analysis also includes analyzing listener characteristics. Judging audience reactions based on racial or ethnic appearances is risky and should be avoided. Speakers should, however, learn whether the audience is voluntary or captive. For captive audiences, acknowledge the attendance requirement and provide additional motivation for listening. Audiences will be more favorably predisposed to the speaker if they believe the speaker is knowledgeable and has the listener's best interests at heart. State your credentials in the introduction or have someone else do it for you in a prespeech introduction.

Audiences with minimal knowledge about the topic require solid justifications, extensive background material, clear definitions, simple language, and clear visual aids. For knowledgeable audiences, much of this is unnecessary.

Persuasive presentations require that the speaker understand the audience's interpretation of the topic. Audiences can be classified into one of five categories. A favorable audience has a positive interpretation of the topic yet has little specific information. The apathetic audience has little knowledge and a negative interpretation of the topic. The neutral audience is neither favorable nor unfavorable and has moderate knowledge about the topic. The active audience is informed and favorably predisposed to the topic. The hostile audience is knowledgeable about the topic and has a negative interpretation. To acquire information about the audience, select relevant questions from the Audience Analysis Checklist. To answer questions, use prior knowledge, or ask members of the audience or their representatives for information.

## Questions and Exercises

1. When conducting a situational analysis, which of the four factors discussed is most critical: the occasion, the organizational culture, the environment, or the time allotted?

2. Why is knowing the size of the audience important for the speaker? Specify what a speaker can do if, instead of speaking before a group of 30, there are 130 people to address. Or what should one do if there are 10, rather than the projected 35, audience members?

3. When can a demographic analysis be revealing and helpful for adapting a speech to an audience?

4. The text identifies several types of audiences and adaptation strategies for each. Can you think of an audience type that is not identified? What specific strategies might be most appropriate for that audience?

5. Bruce Evans is a political candidate running for Congress in the Pacific Northwest. He believes that the needs of the environment must be balanced with economic and job issues. Bruce's opponent, Patti James, is a staunch environmentalist. She believes that the long-term environmental issues should not be compromised at all, especially when

it comes to short-term issues like job loss. The two candidates are set to square off in a series of three debates. One debate is in front of a general audience sponsored by the League of Women Voters, held in a local high school auditorium. A second debate is for business leaders and employees of the largest factory in the region, sponsored by the Chamber of Commerce. The third debate is in front of environmental activists in the community, sponsored by the Sierra Club.

Both speakers must consider the varied audiences and how best to present their messages to fit audience interests. What strategies might each speaker use for the debates? Because Bruce Evans believes in "balancing" the varied interests, would

it be acceptable for him to deliver a "proeconomic" message to the Chamber of Commerce meeting and a "proenvironmental" message to the Sierra Club? Why or why not? What is the difference between adapting to the audience and pandering to an audience? When, if ever, is it acceptable to do the latter?

6. Pick out an advertisement from any popular magazine at the supermarket. Identify the target audience—the specific group of readers out of the entire magazine's readership—that the advertisement seeks to persuade. What is it about the advertisement that suggests a particular target audience? Identify the specific strategies that are used to adapt to that target audience.

## *Notes*

1. Pepper, G. L., *Communicating in Organizations: A Cultural Approach* (New York: McGraw-Hill, 1995).
2. Victor, D. A., *International Business Communication* (New York: HarperCollins, 1992).
3. Begley, S., "East Vs. West: One Sees the Big Picture, The Other Is Focused," *Wall Street Journal*, 28 March 2003, B1.
4. Zachary, G. P., *The Global Me: New Cosmopolitans and the Competitive Edge* (New York: Public Affairs, 2000).
5. Simons, H. W., *Persuasion: Understanding, Practice, and Analysis* (New York: Random House, 1986).

6. Elsea, J. G., "Strategies for Effective Presentations," *Personnel Journal*, September 1985, 31–33.
7. Simons.
8. Ibid.
9. Ibid.
10. Ibid.
11. Elsea, 33.
12. Ibid.
13. Ibid.

# 7

# *Preparing and Delivering Presentations*

According to William K. Rawlins, a communication professor at Ohio University, the fastest route to professional success is to accept every possible opportunity to speak in public. Presentations allow the audience to associate your ideas with your face, personality, and style.[1] Successful people stand out, and making presentations is one of the best ways to stand out in any organization. This chapter focuses on the steps involved in preparing and delivering professional presentations, including phrasing goals, researching the topic, structuring, outlining, developing introductions and conclusions, and delivering the presentation.

Unfortunately, many people believe delivery is the most important factor when preparing to speak. Nothing could be further from the truth. The needs of most professions emphasize command of subject, thorough research, and clear organization, rather than delivery. Decision makers rely on the quantity and quality of the information they are presented. If forced to make a choice, most professionals prefer a well-researched, well-organized speech, with plodding delivery, over thin content in a flashy package. Of course, the ideal presentation includes both excellent content and excellent delivery. Creating an ideal presentation starts with the general purpose.

## *Decide on the General Purpose*

There are two **general purposes** common to speaking in business and professional situations: to **inform** and to **persuade.** Informative speeches teach, demonstrate, or instruct an audience on some topic or process. Persuasive speeches, on the other hand, induce an audience to accept a belief or action. Although some speeches include a bit of both, it is usually possible to settle on one overriding purpose.

The general purpose in professional settings is often determined for the speaker in advance. Everyone knows that sales presentations are persuasive and that corporate training seminars focus on instruction. However, there are situations in which it is up to the speaker to determine the purpose. For example, should a speech to the sales staff merely review performance or attempt to stimulate improvements? In these cases, it's up to the speaker to decide on an appropriate general purpose by combining personal goals with knowledge of what the audience expects. In later chapters we will cover specific kinds of informative and persuasive presentations. Whereas technical presentations are primarily informative, proposal presentations, sales presentations, and crisis briefings are largely persuasive. Risk communication can be either informative or persuasive, depending on the situation. Whatever the topic, the presenter must know whether the primary goal is informative or persuasive.

## *Select a Topic*

Many—perhaps even most—business or professional **topics** are determined by superiors, the organization, or the expectations of the audience. If you sell office supplies to local business owners, then the topic is the product you sell. If you address an organizational crisis, then the organization's response is the topic.

On other occasions, speakers are afforded the opportunity to develop their own topics. Addressing employees at a rally or giving a talk to the local Rotary Club are two such occasions. Topic ideas for such speeches are limitless but may include

Conducting Market Segmentation
Clean Water
Rain Forest Destruction
Opening Markets in the Middle East
Diversifying Our Local Economic Base
Attracting New Retailers to Town
Funding Local Business Expansion

Terrorism
Local Superfund Sites

When selecting a topic for a presentation, speakers should consider **personal experience and interests.** It is difficult to create interest in an audience if you are bored by the topic or lack the necessary experience to address it. **Audience interests** are also crucial. Is the audience interested in the subject? At a minimum, can an interest be developed? Audiences are usually interested in novel, timely, or useful topics. If audience interest can't be generated, the topic should be reconsidered.

Finally, as we mentioned in the previous chapter, the speaker should consider the **audience's expectations about the occasion.** If the presentation is part of a serious discussion of an agency's problems, a lighthearted, informative presentation is clearly inappropriate. If the audience expects a brief review of last year's sales figures, an extensive persuasive appeal is also wrong. Consider the audience's expectations about the occasion before selecting a topic.

## *Develop the Specific Purpose Statement*

Once a speaker has a topic, the real work of creating the presentation begins. The next step in the process is the **specific purpose statement,** which focuses the speech on one aspect of a larger topic. According to Dorothy Leeds, president of New York City–based Organizational Technologies, Inc., the specific purpose statement does not specify what the speaker intends to say in the body of the speech.[2] Instead, it states the **audience outcome** that the speaker desires. The outcome is related to the general purpose of the speech and may include understanding (if the general purpose is to inform) or belief or action (if the general purpose is to persuade).

For example, consider the general topic of globalization, the worldwide movement of capital, trade, people, and culture, which is challenging business and political leaders in almost every nation. For this general topic, a host of specific purpose statements could be developed.

I want my audience to understand the effects of globalization on our local economy.
I want my audience to understand the economic and cultural engines that are driving globalization.
I want the audience to understand the probable impact of globalization on local manufacturing operations.
I want to persuade the audience to take advantage of the export opportunities created by global trade.
I want to convince my audience not to fear the changes that globalization is creating.
I want to persuade the audience that globalization is bad for organized labor.

As these examples demonstrate, the specific purpose statement helps the speaker narrow a broad topic to a manageable subject. Notice also the phrasing of the statements, each of which focuses on a single audience outcome for the presentation. The first three purpose statements focus on informative outcomes, and the last three on persuasive outcomes. When phrased as an outcome, the specific purpose statement provides a clear criterion against which to measure success or failure, which is vital in professional settings.

The following guidelines should be used to formulate a clear specific purpose statement. First, purpose statements should be written as full infinitive sentences, not as phrases or questions.[3] For example, this specific purpose only announces the speaker's topic.

*Specific Purpose:* Nuclear waste.

This purpose doesn't refer to the audience and doesn't specify the speaker's objective. The next example is stronger.

*Specific Purpose:* I want my audience to understand the four different categories of nuclear waste.

This statement narrows the topic to an informative one and clearly states the objective: learning about the different categories of nuclear waste.

Limit your specific purpose statements to one distinct idea. The following example is not limited to a single idea:

*Specific Purpose:* I want my audience to understand how the global positioning system works and the history of its development.

A better purpose statement focuses on a single, distinct idea.

*Specific Purpose:* I want my audience to understand how the global positioning system of earth-orbiting satellites operates to locate people on the ground.
*Specific Purpose:* I want to convince my audience that synthetic carpet is superior to wool.

Finally, specific purpose statements should be worded so they are sharp and precise. The purpose statement below is too vague.

*Specific Purpose:* I want my audience to understand pollution.

The most important term in the statement, *pollution,* is vague. What kind of pollution will the speech cover—surface water, groundwater, soil, subsurface soil, or air pollution? A better example follows.

*Specific Purpose:* I want my audience to understand the sources of groundwater pollution in our town.

This purpose is precise because it narrows the subject to local sources of groundwater pollution.

## *Develop the Main Idea Statement*

After the specific purpose has been clarified, it is time to consider the main ideas. The **main idea statement** is a precise statement of the two to five main ideas in the speech body.

*Main Idea:* In this speech I will cover the five categories of nuclear waste including: high-level, low-level, transuranic, mill tailings, and mixed waste.

*Main Idea:* In this speech I will define "tort" law and then explain the major categories of tort law.

Often, the main idea statement emerges only after extensive research on the subject. The main idea statement serves as a guide for outlining the body of the speech. With minor word changes, the main idea statement can be used as the preview of main ideas in the introduction. The main idea should be stated precisely in a declarative sentence, not a question. For example, the following main idea is not precise.

*Main Idea:* For this speech I will cover theories about why the body ages, including random damage and hormonal influences, as well as genetic programs.

The wording of this statement is unclear for several reasons. How many theories are there? Do hormonal influences and random damage constitute one or two theories? An improved version follows.

*Main Idea:* In this speech I will cover three theories about why the human body ages: first, random damage; second, hormonal influences; and third, genetic programs.

This statement clarifies the three theories by distinctly stating each one. Enumeration can improve the clarity of a main idea statement.

## Gather Supporting Material

As you develop and refine the main idea statement, it is appropriate to collect **supporting material.** Main ideas need examples, statistical support, and quotations from experts for clarity and proof. This section defines and explains the use of supporting material.

*A good presentation requires hours of careful preparation.*

Credit: Bill Burke

## *Examples*

**Examples** are specific instances that illustrate a larger point. An example can be factual, meaning that the instance really happened, or hypothetical, meaning that the instance is a composite of real incidents or the speaker's guess about a future event. When discussing the fire risk at a chemical plant, the speaker may decide to use a factual example.

> The major risk in area five involves the large compressors. As many of you recall, five years ago a malfunction in one of the large compressors caused it to begin belching smoke. When an employee entered the building to investigate, the compressor exploded, causing second-degree burns to 20 percent of the employee's body and a fire in the building that shut down the plant for two days.

This example dramatically illustrates the fire risk in the compressor room. If a factual example cannot be found, a hypothetical illustration can be employed.

> What would have happened if you had invested $5,000 in a mutual fund last year, and over that year the fund had risen from a value of $21 a share to a value of $32? That equals more than a 52 percent increase in the value of your stock. A 52 percent increase on $5,000 equals $2,600.

Hypothetical examples are more useful for illustration than persuasion because they do not prove anything. If you have a choice, use factual rather than hypothetical examples.

## *Statistics*

**Statistics** are a collection of individual examples delivered as raw numbers or averages. Economists used the following raw figure to dramatize the weakness of the U.S. economy.

> Certainly, July saw no turnaround in the job markets. Payrolls in the private sector declined last month by 73,000 workers, the third drop in the past four months.[4]

In other cases, raw numbers are averaged in some manner.

> If you want a vivid illustration of America's role in the global slowdown, consider that the U.S. buys up nearly one-fourth of the rest of the world's exports. And the growth rate of the volume of goods coming into the U.S. has swung from a 17% annual pace last autumn to a –5% pace currently. No wonder many economies abroad are struggling.[5]

The typical method of averaging raw numbers is by calculating the mean: the mathematical average of a list of figures. Speakers should avoid confusing listeners with too much statistical information. If your speech includes many statistics, use visual aids to make the data concrete (see Chapter 8).

Statistics are more meaningful when combined with **comparisons.** For example, in a news story about the Snake River Plain Aquifer in Idaho, various statistics were used to indicate its approximate size. The aquifer is 5,500 feet deep and 100 miles long, and provides water for 130,000 Idahoans. Although interesting, these figures don't help an audience visualize the enormous size of the aquifer. The story added that, if it were completely drained, the water in the aquifer would fill Lake Erie.[6] Bud Mandeville, the assistant plant manager at a potato processor, uses a statistical comparison to describe his plant's processing capabilities. Every day, 3 million pounds of potatoes are turned into French fries. This is equivalent to two and one-half semi–truck trailers full of potatoes every hour.[7] Look for comparisons that make statistical information more meaningful.

### Testimony

**Testimony** is a direct quotation or paraphrase of witnesses, experts, or other informed people. Quotations can make ideas memorable or add credibility to your persuasive appeal.

The use of quotations can add interest and impact to presentations. To emphasize that business leaders should expect continued protests over globalization, *BusinessWeek* used a direct quotation.

> Meanwhile, protest groups intend to keep up their activities against specific companies, from garment makers to drug manufacturers. "We have a commitment to talk about corporate globalization in the U.S. and around the world," says Fred Azcarate, the head of Jobs with Justice, a grassroots labor group in Washington, that, along with churches and environmentalists, plans to protest September's meeting.[8]

The quote clearly supports the magazine's contention that globalization protests will continue for the foreseeable future. Build your credibility by selecting testimony from sources your audience considers expert. Briefly cite the source of your testimony so the audience can evaluate its strength. Developing supporting material requires an understanding of basic research techniques.

## Research the Topic

**Research** involves collecting supporting material for the specific purpose and main idea statements. Typical research tools for professional presentations are the library, the Internet, and the interview.

### Using the Library

Your library's **computerized catalog** can run book searches by title, author, or subject. More advanced systems at most libraries allow combined searches, such as a subject and title search or a subject and author search. Check with the librarian about the most efficient means of locating books on your topic.

An effective search of any online catalog depends on developing a list of **key terms** or **phrases** from your specific purpose statement. For example, for a speech on PM-10 (particulate matter smaller than 10 microns in size) pollution, different terms will assist a catalog search. Such terms as "PM-10" or "PM-10 pollution" might be a good start. Similar phrases might also be useful, including "particulate pollution" or "particulate." Popular terms, such as "air pollution" or "smog," might also lead to important sources. In any search, it is vital that you become familiar with the key words or phrases used to describe your topic.

In addition to the online catalog of books, most libraries include various periodical indexes or abstracts. **Periodical indexes** and **abstracts** are paper or electronic databases that list and/or abstract (summarize) articles in popular and academic periodicals. There are numerous indexing and abstract databases that libraries subscribe to, most of which are now available in electronic form. For example, *The Reader's Guide to Periodical Literature* indexes articles in a variety of popular magazines, including *Time* and *Newsweek.* More specialized periodicals are indexed by *General Science,* covering the physical sciences; the *Political Science Index;* or the *Social Science Index.* Searches for most professional speech topics should probably start at a general index such as *The Reader's Guide* and then seek out at least one other specialized index.

Many university and community libraries now subscribe to EBSCO Information Services, which provides access to a huge number of electronic and print sources through a variety of "databases" that can be searched using your topic's key words and phrases. These databases range from the broad and general, such as Academic Search Premier —(which includes full-text electronic articles from more than 4,500 journals and periodicals including the *Journal of Education* and *Political Science Quarterly*) to more specific databases, such as the Business Source Premier—(which includes full-text articles from journals such as *Harvard Business Review* and *Administrative Science Quarterly*). Other EBSCO databases include Biomedical Reference Collection, for doctors, research scientists, and clinical specialists; Corporate ResourceNet, which indexes 1,200 corporate and trade journals; and PsycINFO, which includes 2.3 million citations in psychology and related disciplines.

When using the EBSCO host at your university or community library, simply choose the database that fits your topic and enter your key words or phrases into the search box. By checking the Full Text box, you limit your search to only those articles that have full-text versions available online. The search options box allows you to set the preferred dates for your results. You can also choose to limit the search to refereed journal articles, thus eliminating popular sources from your results. Talk to your library's research specialist to help you expand or contract your results as needed.

## *Using the Internet*

The **Internet** is a set of linked computer networks that began as a federally funded project to maintain military communication during a nuclear war. The Internet is not run by anyone, but exists as a few committees who establish the languages by which computers interact with one another. As such, the Internet is "a bit like the old Wild West—anything and everything goes, and there's no sheriff to keep law and order."[9]

On one hand, the Internet is a valuable addition to effective library research. First, the Internet is excellent for finding recent articles in newspapers and popular magazines. Because many news organizations such as the *Washington Post* and *USA Today* put their material on the Internet, it is easy to search for recent articles. Some newspapers, such as the *Wall Street Journal,* force researchers to pay a fee for downloading their content.

The Internet is also excellent for finding up-to-date information about particular organizations, local happenings, government agencies, and national and international trends. Want to find out how the Targhee National Forest in Idaho handled recent land closures? See if an update is included on its Web page, or search for the forest supervisor's e-mail address and ask your questions directly. If you want to know how many U.S. manufacturing jobs have been lost to outsourcing (the movement of jobs to overseas locations where labor is cheap) in the past five years, the Internet is an ideal source. The Internet is also an excellent place to find the latest information on local happenings or public information about companies and government agencies—information that doesn't get into print because it's too limited, too local, or too ephemeral.

On the other hand, finding books and many journal articles through the Internet is more difficult. Although some periodicals and publishers make their content available to Web users, they may require that you pay for immediate access in order to protect their subscription base or royalty revenue. Because of these limitations, the best research strategy includes a combination of Internet and library sources.

The most useful part of the Internet is the **World Wide Web,** a series of Internet linkages used by millions of people around the globe. Navigating the Web requires a Web browser program. A **browser** is a series of operating instructions that allows your personal computer to interact with the documents stored on the Web. The most popular Web browsers are Netscape, Microsoft's Internet Explorer, and Firefox.

Browsing allows a person to access **Web pages,** which are sites on the World Wide Web created by universities, publishers, companies, and individuals. Each contains links to another place in that same page or to other, related pages. The page's author decides on these links, which are indicated by underlined or colored words or images. Clicking on these words or images automatically downloads the new page for viewing. Once you find a site that contains useful information, you can follow the links to other relevant sites.

Each site on the Web has a **uniform resource locator,** or **URL,** which starts with the letters *http://.* The URL is similar to a post office box address.

Browsing, however, is not an efficient way to do research, because there are millions of pages. The solution to this problem is a search engine. A **search engine** is a program that sifts through an enormous index of Web pages for key words or phrases. The index is created by "spider programs" that crawl over the Internet collecting and organizing Web pages. Popular search engines include Yahoo!, About.com, AltaVista, Dogpile.com, Google, and go2.com. Every search tool organizes the results of its work differently. Some engines, including Yahoo!, and About.com, use human editors to review and categorize Web sites. For example, on Yahoo! the Web pages under the topic "Ford Mustang" are divided into categories that include classified ads, message boards for Mustang aficionados, general information about the car, and worldwide Mustang clubs. On the other hand, Google ranks page results by how many other sites are linked to them, and go2.com gives priority rankings to the highest bidder.

The search engine you choose depends on your research needs. For example, if you have very little knowledge about your topic, the engines that use human editors (Yahoo! and About.com) are easier because results are categorized in an intuitive manner. On the other hand, because Google and AltaVista have a larger database of Web pages than most other search engines, they work better for very narrow topics or for the researcher who wants to find everything possible on the subject. Because of its large database and the fact that it does not accept money to place certain Web pages above others on its results list, Google has become the preferred search engine for many people.

Let's run a search using two of the most popular search engines, Yahoo! and Google. Imagine you need to create a corporate training program in risk communication. Risk communication is any communication about uncertain physical or environmental hazards.[10] Go to the Yahoo! home page (www.yahoo.com) and click on the Advanced Search button. The advanced search provides several options to expand or narrow research results. The use of AND in your key phrase can narrow your topic and avoid irrelevant results. For example, if we were creating our training program for professionals in the nuclear industry, it might be useful to limit our research to that industry. Entering the phrases "risk communication" AND "nuclear power" exactly as shown here, including the quotation marks, asks the computer to limit the search to those documents that include both the phrases "risk communication" and "nuclear power." Web pages that include only one or the other phrase will not show up in the search results. (The use of quotation marks tells the computer to search for the exact phrase in a document rather than the individual words *risk* and *communication*.) However, if you want to expand your search beyond risk communication issues, you can use the OR function. Entering the phrases "risk communication" OR "risk analysis" tells the computer to expand the search by including documents that include either phrase. Because risk communication is a fairly common phrase in the social sciences, enter that phrase in the search box and click on the third option, the Exact Phrase button. The computer will now search for all documents that include the phrase "risk communication." When we tried this it produced five "hits," including an extensive bibliography of risk communication sources created by someone at the University of Cincinnati and a discussion of how to release information to the public about a nuclear accident, written by the Department of Energy. The third hit is the Society for Risk Analysis, a group devoted to risk analysis and communication. The last two sites include a university department and a consulting company also devoted to risk communication. Yahoo! searches are quick and easy to navigate.

Let's run a similar search on the Google engine. Once at the Google site (www.google.com), a click on the Advanced Search button reveals the same search options as on Yahoo!. Entering the phrase "risk communication" in the exact phrase box reveals approximately 171,000 references. The large number of hits is the result of Google's very large database. A quick glance at the first twenty Web pages shows a number of basic primers on risk communication from the National Cancer Institute, the U.S. Department of Public Health, and the consulting company Battele. Almost every one of the first twenty hits is a useful site for our training program. Google represents a thorough method of searching the Internet.

One final search engine that is especially useful for business presentations is Ask Jeeves. Unlike other engines, which search documents for key terms, Ask Jeeves responds to questions. Imagine, for example, that you need to find out how many U.S. manufacturing jobs have been lost to outsourcing in the past ten years. By entering the URL address "Ask.com," you are taken to the Ask Jeeves search engine. Enter the question "How many U.S. manufacturing jobs have been lost to outsourcing?" in the search box. The Ask Jeeves search engine organizes results into two categories. Sponsored results include companies that pay for product placements. In this search the sponsored results include several firms that specialize in outsourcing, as well as the Monster.com jobs site. The second category, Web results, includes relevant sites that have not paid for product placements. When we did this search, we found two articles, one from Yahoo! News, India, and a second from Lou Dobbs, a CNN anchor, both of which claim that 2.7 million U.S. jobs have been lost to outsourcing since July 2001. Finding the same statistic in two different sources convinces you that it is worthy of inclusion in your presentation. Ask Jeeves is an ideal way to fill in missing information, find important quotes, or identify vital facts you need to support any business speech.

Because Web pages can be created by almost anyone with a computer, the Web includes both experts with something to say as well as "Charlatans, extremists, and malcontents."[11] Careful scrutiny of your research content is vital for any business presentation. Figure 7.1 offers a series of questions to test the credibility of Internet Web pages. The questions focus on the qualifications and relative bias of the author and institution and the recency of the Web page.

**FIGURE 7.1**   *Assessing the Credibility of Internet Sources*

*Authority*

> Who authored the Web page?
> Are the author's credentials included on the Web page?
> Is the author qualified to publish a page on this topic?
> What, if any, institution supports the Web page?
> Is the institution qualified to support a Web page on this topic?

*Objectivity*

> What are the goals or objectives of the Web page?
> Are these goals likely to lead the author or institution to slant information?
> Given what you know about the author or institution, are they relatively free of bias?

*Recency*

> When was the Web page produced?
> When was the Web page last updated?

## Conducting Interviews

**Interviews** are face-to-face, telephone, or Internet conversations with experts. In general, they should wait until the end of the research process so you have thorough knowledge of the topic prior to taking someone's time with an interview.

You should clearly define the purpose of the interview prior to contacting potential interviewees. The purpose should relate closely to the specific purpose statement or one of the main ideas in the body of the presentation. Develop questions prior to the interview so you have something to show if the interviewee wants to see the questions in advance. The questions will also keep the interview on track and prevent wasted time. Avoid yes and no questions, because these answers can be found in other sources.

To save time, many interviews can be conducted over the phone. An even better source of interview information is e-mail. After receiving permission to conduct the interview, the researcher can e-mail her questions, and the respondent is free to reply at his or her convenience. A final e-mail may be necessary to probe for details and ask follow-up questions. A written thank-you note is a vital courtesy following any interview.

# Apply the Information Learned from the Audience Analysis

After the initial research, it is time to consider audience feedback. The previous chapter demonstrated how to analyze audience features relevant to professional presentations. The questions on the Audience Analysis Checklist provide a set of guidelines for asking relevant questions about audience needs and expectations. To apply that knowledge, speakers should use the Speech Adaptation Checklist in Figure 7.2. The questions in the Speech Adaptation Checklist will help you adjust the content and delivery of your presentation to your specific audience. To answer the questions, use your knowledge of the audience from the Audience Analysis Checklist as a guide. Be specific in your answers. Try to think of specific examples, structures, persuasive appeals, and delivery styles that will be most interesting or convincing to the particular audience. Figure 7.2 demonstrates how to answer the questions for the sample speech on tort law that appears later in this chapter.

**FIGURE 7.2    *Speech Adaptation Checklist***

**ADAPTING TO THE SITUATION**

*Occasion*

Does your specific purpose statement match audience expectations?
*(This is a classroom speech in Business and Professional Communication. The audience expects a business-related topic. I will use examples and stories throughout the speech that emphasize how tort laws affect businesspeople.)*

Does your central idea statement match audience expectations?
*(Because this is a classroom speech, there are not many expectations here.)*

Will your delivery create the appropriate level of formality for the audience and the situation?
*(Little formality expected. Emphasize conversational style and eye contact.)*

If it is expected, have you connected your specific purpose to the theme the audience expects to hear about?
*(N/A)*

If expected, have you made an effort to refer to other speakers and their content in your speech?
*(N/A)*

*Organizational Culture*

Have you adapted your content and delivery to local conventions and norms?
*(N/A)*

Have you adapted to the organization's mode of asking questions?
*(N/A)*

Will you be talking to the ultimate decision maker?
*(N/A. No decision required for classroom speech.)*

*Environment*

Have you prepared your delivery for the size of the room and the number of people expected?
*(Yes. Minimal formality for a night class of business professionals.)*

Can your visual aids be seen in all parts of the room?
*(N/A. No visual aids in this speech.)*

Have you prepared for any unusual limitations in the room?
*(N/A)*

Have you prepared for any noise or other distractions possible in this room?
*(N/A)*

*Time*

Will the speech fit within the given time limit?

**ADAPTING TO AUDIENCE TRAITS**

*Demographics*

Have you adapted to relevant audience demographic features?

*Captivity*

Is this audience captive or voluntary? If it is captive, have you adapted to the members' needs?

*(Captive. I want to open with an interesting, business-related story. I will try to provide some hypothetical examples that are common enough to happen to anyone in the audience. Perhaps*

**FIGURE 7.2    *Continued***

*I can also refer to the O. J. Simpson criminal and civil trials as examples. I will use "you" and "we" pronouns to remind them that tort laws apply to everyone. I will keep the delivery lively.*)

*Predisposition Toward the Speaker*

Have you arranged to provide credibility information for the audience?
*(I will mention my business law class to build my credibility.)*

Have you built proof of your goodwill into the presentation?
*(I will mention that I want to protect them from lawsuits.)*

*Predisposition Toward the Topic*

What, if any, interest does this audience have in the topic?
*(Very little. I need to remind the audience that everyone in business needs to know this information.)*

What, if any, knowledge does the audience have about this topic?
*(Almost none. Most audience members haven't had business law. I will start out by making a distinction between civil and criminal law. I will clearly define all terms, including* tort law, civil law, *and* criminal law. *I will provide numerous examples. I must carefully define each category of tort.)*

What kind of audience are you facing: favorable, active, neutral, apathetic, hostile, or mixed?
*(N/A)*

Have you incorporated the specific content and delivery suggestions for each kind of audience in the previous chapter?
*(N/A)*

## Structure the Main Ideas in the Body of the Speech

Research shows that people will understand and remember data if they are clearly structured rather than presented chaotically. According to Dorothy Leeds, structure is equivalent to leadership. Speakers lead by taking command of the audience and guiding listeners to conclusions. "However, nothing diminishes your leadership potential faster than disorganization. If your listeners can't follow you, you lose their respect and attention."[12]

Speeches are divided into three major parts: the introduction, the body, and the conclusion. The **introduction** should gain attention, justify the topic, clarify the speaker's credibility, and preview the main points in the body of the speech. The main ideas reside in the speech **body.** Finally, the **conclusion** reviews main ideas and emphasizes the specific purpose statement. We will cover introductions and conclusions later in this chapter. Here we address structuring the main points in the speech body.

Because most business audiences demand detailed information, speakers rarely have time to cover more than two to five **main ideas.** These should be stated in full sentences rather than phrases or key words. For example, in a classroom speech on bacteria-contaminated food, Jacob M. Lewis started with the following main ideas:

> *Specific Purpose Statement:* I want my audience to understand how bacteria-contaminated food makes people sick.
>
> *Main Idea:* Bacteria contaminate and propagate in food in different ways.
> *Main Idea:* Bacteria can produce enzymes that make people sick.
> *Main Idea:* Bacteria can produce exotoxins that make people sick.
> *Main Idea:* Bacteria can produce endotoxins that make people sick.

*Main Idea:* Government regulations are designed to protect people from contamination.
*Main Idea:* The following are examples of companies that had serious contamination problems.

Developing main ideas should be a freewheeling exercise similar to brainstorming. Record every idea, no matter how silly it may appear; then eliminate main ideas that are unrelated to the specific purpose statement. Some points can be subsumed under other main ideas as supporting material. Because the main idea on government regulation isn't related to the way bacteria make people sick, it can be eliminated. Because the last main point is a series of examples, it is better used as supporting material for other points.

Once the main ideas have been narrowed, they must be structured. There are five patterns for structuring speech content.

## *Chronological Structure*

The **chronological structure** follows a time pattern that moves from earliest to latest or first to last.

*Specific Purpose:* To inform the audience about how the El Niño phenomenon affects winter weather in the Northwest United States.

    **I.** Water temperature in the Pacific Ocean off Peru warms.
   **II.** This warming creates high pressure in the Pacific off the West Coast.
  **III.** The ridge prevents storms from entering the region by splitting the jet stream.

The chronological structure is used in historical speeches that narrate events or in process speeches that demonstrate how something is done.

## *Spatial Structure*

The **spatial structure** follows a geographic or directional pattern when someone covers something from top to bottom or right to left. For example, one could describe the major tribal groups in Idaho by moving from north to south.

*Specific Purpose:* To inform the audience about the major Native American tribes in Idaho.

    **I.** Northern Idaho includes the Nez Pierce and the Coeur d'Alene tribes.
   **II.** Southern Idaho includes the Shoshone and Bannock tribes.

A speech to convince a sporting goods store to carry your company's tennis racket can be organized spatially.

*Specific Purpose:* To convince the sporting goods retailer to carry our racket.

    **I.** The grip on the racket is superior to our competitors' grips.
   **II.** The frame of the racket is made of graphite for superior durability and power.
  **III.** The head of the racket has a specially designed shape for more ball control.

*An effective presentation is more than just good delivery. It involves clear structure and a detailed outline.*

Credit: Kevin C. Wellard

## Cause–Effect and Effect–Cause Structures

The **cause–effect structure** describes how one event leads to another. This structure is especially useful in technical presentations.

> *Specific Purpose:* I want my audience to understand how bacteria-contaminated food can make people sick.
>
> **I.** Improper processing or storage can induce bacteria growth in food.
> **II.** Once on the food, bacteria produce three toxins that result in illness.

Some topics warrant placing the effect first and the cause second.

> *Specific Purpose:* To help our marketing people understand why the manufacturing process is introducing flaws into some of our tennis rackets.
>
> **I.** Customers have noticed three flaws in our rackets.
> **II.** The cause of these flaws is the way materials are extruded during manufacturing.

As the examples above illustrate, a cause–effect structure should be limited to two main ideas, one dealing with the cause and the other covering the effect. If there are several causes or effects, these should be grouped as subpoints under the main idea.

### Problem Solution Structure

The **problem solution structure** defines a difficulty and suggests a remedy. Extremely popular in proposal and sales presentations, the problem solution structure can also be employed in technical and risk communication. As with the cause–effect structure, problem solution structures should include two, and only two, main ideas.

> *Specific Purpose:* I want to persuade my audience that a perpetual inventory system is superior to a periodic system.
>
>   I. There are three major problems with a periodic inventory system.
>  II. The solution to these problems is a computerized perpetual inventory system.

### Topical Structure

When the speaker divides a topic into logical categories, he or she is using a **topical structure.** Each topical category becomes a main point in the speech. For example, a speech detailing the nutrition content of fast food could divide the topic into different kinds of food, including chicken restaurants, hamburger restaurants, and taco restaurants. A speech on nuclear waste can also be organized topically.

> *Specific Purpose:* I want my audience to understand the different kinds of nuclear waste.
>
>    I. Low-level nuclear waste emits relatively small amounts of radioactivity.
>   II. High-level nuclear waste emits high amounts of radioactivity.
>  III. Transuranic waste includes materials such as tools and clothing that become contaminated with human-made radioactive particles chemically heavier than the element uranium.
>   IV. Finally, mill tailings are soils left over after radioactive elements have been mined.

The speech on contaminated food can be organized topically.

> *Specific Purpose:* I want my audience to understand how bacteria-contaminated foods can make people sick.
>
>    I. Bacteria produce enzymes that make people sick.
>   II. Bacteria produce exotoxins that make people sick.
>  III. Bacteria produce endotoxins that make people sick.

A clear structure organizes information logically so the speaker can lead the audience to the desired conclusion.

## Outline the Speech

Creating any kind of presentation involves two somewhat contradictory challenges. First, professional audiences demand well-structured presentations. This requires a thorough, full-sentence outline of all the main and subideas in the presentation. A full-sentence outline compels the speaker to examine the underlying structure and logic of the speech. On the other hand, audiences also demand enthusiasm and a sense of spontaneity that can rarely be produced by reading from a full-sentence outline. We therefore recommend using two outlines: one for preparing the speech and a second for delivering the speech.

## *The Preparation Outline*

The **preparation outline** is a full-sentence outline of virtually everything the speaker intends to say. It allows the speaker to test the structure, the logic, and the persuasive appeals in the speech. Use the following guidelines for creating the preparation outline. These guidelines are exemplified in the sample speech outline on tort law in Figure 7.3.

The preparation outline should include the general purpose, the topic, the specific purpose, and the main idea statements. Next, label the parts of the speech—introduction, body, and conclusion—and start with a new set of Roman numerals in each of the three parts of the speech. Develop a consistent pattern of symbolization for main and subpoints. The traditional pattern of symbolization is as follows:

- Main headings are designated with Roman numerals.
- First-level subheads are indicated by capital letters.
- The following subheads are in Arabic numerals and lowercase letters in that order:

Because phrases and questions are unclear, state main and subpoints in full declarative sentences. Consider the following example:

> *Specific Purpose:* I want my audience to understand the damage free radicals do to the body.

> **I.** Free radicals
> **II.** What's to be done?

What does the speaker intend to discuss in the first main idea? Is he or she defining free radicals, explaining the problem of free radicals, or describing the source of free radicals? The answer is unclear. Stated as a question, the second main idea is also unclear. Will the speaker inform the audience about a variety of solutions or present a single solution? The following example is stronger:

> **I.** Free radicals are electrically charged molecules that damage the cells in our body.
> **II.** Free radicals can be reduced by taking certain vitamins.

Use one symbol for each main or subidea. Can you spot the logical flaw in the outline below?

> **I.** There are several sources of PM-10 pollution.
>   **A.** Smoke from combustion and fumes from chemical reactions are common sources.
>   **B.** Dust is another source of PM-10.
>   **C.** Mist from spraying or condensing water vapor is another PM-10 source.

**FIGURE 7.3**   *Sample Speech Outline*

Tort Law

By Lori Braase

| | |
|---|---|
| Topic: | Tort law |
| General Purpose: | To inform |
| Specific Purpose: | To inform the audience about three kinds of tort law |
| Main Ideas: | First, I will define what tort law is, and then I will explain the major categories of tort law. |

**INTRODUCTION**

I.   A six-year-old boy lights his shirt on fire with a Bic lighter and suffers severe burns. His mother sues the Bic Corporation for damages and wins. An 81-year-old woman orders coffee from a McDonald's drive-through and accidentally spills it in her lap, causing severe burns. She sues the McDonald's Corporation and wins $640,000 in damages.

II.  It is hard to pick up a newspaper today without reading about liability lawsuits that involve millions of dollars in awards.

    **A.** Tort law is the part of the legal code of this country that addresses issues of liability.

    **B.** Everyone needs a basic understanding of tort law to understand the reasoning behind the judgments you read about in the paper.

    **C.** As future businesspeople, you will need a knowledge of torts to protect yourself and your company from lawsuits.

    **D.** Today I will inform you about some of the basic concepts of tort law.

III. My name is Lori Braase, and I am currently enrolled in a business law class that focuses in part on tort law.

IV.  Tonight I will define the concept of a tort and then explain the major categories of tort law.

(Trans: Let's start by defining a tort.)

**BODY**

I.   *Tort* is a French word for "wrong," and it has to do with wrongful conduct by one person that causes injury to another.

    **A.** Tort law is an area of civil law, not criminal law.

        **1.** Criminal law is concerned with wrongs or crimes against society as a whole.

            **a.** The state prosecutes a person who commits a criminal act.

            **b.** If convicted, those who commit criminal acts are punished by the state.

                **(1)** Robbery is a criminal offense.

                **(2)** The same is true of murder.

        **2.** On the other hand, torts are an area of civil law, which is concerned with the responsibilities that exist between people or between citizens and their government.

            **a.** In the case of torts, victims, not the state, initiate the lawsuit.

            **b.** Those who are found guilty of civil violations usually compensate the victim financially.

                **(1)** If, for example, you slip in the grocery store and break your leg, you could sue the grocery store to recover your medical bills.

                **(2)** Although O.J. Simpson was found not guilty in a criminal court, Fred Goldman, the father of murder victim Ronald Goldman, sued Simpson in civil court and won damages of 33.5 million dollars. (Simpson was back in the news in 2007, when he was arrested in Las Vegas for allegedly attempting to steal sports memorabilia related to his football career).

**FIGURE 7.3**     *Continued*

---

**B.** As you can see, a tort is an area of civil rather than criminal law.

(Trans: Now that you know the definition of a tort, let's get to the different kinds of torts.)

**II.** There are three broad categories of torts: intentional torts, negligence torts, and strict liability torts.

    **A.** First, intentional torts are concerned with the intent to commit an act that interferes with another person's rights, such as physical injury, physical security, trespassing, property damage, reputation, privacy, dignity, etc.

        **1.** For example, assault and battery is an intentional act that may cause physical injury.

            **a.** Assault occurs when George threatens to hit Mike with a baseball bat.

            **b.** Battery is the completion of the act that occurs when George hits Mike in the arm with the bat.

        **2.** Defamation of character is a tort that occurs when someone wrongfully hurts another's good reputation through libel or slander.

            **a.** You could be charged with a tort of slander if you orally defame another person by saying they have a loathsome communicable disease.

            **b.** You could be charged with a tort of libel if you publish an article in the local paper falsely describing an attorney's unethical behavior in a nightclub.

    **B.** The second category of torts involves negligence that can occur when the conduct of a person or business creates a risk of negative consequences.

        **1.** Negligence occurs when someone suffers injury because of another's failure to live up to a required duty of care or responsibility for our actions.

            **a.** Allowing a friend to leave your home too drunk to drive may be considered a breach of duty if she or he becomes involved in an auto accident.

            **b.** If someone slips and breaks his or her leg on your icy front steps, you may have committed a breach of duty and be sued under the negligence tort.

        **2.** Both individuals and businesses are open to suits under the negligence tort.

    **C.** Finally, the third category of torts involves strict liability, sometimes referred to as "liability without fault," and these involve business or manufacturing operations.

        **1.** Strict liability torts are governed by three assumptions.

            **a.** First, consumers should be protected against unsafe products.

            **b.** Second, manufacturers and distributors should not escape liability for faulty products.

            **c.** Third, manufacturers are in a better position to bear the costs associated with injuries caused by their products than are consumers.

        **2.** For example, the Bic Corporation was held liable for severe burns on the six-year-old boy who lit his shirt on fire.

            **a.** According to the jury, the Bic Corporation was in a better position to bear the costs of the boy's injuries than the family.

            **b.** As a result of the judgment, Bic modified its lighters to stop young children from using them.

(Trans: Understanding these three broad categories of torts provides you with the ability to understand an important portion of our legal code.)

**CONCLUSION**

    **I.** In conclusion, I have covered two major points about tort law. I have defined a tort and explained the three major categories of torts.

    **II.** Now you can apply your own legal reasoning to understand more about the liability lawsuits you hear about in the media.

(Bibliography)

Point A includes two ideas, combustion and fumes, under a single symbol, which makes the sources of PM-10 difficult to follow.

Once the major features of the outline are solidified, it is time to insert appropriate connectives throughout the body of the speech. **Connectives** are linguistic devices that link ideas. Connectives serve as maps; they let audiences know where they have been and where they are going. Five kinds of connectives are common in business presentations. **Transitions** are full-sentence statements that are inserted in parentheses between the introduction and the body, between the body and the conclusion, and between all main ideas in the body of the speech. The appropriate locations are shown:

INTRODUCTION
    **I.**
    **II.**
    **III.**
    **IV.**
(Transition)

BODY
    **I.**
(Transition)
    **II.**
(Transition)
    **III.**
(Transition)

CONCLUSION
    **I.**
    **II.**

Generally, transitions state both the idea that the speaker is leaving and the upcoming idea. A speech on nuclear waste should include several transitions.

*Specific Purpose:* I want my audience to understand the different kinds of nuclear waste.

INTRODUCTION
    **I.**
    **II.**
    **III.**
    **IV.**

(Trans: Let's begin by examining low-level waste.)

BODY
    **I.** Low-level nuclear waste is material that emits relatively small amounts of radioactivity.
    (Trans: Whereas low-level waste emits small amounts of radioactivity, high-level waste is quite different.)
    **II.** As the name suggests, high-level waste emits high amounts of radioactivity.
(Trans: The third category of waste, transuranic waste, is different from high-level waste.)
    **III.** Transuranic waste includes materials such as tools and clothing that become contaminated with human-made radioactive particles chemically heavier than the element uranium.

(Trans: The fourth category of waste, mill tailings, is the result of mining.)

**IV.** Mill tailings are materials of the earth left over after radioactive elements have been mined.

(Trans: Now that you understand the four varieties of waste, let me finish with a few points.)

CONCLUSION

    **I.**

    **II.**

A second form of connective is **forecasting,** in which a speaker develops main ideas such that they preview subpoints. Although not necessary for all main ideas, forecasting is a valuable source of clarity for listeners. For example,

> *Specific Purpose:* I want my audience to understand what particulate pollution is and why it is a concern.

BODY

    **I.** In the first part of the speech, I will define particulate pollution by explaining what it is and where it comes from.

        **A.** First, air pollution exists as solid matter, liquid droplets, or gas.

        **B.** Second, particulate pollution can come from a variety of sources that are both natural and human.

(Trans: Knowing what particulate pollution is, you can now begin to understand why it is a problem.)

    **II.** To understand why particulates are an air pollution problem, you must understand how small this kind of pollution really is and how it is classified by scientists.

        **A.** First, particulate pollution is so small that it is measured in terms of microns.

        **B.** Second, based on the size of the particles, particulate pollution is classified into one of two categories: coarse and fine.

Both the main points in this example clearly forecast the subpoints.

**Parallel order** is an organizational device that should be used throughout the speech. If, for example, a speaker forecasts two subpoints in the first main idea, then those subpoints should appear in that same order. **Parallel language** means that the same words or phrases are repeated in previews, main ideas, and subpoints. In the previous example, the speaker uses parallel language in the first main idea by saying he or she will cover where particulate pollution "comes from," and that same phrase is used below in the second subpoint. In the second main idea, the terms *small* and *classified* are used to forecast the subpoints, and these terms are employed again in the subpoints themselves.

Finally, **transitional phrases** indicate the relationship between subpoints. Some transitional phrases illustrate such relationships as comparison and contrast: "in comparison," "similarly," "instead," "in contrast," and "nevertheless." Other transitional phrases list things in sequence: "first," "second," "after," "before," "during," and "finally." Physical description is another form of transitional phrase: "above," "below," "on the left," "on the right," and "alongside." Finally, transitional phrases can indicate cause and effect: "as a result of," "because of," "cause," "effect," "leads to," "If . . . then," and "as a consequence of." Insert transitional phrases at various points throughout the body of the speech. See the sample speech in Figure 7.3 for its use of transitional phrases.

## *The Delivery Outline*

The **delivery outline** is an abbreviated version of the preparation outline. Its brevity forces the speaker to select words and phrases on the spot, enabling a more spontaneous presentation than if the speaker read from the preparation outline.

Apply the following suggestions to your delivery outline. First, the delivery outline should use the same outline framework as the preparation outline. Thus, if the preparation outline includes three main ideas and two subpoints under the first main idea, so should the delivery outline.

Second, write the delivery outline legibly or use a computer-printed version. Scribbled notes are difficult to read, especially with the stress associated with public speaking. Many speakers prefer an extensive delivery outline, but this is a mistake. Speaking from an extensive outline is the same as reading from a manuscript. Delivery suffers, and the presentation becomes boring. Keep the delivery outline brief.

Finally, write important **speaking directions** in brightly colored ink. Speaking directions include underlines for points that require emphasis, two lines (//) for important pauses, or words in the corner that correct common delivery errors such as going too slowly, too rapidly, or filling dead space with such vocalized pauses as "um . . ." and "ah . . ." A sample delivery outline can be found in Figure 7.4.

---

**FIGURE 7.4   *Sample Delivery Outline***

---

**INTRODUCTION**

    **I.** Six-year-old boy lights shirt Bic. An 81-year-old woman orders coffee McDonald's, $640,000.

    **II.** Difficult see newspaper w/o reading liability lawsuits involve millions in damages.

        **A.** Tort law is part of legal code address liability.

        **B.** Everyone needs basics to understand decisions.

        **C.** As future businesspeople, need avoid lawsuits.

        **D.** Today inform you tort law.

    **III.** Name, BLE class focuses on tort.

    **IV.** Tonight define concept of tort, explain the major categories tort law.

(Trans: Start with definition tort.)

**BODY**

    **I.** *Tort* French wrong and with wrongful conduct one person cause injury another.

        **A.** Civil not criminal.

            **1.** Criminal with wrongs against society.

                **a.** State prosecutes criminal acts.

                **b.** If convicted, punished by state.

                    **(1)** Robbery

                    **(2)** Murder

            **2.** On the other hand, tort is civil law, which concerns responsibility btw. people or btw. citizens and gov.

                **a.** In the case of torts, victims, not state, lawsuit.

                **b.** Guilty usually compensate victim $.

                    **(1)** Grocery store

                    **(2)** O.J. Simpson, 33.5 million

        **B.** As you can see, civil not criminal.

FIGURE 7.4 *Continued*

(Trans: Know that definition, different kinds.)

**II.** Three categories: intentional, negligence, strict liability.
    **A.** First, intentional are intent commit an act interferes with another person's rights: physical injury, trespassing, property damage, reputation, privacy, dignity.
        **1.** Assault and battery is intentional act of physical injury.
            **a.** Assault is George threatens.
            **b.** Battery is completion.
        **2.** Defamation character offers hurt reputation: libel or slander.
            **a.** Loathsome communicable disease.
            **b.** Publish article unethical.
    **B.** The second category is negligence, conduct creates risk negative consequences.
        **1.** Negligence is suffer injury b/c failure live up to duty, care, or responsibility.
            **a.** Friend drive drunk.
            **b.** Slips on steps.
        **2.** Both individuals and businesses open to this.
    **C.** Finally, the third category is strict liability, liability without fault, usually business or manufacturing.
        **1.** Governed three assumptions:
            **a.** Consumers protected.
            **b.** Manufacturers/distributors not escape liability.
            **c.** Third manufacturers in better position pay.
        **2.** For example, Bic held liable burns on boy.
            **a.** Jury said Bic in better position to pay.
            **b.** As a result, Bic modified lighters.
(Trans: Know three categories provide ability understand legal code.)

**CONCLUSION**
    **I.** In conclusion, covered two major points: define tort law, and explained three major categories.
    **II.** Now can apply legal reasoning to stories in paper.

## *Develop the Introduction and Conclusion*

Many speakers become stalled trying to develop the introduction and conclusion prior to the body. This can be avoided by saving the introduction and conclusion until last.

### *The Introduction*

The basic introduction should accomplish four purposes.

      **I.** Gain the audience's attention.
      **II.** Justify the importance of the topic to the particular audience.
      **III.** Build the speaker's credibility or authority on the subject.
      **IV.** Preview the main points in the body of the speech.

It is not necessary to gain attention or justify the topic if the audience is already familiar with and interested in the subject. If the audience believes the speaker is knowledgeable and trustworthy, a credibility step isn't necessary.

***Gain Attention.*** In many presentations, it is important to gain the audience's attention. This can be done by opening with a rhetorical question, one that does not require a verbal answer, or one that requests a response from the audience. Questions encourage the audience to consider issues relevant to the presentation. In some cases, a series of questions will focus the audience on the subject. In a speech on juvenile crime, a local judge opened her speech with a series of questions.

> **I.** How many of you have ever been victims of juvenile crime? How many of you have ever visited one of our local high schools? How many of you have children who are now or will be attending one of our local high schools?

Because more audience members can respond affirmatively to each successive question, they become progressively more involved in the topic.

Another way to gain attention is to make a **startling statement.** For example, in a classroom speech to persuade people to buy credit life and credit disability insurance when purchasing a car, Cade Rindfleisch said,

> **I.** Last year, more than 1 million Americans declared bankruptcy, a 29 percent increase over the previous year.

Opening with a **quotation** can draw an audience into the speech. For example, a speech critiquing the findings of quantitative social science could open with a quote from the anthropologist and communication theorist Gregory Bateson.

> **I.** Of attempts to measure human behavior with numbers, the anthropologist and communication theorist Gregory Bateson said, "If it's not worth doing, it's worth doing well."

Make quotations short and directly relevant to the topic.

**Stories** are examples that almost always draw an audience into a speech. Stories have protagonists, antagonists, and a problem to be resolved. The story may be hypothetical or real, but if the former choice is made, the audience must be informed that the tale isn't real. A speech persuading people to check their homes for carbon monoxide opened with this story:

> **I.** Last year, while renting a basement apartment in town, I noticed that I spent most of the winter tired, nauseated, and sick with colds and flus. After moving out, I spoke with my former landlord, who told me that he had the furnace replaced because it was leaking carbon monoxide into the air. I quickly realized that I had been suffering from a mild form of carbon monoxide poisoning. Had the furnace been in worse shape, I might have died.

Keep stories brief and to the point. Make careful language choices so the story creates the appropriate emotional response.

***Justify the Topic.***    In some business and professional presentations it is necessary to **justify the topic** by informing the audience why the issue is important or relevant. The justification step relates the topic to the audience by explaining how it affects their interests. In the speech persuading new car buyers to purchase credit life and credit disability insurance, Cade continued his introduction with the following justification:

> **II.** According to *USA Today,* the typical filer for bankruptcy is a white, married homeowner, working full time.
> **A.** As such, this growing problem can affect each of us sitting in this room.
> **B.** We don't anticipate bankruptcy; it slowly creeps up, suddenly strikes, and by then it is too late to do anything about it.

Cade used several techniques to justify the topic. First, the *USA Today* testimony reminded his mostly white, married audience that they are not immune from bankruptcy. He made a direct appeal to the audience, stating that any of us could go bankrupt. He made use of "us" and "we" pronouns that remind the audience the topic is vital to our interests. Of course, in many business settings, a justification step is not required because the audience members are either naturally interested or must know the topic as part of their jobs.

Somewhere in the attention or justification steps, the speaker should clarify the specific purpose. People want to know why you are speaking and what you want them to understand, believe, or do at the end of the speech.

> **I.** Last year, more than 1 million Americans declared bankruptcy, a 29 percent increase over the previous year.
> **II.** According to *USA Today,* the typical filer for bankruptcy is a white, married home-owner, working full time.
>     **A.** As such, this growing problem can affect each of us sitting in this room.
>     **B.** We don't anticipate bankruptcy; it slowly creeps up, suddenly strikes, and by then it is too late to do anything about it.
>     **C.** Today I want to convince you to purchase credit life and credit disability insurance when you buy your next new car, so that you can avoid becoming another bank-ruptcy statistic.

In this example, subpoint C clarifies the speech goal. In most cases you can modify the specific purpose statement for use in the attention or justification step. In cases where an attention and justification step are not required, the speaker can open the speech with the specific purpose statement.

***Establish Credibility.*** The third objective of the introduction is to establish credibility. **Source credibility** is the audience's perception of the speaker's expertise, trustworthiness, and dynamism. If the audience is unfamiliar with the speaker's expertise or, worse yet, if the audience has a negative view of the speaker's competence, then a credibility step is a vital part of the speech introduction. As such, the speaker's source of expertise on the topic should be cited in the credibility step. For example, in a speech to persuade state law makers to create contractor licensing requirements, Tari Jensen made the following credibility statement:

> **III.** My name is Tari Jensen. I have been involved in the construction industry for over 20 years.
>     **A.** Our company is named Jensen Bros. Builders. We build 10 to 20 residential homes per year and have gross sales of $1.5 million to $2 million per year.
>     **B.** I have been president of the Building Contractors Association for Southeast Idaho and received the state association's Builder of the Year Award for 1995.
>     **C.** To prepare this speech, I interviewed Dave LeRoy, the past attorney general of Idaho; Dave Wilson, the national representative for the Building Contractors Association for the state of Idaho; Evan Frasure, our district senator; and Jack Robinson, a local real estate attorney. I read and reviewed many articles and books from the ISU (Idaho State University) library, the Marshall Public Library, and trade magazines.

This statement makes numerous references that support Tari's source credibility.

Of course, some professional presentations are made among people who know and have a high opinion of the speaker. As such, a credibility step may not be necessary.

***Preview the Main Ideas.***    The fourth goal of the introduction is to **preview the main ideas** in the body of the speech. Like connectives, previews provide a helpful mapping function for listeners. The main idea statement can be modified to serve as the preview statement. In his classroom presentation about wool versus synthetic carpet fiber, Joseph Wilcox included the following preview:

> **IV.** I will cover these different carpet fibers in four main steps: First, I will acknowledge that many people think wool is the best carpet fiber. Second, I will discuss why people think wool is better. Third, I will state that wool is not superior. And fourth, I will illustrate why synthetic fiber is superior to wool.

It is often useful to enumerate each point in the preview, as Joseph did in his speech. The points in the body of the speech should be covered in parallel order and written in parallel language to those in the preview. Examine the sample speech outline in Figure 7.3 for a well-crafted introduction.

## The Conclusion

The **conclusion** puts the speech back together by tying the end back to the beginning. It does this in two steps: The conclusion reviews the main ideas in the body of the speech and ends with a capstone statement.

***Review the Main Ideas.***    Like the preview, the **review** ties the speech together by summarizing the main ideas. For example, in Joseph Wilcox's speech on carpet fiber, he reviewed his main ideas as follows:

> **I.** To conclude, I have stated that most people think wool is the best fiber for carpets and explained why people think wool is superior. I then rejected the idea that wool is superior to synthetics and listed reasons why synthetic fiber is superior to wool.

Almost all business presentations should include a brief restatement of the main ideas in the body.

***End with a Capstone Statement.***    Close the speech with a **capstone statement** that reinforces the specific purpose. There are many ways to do this, including any one of the methods of gaining attention previously mentioned. To close his speech on bacteria, Jacob M. Lewis used a hypothetical story.

> **II.** So, the next time you feel queasy after eating week-old potato salad, you'll at least understand why you are rushing to the bathroom.

This humorous anecdote reminds the audience about Jacob's specific purpose: the way bacteria make people sick. Strong capstone statements can also employ questions, startling statements, or quotations.

Another effective way to tie the speech together is to refer listeners back to the introduction. In the introduction to her speech on contractor licensing, Tari Jensen described a family who lost their life's savings at the hands of an inexperienced, unlicensed contractor. Her conclusion referred the audience back to the plight of that family.

> **II.** We should never allow the heartache, frustration, and years of suffering of our family in Pocatello to happen to anyone else in the state, ever again.

The capstone statement for a persuasive presentation should make an appeal to belief or action. An appeal to belief emphasizes the persuasive outcome in the specific purpose statement. In so doing, the speaker emphasizes the attitude or belief he or she wants the audience to adopt. In a speech protesting the killing of bison outside Yellowstone National Park, the capstone statement emphasizes the speaker's interpretation of events.

> **II.** As I have made clear in this presentation, many of the bison in Yellowstone are not infectious, and the chances of disease transmission to cattle are almost nonexistent. There is therefore no legitimate reason to kill these animals.

The emotional tone of the clincher should be consistent with the content in the body of the speech.

A call to action is necessary in some persuasive speeches. State exactly the action you want the audience to take.

> **II.** I encourage all of you who feel the way I do to make your voice heard by contacting the superintendent of Yellowstone National Park, Mike Finley.

Speakers must do more, however, than simply call for action. They should take steps to make the action easy for the audience. We will discuss methods of encouraging action in Chapter 10, on persuasive proposals. Examine the sample preparation outline in Figure 7.4 for its conclusion.

## Rehearsal and Delivery Considerations

As we mentioned in Chapter 2, the verbal portion of the message accounts for as little as 10 percent of the total meaning of that message; nonverbal cues account for the rest.[13] As a consequence, delivery is a crucial component of any speech.

John Gribas, a professor of communication and organizational consultant, says that attending to a few vocal and physical cues will ensure strong delivery. First among the vocal cues are appropriate volume and rate. Presentations always need to be louder and slower than normal conversation. Although it is sometimes thought that slow speakers are boring, it is actually the lack of vocal energy that makes a speaker dull. Gribas reminds us that it is possible to speak slowly yet do so with energy, enthusiasm, and variety. Slowing down also allows the speaker to clearly articulate and correctly pronounce words. When they're doing it right, many speakers feel they are overarticulating their words.

In addition, a single mispronunciation can destroy a speaker's credibility. Make sure that you can correctly pronounce all the terms in your presentation. Finally, speakers should use changes in their voice to stress important points. Changes in the vocal pattern, such as becoming louder or softer, going faster or slower, can be used to signal an important point in the presentation.[14]

Speakers can make themselves aware of several elements of their physical delivery. A presenter's eye contact should be direct, rather than over people's heads, and inclusive of the entire audience. Generally, speakers should stand still, with both feet planted on the ground and their body weight evenly distributed. Stand straight rather than slouching or leaning on the lectern. Move toward the audience to emphasize a point. Finally, speakers should rest their hands and arms at their side or lightly on the lectern and use gestures to reinforce important ideas.[15] Think about these guidelines as you develop and practice your presentation.

Delivery is always improved by thorough familiarity with the message. To improve your delivery, focus on rehearsal and attitude adjustment. Mastering the message involves practicing the presentation at least 12 to 15 times. The first few rehearsals will be halting and unsatisfactory. But, as rehearsal proceeds, your self-confidence with the delivery outline will grow. You will be able to stick to the outline enough to maintain logical consistency but also choose words and phrases on the spot, creating spontaneity. Rehearsal is one of the steps that many students ignore in their classroom speeches, and it clearly shows.

The second way to improve delivery is developing the proper attitude toward the topic and the audience. If you have enthusiasm for your topic and an intense desire to be understood by the audience, these emotions will be reflected in your nonverbal cues. According to Joel D. Whalen, a business professor at DePaul University, the most important emotion for business and professional presentations is enthusiasm.

> Of all the emotions that will move your audience to embrace your point of view, enthusiasm is the most important. It's the emotion that you should adopt as your primary tool in communication.[16]

Develop an intense enthusiasm for your topic, and it will naturally show in the presentation. The audience, having no doubt listened to many dull presentations in the past, will be grateful for your effort and more interested in and persuaded by your ideas.

In addition to enthusiasm, develop a concern for audience comprehension. Too many speakers devote too little attention to helping audiences understand their ideas. Their main goal is to complete the presentation and sit down. When you really care about audience comprehension, you can stop the speech in the middle and go over something again if you see quizzical expressions. You naturally highlight main ideas with your voice because you want the audience to understand, and you naturally exhibit appropriate nonverbal cues. Finally, learn to have fun. A sense of fun communicates competence and dynamism, two important elements of credibility. Let your nonverbal communication flow from the attitudes of enthusiasm, goodwill, and fun.

*Enthusiasm is the key to strong delivery.*
Credit: Comstock

# *Summary*

A good presentation involves solid preparation and enthusiastic delivery. Preparing a presentation begins with deciding whether the general purpose is to inform or persuade. The specific purpose statement clarifies the primary outcome the speaker desires, whereas the main idea statement clarifies the two to five main ideas in the body of the presentation. Supporting material includes examples, statistics, and testimony. Research to collect supporting material involves using the library, the Internet, and interviews.

After library research, take the information from the Audience Analysis Checklist and apply it to the presentation. The Speech Adaptation Checklist provides a list of relevant questions that help speakers apply the results of their audience analysis. Structure is vital to clear presentations. The speech body may be structured using one of the following patterns: chronological, spatial, cause–effect, problem solution, or topical. The preparation outline helps the speaker flesh out the content of the speech. The preparation outline is a full-sentence outline of all the ideas in the presentation. The outline should employ a consistent pattern of symbolization and appropriate connectives. Connectives are linguistic devices that link ideas. Transitions, forecasting, parallel order, parallel language, and transitional phrases are five commonly used connectives. The delivery outline is an abbreviated version of the preparation outline for making the presentation.

The speech introduction should gain attention, justify the importance of the topic, build the speaker's credibility, and preview the main ideas in the presentation. The conclusion should review the main ideas in the body of the speech and finish with a capstone statement. Delivery is important to an effective presentation. Delivery is improved through rehearsing and developing enthusiasm for the topic.

## *Questions and Exercises*

1. Examine the sample preparation outline in this chapter. Was the introduction handled well? Label the main steps in the introduction. Are all four steps there? Is there anything you would have done to improve this introduction?

2. Look at the body of the speech in the sample preparation outline. What structure is used to organize the main ideas? Was this structure effective? Label the different kinds of supporting material in the body. Does the supporting material help clarify Lori's points? Is there anything you would have done

differently to improve the use of supporting material? Label the different connectives in the presentation, including transitions, forecasting, parallel order, parallel language, and transitional phrases. Were the connective devices easy to identify? Do they help the listener follow the presentation? Were there other places that needed connectives for clarity?

3. Examine the conclusion of the speech in the sample preparation outline. Was the conclusion handled well? How did the author draw the speech to a close? Was this effective?

## *Notes*

1. Rawlins, W. K., personal communication, October 1988.
2. Leeds, D., "No-fault selling," *Folio,* 1 December 1996.
3. Sprague, J., and D. Stuart, *The Speaker's Handbook* (Fort Worth, TX: Harcourt Brace, 1996), 127.
4. Cooper, J. C., and K. Madigan, "What Surprising New Data Reveal About the New Economy," *BusinessWeek,* 27 August 2001, 44.
5. Cooper, J. C., and K. Madigan, "U.S. Growth Slows—and Foreign Economies Feel the Pain," *BusinessWeek,* 6 August 2001, 23.

6.  Robertson, R. G., "Layers of Basalt Hide Water at Craters," *Idaho State Journal,* 10 May 1995.

7.  Mandeville, C., phone conversation, January 1998.

8.  "Time to Regroup," *BusinessWeek,* 6 August 2001, 27.

9.  Doyle, T. A., *Allyn & Bacon Quick Guide to the Internet* (Boston: Allyn & Bacon, 1998), 1.

10. Renz, M. A., "Communicating About Environmental Risk: An Examination of a Minnesota County's Communication on Incineration," *Journal of Applied Communication Research* 20 (1992): 1–18.

11. Lucas, S. E., *The Art of Public Speaking* (Boston: McGraw-Hill, 1998), 149.

12. Leeds, 75.

13. Whalen, J. D., *I See What You Mean: Persuasive Business Communication* (Beverly Hills, CA: Sage, 1996).

14. Gribas, J., personal communication, September 2000.

15. Ibid.

16. Whalen, 124.

# 8

# *Creating and Using Visual Aids*

We live in a visually oriented society! We derive most of our entertainment from television and film. Most Americans stay informed about current events through television and the Internet rather than newspapers. To compete, newspapers have "gone visual," offering color pictures as well as more charts and graphs than in the past.

Our penchant for images affects all forms of communication, including business and professional presentations. Yearly reports to stockholders have become multimedia events incorporating giant video screens, computer-generated graphics, and live video feeds from remote locations. Today, college graduates are "expected to enter the business world with a good understanding of essential business practices and with decent communication skills as well," says Dianne Porter, a writer for *Presentations* magazine. Students must have an understanding of "lighting, sound systems, video, and PowerPoint slideshows."[1]

The information in this chapter will help you create and use visual aids. We have divided the chapter into three parts. First, we review the various types of visual aids available and explain guidelines for creating effective graphics. In section two, we discuss guidelines for the effective use of visual aids during the presentation. Finally, because computer-generated graphics are standard in most business and professional organizations, the third section focuses on integrating this material into the presentation.

When using visual aids, it is important to remember one guiding principle: Professional presentations are a chance to exchange information and share ideas with an audience; therefore, visual aids should support rather than supplant speaker and content. Marya Holcombe and Judith K. Stein, authors of *Presentations for Decision Makers,* assert that a presentation "is not a picture show for which you provide the voice-over."[2] The purpose of any visual is to make the content more understandable or persuasive. Using a visual aid without any clear informative or persuasive purpose is, at best, distracting. Throughout this chapter we encourage the use of visual aids that support the speaker and the content.

## *Types of Visual Aids*

A **visual aid** is any pictorial, textual, or graphic image that is presented visually rather than orally. Visual aids can add to the effectiveness of a presentation in three ways. First, visual aids increase the clarity of complicated pictorial, statistical, or conceptual material.[3] Think about the difficulty of describing earnings trends over several years without the use of line graphs. When they are well constructed, visual aids communicate complicated information clearly and quickly.

Second, visual aids increase the persuasiveness of a message.[4] In a study conducted at the University of Minnesota, the use of computer-generated overhead transparencies increased a presenter's persuasiveness by 43 percent.[5] Other research showed that the addition of tables and pictures in a speech made the content more persuasive and increased the audience's perception of speaker credibility.[6]

Finally, visual aids make a presentation more dynamic, motivating the audience to pay attention.[7] There are, however, many different forms of visual material to choose from. What are the different types of visual aids, and how can they be designed for the greatest effect? These questions are addressed in the following text, where we explain the ten types of visual aids commonly used in business and professional presentations.

*Well-constructed visual aids make a presentation clearer and more interesting.*
Credit: Bill Burke

## Objects

Using an **object** is an excellent way to add interest and clarity to your ideas. For example, Jesse works for a tennis racket maker and needed to explain how a manufacturing problem created blemishes on the surface of many rackets. He brought in several rackets to show the audience the location and severity of the scarring. Objects are used in sales presentations when the speaker brings in the item for display or demonstration.

Objects might be the ideal visual aid, but for one problem—size. Many objects are too large to fit into a room or too small to be easily seen by the audience. For large objects, photographs or slides may serve as adequate visual representations. A scaled-down model is another means of displaying a large object.

If, on the other hand, the object is too small to be seen, resist the temptation to pass it around the room. Audience members will not be listening to you as they manipulate and look at the object. Instead, use photographs or slides for easy viewing. If you must show the object by passing it around, temporarily suspend the presentation and give the group a chance to clearly examine the object and discuss its characteristics. Once this is completed, you may reconvene and continue with the presentation.

## Models

**Models** are scale, two-dimensional drawings or three-dimensional constructions that represent very large or very small objects. Models are an excellent substitute for objects that are too large or too small for easy viewing. For example, a model of the human heart is a useful way to show the placement and functions of a pacemaker. Models should be large enough for easy viewing by the entire audience. If you must pass around the model, follow the same guidelines previously stated for passing around objects.

## Chalkboard/Whiteboard/Flip Chart

The chalkboard, or its more modern equivalents, the whiteboard and the flip chart, are useful in some professional forums. The value of these items is limited because they are "low tech" and not very impressive. Also, unless they are prepared in advance, the time it takes to write things on the board or flip chart interrupts the smooth flow of ideas in a presentation. Finally, if the chart is not flipped to a blank page or the board erased (both of which interrupt the presentation) the information remains in view and distracts audience members long after it's covered.

Given these limitations, we recommend the use of boards and flip charts only for extended presentations (e.g., lectures) or in group brainstorming sessions where ideas must be written down, narrowed, and solidified in front of the entire group. In both cases, audience input makes it impossible to prepare visual aids pre-demonstration.

## Handouts

Very common in college classrooms, **handouts** are also an indispensable part of business and professional presentations. Handouts can summarize information and provide a handy reference guide to audience members long after the presentation. Any visual aid shown to the entire audience can be reduced and included on handouts.

The disadvantage of handouts is the same as for passing objects or models around the room—they distract the audience. With handouts, audience members may move ahead of the speaker by considering information not yet covered or miss important information by stopping to focus on one part of a handout. As a result, most business communicators recommend providing handouts after, rather than during, the presentation. If you must use handouts to explain complicated information, provide the handout only at the point in the speech when it's relevant, go over the handout thoroughly, and then move on with the rest of the presentation.

## *Photographs*

**Photographs** improve understanding and retention of complex information. As previously explained, photos are an excellent substitute for objects that are too large or too small for the audience to see. Digital photos are easy to incorporate into presentation programs like Microsoft's PowerPoint or Corel Presentations.

## *Charts and Graphs*

**Charts** and **graphs** include any kind of two-dimensional visual aid that clarifies complicated statistical or relational information. As we said in the last chapter, statistics are a collection of individual examples delivered as raw numbers or averages. Relationships compare or contrast the performance of two or more variables.

Every chart or graph should include a title that communicates and emphasizes the meaning you want the audience to accept rather than merely what the chart represents.[8] For example, look at the titles of the two pie charts in Figure 8.1. Although the title of the first chart merely describes it as the "Department Budget," the second title clearly explains the speaker's central meaning—that duplication has grown too large in comparison to the other budget items. Create titles that clearly state the interpretation you want the chart or graph to communicate.

*Charts.*   **Charts** are particularly useful for summarizing statistical information. The data in Figure 8.2 indicate the amount, in tons per year, of six different kinds of pollution emitted by various sources in a hypothetical town. The chart's numerous categories make it easy to compare the output of various sources.

Despite the usefulness of this chart to a decision maker in the privacy of his or her office, it is too extensive and too detailed for most presentations. Speakers should simplify charts so they clarify only the most important information. This means eliminating irrelevant data or grouping information into larger categories. For example, in a presentation about air pollution in her area, Sue Yang decided to simplify the chart (from Figure 8.2). Because she was interested mainly in pollution contributions by the top two firms, she added the contributions from all the other sources and put these into a row called "All Others" (see Figure 8.3 on page 000). This created a simpler, cleaner chart, one that is easier for the audience to scan and comprehend.

*Line Graphs.*   A **line graph** is a useful way to show changes in one or more variables over time. Figure 8.4 depicts a two-day measurement of particulate matter in a large city experiencing an air inversion. The vertical axis depicts the number of micrograms of particulate matter per cubic meter of air. The horizontal axis depicts the time of day in six-hour increments. The graph clearly shows a buildup of particulate matter from 40 to 140 micrograms between 12:00 A.M. and 12:00 P.M. The levels drop off slightly during the next 18 hours.

The rules for creating line graphs are similar to those for charts. Keep the information simple. Too many lines (each representing a different variable) cause confusion. Examine the

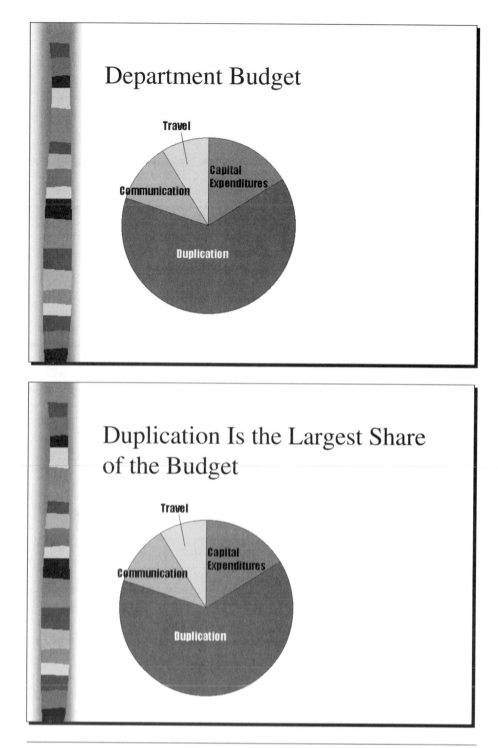

FIGURE 8.1   *Effective (below) and Ineffective (above) Titles*

## 2006 Emission Inventory (Point)

All Figures in Tons per Year

| Source | PM-10 | PM-2.5 | SO₂ | NOₓ | CO | NH₃ |
|---|---|---|---|---|---|---|
| Chem. Plant | 724.88 | 59.39 | 4164.86 | 1719.18 | 2156.47 | 1.01 |
| Steel Mill | 482.30 | 91.78 | 2554.51 | 755.79 | 181.75 | 132.91 |
| Cement Co. | 65.43 | 29.71 | 48.00 | 337.00 | 510.20 | 0.00 |
| Paving Co. | 35.46 | 11.63 | 15.34 | 3.49 | 0.32 | 0.00 |
| Railroad | 34.19 | 26.97 | 54.17 | 286.14 | 88.02 | 3.20 |
| Assembly Plant | 19.42 | 8.30 | 0.11 | 19.48 | 5.69 | 0.20 |

PM-10 = particulate matter smaller than 10 microns
PM-2.5 = particulate matter smaller than 2.5 microns

$SO_2$ = sulfur dioxide
$NO_X$ = various nitrogen oxides
CO = carbon monoxide
$NH_3$ = ammonia

FIGURE 8.2   *Chart for Summarizing Statistical Information*

## 2006 Emission Inventory (Point)

All Figures in Tons per Year

| Source | Particulates | | Gases | | | |
|---|---|---|---|---|---|---|
| | PM-10 | PM-2.5 | SO₂ | NOₓ | CO | NH₃ |
| Chem. Plant | 724 | 59 | 4164 | 1719 | 2156 | 1 |
| Steel Mill | 482 | 91 | 2554 | 755 | 181 | 132 |
| All Others | 163 | 65 | 117 | 654 | 592 | 3 |

PM-10 = particulate matter smaller than 10 microns
PM-2.5 = particulate matter smaller than 2.5 microns

$SO_2$ = sulfur dioxide
$NO_X$ = various nitrogen oxides
CO = carbon monoxide
$NH_3$ = ammonia

FIGURE 8.3   *Simplified Chart*

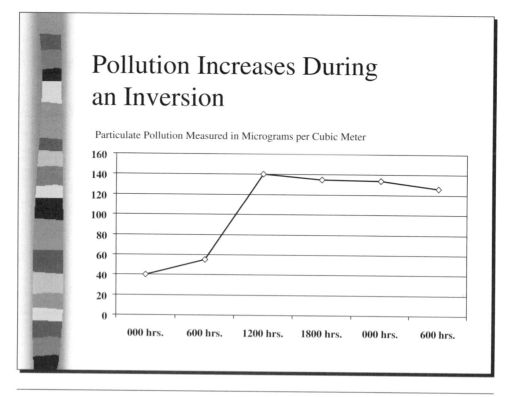

**FIGURE 8.4** *Line Graph*

first line graph in Figure 8.5. This slide depicts percentage changes for the gross domestic products of seven nations. The speaker wants to demonstrate that U.S. economic downturns hurt other economies throughout the world. If, however, the speaker averaged the changes in the three European and Asian economies, the slide communicates the same meaning with fewer lines. This improved slide is also depicted in Figure 8.5. If, however, all the lines are absolutely necessary, it's best to display each, one after the other. This requires the construction of several line graphs for the presentation, each new graph adding a new line to the total. The speaker can then discuss each line as it is presented on the screen, which prevents the audience from being overwhelmed by a complicated graph.

Speakers should use different colors for each line and clearly label which variable is represented by which color. Use the darkest, heaviest line for the most important variable. As with all visual aids, include only the information absolutely necessary to make your point.

**Pie Charts.** The **pie chart** displays the relationship of various parts to a whole.[9] For example, Figure 8.6 shows the relative contributions of various sources to total particulate pollution in a hypothetical town. The pie represents the particulate emitted into the air each summer, and every wedge of the pie represents a significant particulate source. The pie chart provides a vivid way to explain the contributions of various polluters to the town's annual air quality.

When constructing a pie chart, try to avoid slicing the pie into more than seven or eight pieces. Small slices are difficult to label and confusing to the audience. Creating too many

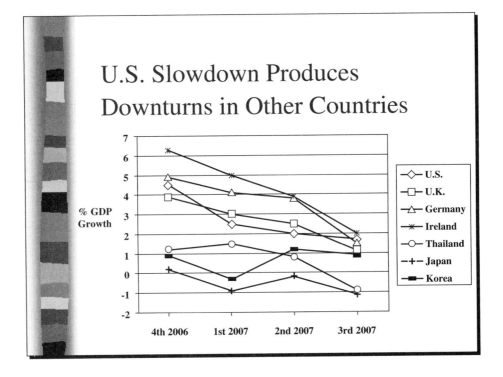

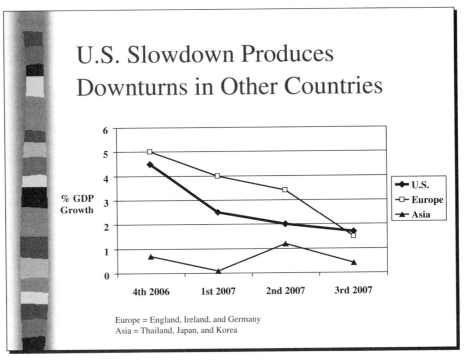

**FIGURE 8.5** *Improving a Line Graph (below)*

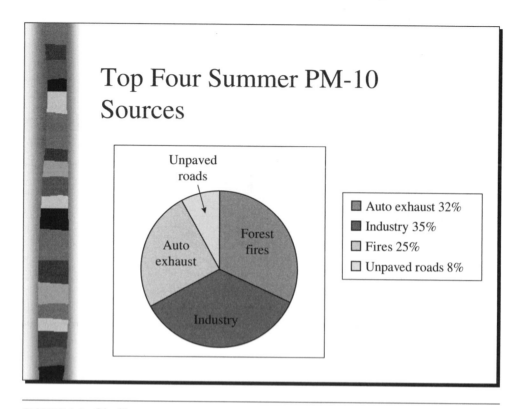

**FIGURE 8.6** *Pie Chart*

slices also sacrifices the impact of the chart, the ability to quickly apprehend proportions of the whole. The first pie chart in Figure 8.7, illustrates the problem of too many slices.

The second pie chart in Figure 8.7 reduces the number of slices by combining several non-refrigeration-related utility expenses (gas, water, and sewer) into a single slice. If the presenter needs to highlight these expenses, a new pie chart that focuses only on utility expenses can be created. Because audiences find it difficult to work between the pie chart and a legend, label pie pieces on or near the slice (see the second slide in Figure 8.7).

Most presentation programs let users highlight slices by separating them from the rest of the pie. In Figure 8.8, Terri believes her company is spending too much money correcting problems after the product is sold (the "Service" slice of the pie) and too little money on research and development. She used the separation feature to highlight the appropriate slices.

***Bar Graphs.*** Finally, the **bar graph** is an excellent way to make comparisons among magnitudes. In Figure 8.9, you can see a bar graph comparing how much five companies spend on research and development. The graph makes it easy to see that the general trend in R&D spending is up. Speakers should try to limit the number of bars and use different colors for different variables. If many bars are necessary, use the animation function of your program to bring up each variable's bars individually.

Like line graphs and pie charts, bar graphs can provide a more interesting and influential way to present information than charts. Examine the chart displayed in Figure 8.10. This

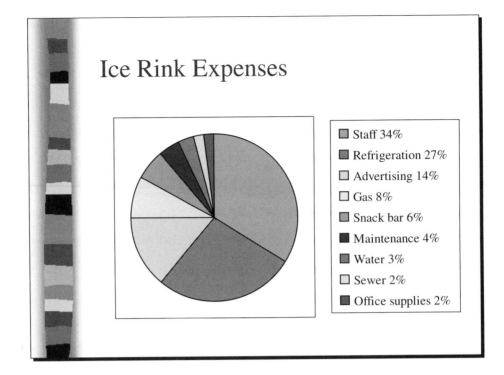

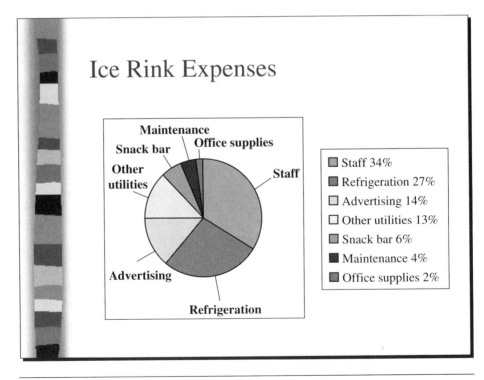

**FIGURE 8.7** *Pie Chart Slices and Labels*

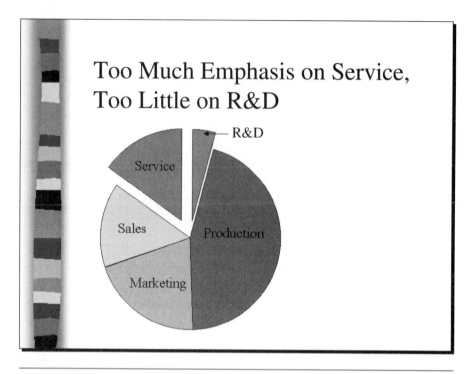

**FIGURE 8.8** *Highlighting Slices*

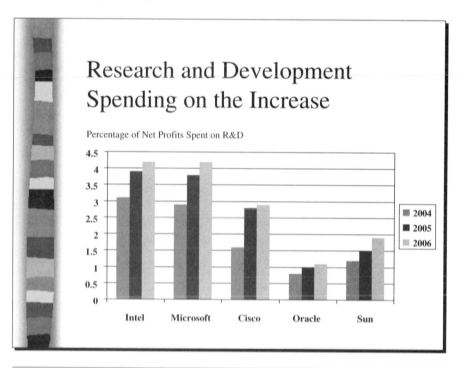

**FIGURE 8.9** *Bar Graph*

## Ford Lags the Industry in Quality

| Auto Maker | Problems per 100 Vehicles |
|---|---|
| Toyota | 115 |
| Honda | 133 |
| Nissan | 145 |
| General Motors | 146 |
| DaimlerChrysler | 154 |
| Volkswagen | 159 |
| Ford Motor Co. | 162 |

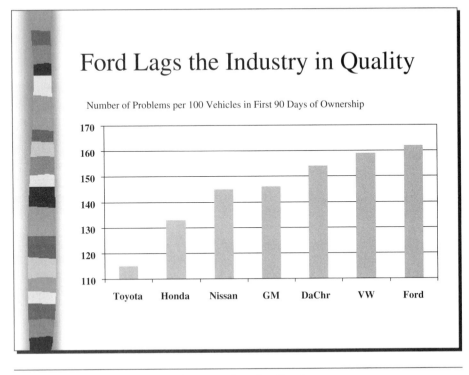

**FIGURE 8.10** *A More Effective Summary in a Bar Graph*

table depicts the number of problems reported by new car buyers during the first 90 days of ownership. Although accurate and easy to read, this information is presented more forcefully in the bar graph that is also depicted in Figure 8.10. Experiment with your charts and graphs to create the most powerful, effective, and persuasive visuals possible.

## Text Visuals

**Text visuals** display the key features of the presentation in words, phrases, and sentences. According to Jean-Luc Doumont, a speech consultant, text visuals are one of the most abused formats of Powerpoint because people include more text than that the audience wants to read.[10]

The problem of too much text is well illustrated in Figure 8.11, from Doumont's article on the subject. "When presented with a slide full of text, we are faced with the dilemma: either read the text or listen to the speaker. We cannot do both, unless the speaker reads the text with us, in which case we might question the added value of either speaker or slide."[11] The second slide in Figure 8.11 reduces the original to only that which is necessary for understanding. Doumont suggests that text visuals should express themselves with short sentences (thus including a verb) and each item should run no more than two lines. The goal is to reach this "with clever rephrasing, not random content truncation."[12]

Whether you choose to use the object itself, a model, board, photographs, or some variety of graphs and charts, well-constructed visual aids can add to the clarity, persuasiveness, and dynamism of any professional presentation.

## Constructed Visuals

**Constructed visuals** illustrate complicated concepts or processes with the simple shapes, lines, and arrows available on PowerPoint or Corel Presentations. These visuals are necessary if you don't have photos or can't find appropriate visuals for downloading from the Internet. Constructed visuals require a degree of imagination and creativity on the speaker's part. For example, examine the two slides in Figure 8.12.

The first slide uses the thermostat to illustrate how simple self-correcting circuits are structured. The slide was created on PowerPoint through the use of the Text Box button and the Arrow button on the Drawing toolbar. This simple combination of words and arrows creates an illustrative visual. The second slide in Figure 8.12 clarifies how a thermostat functions to regulate temperature around a calibration. This slide was also created through the use of text boxes and lines. The curved line between the parameters was created with the AutoShapes button, which can be found in PowerPoint's Drawing toolbar.

A little creative thought can produce even more elaborate visuals to illustrate highly complicated processes. The slide in Figure 8.13 illustrates the way an experimental drug, IMC-C225, halts the spread of cancer.

Normal cells divide to produce more cells only when the body needs them. This process is controlled by oncogenes, the genes that direct cell duplication, and tumor suppressor genes, which are in charge of cell death. As shown in Figure 8.13, many cancers occur when a defective oncogene sends out a flood of protein signals that attach themselves to receptors on the cell wall. This produces enzymes that tell the cell to embark on a rapid course of cell division. The resulting cancerous cells proliferate, and the tumor suppressor genes are overwhelmed. In the slide, the cell, oncogenes, tumor suppressor genes, and growth proteins were created with the repeated use of the Oval button on the Drawing toolbar. The receptors were created with the AutoShapes button, as were the various curved and straight arrows. The right side of the slide

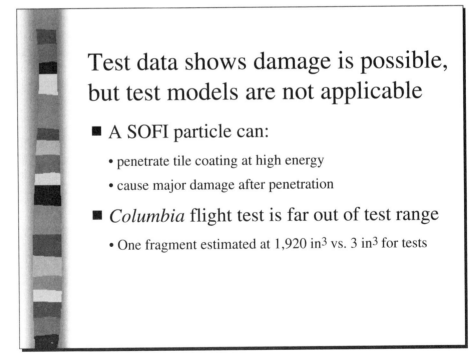

## Review of Test Data Indicates Conservatism for Tile Penetration

- The existing SOFI on tile test data used to create Crater was reviewed along with STS-87 Southwest Research data
  - Crater overpredicted penetration of tile coating significantly
  - Initial penetration to described by normal velocity
  - Varies with volume/mass of projectile (e.g., 200 ft/sec for 3 cu in)
  - Significant energy required for the softer SOFI particle to penetrate the relatively hard tile coating
  - Test results do show that it is possible at sufficient mass and velocity
  - Conversely, once tile is penetrated SOFI can cause significant damage
  - Minor variations in total energy (above penetration level) can cause significant damage
- Flight conditions is significantly outside the test database
  - Volume of ramp is 1,920 cu in vs. 3 cu in for test

## Test data shows damage is possible, but test models are not applicable

- A SOFI particle can:
  - penetrate tile coating at high energy
  - cause major damage after penetration
- *Columbia* flight test is far out of test range
  - One fragment estimated at 1,920 in³ vs. 3 in³ for tests

FIGURE 8.11   *Avoid Test-Heavy Visuals*

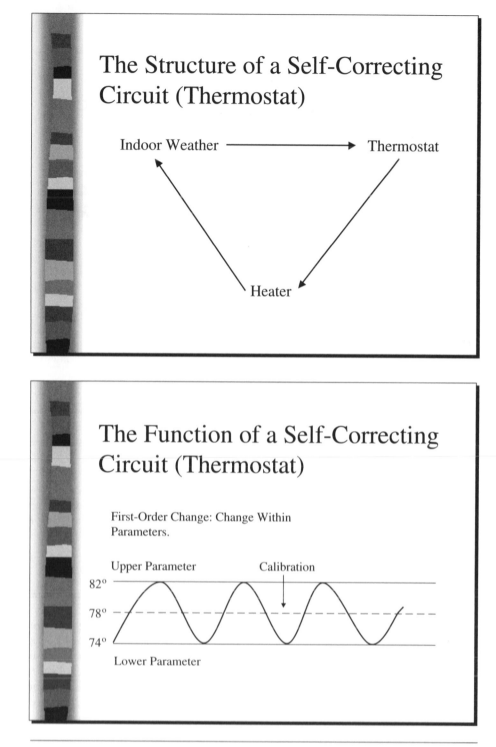

FIGURE 8.12  *Constructed Visuals*

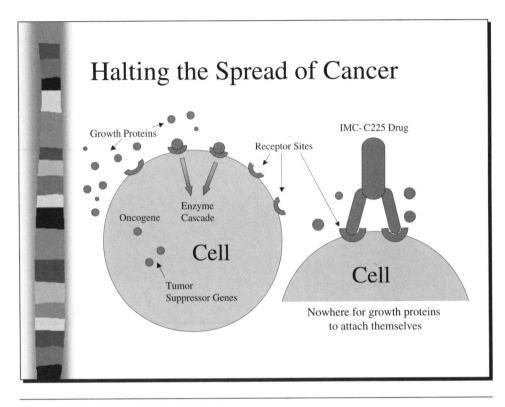

**FIGURE 8.13**    *A More Elaborate Visual*

shows that the cancer drug works by plugging up the cell's receptor sites. This prevents the growth proteins from attaching themselves to the cell, which prevents the uncontrolled division that is cancer. The pill-shaped figures represent the cancer drug, which were found in the AutoShapes section of the Drawing toolbar. As you can see in Figure 8.13, the creative use of the simple shapes can lead to interesting and illustrative visual aids.

### Formatting Computer-Generated Charts, Graphs, and Visuals

This section offers recommendations for formatting graphics generated with Microsoft PowerPoint, or any other computer graphics program. First, decide on a consistent style, font, and color scheme for the visuals throughout the presentation. When selecting a background design for the slides, the computer automatically selects colors for the text, charts, and graphs based on visibility and aesthetic qualities. Changing colors should be done with care to avoid slides that clash.

We think that light or white backgrounds function better than dark ones for several reasons. Dark text, graphs, and clip art show up better against a light background. In addition, bright backgrounds throw more reflected light on the speaker and the audience, which partly compensates for the dim overhead lighting required for many LCD projectors.

Second, exercise discretion when using animation effects. Because the programs are fun to work with, it's tempting to experiment with everything available, such as flying clip art or the sound effects of screeching wheels or laser blasts when bulleted text enters the slide. Such effects do not reflect the conservative nature of business and professional audiences. Do not let technical sophistication interfere with the basic message. Instead, use the animation effects to help make your point. If you have a lot of text on a slide but don't want the audience to read ahead, the Custom Animation button on the Slide Show toolbar allows you to bring in each bulleted point one at a time. The same procedure allows you to animate clip art. Use animation to augment your point, not for empty flash.

Third, use the clip art in the computer program or images from the Web to reinforce your points. Nothing is more boring than an endless series of text visuals. The clip art provided with the program or available on the Web is a fun way to reinforce a point. The slide in Figure 8.14 explains how a smokestack scrubber works. The visual aid on the right illustrates two stacks—one with a scrubber, one without. Although the clip art isn't designed to depict the operation of a scrubber, by tying an image to a particular point, it makes that point more memorable.

When using the PowerPoint graph and chart function, avoid the three-dimensional options for line graphs, pie charts, and bar graphs. Most statisticians suggest that charts remain two-dimensional unless the data being depicted are three-dimensional. Aside from this concern, the speechwriter's argument for two-dimensional charts is simpler; in PowerPoint and the other presentation programs, the three-dimensional charts are very difficult to read. Examine the line graph and bar graph in Figure 8.15. These charts are three-dimensional reproductions of those depicted in Figures 8.5 and 8.9. Look how much more difficult the information is to see and understand in the three-dimensional version. Unless the data merit something more, stick with two-dimensional charts.

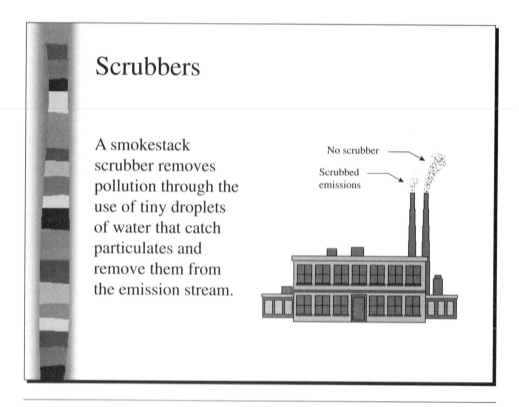

**FIGURE 8.14**    *Clip Art in a Computer-Generated Slide*

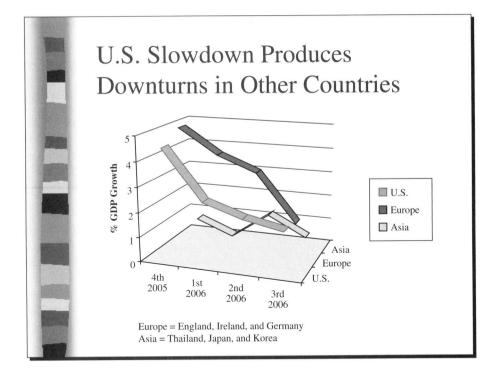

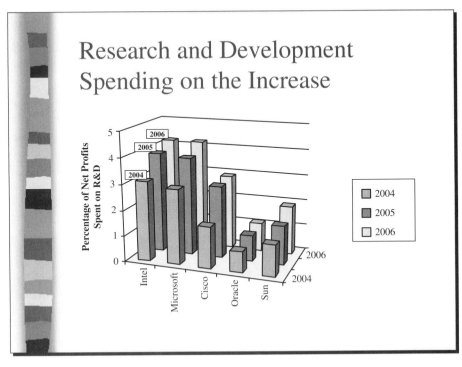

**FIGURE 8.15** *Three-Dimensional Graphs*

### *Videotape/DVD*

**Videotape** or **DVD** can add dynamic impact to a presentation. For example, a speech reporting on the relative success of various television commercials should show those commercials. However, those commercials that are not directly relevant to the specific purpose are time consuming and distracting. Cue the tape or DVD to the proper location and familiarize yourself with the VCR, DVD player, and TV monitors at the site prior to the presentation. If you use video from a variety of sources, have the tape/DVD professionally edited so that the cuts between excerpts are clean.

## *Presenting Visual Aids to the Audience*

The following suggestions are essential for the effective use of any visual aid. The effort to create a visual aid is wasted if it is poorly presented. First, use visual aids only when they are justified; do not try to "jazz up" a presentation with unnecessary ones. Empty vigor and verve distracts or annoys conservative, bottom-line-oriented professional audiences. Visual aids are useful for clarifying information, but they are no substitute for solid research and accurate content.

Second, if you do decide to create visual aids, make sure they are large enough for the entire audience to see. It's annoying to listen to a presentation that has numerous carefully prepared visual aids that cannot be seen from all locations in the room. A visual aid that can't be seen will not add to your clarity, persuasiveness, or dynamism.

Third, position yourself in such a way that the entire audience has a clear view of the visual aid. Never obscure or block the visual with your body. If you have to point to the visual, use a laser pointer so as not to obscure people's view. Laser pointers, which project a red dot, are an effective way of pointing to important items without getting in the audience's line of sight.

Next, display the visual aid only when you come to the relevant place in the speech, and remove it from view before moving on to new information. Leaving the visual aid in sight distracts audience members who continue to examine it instead of listening to your next point. When you are in the PowerPoint slide show mode, hitting the B key will take you to a black screen and the W key to a white screen. This function allows you to pause the slide show while you move on with the presentation. Hitting any key on the keyboard will bring the show back by automatically advancing to the next slide.

Fifth, visual aids need to be explained and interpreted for the audience. As we mentioned in Chapter 1, people do not automatically assign the same meaning as the speaker to a visual aid. The speaker's goal is to manage the meaning the audience assigns. This is done by explaining all major parts of the visual aid, pointing out the important statistical comparisons or graphic features. Leave nothing to chance; lead the audience to the interpretation you desire.

Sixth, when explaining the visual aid, use the same words from the visual aid's title and labels. Using different labels is a form of mixed message that can be confusing for the audience. Parallel language, in both order of coverage and grammatical form, is vital for complete understanding.

Finally, because the goal is communication with audience members, talk to them and not to the visual aid. Turn no more than one-third of your body toward the display.

## *Summary*

When used correctly, visual aids can increase the clarity and persuasiveness of a message, and increase audience perceptions of the speaker's credibility and dynamism. Objects and models are excellent ways to add interest to a speech. They should be easy for the entire audience to see.

Avoid passing around objects or models to the audience. The chalkboard, whiteboard, and flip chart are excellent for keeping track of ideas during group brainstorming and discussion. Pass around handouts only when they are needed during the speech, and go over them thoroughly with the audience. Photographs should be downloaded to a computer for easy viewing.

Charts are useful for summarizing statistical information. Line graphs display changes in variables over time. Pie charts display proportions of a whole distribution. A bar graph makes comparisons among various magnitudes. Simplify charts and graphs by eliminating or combining unnecessary information. Text visuals display key information in brief words and phrases. Constructed visuals illustrate complicated processes with simple lines and shapes.

Use visual aids only when they are justified. Make sure they are large enough for everyone to see. Position yourself so that the entire audience has an unobstructed view. Display the aid only at the relevant place in the speech, and remove it from view when you are finished. Explain and interpret all the important elements of the visual aid for the audience.

## Questions and Exercises

1. Television has obviously contributed to our preference for visual information. In what specific ways has television influenced our preference for visual images? How do you think computers contribute to this preference for visual material? Besides television and computers, are there other things that have contributed to our preference for visual information?

2. Are there other means of adapting to visually oriented audiences without becoming the narrator of a picture show? What can you do to keep the audience stimulated and interested despite the fact that your presentation does not contain "souped-up" visual aids? Develop ways to compensate for a presentation that is heavy on verbal information and light on visual aids.

3. Get several *USA Today* newspapers and examine the informative charts and graphs in the lower left side of the front page. What makes the graph clear or unclear? Which rules for developing charts and graphs are employed in the newspaper chart? What changes would you make in the chart to make it clear to the audience in a presentation?

4. Examine your local weathercaster's use of visual aids during the nightly newscast. Does the weathercaster use unnecessary visual aids? Is the weathercaster positioned in such a way that the visual aid is not obscured? Is each visual explained clearly, and of what quality is that explanation? What, if anything, does your local weathercaster do to lead you to the correct interpretation of each visual aid? What does your weathercaster do to avoid talking to the visual aid?

## Notes

1. Porter, D., "Classworking: How Today's Colleges and Universities Are Preparing Tomorrow's Presenters," *Presentations,* January 2001, 42.
2. Holcombe, M. W., and J. K. Stein, *Presentations for Decision Makers* (New York: Van Nostrand Reinhold, 1996), 95.
3. Grice, G. L., and J. F. Skinner, *Mastering Public Speaking* (Boston: Allyn & Bacon, 2004).
4. Ibid.
5. Antonoff, M., "Meetings Take Off with Graphics," *Personal Computing,* July 1990, 62.
6. Seiler, W. J., "The Effects of Visual Materials on Attitudes, Credibility, and Retention," *Speech Monographs* 38 (1971): 331–334.
7. Grice and Skinner.
8. Ibid.
9. Clayton, J., "How to Make a Picture Worth a Thousand Words," *Harvard Management Communication Letter,* October 2002, 3–5.
10. Doumont, J., "The Cognitive Style of PowerPoint: Slides Are Not All Evil," *Technical Communication* 52 (2005): 64–70.
11. Ibid., 65.
12. Ibid., 69.

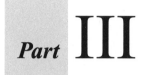

*Part* III

# *Types of Business and Professional Presentations*

# 9

# *Technical Presentations*

Several trends in professional life make informative communication more difficult than in the past. According to Peter Huber, author of *Judging Science,* "Major industries in our modern economy are built on a vast, fast-growing infrastructure of systematized knowledge . . . . New science, newer technology, vast databases, statistical analyses, and computer simulations have overtaken old wing-and-a-prayer ways of doing business."[1]

Increasingly, the language and methodology of every industry and discipline have developed along individual paths, making it virtually impossible for a single person to be an expert in more than one field. Specialization makes it difficult for people to communicate with each other across disciplines. If this weren't bad enough, specialization has made communication with lay audiences all but impossible.

Although increased specialization has made communication difficult, the interconnected nature of society necessitates greater, rather than less, communication with nonexperts. Managers in private, public, and government organizations need information from technical experts to make decisions. In Pocatello, Idaho, for example, the city council needed to select a method of removing trichloroethylene (a solvent) from the city's wells, despite the fact that neither the council members nor the mayor had any expertise in hydrology. Managers in organizations make decisions that require technical knowledge from a variety of fields. But managers are not the only consumers of technical information.

Because communities are affected by layoffs, industrial accidents, and pollution, they demand more information and greater input into business decisions than in the past. As a result, organizations must provide technical information about their operations to the lay public. Also, whenever the Park Service, the Forest Service, or the Environmental Protection Agency propose changes in policy, they are required to communicate the reasons for the change to interested publics.

These two trends have conspired to create a communication problem. Just as increased specialization makes communication outside narrow disciplines more difficult, managerial needs and public demands have made communication more vital. Most professional positions require strong informative communication skills. And most informational presentations require communicating technical information to someone outside a particular field or to a lay audience.

**Technical communication** is communication about scientific, engineering, technological, business, regulatory, legal, managerial, or social scientific information. A **technical presentation** is a prepared formal presentation on one or more of these topics to a nonexpert audience. A variety of common presentations fit under the rubric of technical communication, including laboratory presentations, feasibility reports, progress/status reports, survey presentations, training lectures, and business reports. This chapter is devoted to improving your technical communication skills.

The two goals of technical communication are accuracy and shared meaning. First, technical communication must be **accurate.** This means that the information must be correct, complete, and detailed enough to fill the needs for the specific audience. The Ethics Brief reviews issues related to accuracy. Accuracy requires solid research, careful reading and note taking, and constant verification of all facts.[2]

The second goal of technical communication is **shared meaning**—the ability to "present information in such a manner that the audience can draw one and only one meaning from the

*The ability to communicate technical information is vital in our increasingly complex society.*

Credit: Kevin C. Wellard

**BOX 9.1 • *Ethics Brief***

In our high-tech society, those with the most technical knowledge are often the only ones empowered to make decisions. Democracy is endangered, and the profit potential of business organizations is diminished when only a few participate in decision making. Technical communication empowers others to act because it spreads the knowledge required for decision making. We accept the following belief: No scientific or technical content is beyond explanation or understanding. If the presenter does an effective job of arranging and explaining the content, and the audience makes a commitment to understanding that content, then a shared understanding between speaker and listener is possible. The technical communicator commits herself to explaining even the most difficult content because it is people's right in a democracy to participate in decisions that affect their lives and because effective organizations take full advantage of their human resources. Although it's a task that requires logical thinking and careful attention to detail, technical communication serves a higher ideal: empowering people to participate in decision making.

Accuracy is the hallmark of ethical technical communication. Accuracy is the degree to which the information presented is correct and complete. Accuracy involves several processes and commitments. First, accurate communication requires excellent research skills. Skimping on research, relying on biased sources, or making up examples hurt the accuracy of a technical presentation. The best technical communicators are experts in their field but, more importantly, are diligent, thorough researchers whose goal is to bring the most up-to-date information to their audience.

Second, ethical communicators are willing to admit the weaknesses and limitations of their data. During a town meeting on the Environmental Protection Agency's (EPA's) proposals to strengthen regulations on particulate emissions, an EPA epidemiologist presented data about the health consequences of particulate pollution. Although she clearly believed the data she presented, she also reminded the audiences that epidemiology studies can look only at association and correlation, not at causation. As such, no study can prove that particulate pollution causes disease or death. Admitting limitations brings an added credibility advantage. The technical communicator who admits the limitations of her knowledge in some areas will command more trust from the audience when she does stand "four square" behind other data.

Third, even hard scientific disciplines are prone to conflicting data and disagreements among experts. When covering a topic that includes such conflicts and disagreements, the technical communicator doesn't gloss over opposition or contrary opinion; rather, he or she includes the full spectrum of opinion in the presentation.

Fourth, ethical communicators commit themselves to maintaining the integrity of the data. They refuse to "dumb down" the content through simplification and distortion. The strategies in this chapter are designed to help communicate complicated ideas without destroying the integrity of those ideas.

Fifth, ethical communication involves avoiding the use of jargon. Jargon is unnecessarily obscure terminology designed to prevent uninitiated members from participating in decision making. Jargon is often used to dazzle the audience, obscure meaning, or mystify the uninitiated, but is antithetical to technical communication's empowerment goal.

Finally, ethical communicators check their facts with other experts in the field. No person is infallible, and no one person can know all there is to know even in a small technical field. Check your content with other experts to be sure there is nothing you have missed and that your information is fair to competing positions and accurate based on the most recent knowledge. Ethical technical communicators commit themselves to the higher purpose and specific procedures outlined in this brief.

communication—the meaning intended by the communicator."[3] In other words, technical communicators seek a close correspondence between the speaker's understanding and the new understanding the audience achieves as a result of the message. The strategies we present in this chapter are designed to increase the likelihood of shared meaning.

This chapter reviews audience factors relevant to technical presentations, covers general guidelines for making technical information clear, explains how to overcome obstacles to shared meaning, and reviews how to structure technical presentations.

## *Understanding the Audience for Technical Information*

Strategic communication requires an understanding of various audience predispositions. In Chapter 6 we discussed methods of analyzing the audience. The Audience Analysis Checklist presented questions to probe the situation and listener traits of the audience. The guidelines in Figure 9.1 explain how to adapt to several audience traits.

For technical presentations it's also wise to consider the psychological meanings people derive from your major terms and concepts. In Chapter 1 we defined psychological meanings as the private associations individuals have for symbols. Some technical topics create reactions of fear (math), concern (pollution), or dread (cancer or radiation). A technical presentation about radiation dangers from a nuclear power plant must take into account the dread that people experience when they contemplate radiation. The audience's psychological meanings should influence how the speaker introduces and justifies the topic, builds credibility, and arranges the content in the speech body.

Obviously, most experts are both knowledgeable and interested in their specialty, which makes it difficult to put themselves in the place of lay audience members and adapt accordingly. However, this is exactly the role-taking skill required to communicate technical information. The effective technical speaker submerges his or her own knowledge sufficiently enough to be able to adopt, temporarily, the perspective of the listener and develop a presentation from that point of view. Use the Audience Analysis Checklist to improve role-taking skills and increase your ability to share technical information. In the next section, we discuss general techniques for making technical information clear.

**FIGURE 9.1**    *Adapting Technical Information to Audience Traits*

| Audience Trait | Adaptation |
|---|---|
| Captive audience: Complicated content makes members' interest difficult to maintain. | Acknowledge the audience is required to attend. Use colorful visual aids. Use interesting examples. Use dynamic delivery. |
| Predisposition toward the speaker: The speaker must be seen as a qualified expert. | Follow prescriptions in Chapters 7 and 10 and build your credibility prior to the presentation. |
| Predisposition toward the topic: Speakers are prone to overestimating audience knowledge. | Adapt explanations, definitions, examples, analogies, and visual aids to the audience's knowledge level. |

# General Guidelines for Communicating Technical Information

The following guidelines are applicable when communicating any kind of technical information. Observing the guidelines will increase the shared understanding between presenter and audience.

## Make Appropriate Word Choices

Word choice can make technical information clear or muddle it beyond recognition. As a general rule, rely on short, two-syllable words as opposed to longer three- (or more) syllable words.[4] Don't add to listeners' struggle to learn complicated information with unnecessarily complicated words. Below are a series of complicated words and their shorter, clearer alternatives.

| | |
|---|---|
| contiguous | connected |
| interface | talk |
| utilization | use |
| effectuation, enactment | operation |
| metamorphose, transfigure | change |
| retrofit | replace |

Nothing is gained by using the more complicated words in the left column. Although it is sometimes necessary to use a technical term because there is no easier equivalent (e.g., photosynthesis), speakers should err on the side of short words.

It is impossible to make word choices in a technical presentation without considering the problem of jargon. Jargon is unnecessarily obscure terminology peculiar to a discipline.[5] Rather than making things clear, jargon obscures meaning and prevents uninitiated members from participating in decision making. In many cases, jargon is designed to obscure meanings and make something bad into something good. For example, one might make a battlefield retreat sound less disastrous by calling it a "tactical redeployment" or make an explosion at a manufacturing plant sound less violent by calling it an "energetic disassembly."[6] Because of its power to confuse, jargon should be avoided.

However, jargon is not the same as technical terms such as *alpha particle, photosynthesis, crystallization, solubility, catalyst, millirem, polymer, anode,* and *cathode.* Technical terms often have one and only one meaning.[7] A term with limited meanings helps scientists, doctors, and engineers communicate with greater accuracy than is possible using a term that has more than one meaning. Technical terms may be necessary in some technical presentations. If so, follow the guidelines for clarifying difficult concepts articulated later in this chapter.

## Make Frequent Use of Examples and Analogies

As we mentioned in Chapter 7, an **example** is a specific instance that illustrates a larger point. A good example is not only more interesting than pages of dry description, it can also help an audience grasp abstract information. For instance, an example can explain the operation of latent viruses. Latent viruses are infections that retreat during recovery but linger in the body for years, only to emerge later and cause disease. Chicken pox is a classic example of a latent virus.

> After initial infection, the virus becomes latent, lying low within the nerve cells of the vertebrae. In most people, the virus remains dormant for life. It can, however, reactivate, causing the painful back rash of a disease called shingles.[8]

Because most people are familiar with chicken pox and may have parents or grandparents who have had shingles, the example provides a useful illustration of latent viruses.

**Analogies** are another powerful method of communicating technical information. An analogy is a comparison between two objects, events, instances, or people, suggesting that what is true of one is also true of the other. Cynthia Crossen, writing in the *Wall Street Journal,* explains that analogies "may be the best way to help ordinary people understand such complex and invisible systems as the Internet and the human genome, not to mention killer viruses and black holes."[9]

To help his audience understand the amount of empty space in an atom, physicist John Gribbon used the following analogy:

> Imagine a pinhead, perhaps a millimeter across, at the center of St. Paul's cathedral, surrounded by a cloud of microscopic dust motes far out in the dome of the cathedral, say 100 meters away. The pinhead represents the atomic nucleus; the dust motes are its retinue of electrons. That is how much empty space there is in the atom—and all of the seemingly solid objects in the material world are made of these empty spaces.[10]

This analogy is not only clear but quite vivid. Frequent use of both examples and analogies will help an audience comprehend complicated information.

### Translate Measurement Scales into Useful Analogies

The measurement scales used in scientific disciplines are difficult for lay audiences to understand. How big is a one-micron particle? What does it mean to say that there are $10^{28}$ atoms in the human body? Is the 10 millirems of radiation we receive from a dental x-ray a lot or a little? Any measurement scale unfamiliar to the audience should include an explanation of that scale. For example, how many is $10^{28}$ atoms? A speaker could explain it by saying it is a one followed by twenty-eight zeros.

However, explanation alone isn't usually enough to help audiences understand the very large or very small scales common to many scientific fields. Saying that the earth is five billion years old or the nearest star as five light-years away is fine, but the audience will not truly understand unless something is done to provide perspective to these figures. For example, the following translations help us comprehend the tremendous density of such astronomical objects as white dwarf and neutron stars.

> In white dwarf stars, where the atoms are compressed so closely together that the electrons in each atom may touch, the density is extremely high. White dwarf stars are so dense that "if a thimbleful of it were brought to Earth, it would weigh more than one million tons!" But white dwarfs are not as dense as neutron stars. The gravity of a neutron star has compressed the atoms so tightly that the electrons have collapsed in on the nucleus of the atom. "A sugar cube of neutron star material would weigh 100 million tons; if dropped, it would fall through to the center of the Earth."[11]

Rather than simply describing density mathematically, the earth-based measures of weight help explain density in a way that any layperson can understand.

The same problem of perspective applies when communicating measurements on a microscopic, atomic, or subatomic level. For example, saying that a 10-micron particle is 1/25,000 of an inch in diameter does not really help the audience picture the particle's size. However, saying the 10-micron particle is ten times smaller than the diameter of a human hair translates the scale into something the audience can relate to. You will note also that translating measurement scales involves the use of analogy. In essence, you compare the measurement scales to something the audience can relate to more easily. Translating measurement scales requires the effective use of analogy.

### Create Relevant Visual Aids

In Chapter 8 we reported research indicating that visual aids increase the clarity of complicated information. As such, visual aids are a must for most technical presentations. It's hard to imagine explaining a complicated process without a visual aid to communicate the essence of the event. Refer to the advice in Chapter 8 when creating visual aids for your technical presentation. In the next section, we review obstacles to shared meaning and present solutions in order to overcome these barriers.

## Overcoming Obstacles to Shared Meaning

As we stated in the beginning of this chapter, shared understanding is the goal of technical communication. One challenge of technical speaking is to analyze the principal obstacle that a topic presents and shape the speech to overcome that difficulty. Katherine Rowan, a communication professor at Purdue University, suggests two major obstacles to understanding informative content: difficult concepts and difficult structures or processes.

### Difficult Concepts

Some technical information is difficult to understand because it involves **difficult concepts.**[12] People may have difficulty understanding the concept of flat versus graduated tax systems. The concept of PM-10 (particulate matter smaller than 10 microns) pollution is difficult to conceive because we don't usually think of smog as particles. Understanding nuclear waste storage is complicated because people don't know there are five different kinds of waste. In these cases, the audience's lack of familiarity with terms is an obstacle to shared understanding.

When people attempt to understand the meaning of technical terms, they struggle to distinguish a concept's **essence,** features that are always present from its **associated features,** features that are frequently but not necessarily present.[13] When trying, for example, to distinguish the difference between a flat and a graduated income tax, the listener needs to comprehend the essential features of a graduated income tax (people who make more money pay a larger percentage of that money in taxes) and the essential feature of a flat income tax (everyone pays the same percentage regardless of income). Although many flat income tax proposals eliminate tax deductions for children, medical payments, and interest payments, this is not an essential feature of the flat income tax. A flat tax can include or exclude a variety of deductions without changing the essential nature of the tax—that everyone pays the same percentage regardless of income.

When trying to understand the difference between coarse and fine particulate pollution, listeners must understand that the size of the particle, not its composition, is the essential feature. Although coarse particulate matter is larger than 10 microns in size, fine particulate is 10 microns or smaller. PM-10 can be a particle, a liquid droplet, or any combination of the two; thus the composition is an associated rather than an essential feature of particulate pollution. New concepts can be clarified by the inclusion of definitions, a typical example, and varied examples and nonexamples.

***Provide a Definition That Lists Essential Features.***    Definitions clarify a concept's essential features. Several kinds of definitions are useful for communicating technical information.

*Logical Definition.*    The most important method of defining a concept is the **logical definition.** Logical definitions include two steps: Place the concept into a general category, then explain the characteristics that distinguish that concept from all other members of the category.[14] For example, a mutual fund can be logically defined as follows:

> Part 1: A mutual fund is one of two ways to invest in the stock market.
> Part 2: Instead of buying individual stocks, the mutual fund investor turns over his or her dollars to the mutual fund manager, who is responsible for overseeing the growth of the money by buying and selling individual stocks. Some mutual funds are organized to buy and sell stocks in a particular area of business, such as biotechnology or high-technology companies.

Some technical speakers make the mistake of skipping step 1. A speech on nuclear reactors defined nuclear fission as follows:

> Nuclear fission occurs when a large nucleus splits into two smaller nuclei.

This will not help the listener who does not have a context within which to understand the definition. The first step of the logical definition creates that context.

> Nuclear reactions are reactions that split or combine the nucleus of an atom. Whereas fusion combines two nuclei, nuclear fission splits a nucleus into two smaller nuclei.[15]

Be sure to include both steps in a logical definition. Logical definitions are the best way to help an audience understand the essence of a concept.

*Operational Definition.*    **Operational definitions** explain how something functions. For example, in defining how the brain is divided into two hemispheres, the right and the left, a speaker could say that

> the right hemisphere is largely responsible for seeing holistic patterns, whereas the left hemisphere is responsible for linear, analytic thinking.

Many operational definitions explain the steps in a process.

> In any list of data, you can find the "mode" by identifying the number that occurs most frequently.

Operational definitions are almost as powerful as logical definitions for clarifying a concept's essence.

*Definition by Etymology.*   Another common way to define a scientific concept is to explain how the word was derived from a historical event or another language. For example:

> The word *plastic* comes from the Greek *plastikos* meaning "fit for molding" [italics in original].[16]

Although etymological definitions are interesting, they should be combined with other definitions for maximum clarity.

Definitions help distinguish the essential features of a concept from its associated features.

**Provide a Typical Example of the Concept or Idea.**   A second way to clarify difficult concepts is to provide a **typical example.**[17] The typical example is representative of the whole group. A speech on investing in the stock market provided the following typical example of a mutual fund:

> A typical example of a mutual fund is the Seligman Communications and Information Fund. The manager of this fund is empowered to use investors' money to buy and sell stocks in various communication companies such as Verizon or AT&T, and various information companies such as Intel and Microsoft. The goal is to buy stocks in these companies at a low price and acquire value when and if the prices of the stocks rise.

**Provide a Series of Examples and Nonexamples.**   Technical speakers should provide a series of examples and nonexamples to aid the audience's ability to distinguish between the concept and things that might be mistaken for the concept.[18] For example, a speech on PM-10 pollution included an overhead to distinguish between a variety of particulates, some of which are smaller than 10 microns, others of which are larger.

*Size Comparison of Particulates*

| | |
|---|---|
| Viruses | .01 to .1 micron |
| Insecticide dust | 1 to 10 microns |
| Bacteria | 1 to 25 microns |
| Pollen spores | 10 to 100 microns |
| Baking flour | 25 to 50 microns |
| Beach sand | 100 to 500 microns |

Figure 9.2 depicts a sample technical presentation where the primary obstacle is difficult concepts. Many people mistakenly believe that the smoke emitted from automobiles and factories is composed entirely of toxic gases. Although gases are a problem, when scientists and regulators discuss air pollution they are usually referring to particles smaller than 10 microns in size. The sample presentation in Figure 9.2 defines and explains the concept of PM-10 pollution. Examine this presentation for its use of definitions, typical examples, and nonexamples.

**FIGURE 9.2** *Speech on PM-10 Pollution*

| | |
|---|---|
| Topic: | Particulate Pollution |
| Specific Purpose: | I want my audience to understand what particulate pollution is and why it is a problem. |
| Main Idea: | This speech will cover the issue of particulate pollution in three main steps: First, I will define particulate pollution; second, I will explain why the small size of this form of pollution is so important; and third, I will explain why particulates are hazardous to human health. |

**INTRODUCTION**

    I. Imagine that this tank represents the Portneuf Valley, Fort Hall area. The water is our air, and the sides of the tank represent the hills that surround three sides of the valley. During an air inversion, a cold air cap seals the tank, trapping pollution in the air. Imagine that this cup of milk is particulate pollution from industrial and individual sources. Under these conditions, our air looks like this (pour milk in fish tank). This soup of gases and particulates is the air we see and breathe until the inversion breaks.

    II. Pollution is a concern to all of us in the valley, whether we live in Fort Hall, Chubbuck, or Pocatello.

        A. There are many forms of pollution that concern citizens and regulators: gaseous pollution like $CO_2$ (a greenhouse gas), or sulfur dioxides, lead from automobile exhaust (once a huge concern prior to the advent of unleaded gasoline), and ozone concentrations from various forms of combustion are all forms of pollution.

            1. However, in our valley one of the most important pollution concerns is PM-10 pollution—very fine particles of dust that come from a variety of natural and human sources.

            2. Although PM-10 is particularly noticeable during our winter air inversions, when the pollution is trapped close to the valley floor, it is put into the air every day of the year.

        B. My goal today is to give you a better understanding of what particulate pollution is and why it is such a concern in our valley.

    III. My name is Jim DiSanza, and I teach in the Communication Department at Idaho State University. For the past three years I have served as the facilitator for the Portneuf Valley Community Advisory Panel, a group of volunteer citizens from Fort Hall, Chubbuck, and Pocatello who advise the FMC Corporation and the J. R. Simplot Company on a variety of issues, including air pollution.

        A. As facilitator of the PVCAP, I have spent three years working with the group on a variety of air pollution issues.

        B. I have heard presentations on particulate pollution from industry representatives, members of the Idaho Division of Environmental Quality, and the U.S. Environmental Protection Agency.

        C. For this speech I interviewed Audrey Cole, at the Pocatello office of the Division of Environmental Quality, and read several books on the subject from the ISU (Idaho State University) library.

        D. Information presented in this speech was checked for accuracy by members of the Idaho Division of Environmental Quality.

    IV. I would like to cover the issue of particulate pollution in three steps: First, I will define particulate pollution; second, I will explain why the small size of these particles is important to pollution experts; and third, I will explain why particulates are hazardous to human health.

(Trans: So, let me start by defining the nature of particulate pollution.)

**FIGURE 9.2** *Continued*

**BODY**

    **I.** In this first part of the speech I will define particulate pollution by explaining what particulate pollution is and where it comes from.

        **A.** First, air pollution exists as solid matter, liquid droplets, or gas (1, p. 30). (OH 1).*

            **1.** Substances such as carbon dioxide (thought to be a greenhouse gas) or sulfur dioxide are gases, not particulates.

            **2.** Solid matter and liquid droplets, however, are referred to as particulates because they combine or chemically react to form particles (1, p. 30).

                **a.** In large communities such as Los Angeles, the air is chock-full of particulate pollution, which reduces visibility and causes human health problems.

                **b.** Here in the Portneuf Valley, particulate pollution, including both solid matter and liquid droplets, although always in the air to some extent, become pronounced during our winter air inversions, which trap particulate matter in the valley for several days at a stretch.

            **3.** Thus particulate pollution includes particles of solid matter or liquid droplets that become suspended in the atmosphere.

        **B.** Second, particulate pollution can come from a variety of sources that are both natural and human (3, p. 23).

            **1.** Natural sources include particles from condensing water, wind-borne pollen, dead and living organic debris, various forms of fungi and mold, wind-blown dust and rust, and particles from forest fires as well as natural volcanic and other geothermal sources (3, pp. 23–34).

            **2.** On the other hand, human sources include:

                **a.** First, smoke from any form of combustion, including coal burning for heating or electricity, automobiles, railroad diesels, aircraft, trucks, heavy industry, and home heating.

                **b.** Second, fumes from chemical reactions such as smelting or refining.

                **c.** Third, dust from innumerable sources in our area including:

                    **(1)** Industrial sources such as phosphorous plants, the paving company, and the cement plant.

                    **(2)** And nonindustrial sources such as agricultural tilling, paved and unpaved roads, even tire and brake wear on our cars.

                **d.** And, fourth, mist formed from spraying or condensing water vapor (1, pp. 31–33).

(Trans: Now that you know more about particulate pollution, let's examine why the size of these particles is so important.)

    **II.** To understand why particulates are an air pollution problem, you must understand how small this kind of pollution really is as well as how it is classified by scientists.

        **A.** First, particulate pollution is so small that it is measured in terms of microns.

            **1.** (OH 2) A micron is equal to 1/1000 of a millimeter or 1/25,000 of an inch (1).

            **2.** A human hair is 10 times larger than a 10-micron particle (2).

                **a.** As you can see in the overhead, the diameter of a 10-micron particle is quite small.

                **b.** Only particles five times larger than 10 microns can be seen by the human eye.

            **3.** (OH 3) To get a comparison, examine the following overhead, which compares the size, in microns, of several kinds of particulates found in or near your household (3, p. 26).

        **B.** Second, based on the size of the particles, particulate pollution is classified into one of two categories: coarse and fine.

---

*OH refers to PowerPoint overhead slides.

*(continued)*

**FIGURE 9.2**  *Continued*

---

1. Coarse particles are pollutants that are larger than 10 microns in diameter.
   a. These larger particles of pollution are, relatively speaking, heavy, and if they get into the air either through combustion or carried aloft by the wind, they settle back to the ground quickly (1, p. 31).
      (1) This sand from a sandbox is approximately 100 microns in size.
      (2) Watch how quickly it falls to the ground as I throw it.
   b. As a result, particulate pollution larger than 10 microns is usually a problem only very near the source of the pollution (1, p. 31).
2. Fine particles, on the other hand, are smaller than 10 microns in diameter.
   a. These particles are lighter than the coarse variety (1, p. 31).
      (1) If you remember from the last overhead, baking flour is about 25 to 50 microns in size.
      (2) I use it because I can't show you PM-10; it is microscopic.
      (3) Watch what happens when I throw this into the air.
      (4) See how it hangs in the air and remains there longer than the sand.
   b. Because of its small size and light weight, PM-10 hangs in the air for longer periods than coarse particles, and this is the basis of many pollution problems in the Portneuf Valley and throughout the country.
      (1) (OH 4) The thing to remember is that coarse particles are larger than 10 microns in size and are not a large pollution concern.
      (2) In contrast, PM-10 is particulate matter smaller than 10 microns and is a serious pollution concern—the 10-micron line is the important distinction.

(Trans: Now that you know why particulates smaller than 10 microns are a problem, let's examine the health consequences of this pollution.)

III. It is the small size of the particle that makes PM-10 dangerous to human health.
   A. The small size of the PM-10 particle makes it dangerous.
      1. First, when substances are broken down into smaller and smaller particles, more of the original particle becomes surface area that is exposed to the air.
         a. Under these circumstances, the particle becomes more attractive to other toxic substances.
         b. Toxins such as sulfur dioxide or oxides of nitrogen can coat the particle and hitch a free ride through the atmosphere (1, p. 33).
      2. If this weren't bad enough, the smaller the particle, the more easily it can become lodged deep in the lungs, toxic coating and all.
         a. Particles between 4 and 10 microns tend to get trapped in the mucus membrane of the nose and cannot then make their way deeply into the lungs.
         b. However, particles smaller than 4 microns pass through the mucus in the nose and lodge deeply in the lungs (4, p. 16).
            (1) These small particles enter the lungs, carrying various gases such as sulfur dioxide and oxides of nitrogen.
            (2) Thus the particle provides an avenue for other toxic gases to be deposited in the lungs.
   B. As a result, breathing particulate matter that is smaller than 10 microns, especially matter below 4 microns, is linked to various forms of respiratory disease, both chronic and acute.
      1. Particulate matter has been linked to breathing problems in children and the elderly.
      2. It has been shown to cause lung tissue damage.
      3. And it is linked to a variety of diseases from asthma to lung disease.

**FIGURE 9.2**   *Continued*

(Trans: To summarize, particulate pollution affects human health because the smaller particles stay in the air, they are the most chemically active particles, and they are the particles most likely to make it deep into our lungs.)

**CONCLUSION**

**I.** To conclude this brief presentation, I have defined what particulate pollution is, described why the size of that particulate is so important, and discussed the human health effects of particulate pollution.

**II.** Remember that PM-10 pollution, particulate matter smaller than 10 microns, is a major pollution concern both here and nationwide.

**III.** The rest of this show is designed to provide you with more information about PM-10.

    **A.** First, Audrey Cole, of the Idaho Division of Environmental Quality, will discuss the various sources of PM-10 pollution in the Portneuf Valley.

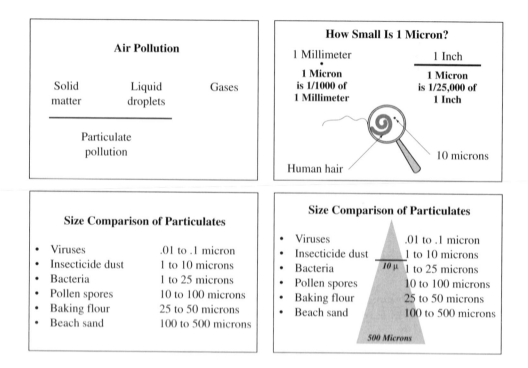

    **B.** Then, Dean Hazen, an employee of the National Weather Service and a member of our Community Advisory Panel, will discuss how air inversions work to trap particulate matter.

    **C.** Finally, the CAP will hold a panel discussion with members of the FMC and J. R. Simplot companies to discuss particulate pollution in our valley.

    **D.** We hope the show is both informative and enjoyable.

*(continued)*

**FIGURE 9.2** *Continued*

### REFERENCES

1.  Natural Tuberculosis and Respiratory Disease Association. *Air Pollution Primer.* New York: 1969.
2.  Idaho Department of Health and Welfare, Division of Environmental Quality (Informative Paper). "What is PM-10?"
3.  Boubel, R. W., D. L. Fox, D. B. Turner, and A. C. Stern. *Fundamentals of Air Pollution.* San Diego: Academic Press, 1994.
4.  Bates, D. W. *A Citizen's Guide to Air Pollution.* Montreal: McGill-Queen's University Press, 1972.

## Difficult Structures or Processes

Some technical information is difficult to understand because it involves **complicated structures** or **involved processes** that are hard for an audience to visualize.[19] How are laser beams created? How are microchips manufactured? How do viruses cause illness? How does the DNA molecule control human growth and development? In these topics, the obstacle to shared understanding is the complexity of key components or processes. The speaker helps the audience visualize the whole by providing a graphic model and an organizing analogy.

### Provide a Graphic Model of the Process.
One of the simplest ways to help an audience visualize the whole is to provide a **graphic model** of the process being described.[20] For example, the FMC elemental phosphorus plant encourages people to tour its massive facility. Prior to touring the various manufacturing areas, visitors stop at a conference room that includes a huge poster displaying a flowchart of the entire process—from the entry of the raw ore into the plant, to the calciners that prepare the ore for burning, to the furnaces that heat the ore, to the place where the liquid phosphorus is loaded onto rail cars for the trip to eastern manufacturing facilities. This graphic model is reproduced in Figure 9.3. While on the tour, representatives frequently refer back to the chart to remind us where we are in the manufacturing process. The graphic model provides a quick way to visualize the entire process. Use the suggestions in Chapter 8 to prepare and show your graphic model.

### Use Organizing Analogies.
An **organizing analogy** communicates the general impression of a structure or process in a nutshell.[21] Read the organizing analogies that follow:

> The atom is like a small *solar system.*
> A laser is created when all the wavelengths of light are made to *line up.*
> To create liquid phosphorus we *cook* raw ore that contains phosphate and capture the *steam.*
> Viruses cause illness by *colonizing* cells.

An organizing analogy communicates the big picture in a way that is easy to grasp and lays the foundation for more detailed explanation. Figure 9.4 displays a sample technical presentation where the primary obstacle is a difficult process. Examine this presentation for its use of definitions, visual aids, and organizing analogies.

The primary obstacle to understanding technical content may be new concepts, difficult processes, or both. For example, the main obstacle to understanding PM-10 pollution is new

Shown below is a simplified diagram of what happens here at FMC's plant.

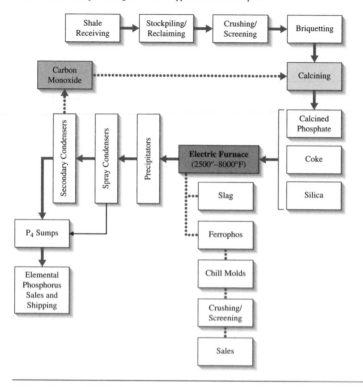

**FIGURE 9.3     *FMC Process***

concepts. Thus, the author focused on strategies for clarifying concepts. The main obstacle in the sunburn presentation is a difficult process. Thus, the author focused on graphic models (through the creation of a variety of constructed PowerPoint visuals) and a solid organizing analogy. A topic that includes both new language and a difficult process requires a combination of strategies. Analyze your topic for the obstacles it presents, and adapt your content accordingly.

## *Structuring the Technical Presentation*

Although there isn't a single best way to structure technical presentations, research indicates that clearly structured messages are understood and remembered better than unstructured messages.[22] Any of the structures discussed in Chapter 7 can be used in a technical presentation. For example, the PM-10 speech in Figure 9.2 includes three main ideas that are arranged topically.

 This simple structure is entirely appropriate for a technical presentation. For presentations on complex structures and processes the cause–effect and problem solution structures may be effective. Whatever structure you select, the technical presentation must be clearly organized for greatest effect.

**FIGURE 9.4**   *Sample Speech on Sunburn Damage*

By Kristal Searle

Topic:                  Sunburn

Specific Purpose:       I want my audience to understand the process the human body uses to repair sun-
                        burn damage to the skin.

Main Idea:              In this speech I will discuss the parts of the skin and the body's initial response to
                        sunburn damage, and I will explain why sunburns create red skin, feelings of pain,
                        and peeling.

**INTRODUCTION**

    **I.** It has happened to all of us. You go to bed after spending a beautiful, warm summer day
outside. When you wake up the next morning, you are in immense pain. You get into the
shower and the water feels like thousands of tiny pins jamming into your flesh. You have
been sunburned.

   **II.** After being sunburned, something remarkable takes place over the next 24 hours: your body heals
and repairs itself.

      **A.** The human body has a very effective self-repair system.

      **B.** Because each of us has experienced sunburn, we should know how the body heals itself of this
condition.

      **C.** By the end of this presentation, each of you will understand how the human body repairs itself
after being damaged by the sun.

  **III.** My name is Kristal Searle and I've done some research on sunburns.

      **A.** The processes that occur within the human body are fascinating.

      **B.** I have researched sunburns by reading dermatology books found at the local library.

      **C.** I have also done some reading in several sections of a popular anatomy and physiology
textbook.

  **IV.** Today I will discuss three main ideas.

      **A.** I will begin by discussing the layers and parts of the skin.

      **B.** I will then discuss the body's initial response to the damage done to the skin.

      **C.** Finally, I will explain how increased cell production causes the symptoms that we associate
with sunburns.

(Trans: I will now discuss the layers of the skin.)

**BODY**

    **I.** In the first part of this presentation I will describe the two main layers of skin.

      **A.** (Slide 1) We can think of the layers of our skin like a building. Every building has a base, and
every building has a roof.

      **B.** (Slide 2) The inner layer of skin is like the base of a building and is called the dermis.

         **1.** Sweat glands are located within the dermis layer.

         **2.** Hair follicles are located within the dermis layer.

         **3.** Capillaries are located within the dermis layer.

            a. The capillaries are like tiny blood vessels.

            b. They contain the oxygen, white blood cells, proteins, and other nutrients that are
necessary for cell production.

      **C.** Like the roof of a building, which shields the lower structure, the outer layer of skin protects
the inner layer of skin. This outer layer is called the epidermis.

         **1.** The outer layer of the epidermis is called the stratum corneum.

            a. The stratum corneum is made up of dead cells.

            b. Look at your hand. What you are looking at is the stratum corneum.

**FIGURE 9.4   *Continued***

---

      **2.** The inner layer of the epidermis is called the Malpighian layer.
        **a.** The Malpighian layer is made up of living cells.
        **b.** The Malpighian layer is where new cells are created.
        **c.** (Slide 3) When skin is overexposed to ultraviolet radiation, cells within the Malpighian layer are damaged and destroyed, resulting in the condition known as sunburn.

(Trans: Now that we are familiar with the layers and parts of the skin, I am going to discuss the body's initial response to the damage done to the skin.)

  **II.** The body's initial response to the damage done to the skin is to begin repairing the damage as soon as possible.
    **A.** (Slide 4) The body's self-repair system can be compared to the events that would take place if a fire was to start within this building.
    **B.** If a fire were to break out in this building, a chain reaction of events would occur.
      **1.** The smoke of the fire will be detected by the smoke detector.
      **2.** The fire alarm will signal to the occupants that they need to exit the building.
      **3.** Finally, the sprinkler system will be activated and begin to extinguish the fire.
    **C.** When ultraviolet radiation has damaged our living skin cells, a process like the one just described occurs within the body.
      **1.** Just as the fire releases smoke that sets off the fire alarm and the sprinkler system, the brain detects these pain signals from the injured portion of the body.
      **2.** Once the signal is received by the brain, it sends out an alarm to the glands throughout the body.
      **3.** The glands release chemical substances called mediators of inflammation.
        **a.** The sprinkler system extinguishes the fire.
        **b.** The mediators of inflammation begin repairing the damage done to the skin.

(Trans: Now that you know the body's initial response to the damaged skin cells, I am going to explain how increased cell production causes the symptoms that we associate with sunburn.)

  **III.** Increased cell production causes the symptoms that we associate with sunburn.
    **A.** (Slide 5) Each day, some of your cells die and new cells are created.
      **1.** (Slide 6) When you get sunburned, a large number of cells have been destroyed.
      **2.** Unlike a building, which requires outside help in order to be repaired, our skin is able to repair itself from the inside.
      **3.** When you get sunburned, physical changes must occur within the skin that result in increased cell production.
      **4.** These changes are made possible by the mediators of inflammation.
    **B.** (Slide 7) The mediators of inflammation cause the capillaries contained within the dermis layer to dilate and to become more permeable.
      **1.** The mediators of inflammation cause the capillaries to dilate.
        **a.** As the capillaries dilate, or in other words, as the capillaries increase in diameter, more blood is moved to the damaged area.
        **b.** This blood contains the oxygen, white blood cells, proteins, and other nutrients that are necessary for the creation of new skin cells.
        **c.** Just as a fire hose is able to carry more water than a garden hose and, thus, will be more effective in putting out a fire, the dilated capillaries carry more nutrients than regular capillaries and, thus, are more effective in repairing cell damage.
        **d.** It is the increased blood flow in the capillaries that makes the skin of the damaged area appear redder and feel hotter than normal.

*(continued)*

**FIGURE 9.4** *Continued*

---

      2. The mediators of inflammation also increase the permeability of the capillaries.

        **a.** (Slide 8) As the permeability of the capillaries increases, additional oxygen, white blood cells, proteins, and other nutrients leave the capillaries and enter the tissue of the Malpighian layer where the new cells will be created.

        **b.** When these nutrients leave the capillaries, the concentration of the inside and outside of the capillaries is no longer in equilibrium.

          **(1)** The outside of the capillaries is more concentrated than the inside of the capillaries.

          **(2)** In order to return back to a state of equilibrium, water is needed on the outside of the capillaries.

        **c.** As water moves to the outside of the capillaries, the tissue swells, resulting in inflammation or swelling.

        **d.** This swelling stimulates neurons and causes the sensation of pain.

    **C.** The mediators of inflammation create an increase in the production of skin cells.

      **1.** (Slide 9) As a result of the dilation and increased permeability of the capillaries, an increase in the production of skin cells is possible.

      **2.** If a building was repaired in the same manner as our skin, new wood cells would be created within the wall of the building, forcing the old, charred wood off of the outside of the building.

      **3.** New skin cells are created in greater-than-normal quantities, and the older cells are forced off of the stratum corneum in greater amounts than we are used to.

      **4.** When we notice the dead skin cell falling off of our body, we say that the skin is peeling.

(Trans: In summary, what we recognize as symptoms of sunburn are actually a result of the increased cell production made possible by the mediators of inflammation.)

**CONCLUSION**

    **I.** This morning I have discussed three main points.

      **A.** I have discussed the layers and parts of the skin.

      **B.** I have discussed the body's initial response to the damage done to the skin.

      **C.** I have discussed how increased cell production causes the symptoms of sunburn.

    **II.** So the next time a day in the sun leaves you screaming in pain in the shower, remember that your red, hot, painful, peeling skin is actually evidence that your body's self-repair system is working properly.

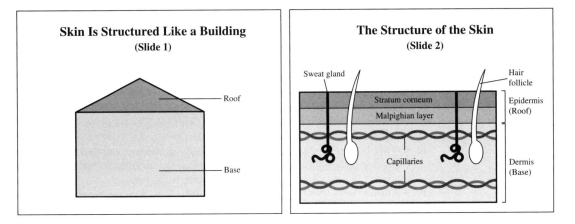

**FIGURE 9.4** *Continued*

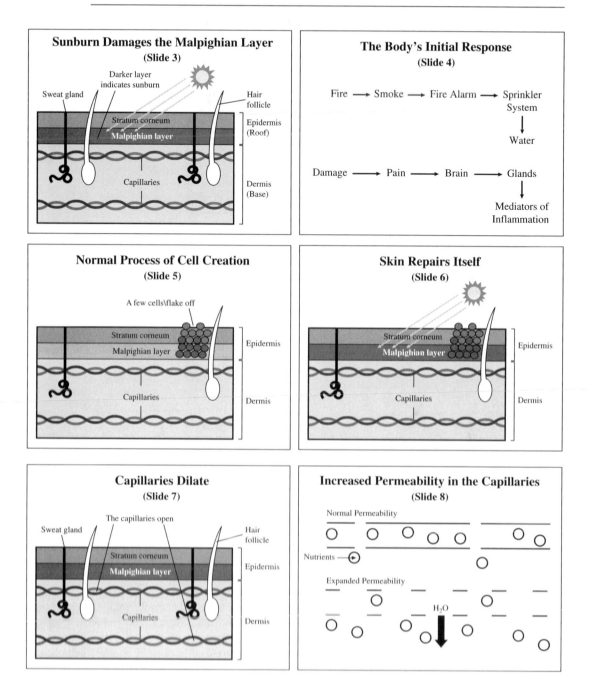

**FIGURE 9.4**    *Continued*

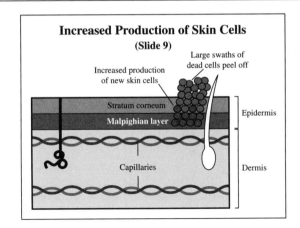

**Increased Production of Skin Cells**
(Slide 9)

Increased production of new skin cells

Large swaths of dead cells peel off

Stratum corneum

Malpighian layer

Epidermis

Capillaries

Dermis

**WORKS CITED**

Howstuffworks. "How Sunburns and Sun Tans Work." 31 Oct. 2003.
    http://travel.howstuffworks.com/sunscreen.htm/printable

Parish, John A., *Dermatology and Skin Care.* New York: McGraw-Hill, 1975.

Seely, Rod R., Trent D. Stephens, and Philip Tate, *Anatomy and Physiology,* 6th ed. Boston:
    McGraw-Hill, 2003.

# *Summary*

Despite the difficulties created by specialization, managerial needs and public demand have increased the need to communicate technical information with lay audiences. Technical communication is communication about scientific, engineering, technological, business, regulatory, legal, managerial, or social scientific information. Technical communicators should strive for accuracy and shared meaning.

The following procedures can increase the chances of shared meaning with an audience. Rely on short words, avoid jargon, and clearly define all technical terms in the presentation. Make frequent use of examples and analogies. Analogies compare an unfamiliar concept or idea with one that is familiar to the audience. Presenters should also translate scientific measurement scales into useful analogies to provide a sense of perspective. Good technical speaking includes visual aids to help the audience grasp complicated ideas.

There are two common obstacles to understanding complex information: new concepts and difficult structures and processes. To teach new concepts, a speaker should include logical, operational, and etymological definitions, typical examples, and a series of examples and nonexamples. Some information is difficult to comprehend because it involves complicated structures and processes that are hard to visualize. The presenter can overcome these obstacles by including graphic models and organizing analogies. Communicators should select a structure that is both clear and fits the content.

## Questions and Exercises

1. Examine the sample technical presentation on PM-10 pollution in Figure 9.2. One of the primary obstacles to understanding technical content is difficult concepts. Does the speech use definitions and typical examples to overcome the language obstacle? Label the places in the outline where these strategies are employed. Explain how the strategies create shared meaning. Was the speech effective or ineffective? What would you change to make the presentation more effective?

2. Following is a list of various technical topics. For each topic, identify the primary obstacle to audience understanding.

How are e-mail messages sent on the Internet?
How does aspirin relieve pain?
How do bacteria come to contaminate meat products?
How do scientists genetically engineer strains of insect-resistant plants?
How does a television screen produce a picture?
What is a laser beam?
What is radiation?

## Notes

1. Huber, P., "Tires, Bees and Expertise," *Wall Street Journal,* 1 April 1999, A22.
2. Alvarez, J. A., *The Elements of Technical Writing* (New York: Harcourt Brace Jovanovich, 1980).
3. Barnette, G. A., and C. Hughes, "Communication Theory and Technical Communication," in *Research in Technical Communication,* ed. M. G. Moran and D. Journet (Westport, CT: Greenwood Press, 1985), 40.
4. Alvarez.
5. Ibid.
6. Satchell, M., "Could you, er, say that again?" *U.S. News & World Report,* 20 April 1987, 71.
7. Eisenberg, A., *Effective Technical Communication* (New York: McGraw-Hill, 1982).
8. Zimmerman, B. E., and D. J. Zimmerman, *Why Nothing Can Travel Faster than Light . . .* (Chicago: Contemporary Books, 1993), 272.
9. Crossen, C., "Analogize This: A Is to B as C Is to . . . ? The Correct Answer Is More Vital Than Ever," *Wall Street Journal,* 22 August 2000, A1, A10.
10. Gribbon, J., *In Search of Schrödinger's Cat: Quantum Physics and Reality* (Toronto: Bantam Books, 1984), 31–32.
11. Zimmerman and Zimmerman, 76–77.
12. Rowan, K. E., "A New Pedagogy for Explanatory Public Speaking: Why Arrangement Should Not Substitute For Invention," *Communication Education* 44 (1995): 236–250.
13. Merril, M. D., and R. D. Tennyson, *Teaching Concepts: An Instructional Design Guide* (Englewood Cliffs, NJ: Educational Technology Publications, 1977).
14. Sprague, J., and D. Stuart, *The Speaker's Handbook* (Fort Worth, TX: Harcourt Brace, 1996).
15. Zimmerman and Zimmerman.
16. Ibid., 258.
17. Rowan.
18. Ibid.
19. Ibid.
20. Ibid.
21. Ibid.
22. Barnette and Hughes.

# 10

# *Proposal Presentations*

Proposal presentations are a way of life for many professionals. Consider the following examples:

- Mario owns a business that manufactures antennas. However, his products are more expensive than the competition's. He must persuade clients to spend more money for his antennas.
- Ramon has identified a problem with the way travel authorizations work in his company. His solution involves a change in company policy.
- Anita is in charge of this year's United Way campaign in her company. How will she encourage donations?
- Terry's committee will apply for a government grant to get new playground equipment at the local school.
- Tony proposes that the city council give his company, Environmental Solutions, Inc., a contract to collect the city's residential trash.

To address each of these problems, the people involved must make effective **proposal presentations.** A business proposal should create shared meaning by persuading others that whatever you have to offer—an idea, a design, a program, new equipment, or a new procedure—is the best solution to their problem. Proposal presentations are a major part of day-to-day operations for many business and professional organizations. Research and development firms survive by presenting proposals to government agencies. For social service and arts organizations, proposals to foundations or government agencies mean the difference between continued operation and folding. In giant corporations, proposals for large government contracts may determine the company's future direction for up to five years. Charles E. Beck of the University of Colorado, and Keith Wegner, president of Quantalex, Inc., claim that "proposals have become vital to organizational success" regardless of the type of business.[1]

This chapter covers proposals in several steps. After a discussion of audience concerns, we explain the use of various proposal structures. Because effective proposals are clearly argued, we discuss the construction and evaluation of logical arguments. We conclude with a discussion of speaker credibility and emotional appeals. Given the importance of proposals in many organizations, it stands to reason that your ability to persuade others is vital to your professional success.

## Audience Analysis for Persuasive Proposals

As always, the audience is the first consideration in a proposal. Your understanding of the audience should guide your tactical choices regarding structure, logical arguments, credibility, and emotional appeals. Bernard L. Rosenbaum, president of MOHR Development, Inc., a training and development firm, contends that effective proposals focus on the issues that "are most important to the people present at the meeting. Too many presentations fail to do this."[2]

In Chapter 6, Figure 6.4, we introduced the Audience Analysis Checklist, a series of questions that guide audience analysis. For proposal presentations, the speaker must address all major categories under situation analysis (occasion, organizational culture, environment, and time) and listener analysis (demographics, captivity, predisposition toward the speaker, and predisposition toward the topic). Once you understand the audience's knowledge and meaning associated with the topic, you can plot the kind of audience you are facing: favorable, apathetic, neutral, active, or hostile. Then follow the guidelines in Table 6.1 to adapt your content, structure, and delivery to the specific audience.

## Proposal Structures

In Chapter 7, we equated structure with leadership. Speakers lead by taking command of the audience and guiding them to the preferred interpretation of an idea, product, or service. Gary Blake, a writing consultant, suggests that preparing a proposal without organizing one's thoughts is like a commercial pilot taking off without a flight plan. Blake says, of all the "problems that plague businesspeople, none is more far-reaching or likely to cripple profits and profitability than lack of organization."[3] This section expands on the basic structures covered in Chapter 7 to include those uniquely suited to the proposal presentation.

Although we usually think of the content of a proposal as the main engine of persuasion, the structure itself can increase or decrease persuasiveness. Because structures emphasize different elements of a proposal, strategically matching the structure to audience concerns allows you to emphasize the elements of your proposal, order of presentation, and persuasive appeals that are most appropriate for a given audience. As such, the structure of a proposal is as important as the content. Table 6.1 (p. 109) in Chapter 6 suggests ways to adapt your structure to five different kinds of audiences.

In this section we explain four strategies for organizing persuasive ideas: the problem–solution structure, Monroe's Motivated Sequence, N-A-R structure, and balance structure. Your choice of structure should be guided by your understanding of the audience and the topic.

### The Problem–Solution Structure

In the **problem–solution structure,** the presenter articulates the problem the company has and provides a solution tailored to that company. Audience members who hear a proposal presentation, writes Richard J. Fulscher, head of the National Institute of Asset Management in Chicago, "want you to show your understanding of their problems, propose solutions, and demonstrate your capabilities" in carrying out the solution.[4]

When Ramon approached his colleagues about travel authorizations, his proposal followed the problem–solution structure. He indicated the problem: The company was losing $10,000 per month through incorrectly booked, reported, and processed travel authorizations. The solution: Employee travel will be booked through a single travel agent, and employees will turn in credit card receipts within three days of completed travel. If the audience is not aware of the need for your proposal, you should focus equally on the problem and the solution. If the audience knows the problem, briefly review it and spend the bulk of the speech emphasizing the solution. The outline for a problem–solution structure should use the following format:

*[handwritten: prob/sol basic format]*

*[handwritten: * business people *]*

INTRODUCTION
I. Gain attention
II. Justify the topic
III. Establish credibility
IV. Preview the main ideas
(Transition)
BODY
I. Problem
(Transition)
II. Solution
(Transition)
CONCLUSION
I. Review
II. Call to action

Because of its no-nonsense focus, this structure is recognized and well liked by most businesspeople.

### Monroe's Motivated Sequence   *[handwritten: *hesitant *]*

*[handwritten: good if, audience is hesitant]*

Developed by professor Alan H. Monroe, the **motivated sequence** is similar to the problem–solution structure, but adds several steps to get the audience involved (hence the label "motivated"), moving them to act on the proposal. This strategy is useful when your audience is hesitant to act on your proposal.

*attention getting* (handwritten)

The steps in the motivated sequence are attention, need, satisfaction, visualization, and action. Monroe knew that effective persuasion grabs the audience's attention. Use the techniques discussed in Chapter 7, including questions, rhetorical questions, startling statements, quotations, or stories, should be used in the **attention step** to hook the audience.

Like the problem step in the problem–solution structure, the **need step** in Monroe's motivated sequence identifies the audience's problem. Business speakers should detail quantifiable problems such as missed deadlines, substandard quality, declining profitability, or customer service. The motivated sequence includes four steps to develop the problem: (1) **state the specific problem**, (2) **illustrate** the problem, (3) **reinforce** the need with additional examples and statistics, and (4) **"point"** the problem to the audience by showing how it relates to them.

While convincing employees to give to the United Way, Anita developed her need step.

I. The problem is that our community lacks programs for the elderly.
   A. There is one program for elderly people on Saturday mornings at the Community Center.
      1. That's it!
      2. Each Saturday more than 50 seniors attend the center, happy to have someplace to socialize.
         a. It's the high point of Sarah Johnson's week.
         b. She said, "I'm so lonely during the week. And I hate being a burden to my family. I wish we had some other senior programs."
   B. Although bad now, the problem is only going to get worse in the future.
      1. Each year our community's senior population grows by 12 percent, or 120 seniors.
      2. There will be more people with no place to go.
   C. Our research indicates that next year more than half of our employees will be directly involved with this problem.
      1. They have elderly parents who also feel lonely.
      2. Some of you may even come to represent those statistics when you retire next year.

Notice that, in this example, the main idea states the problem, the first subpoint illustrates the problem, the second reinforces the problem, and the third points the problem to the audience.

The **satisfaction step** answers the question: What can be done to solve the problem? The satisfaction step is a two-stage process: (1) provide **support** for the claim that your plan will solve the problem, and (2) **address the objections** leveled against your plan. Anita's satisfaction step included supporting material from the United Way.

I. The United Way has plans to solve the problem I just described.
   A. Funds raised for this year's campaign are earmarked for a senior day-care center.
      1. The center will be a place for seniors to visit from 9:00 A.M. to 9:00 P.M. to do craft projects, join dance or exercise programs, and eat healthy meals.
      2. (Other supporting material.)
   B. One major objection to a senior day-care center involves the costs of building the center.
      1. Well, in our case, the solution is simple—the day-care center will be in an old elementary school, so the facility already exists.
      2. The United Way needs only $20,000 more to finish the renovations and furnishings.
   C. The objection to additional costs for upkeep is easily addressed because the center will be self-supporting.

D. Last year our company contributed $17,825 to the United Way. All we need to do is each commit $10 more a month, and we will have a new senior day-care center in our community.

Points B, C, and D address objections to the plan. We explain several strategies for refuting objections later in this chapter.

The fourth step in the motivated sequence is the **visualization step,** in which the speaker paints a visual picture of the future if the plan is adopted. Use vivid verbal descriptions, visual pictures, charts, and graphs to clearly illustrate the effects of your plan. Anita's visualization step included projections about the kinds of productive things seniors could accomplish at the day-care center, as well as illustrations from people who would benefit from the center. Specific projections and concrete examples make the audience more willing to adopt the proposal.

The **action step** moves the audience to adopt the proposal. The appeal to action should be as direct and specific as possible. For example,

II. Each of you received your United Way donor card in your paycheck this morning.
A. If you need another card, please raise your hand, and I will hand it to you now.
B. In the space marked "Amount to Contribute," consider writing $20 per month or a one-time donation of $240.
C. That's only $10 a month more than last year's average contribution.
D. Fill out the form and give it back to me by tomorrow. Let me know if I can answer any questions.

The outline for a motivated sequence proposal should follow this basic format:

INTRODUCTION
I. Gain attention
II. Justify the topic
III. Establish credibility
IV. Preview the main ideas
(Transition)
BODY
I. Need step
(Transition)
II. Satisfaction step
(Transition)
III. Visualization step
(Transition)
CONCLUSION
I. Review
II. Action step

### The N-A-R Structure

The **N-A-R structure,** which was first developed in ancient Greece, is named for its three key components: narrative, argument, and refutation. Like other structures, the introduction to the N-A-R should gain attention and establish credibility. Unlike other structures, however, the introduction should not justify the topic or preview the main ideas. The preview ruins the effect of the pattern by eliminating the element of surprise.

Much like a trial lawyer's opening statement, the **narrative** tells a story that emphasizes the speaker's interpretation of an event or situation. Most people are naturally interested in stories because they depict protagonists, antagonists, and a plot line. The narrative part of a proposal presentation must portray the facts in such a way that the speaker's preferred interpretation is emphasized. Compare these two stories:

1. Children at an elementary school have no playground equipment to play on. As a result, they occupy themselves in noneducational and sometimes dangerous games.
2. The "playground" is a big empty field. There is no playground equipment for the children to play on. Louisa stands ankle deep in mud, using a stick to draw pictures. Joey throws mud at Mickey and Sam. Three children stand a few inches from the busy street; one waves at cars that pass, while the other two push each other back and forth.

Although the first narrative is accurate, it does little to communicate Terry's concern for what she saw. The second story is also accurate, but its detail better depicts the speaker's meaning. Use detailed description, vivid language, and forceful delivery to emphasize your meaning in the narrative. Because hypothetical narratives are easily dismissed, use real, documented stories.

The third step in the N-A-R structure is the argument section. An **argument** is a line of deductive (or inductive) reasoning. The next section illustrates how to develop and strengthen arguments. Fourth, after the arguments comes the refutation section. **Refutation** addresses the objections to your proposal and is covered later in this chapter.

In the conclusion, the suspense is over, so the main ideas can be reviewed. In addition, the conclusion should make a call to action.

Because of its inclusion of a narrative, the N-A-R structure is appropriate for proposals that include dramatic testimonials or experiences. The emotional potential of the narrative makes it excellent for neutral audiences. Further, the argument and refutation sections allow speakers to both make their case and answer key objections. The outline for a proposal using the N-A-R structure should follow this format:

INTRODUCTION
I. Gain attention
II. Establish credibility
NARRATIVE
(Transition)
ARGUMENTS
I. Argument 1
(Transition)
II. Argument 2
(Transition)
REFUTATION
I. Refutation 1
(Transition)
II. Refutation 2
(Transition)
CONCLUSION
I. Review
II. Call to action

*and = undecided*

## The Balance Structure

Some proposals require you to address competing solutions and explain why your solution is superior. The audience for such proposals understands the nature of the problem but is undecided about solutions. For instance, a retail company may agree that the current antenna supplier is not working out but disagree about whether it's best to find another supplier or manufacture the antennas internally.

The balance structure eliminates all the competing solutions until only the speaker's proposal is left.[5] The introduction to the balance structure should grab the audience's attention and justify the topic. A credibility statement may also be included, depending on the audience. Because it detracts from the structure's persuasive power, do not include a preview of main ideas in the introduction. In the body, the presenter develops each alternative or solution by first acknowledging its positive attributes, because there are undoubtedly merits to each choice. Acknowledging positive qualities demonstrates your objectivity (hence the label "balance") and goodwill toward individuals who prefer the solutions you reject. After the positive qualities are cited, the majority of the time is devoted to demonstrating the plan's drawbacks.

*do NOT preview*

*be objective*

Once you have offered and indicted each alternative, develop your solution, by citing arguments in its favor. The audience will not know that this is your proposal. Next, mention some drawbacks to balance your presentation. Finally, state additional reasoning and evidence to support your proposal. To be effective, the speaker must clearly refute all of the reasonable alternatives. Thus Mario's proposal to become the new supplier of cell phone and CB antennas for an electronics retail chain must explicitly address and dismiss all the chain's alternatives. In the introduction, Mario briefly restated the problem: "We all agree that your current supplier is inept: Supplies are consistently back-ordered, the product is poorly manufactured, and returns are high." Mario then went on to eliminate alternatives, and concluded with his alternative.

BODY
I. One alternative is to discontinue this product line.
   A. This would obviously solve supply and return problems.
   B. However, it would do so at the cost of more than $300,000 of annual net profit.
   C. In addition, customers wanting this product would stop shopping in your outlets, possibly cutting into other sales as well.
   (Trans. I have spoken with some people in your company who favor another solution.)
II. You could get a new, more dependable supplier overseas.
   A. This solution is workable, and given the currency exchange rates overseas, the product could be acquired more cheaply than from the present supplier.
   B. However, delivery from most overseas suppliers has been less—rather than more—reliable than from your present supplier.
   C. Quality control on products from the presently available list of overseas suppliers is no better than the current supplier.
   (Trans. So, looking for overseas suppliers is not a viable alternative. What other solution is available?)
III. There is a new supplier available who is both dependable and of high quality.
   A. I am a dependable supplier, as my current clients will attest.
   B. My products have superior quality engineering.
     1. We have patents on designs to increase antenna range.
     2. We have two patents on methods to allow adjustable tuning.

**C.** Although my antennas cost a bit more, selling my antennas will actually increase your profits.

    **1.** The quality of the antenna is superior to any on the market.

    **2.** My dependable record ensures that you will always have what the customer wants in stock.

The outline for the balance structure should follow this format:

INTRODUCTION
   I. Gain attention
  II. Justify the topic
  II. Establish credibility
    (Transition)
BODY
   I. Option A
    (Transition)
  II. Option B
    (Transition)
 III. Option C
    (Transition)
 IV. Option D
    (Transition)
CONCLUSION
   I. Review
  II. Call to action

## Developing Persuasive Arguments

If the audience is to share your interpretation of the proposal, the members must hear adequate reasons and evidence. Imagine Tony suggesting that the city give his company a contract "just because." Without reasons, no one will adopt your proposal. The best proposals use a variety of reasoned arguments, both deductive and inductive, to support each claim.

### Deductive Arguments

A **claim** is a particular interpretation you want the audience to accept. Claims will not be accepted unless supported by some kind of reasoning. **Arguments** are lines of deductive or inductive reasoning that retrace your original thought process for the audience and answer the question: Why should the audience accept my claim?[6] **Deductive arguments** move from general principles to the application of those principles in specific cases.[7] If we know how two terms, concepts, events, or characteristics are related, we can discover other relationships that are logically implied.[8] We discuss three types of deductive reasoning in the following text.

***Causal Reasoning.*** **Causal reasoning** connects two events and claims that the second event is produced by the first. Common causal arguments include

Interest rate increases lead to declining home and car purchases.

Terrorist attacks and political instability in Saudi Arabia lead to higher oil prices.

Lower interest rates lead to increased consumer spending on large-ticket items such as homes and automobiles.

Causal reasoning should do more than state the linkage between events; it should also explain the way the causal connection operates. For example, the causal connection in the third example is as follows:

> Declining interest rates reduce the cost of borrowing money, which makes people more likely to invest in products that require loans.

There are three tests to check the validity of causal arguments. Use these tests to critique and strengthen your reasoning prior to delivering your proposal presentation.

First, the speaker should ask, *"Does a causal relationship really exist?"* Just because one event precedes another does not mean that the first event caused the second. Thus "I washed my car, so it rained" is invalid reasoning because car washing cannot cause a rainstorm.

Second, the speaker should ask, *"Is the cause sufficient to bring about the effect?"* The relationship between the two events needs to be significant. Thus the claim that "An increase in the price of potatoes for potato chips lead to nationally higher inflation" uses invalid reasoning.

Third, the speaker should ask, *"Could the effect result from other intervening causes?"* Although some events are related, there are often intervening causes that also account for the effect. Thus claiming the lack of cardiology equipment at the local hospital led to a higher-than-average death rate from heart attacks in the community is partly true, but the higher rate could also be related to the community's diet and exercise habits, individual heredity, hypertension, or age. The deaths do not result solely from the lack of equipment. Presenters strengthen their arguments when they demonstrate that the cause contributed significantly to the effect.

***Argument from Sign.*** **Argument from sign** is based on the idea that, when we see something, we infer that it represents or stands for the occurrence of something else. But, unlike causal arguments, reasoning from sign does not assume that the relationship between the two events is causal, only that they are related.[9] When a physician, for example, examines you and sees a red, irritated throat with white blotches, it is a sign of a bacterial infection. Look at these examples.

*Persuasive proposals are vital to the survival of most organizations.*

Credit: Bill Burke

Mario may argue that late deliveries, poor communication, and higher customer returns are a sign that the current antenna supplier is not interested in servicing small accounts.

When Jackie sees people driving 15 minutes downtown for coffee, she infers that the area will support a new coffee bar.

If signs always stood for something, then the connection between them would be certain. Unfortunately, this is not always the case. Simply because people drive downtown does not mean they will support a closer coffee bar. They may drive because the downtown bar is close to other work-related stops or because they like to get away from the office. Use the following three tests to strengthen your arguments from sign.

*First, is there another explanation that makes the relationship between events believable?* It's possible Jackie jumped to a conclusion when she decided that driving downtown means people will support her establishment. If there are reasonable alternative explanations for the signs, then the argument loses its strength.

*Second, are sufficient signs presented?* Signs come in clusters, so that various signs must consistently signify a relationship between things or events. If only a few signs are present, it may not signal the relationship. Seeing only a few antennas on the retail store's shelves may not signal problems with the supplier. It may signal a move to "just-in-time" delivery by the retailer. Such additional signs as poor service, inadequate supplies, and a high rate of return strengthen the conclusion about the supplier. Clearly, the more signs one has to draw on, the stronger the argument.

*Third, are contradictory signs considered?* Contradictory signs reduce the strength of the conclusion. For example, Mario may have failed to consider the popularity of the antenna and that no manufacturer could keep up with current demand. By considering and addressing contradictory signs, a speaker is better able to test the strength of the argument. The tests for causal argument, argument from sign, and syllogistic arguments are summarized in Figure 10.1.

**Syllogistic Arguments.** **Syllogistic arguments** involve three statements that lead the audience from general categories to conclusions about specific instances. These statements are referred to as the major premise, the minor premise, and the conclusion.

> *Major Premise:* All managers need to develop time management skills. *[handwritten: gen. assump]*
> *Minor Premise:* Olivia is a manager. *[handwritten: applies to specific case]*
> *Conclusion:* Olivia needs to develop time management skills. *[handwritten: links]*

*[handwritten left margin: Major / Minor / Conclusion]*

The major premise is based on an assumption or general principle. The minor premise applies the general principle to a specific group, person, or event. The conclusion links the major and minor premises by saying that what is true of the general class is true of the specific instance. Taken together, the statements form a line of reasoning that is clear and compelling.

Lacking complete data, leaders make decisions based on a variety of assumptions. These assumptions usually represent the major premise of a syllogism. The strength of the syllogism is based on the degree of certainty in its premises. If listeners accept the premises, they must accept the conclusion. The problem is that most business premises are far from absolute and may not be accepted by an audience. When they are built on probable rather than absolute certainties, syllogisms lose some—but not all—of their persuasive value. Speakers can compensate for some uncertainty by building on premises the audience shares. Thus knowing your audience is important to persuasive reasoning. Learn the three kinds of syllogisms to become a critical listener and persuasive speaker.

**FIGURE 10.1    *Tests for Causal Argument, Argument from Sign, and Syllogistic Arguments***

**Tests for Causal Argument**
1. Does a causal relationship really exist?
2. Is the cause sufficient to bring about the effect?
3. Could the effect result from other intervening causes?

**Tests for Argument from Sign**
1. Is there another explanation that makes the relationship between events believable?
2. Are sufficient signs present?
3. Are contradictory signs considered?

**Tests for Deductive Syllogisms**

*Categorical Syllogisms*
1. Three terms and only three terms may appear.
2. Each term must be used twice.
3. The middle term must be used in its universal or unqualified sense.
4. The middle term must be used for the second time in the minor premise.
5. At least one premise must be affirmative.
6. If one premise is negative, then the conclusion must be negative.
7. The major and minor premises must be accurate.

*Hypothetical Syllogisms*
1. The minor premise must either affirm the antecedent or deny the consequent.
2. If the minor premise denies the antecedent or if the minor premise affirms the consequent, no logical conclusion can be drawn from the syllogism.
3. The major and minor premises must be accurate.

*Disjunctive Syllogisms*
1. The major premise must include all reasonable alternatives.
2. The alternatives must be mutually exclusive.
3. The minor premise must eliminate all but one of the alternatives.
4. The major and minor premises must be accurate.

*Categorical Syllogism.*    The major premise of a **categorical syllogism** classifies without qualification, and is phrased with words such as *all, every, none,* or *no.* Mario structured the following syllogism to sell his antennas:

> *Major Premise:* Any company that holds patents for its products demonstrates superior engineering.
> *Minor Premise:* 10Com has several patents on this antenna.
> *Conclusion:* 10Com's antenna demonstrates superior engineering.

To evaluate a categorical syllogism, it's crucial to identify the major term, minor term, and middle term. The **major term** is the predicate term (the term acted on) in the major premise. It is usually the last term in the major premise ("demonstrates superior engineering"). The **minor term** is the subject of the minor premise ("10Com"). The **middle term** is the subject of the major premise ("Any company"). To test a categorical syllogism, apply the seven standards depicted in Figure 10.1.

1. Three terms and only three terms may appear.
2. Each term must be used twice.
3. The middle term must be used in its universal or unqualified sense.
4. The middle term must be used for the second time in the minor premise.
5. At least one premise must be affirmative.
6. If one premise is negative, then the conclusion must be negative.
7. The major and minor premises must be accurate.

Of these standards, number three causes the most confusion. Using a term in its universal sense means two things. First, the term must include all members of the class to which it refers. A logical syllogism cannot be created from the following middle term:

> *Major Premise:* Some businesspeople are unethical.
> *Minor Premise:* John is a businessperson.

Does John fall into the category of ethical or unethical businesspeople? We don't know. Thus, the middle term must cover all the members of the class.

Second, the middle term must accurately describe the individuals in that class.

> *Major Premise:* All businesspeople are unethical.
> *Minor Premise:* John is a businessperson.
> *Conclusion:* John is unethical.

Although structured properly, the middle term does not accurately describe individuals who belong to the class "businesspeople." The universal statement in the middle term must be accurate for the conclusion to be valid.

*Hypothetical Syllogism.*   The major premise of a **hypothetical syllogism** is concerned with uncertain or conditional instances and is phrased with words such as *if, when, assuming,* or *in the event of.* In Chapter 5, we emphasized the following hypothetical syllogism:

> *Major Premise:* If you have grammatical and typographical mistakes on your résumé, you probably won't be hired.
> *Minor Premise:* Tom has grammatical and typographical mistakes on his résumé.
> *Conclusion:* Tom won't be hired.

Testing the hypothetical syllogism involves two terms. The **antecedent term** is the "before term," usually linked to the "If," "Assuming," or "In the event of" statement ("If you have grammatical and typographical mistakes on your résumé ..."). The **consequent term** is the "after term," describing what will happen if the antecedent occurs ("you won't be hired"). To test the validity of a hypothetical syllogism, apply the three standards depicted in Figure 10.1.

1. The minor premise must either affirm the antecedent or deny the consequent.
2. If the minor premise denies the antecedent or if the minor premise affirms the consequent, no logical conclusion can be drawn from the syllogism.
3. The major and minor premises must be accurate.

When either of the first two standards is violated, we encounter the problem of necessary, but not sufficient conditions for the conclusion. Examine the following syllogism:

> *Major Premise:* If you have grammatical and typographical mistakes on your résumé then you probably won't get hired.
> *Minor Premise:* John has no mistakes on his résumé.
> *Conclusion:* John will get hired.

The minor premise denies the antecedent because it says that there are no grammatical or typographical errors on the résumé. But the conclusion does not follow from this reasoning. A clean résumé is a necessary—but not a sufficient—condition for getting a job.

*Disjunctive Syllogism.*    The major premise of the disjunctive syllogism presents alternatives, usually with terms such as "either . . . or," "neither . . . nor," or "but." Tony proposes that his company, Environmental Solutions, Inc., be given the town's residential trash collection responsibilities and includes this disjunctive syllogism:

> *Major Premise:* Either you use a private collection firm, or you will continue to run a budget deficit.
> *Minor Premise:* Give my company the contract to collect residential trash.
> *Conclusion:* You will stop running a deficit.

Test the strength of disjunctive syllogisms by applying the four standards depicted in Figure 10.1.

1. The major premise must include all reasonable alternatives.
2. The alternatives must be mutually exclusive.
3. The minor premise must eliminate all but one of the alternatives.
4. The major and minor premises must be accurate.

Examine the following disjunctive syllogism:

> *Major Premise:* Either you get a college degree, or you end up a useless bum.
> *Minor Premise:* You have said you will not go to college.
> *Conclusion:* You will be a bum.

There are several problems with this syllogism. First, all the reasonable alternatives are not included, because there are many life possibilities apart from going to college or becoming a bum. In addition, the alternatives are not mutually exclusive. Some people who go to college are still bums, and some who do not go to college are millionaires.

In organizations and interpersonal interactions, syllogisms usually appear as **practical syllogisms,** where one of the premises or the conclusion is not presented. Rather, the clarity of the reasoning is evident so that the audience supplies the missing information. Such arguments are very effective because they involve the listener in the reasoning process. For example, Mario might leave out the major premise of his syllogism, presuming the audience already shares this assumption.

> 10Com has several patents on this base station antenna. As such, our base station antenna demonstrates superior engineering.

The audience probably assumes that any company that holds patents has well-engineered products. Other syllogisms can be abbreviated in practical form.

- These cost-cutting strategies should be implemented because they save money.
- If you use my company for residential collections, you will stop deficit spending.
- Because John has mistakes on his résumé, it's doubtful he will be hired.
- If oil prices remain high, people will begin searching for alternative energy sources.

However, if there is any doubt that the audience shares your assumptions, state all the premises in the syllogism and support each with appropriate evidence. When listening to arguments from others, pay attention to the assumptions they use in their reasoning. Embedded in these assumptions are a series of claims that form a syllogism. Apply the tests for syllogisms to test that reasoning.

### Inductive Arguments    *Observation → gen conclus.*

Inductive arguments move from particular observations to general conclusions. Thus a report may cite the following finding:

> In an independent salary audit of 50 major corporations, male accountants were paid an average of 17 percent more than their female counterparts.

The speaker uses the statement to conclude that many corporations pay male workers more than female workers. Inductive arguments make a leap beyond the evidence to draw a conclusion that is more or less probable. The goal is to collect enough specific instances to establish a pattern. The tests for inductive arguments are depicted in Figure 10.2. We will discuss four types of inductive reasoning.

---

**FIGURE 10.2    *Tests for Inductive Arguments***

---

**Tests for Analogy**
1. Are the compared cases essentially alike?
2. Are the compared traits in the analogy accurate?

**Tests for Examples**
1. Are the examples typical?
2. Is the example relevant to the claim?
3. Are enough examples used to support the claim?

**Tests for Testimony**
1. Does the authority have expertise in the subject area?
2. Is the authority free from bias?

**Statistics**
1. Is the source of the statistic recent and valid?
2. Are the statistics based on an adequate sample?

---

*Analogy.*    **Analogies** are comparisons between two similar objects, events, instances, or people and suggest that what is true of one is also true of the other. If the audience accepts the similarity, then it will accept the conclusion. A consultant suggests that Jeffrey, the bank manager, use peak-time tellers to sell bank products and services. He supports his suggestion with the following analogy:

> First National Bank is similar to your bank in almost every way. It has branches in neighborhoods such as this one, it does similar volume, and its line of products and services is similar. It went to the peak-time process last year and has been very successful. The same process will work for you.

Use the standards depicted in Figure 10.2 to test your analogic reasoning. It's important to ensure that the comparisons are alike in the most critical characteristics. In the previous analogy, Jeffrey must consider whether the two banks are really alike. The consultant didn't mention an important area in which the two banks must be alike. If the part-time tellers at Jeffrey's bank are significantly less educated or motivated than the tellers at the other bank, it hurts the strength of the analogy and makes it difficult to determine if the plan will work.

It's also important to know whether the comparisons are accurate. If the products and services at Jeffrey's bank are really more complicated or less helpful to customers than at the other bank, it will be more difficult for the tellers to sell those products.

*Example.*    **Examples** are specific instances that illustrate a larger point. Arguing from example uses a specific instance to draw conclusions about a larger event or class. A story in the *Wall Street Journal* used several examples to argue that American citizens are more interested in "high culture" now than in the past.

> More than 110 American symphonies—including the Louisiana Philharmonic in New Orleans and the Northwest Symphony near Seattle—have been founded since 1980.
>
> Public radio stations, broadcasting a once exotic blend of classical music and introspective news, have more than tripled in number since 1980 to nearly 700.[10]

Use the questions in Figure 10.2 to strengthen your examples.

First, are the examples typical? Typical examples exhibit most of the traits of the larger class. Examples must not be extraordinary but should reflect a general trend to qualify as typical and sufficient. The inclusion of raw statistical information in the two examples helps ensure that they are typical.

Second, is the example relevant to the claim? Examples must also belong to the class about which the claim is made. Because sporting events are not considered high culture, citing increased attendance at such events is not relevant to the claim that Americans are more cultured than in the past.

Third, are enough examples used to support the claim? To support its claim, the *Wall Street Journal* provided numerous additional examples, ranging from attendance at theatrical presentations to book sales.

*Testimony.*    **Testimony** is a direct quotation by or paraphrase of witnesses, experts, or other informed sources. Arguing from testimony assumes that an idea is valid because it's supported by an authority on the subject. Tony used testimony to support his bid for residential trash collection.

> According to Brant Brown, mayor of nearby Fairfield, "Since having our trash collected by Environmental Solutions, Inc. our municipality has saved $25,000 over the projected savings."

The tests for testimony are found in Figure 10.2. As shown in that figure, to be valid a source must have credentials related to the topic. Citing a mayor with no experience with private trash collection is meaningless.

It's also important to consider the self-interest of the authority to understand the relative degree of bias. Positive comments from your own company's CEO won't bolster a claim because he or she wouldn't make anything but positive claims. On the other hand, **reluctant testimony** defines the rare instance when a person does say something against his or her self-interest. Because of that negative impact, reluctant testimony is very persuasive.

Quoting sanitation officials in the city who agree that switching to Environmental Solutions, Inc., will save money is strong, because it works against self-interest.

*Statistics.*     **Statistics** are a collection of individual examples delivered as raw numbers or averages. When arguing from statistics, we assume that what is true of the collected data can be extrapolated to similar circumstances where no data were collected. Tony should use statistics to quantify the savings the city can achieve by contracting with Environmental Solutions.

> Based on my work in two similar communities, my proposal will save you from 12 to 20 percent each year.

Contrary to the common axiom "Numbers speak for themselves," numbers cannot talk. As such, statistical information must be interpreted for the audience. Tony can translate his numbers into concrete terms to show the audience how large his projected savings really are.

> That means that every person's bill would decrease an average of $12.50 per month, resulting in savings of $150.00 per household per year. I think you'll agree that this is significant.

Figure 10.2 includes tests for statistical evidence. As you can see, statistics must be recent to be valid. The professional world turns quickly, and statistics rapidly become outdated. Cite the source and date of your statistics and use recent information to avoid undermining your point.

Statistics must also be based on adequate samples, and it's important to know how the sample was gathered, as well as its size. Tony cited his sample size—two cities—in his presentation.

Effective proposals support their claims. If you suggest that your proposal is the best because it increases profitability, reduces overhead, and promotes better employee relations, you must demonstrate the claims with good reasoning and evidence. Strong proposals also anticipate and refute audience objections.

## Refutation Tactics

Three of the four persuasive structures carve out space for answering the audience's objections. **Refutation** is an argument that addresses and eliminates objections to the proposal. Use the questions under "Meaning" in the Audience Analysis Checklist (Figure 6.4, p. 114) to learn about the audience's objections.

Lead the audience into a refutation by stating the audience's objection in a phrase, and then state your response in a phrase. For instance,

I. I know that many of you resist the city's proposal to go to automated garbage collection trucks because it's too expensive, but this perception is untrue.

II. I know that some are against the proposal to expand our operation because of the health risks to nearby communities, but I assure you that the risks are infinitesimal.

Although there are many ways to address objections, we will introduce four of the most common strategies. **Denial** counters an objection by saying it is not true. In his proposal to change travel authorization procedures, Ramon anticipated the key argument against his suggestion and stated, "Although some are concerned that this idea will require more paperwork, this is untrue."

The **minimization** strategy suggests the counterargument is true, but that its significance in relation to other issues is minimal. Mario may refute the objection that his antennas cost more by demonstrating that quality and dependability outweigh the higher price.

A very powerful refutation technique is **exposing inconsistent statements,** beliefs, or actions by the opposition. Demonstrating inconsistency undermines the opposition's credibility, thereby bolstering your case. People believe that words and actions should be consistent. For instance, Anita may point out that, although her coworkers pay lip service to supporting the community, declining donations reflect indifference. Truly caring people should contribute more to United Way.

**Turning the tables** suggests that, although the objection is accurate, it actually supports rather than denies your proposal. "Indeed," the salesperson said, "the Lexus or BMW is an expensive automobile, but that is what makes it distinctive." As such, the cost becomes part of the product's appeal.

Think of each refutation strategy as a label for a claim, and like any claim, it needs inductive and deductive reasoning for support. It is usually impossible to address all the objections to your proposal in a single presentation. Although easy to accomplish, refuting weak objections isn't persuasive, because the audience will still have strong reasons for opposing your proposal. Therefore, select the two or three strongest objections and address those.

## *Outlining Your Points to Show Logical Relationships*

Structuring your arguments can be challenging because there are many different ways to outline an argument. Sometimes your main idea is a single claim supported by a single line of reasoning. For example, examine the following claim in the motivated sequence outline:

I. You should stock 10Com's CB antennas because they demonstrate quality engineering.
  A. Any company that holds patents for products demonstrates superior engineering.
  B. 10Com has several patents for this CB antenna.
    1. Example of patent
      a. Advantage of patent with syllogism or cause–effect reasoning
      b. Advantage of patent with syllogism or cause–effect reasoning
    2. Example of patent
      a. Advantage of patent with syllogism or cause–effect reasoning
      b. Advantage of patent with syllogism or cause–effect reasoning
  C. 10Com's CB antenna demonstrates superior engineering.

In this example, the main idea makes a single claim, and the three subpoints constitute a practical syllogism in support of the claim.

  In other cases, the main ideas make several claims, and the subpoints support each claim.

> **II.** You should carry 10Com antennas because they demonstrate quality engineering and excellent quality control, and we guarantee rapid, on-time delivery.
>  **A.** 10Com CB antennas demonstrate quality engineering.
>  **B.** 10Com exercises superior quality control for its CB antenna.
>  **C.** At 10Com, we guarantee rapid and timely delivery.

In this example, the main idea makes three claims, and each subpoint supports each claim.

  If the reasoning to support a claim requires extensive explanation, it's useful to use a main idea for each claim.

> **I.** 10Com's CB antennas demonstrate quality engineering.
>  (Extensive supporting material)
> **II.** 10Com exercises superior quality control.
>  (Extensive supporting material)
> **III.** 10Com guarantees rapid and timely delivery.
>  (Extensive supporting material)

  Finally, claims are usually stated before supporting reasons and evidence. Listeners may easily get lost as the steps of an argument unfold, and evidence and reasoning are added. To avoid confusion, restate your claim as an internal summary at the end of a main point.[11]

> **II.** 10Com exercises superior quality control of its CB antennas.
>  (Extensive deductive and inductive reasoning for support)
>  (*Internal Summary:* For the reasons just mentioned, 10Com exercises superior quality control on its CB antennas.)

Logical organization helps lead the audience to the "correct" interpretation and increases the chances of shared meaning. Once the logic of an argument is understood and articulated, you need to consider speaker credibility.

## Developing Effective Credibility Appeals

*[handwritten annotation:] Competence = knowledge*
*Credibility = Trustworthiness + dynamism*

Audiences respond not only to the arguments people make, but also to the person making the arguments. If the audience doesn't believe you, then even the best arguments are irrelevant. **Credibility** is the audience's perception of the speaker's competence, trustworthiness, and dynamism. **Competence** is the audience's perception of the speaker's knowledge and expertise on the topic. If the audience is unaware of your competence or, worse yet, believes that your reputation is poor, steps must be taken prior to and during the presentation to improve these perceptions. Have someone introduce you who will tout your experience and expertise. Use the credibility step in the introduction to enhance your competence, and demonstrate your competence by knowing your subject and providing evidence of your research. When challenged about the effectiveness of his travel changes, Ramon included testimony from reputable accounting firms about the desirability of his proposal. The testimony beefed up audience perceptions of Ramon's competence. Cite only those sources the audience views as credible. Tari Jensen's sample speech in Figure 10.3 works to build audience perceptions of her competence on the subject.

**FIGURE 10.3** *Sample Proposal Presentation*

Consumer Protection and Contractor Licensing

By Tari Jensen

| | |
|---|---|
| Topic: | Contractor Licensing |
| General Purpose: | To persuade |
| Specific Purpose: | To persuade the audience to support a contractor licensing law. |
| Main Idea: | I will persuade the audience that a public works license will protect consumers and that there are no legitimate objections to licensing. |

## INTRODUCTION

   **I.** In Idaho it is sometimes said that, if you have a dog and a truck, you are a contractor. Contractor licensing has been the subject of debate in the Idaho legislature for many years. Pocatello and Idaho Falls are the only cities that require a license. I propose that anyone involved in new construction or remodeling work be required to have a public works contractor's license. A public works contractor's license will protect consumers and increase the respectability of the construction industry.

   **II.** My name is Tari Jensen, and I have been involved in the construction industry for over twenty years.

     **A.** Our company is named Jensen Bros. Builders.

       **1.** We build ten to twenty residential homes per year.

       **2.** We have gross annual sales of $1.5 million to $2 million per year.

     **B.** I have been president of the Building Contractors for Southeast Idaho and received the state association's Builder of the Year Award for 1995.

     **C.** To prepare this speech, I interviewed Dave LeRoy, the past attorney general of Idaho; Dave Wilson, the national representative for the Building Contractor's Association for the State of Idaho; Evan Frasure, our district's senator; and Jack Robinson, a local real estate attorney. I read and reviewed many articles and books from the ISU library, the Marshall Public Library, and trade magazines.

(Trans: Let me tell you a story about a local family that wanted to start a business in residential construction.)

## NARRATIVE

This family decided to start a new business. All of their hopes and dreams for a better life were wrapped up in this goal. They wanted to become log home dealers. The log home dealership would set the logs, and the family would finish the structure. This family sought a contractor who was willing and able to finish the homes.

The gentleman they found started the foundation of the first home in May 1995 and committed to finishing in October. On October 31, the home was not near completion. Cursory inspections of the incomplete home revealed numerous flaws. In the middle of December, the contractor left a note on the door saying he quit. The mother of the family told me that she felt as if she had been raped by the contractor.

This family borrowed more than $50,000 above their original bank loan on credit cards to finish the house. The general contractor declared bankruptcy.

Two years and thousands of dollars over budget, the family finally moved into their first log home. A public works contractor's license would have prevented this situation because their contractor would have been disqualified to bid on the log home job because he lacked the appropriate financial solvency. The license would have protected this contractor from getting in over his head and would have prevented the embarrassment and devastating losses this project cost. The family would not have hired the man and had their dreams butchered by someone lacking the proper skills, qualifications, and financial backing.

**FIGURE 10.3    *Continued***

---

*Definition:* A public works license law was written many years ago to certify contractors who work for the state on publicly owned projects. The "Public Works Contractor's License Act" handbook states, "The Board believes the legislature in providing the License Act and subsequent amendments thereto, intended to afford some protection [for the state] .... A 'Public Works Contractor' shall give to the investing public body some assurance of the contractor's reputation, ability, qualification, experience, and financial responsibility." (24)

(Trans: There are two main arguments in support of using the existing public works contractor's license law in residential construction.)

**ARGUMENTS**

I. A public works license would protect consumers by documenting a contractor's ability, qualification, experience, and financial responsibility.
   A. Licenses are granted to contractors based on their good reputation among peers, bankers, and the bonding company (Public 12).
   B. Licenses are granted on a graduated scale according to financial solvency, which protects the consumer by making sure the person hired can afford to pay damages.
      1. The amount you are allowed to bid on is determined by your financial statement.
      2. The law allows a maximum net worth of $300,000 and liquidity of $60,000, and a minimum net worth of $10,000 and liquidity of $2,000 (Public 27–28).
   C. The license requires an examination, which ensures that the contractors know the law and the penalties for violating the law.

(Trans: Not only will licensing protect consumers, it will protect contractors too.)

II. A public works license will protect small contractors (the "little guys") entering the industry.
   A. Construction is a very complicated industry, and a contractor needs vast knowledge to survive.
      1. Would we allow someone to calculate the trajectory of a spacecraft, which requires complicated trigonometry, before he or she has learned to add and subtract?
      2. In a complex industry, it is necessary to learn the business one step at a time, not by taking on all the steps at once.
   B. We must regulate by creating a graduated scale of qualifications, reputation, skills, and knowledge.

(Trans: So, if licensing will protect the consumer and help the "little guy" succeed, what could be wrong with this proposal?)

**REFUTATION**

I. The first objection to licensing is that it increases government regulation, but this is inconsistent with the facts.
   A. The State of Idaho requires that, before you do construction work for any publicly owned property, you must have a public works license.
      1. If the state needs protection with licensing, then citizens need protection with licensing.
      2. Residential construction should also require licensing.
   B. Professional money managers such as stockbrokers, bankers, real estate agents, and insurance agents must be licensed.
      1. If construction workers handle a lot of money, they should also be licensed.
      2. This leads me to a passage in *Modern Real Estate Practice,* which says, "Buying a home is usually the biggest financial transaction in a person's life. The home buyer pays out more cash, undertakes more debt, and has a deeper personal interest in this transaction than any other purchase made during his or her lifetime" (p. xvii). [As you can see, contractor licensing is consistent with licensing requirements for people who handle public money and for people who manage large amounts of other people's money.]

(Trans: Government regulation is one objection to licensing, but there are other objections.)

*(continued)*

**FIGURE 10.3**  *Continued*

II. Others say that this restriction prevents the "little guy" from entering the construction industry; I argue that these restrictions will actually help the "little guy."
  A. The public works license does restrict the "little guy" by limiting the jobs he can do according to his ability to pay for possible damages.
    1. But it also prevents him from getting in too deep too fast.
    2. A law would create a loose apprenticeship by encouraging the "little guy" to start out where he can afford to pay for losses.
    3. As his solvency increases, so could his license.
  B. Limiting competition to businesses that can afford to cover damage is not bad, because it protects the "little guy" from judgments from which he could not recover.

(Trans: So, if we agree that licensing would protect the "little guy," we need to look at how much this process will cost.)

III. The third objection is the expense of creating a new agency and writing a new law, but costs can be cut by using already-existing laws and agencies.
  A. Modifying the public works license law to fit residential builders would be easy and inexpensive.
  B. The Public Works Licensing Board already exists and could be modified to license residential builders.
    1. The board would require only additional secretarial help to handle the increased license volume.
      a. Gaylord Lake, at the Public Works Licensing Board, told me that he has tried to get this law amended and applied "statewide for years and would encourage [me] in this endeavor however he could."
    2. The city and county building departments already collect information for permits and would merely add a requirement to see proof of license when a builder buys a building permit.

(Trans: Because the costs to implement this law are minimal, let's look at the last objection.)

IV. Finally, some say that the industry is not in favor of licensing, but this is inaccurate.
  A. The Idaho Building Contractor's Association, which has well over 1,500 businesses as members, has written, sponsored, and lobbied for licensing for over ten years.
  B. The full-time, legitimate contractors in the industry see the problems created by unskilled, inexperienced, and underfunded part timers and have begged for rules and legislation (Allen 3).
  C. When I interviewed Dave LeRoy, Dave Wilson, and Evan Frasure, they said that the main objectors against licensing are the part-time contractors. These are the very people in need of protection and from whom consumers must be protected.

(Trans: If we review the objections against licensing, we see that they are not persuasive and that modifying the public works license is an effective solution to the problem of fly-by-night contractors.)

**CONCLUSION**

I. To create regulations for the single most expensive purchase consumers make in their lifetime seems only sensible.
  A. The regulation will not prevent newcomers from entering the industry, but would force them to enter at a level they can afford and protect the consumer in the process.
  B. It is not expensive or difficult to implement this law.
  C. The full-time, qualified, knowledgeable, experienced, and financially solvent contractors are united in favor of this law.
II. We should never allow the heartache, frustration, and years of suffering that happened to our family in Pocatello happen to anyone else in the state of Idaho ever again.

**DISJUNCTIVE SYLLOGISM**

*Major Premise:*  We can either take the costly approach and develop a new agency to enforce the law or we can use an existing agency at low cost.
*Minor Premise:*  Creating a new agency is too expensive.
*Conclusion:*  We should use the existing agency.

**FIGURE 10.3** *Continued*

---

## CATEGORICAL SYLLOGISM

*Major Premise:* We regulate people who work in complex jobs that control or manage a lot of money for individual citizens.

*Minor Premise:* A contractor's job is complex, and they control the largest investment most citizens ever make.

*Conclusion:* Therefore, contractors should be regulated.

## HYPOTHETICAL SYLLOGISM

*Major Premise:* If the state feels the need to protect its own financial affairs from inexperienced and insolvent contractors, then citizens should also be protected.

*Minor Premise:* The state has enacted laws to protect itself from inexperienced and insolvent contractors.

*Conclusion:* Laws should be enacted to protect the citizen from inexperienced and insolvent contractors.

---

**Trustworthiness** is the audience's perception of the speaker's honesty, objectivity, fairness, and concern for the audience. Perceptions of trustworthiness can be improved by establishing common ground with the audience. Let audience members know you share their values and understand their goals. Trustworthiness can also be increased by demonstrating objectivity. Focus on a variety of sources rather than a single source. Use unbiased authorities for your research and acknowledge the benefits of competing proposals.

**Dynamism** is the audience's perceptions of the speaker's energy, confidence, and enthusiasm. Although good listeners focus on speech content, it is difficult to follow a monotone presentation. Audiences view dynamic speakers as concerned, committed, and confident. It's easier to persuade an audience to commit to a proposal if you demonstrate your commitment with a dynamic presentation style.

## Developing Effective Emotional Appeals

Effective proposals include emotional appeals. Emotional appeals encourage active listening and make listeners more willing to complete practical syllogisms. A persuasive proposal may wish to arouse a variety of emotions:

| | |
|---|---|
| envy | pride |
| fear | dread |
| compassion | anger |
| shame | security |
| commitment | frustration |

Decide on the emotional responses you want from the audience, and use the following techniques to enhance these responses.

Emotions can be aroused through **emotional examples** and **effective delivery.** Use vivid stories to help the audience identify with the topic. Alexis used the following example to get her audience emotionally committed to giving money for new cardiology equipment at her hospital.

> Can one person really make a difference in a community? Sue Finch did. Sue Finch represents what many of us would like to be—one who gave of herself to help others live better lives. She volunteered at the local homeless shelter, spoke as a child advocate in court proceedings, and belonged to the Optimist Club, where she was the driving force behind scholarships for entering college freshmen. Sue Finch celebrated her 44th birthday on August first. And on August fifth, Sue died tragically of a heart attack. The real tragedy is that Sue's death could have been prevented if our community had a heart catherization machine. But we don't have one, and Sue died as many of us watched—helplessly. Sue's death was not an isolated one. Fully 75 people in our community die each year from similar heart failure. With your support, we could help reduce that significant number.

Alexis used emotional images of service and volunteerism to create a picture of an upstanding, ethical community member. She then used **vivid language** such as "tragedy" and "helplessly" to emphasize the sorrowful nature of the death. The **descriptive detail** of Sue Finch's contributions further raises emotional awareness and involves the audience in the tragedy.

## Summary

Persuasive proposals should create shared meaning by persuading others that whatever you have to offer is the best solution to their problems. The problem–solution structure and Monroe's motivated sequence articulate a problem or a need and provide specific solutions. In the N-A-R structure, the narrative tells a story that emphasizes the speaker's meaning for the issue, problem, or situation. The arguments and refutations offer inductive and deductive support for the proposal. The balance structure eliminates competing solutions until the speaker's proposal is the only one left.

A claim is any interpretation a speaker wants the audience to accept. Arguments are lines of deductive or inductive reasoning that retrace your original thought process for the audience. Causal arguments connect two events and claim that the second event is produced by the first. When we infer that one thing or event stands for the occurrence of something else, we are arguing from sign. Syllogistic arguments involve three statements that lead the audience from general categories to conclusions about specific instances. The categorical syllogism classifies without qualification. A hypothetical syllogism is concerned with uncertain or conditional instances. The disjunctive syllogism presents alternatives, all but one of which are logically eliminated.

Inductive arguments move from particular observations to form general conclusions. Inductive arguments make a leap beyond the evidence to draw a conclusion. Analogies are comparisons between two similar objects, events, instances, or people and suggest that what is true of one is also true of the other. Examples are specific instances that illustrate a larger point. Testimony is a quotation by or paraphrase of a witness, expert, or other informed source. Statistics are a collection of individual examples delivered as raw numbers or averages. Refutation addresses and eliminates objections to the proposal. Four kinds of refutation are denial, minimization, exposing inconsistent statements, and turning the tables.

Credibility is the audience's perception of the speaker's competence, trustworthiness, and dynamism. Use examples, vivid language, descriptive detail, and effective delivery to raise emotional support for your proposal.

## Questions and Exercises

1. Which of the four structures identified here (problem solution, Monroe's motivated sequence, N-A-R, and balance) would you use for the proposal presentations described at the beginning of this chapter? Consider the topic, the audience, and the types of arguments for each presentation.

2. Describe the advantages of proposals that include only one kind of argument (e.g., argument from sign, causal argument). What are the disadvantages of reliance on a single line of argument?

3. Describe the advantages of deductive reasoning over inductive reasoning. Why are well-constructed deductive reasons more convincing than inductive reasons? What prevents speakers from relying exclusively on deductive reasoning for persuasion?

4. Many theorists, both ancient and modern, believe that credibility is the most important kind of persuasive appeal. Is this true in your opinion? Why or why not?

5. Read each of the following practical syllogisms. For each statement: (a) structure the statement as a complete syllogism; (b) identify the type of syllogism it represents; and (c) apply the appropriate tests to determine its validity.

   - Of course he supports lower taxes; he's a Republican.
   - If you major in accounting, you are assured a job when you graduate.
   - Mary is a racist because she opposes affirmative action in corporate hiring decisions.
   - If a company makes a poor product line, it will go bankrupt, and Techware has poor products.
   - The damage the hacker did to your computer system indicates its vulnerability.
   - The movement of goods is the lifeblood of the economy. If the movement is cut off because of a trucker strike, the economy will collapse.

   - Rather than fire the employee, I guess we'll provide the remedial training he needs to do the job.
   - The governor is unethical because he actively deceives the public about policy initiatives.
   - This oil improves gas mileage because it includes silicon additives.
   - The ability to persuade others is vital to your career.

6. Look for the practical syllogisms in the sample speech in Figure 10.3. These can be found by scanning for assumptions (usually the major premise of a syllogism) or conclusions the author draws. Draw out the entire syllogism by writing the major premise, the minor premise, and the conclusion. Compare your syllogisms to the three the author drew out at the end of the speech. Did you find additional syllogisms? Apply the logical tests described in this chapter to the syllogisms. Are they logical and persuasive? Why or why not?

7. Examine the sample speech in Figure 10.3 for causal arguments, arguments from sign, and arguments from analogy, statistic, testimony, and example. Apply the tests to each argument. Is each argument persuasive? Why or why not? Overall, are you persuaded by the arguments in this presentation? Why or why not?

8. Examine the credibility appeals in the sample speech in Figure 10.3. How do the various credibility appeals affect your perceptions of the speaker's competence and trustworthiness? Do you see the speaker as credible? Why or why not?

9. Examine the refutation strategies used in the sample speech in Figure 10.3. Label each of the strategies the speakers uses to refute objections. How persuasive are these refutations? Why?

## *Notes*

1. Beck, C. E., and K. Wegner, "Toward a Rhetoric of Technical Proposals: Ethos and Audience Analysis," *Technical Communication* 39 (1992): 122.
2. Rosenbaum, B. L., "Making presentations: how to persuade others to accept your ideas," *Supervision,* May 1992, 9.
3. Blake, G., "It Is Recommended That You Write Clearly," *Wall Street Journal,* 3 May 1995, A24.
4. Fulscher, R. J., "A No-Fail Recipe: Winning Business Proposals," *Journal of Property Management,* January/February 1996, 62.
5. Ryan, H., *Classical Communication for the Contemporary Communicator* (Mountain View, CA: Mayfield, 1992).
6. Sprague, J., and D. Stuart, *The Speaker's Handbook* (Fort Worth, TX: Harcourt Brace, 1996).
7. Ziegelmueller, G. W., and J. Kay, *Argumentation: Inquiry and Advocacy* (Boston: Allyn Bacon, 1997).
8. Sprague and Stuart.
9. Ziegelmueller and Kay.
10. Blackmon, D. A., "Forget the Stereotype: America Is Becoming a Nation of Culture," *Wall Street Journal,* 17 September 1998, A1.
11. Sprague and Stuart.

# 11

## *Sales Presentations*

Without sales a business will eventually close its doors. Sales presentations can take many forms. Commercial advertising on radio, television, newspapers, and the Internet are all forms of the sales presentation. Retail selling, from small shoe stores to large automobile dealerships, requires sales presentation skills. Businesses make sales presentations to other businesses when, for example, a laundry service acquires a contract to clean linens for a large hotel chain.

Because commercial advertising is a specialized field, it is not considered in this book. Nor is retail selling, which represents informal, interpersonal communication. Instead, we focus on **sales presentations** between organizations, where a salesperson persuades a business to buy products or services for use in the business or for eventual sale to retail customers. Such presentations may be given to a single person or to a group responsible for corporate purchasing. The salesperson's goal is to create shared meaning so that the receiver shares the sender's interpretation of the product or service. This is achieved through thoughtful strategic and tactical choices.

We begin this chapter by discussing the significance of sales presentations in business and the professions. Second, we address audience analysis for sales presentations. In Chapter 1, we said that effective communication requires the ability to adapt to audience needs and concerns, and nowhere is this more vital than in selling. Next, laptop computers and graphics software give salespeople the ability to create appealing, interactive presentations that can be adapted to meet the needs of individual clients. The content of sales presentations must contain

**215**

persuasive logical, credible, and emotional appeals. Finally, the chapter closes with a discussion of the delivery qualities required in selling and structures specific to the sales setting.

## The Significance of Sales Presentations in Business and the Professions

On any given day, salespeople make thousands of sales presentations to a variety of industries. Large manufacturing outfits hear numerous presentations encouraging them to buy raw materials and equipment for manufacturing, office supplies for daily operation, contracting services to retool areas of the plant, and consulting services for the company's management. In other cases, salespeople try to convince wholesale and retail outlets to carry their products. Companies such as Hallmark and Radio Shack, to name just two, must purchase merchandise that they do not manufacture themselves. Small retailers in your town hear a variety of sales presentations from suppliers of business or retail goods and services. Even government agencies and social service organizations are becoming more customer oriented.

Moves to privatize government mean that agencies such as your city's water or sanitation department may be forced to bid for city services against for-profit businesses. In the city of Indianapolis, almost all city services except police and fire protection are put up for bid. If city departments want to provide services and employ their people, they must make competitive sales presentations.[1] Cities, counties, and states compete fiercely for new manufacturing plants or to persuade organizations to schedule conventions in their communities. For example, Marcy Roitman, the national sales manager for the Grapevine, Texas, Convention and Visitors Bureau, works to recruit convention business to Grapevine. A typical presentation is to the American Society of Law Enforcement Trainers to sell her small town as a convention and training site.[2] As such, sales presentations have become vitally important to local and state governments.

Sales situations come in two varieties. In a **one-time buy**, a company or government agency preparing to make a large purchase (new software, mainframe computer, new manufacturing process for an entire plant) lines up potential suppliers to hear their presentations. Suppliers present before large audiences, all of whom are involved in the purchase. The presentation team might include members of the sales staff, the marketing department, and engineers and other technical support staff. Competition for these sales is usually intense, requiring months of research and preparation.

When companies buy parts or supplies crucial to their day-to-day process, they make **continuing requirement purchases.** Manufacturing plants need raw materials such as steel, natural gas, or calcium carbonate to produce their products. Companies that make things such as autos and airplanes contract with outside suppliers for the parts they include in their finished goods, and every organization needs desks, chairs, computers, copiers, fax machines, and basic office supplies to maintain its operations. If purchases are small, like many office supplies, sales presentations are made over the phone or through the Internet. The purchasing agents will not spend much time assuring rapid delivery or top-quality products; instead, price is the most salient quality. For other purchases, however, so much is riding on the arrangement that sales aren't based on presentations, but depend on the salesperson's ability to establish a relationship of trust with the client. Today's manufacturing processes are so tightly scheduled that late delivery will grind production to a halt. Inferior materials can cost the company millions in backlogged production and product recalls. Buyers may be putting their careers on the line when they switch from one supplier to another, and they won't commit if they don't trust the salesperson who makes the promises.

Gaining the buyer's trust often begins with a **cold call**, a first-time visit or telephone call from a salesperson to a potential customer. The goal for a cold call is to find out who controls the purchase and to meet, at least briefly, with that person.

The most important thing to remember about cold calls is that you will receive a lot of rejections, and some of those may not be very friendly. But, even the most successful sales-people in the world receive many more turndowns than orders. "The only people who act a little short [with you] will be those who don't need what you sell anyway, so why let that bother you?"[3]

If the product you sell is a commodity (natural gas, coal, gasoline), then someone in the purchasing department probably controls the buy. If, on the other hand, the product is a technical item with strict specifications, an engineer or other technical person is usually in charge, as well as an assistant plant manager or purchasing manager.

After the cold call, the salesperson's goal is to ingratiate herself with the person who controls the purchase and keep peripheral members positive about, or at least neutral to, the buy. This can happen only if the potential client believes the salesperson is trying to help him save money or solve a problem. To create this kind of relationship, the salesperson must call on the client every few months to discuss improvements in the product, recent price cuts, or lab results that confirm the product's value. When you visit with the prospect, try to learn a little about his or her personal life. Is he or she married? Does he or she have children? What sports does he or she play? Is the client an avid gardner? A birthday card for the client, a souvenir hockey puck for his or her daughter, or an article on gardening are nice gifts that help create a connection with the prospect. If several clients offer approximately equal products, the relationship you develop with the prospect may make the difference. The interview in this chapter discusses the importance of creating relationships with clients.

As your relationship with a purchasing agent develops, stay in touch with occasional e-mails or phone calls that provide new information about the product. The salesperson should also work to neutralize potential opposition from others involved in the purchase. This means keeping the purchasing manager or assistant manager up-to-date about your activities in the organization. If you schedule plant trials or product tests, let the purchasing manager know what you are doing. Even the lowliest persons in the purchasing department can wreck your sale if they become angry or aren't kept informed.[4]

In today's era of global competition, it's more difficult than ever to form a relationship with prospects. For many continuing requirement purchases, the liability involved in changing from one supplier to another is enormous, and people simply refuse to put their career on the line for minor benefits. The salesperson must prove the product is truly superior. Getting people to even speak with a salesperson is difficult. Staffs have been cut, and layoffs mean that many managers are doing the job that two or three people did only five years ago. In addition, companies are ferocious about defending their customer base. If another firm knows you are investigating its client for a sale, it may immediately drop its prices, sign the client to a long-term contract, or develop quality improvements to keep the business. Convincing people that you have real value to sell is more difficult than ever before. The techniques we articulate in this chapter are designed to give salespeople a competitive edge in an increasingly cutthroat business climate.

## BOX 11.1 • *Interview: Tony Ciampa (Global Market Manager for the Automotive Business, Lord Corporation, Erie, Pennsylvania)*

(Lord is a supplier of adhesives, coatings, and shock, noise, and vibration control devices to various aerospace, industrial, and commercial manufacturers.)

*Give me an overview of the sales process.*

There are two basic components to the sales process. The first is the mechanics of making a sale. Mechanics involves preparing what you want to say, which can involve preparing literature, brochures, or PowerPoint presentations. Most of these materials make a case for your product based on its technical specifications.

*How do you adapt your presentations to the client's needs?*

To meet the client's needs you must go through a process of investigation by asking the potential client what technical parameters the product needs to meet. You may ask the client to send samples to your lab for testing to see how your product performs with their materials. In other cases, this involves taking a site tour with your own company's technical people to get a better handle on how the parts or product are used in the manufacturing process.

*Are companies generally forthcoming with this information?*

Sometimes they are very up front. If you ask them questions they will give you all the information you need. However, some industries, like the auto industry, are more secretive because they've developed processes or techniques that are revolutionary and they don't want the competition to learn about their innovations. They know we deal with their competitors and no matter how much any company promises confidentiality, there's always a chance that information could leak back to competitors. In such cases, the salesperson has to take a different approach. I find that questions that pose alternatives may work. For example, if I was trying to learn about the requirements one of my adhesives has to meet, I might ask, "Is this a short-cycle drying period (high temperature, short drying time) or a long-cycle drying period (low

temperature, long time)?" This way, the client can give me the specific response I need without giving away too much about the larger process.

*So these questions give you a handle on the prospect's needs?*

Yes. It's also important for the salesperson to understand the "values" the customer needs in the product and sell those values as part of the sales equation. You need to know what the client's "hot button" needs are. Is reliable delivery important? Do they care that you have continuous quality improvement in your production process? Is the firm trying to make its products more environmentally friendly? Do they need a global company that can supply product no matter where the prospect's manufacturing operations are located? If these are the values the company desires, then these are the elements of the company or product the salesperson must pitch to that client.

*What's the second element of the sales process?*

The second element is the human element. You have to establish your credibility with the customer. If you can't sell yourself first, you're going to have a hell of a time selling your product. You can establish your credibility by staying in touch. If you tell a client you're doing a lab test and you'll report back on the 10th, and there is a delay, don't ignore the issue. Call the client back and say you promised the 10th, but the lab is tied up and it will be a few days later. That's usually all the person wants to know. Salespeople must also avoid overpromising anything in terms of delivery or technology. If you promise something and don't deliver, that kills your credibility.

In addition, it's important to take time and find out something about the people you are dealing with. Are they married? What hobbies do they have? If you find an article related to the person's hobby in an airline magazine, copy the article and send it to the client with a nice note saying you remembered their interest and thought they might find the article interesting. I think that electronic cards for birthdays or anniversaries are a nice way to make contact. Some people say this stuff is fake, but if you work with a person long enough, it usually becomes sincere. Of course, no matter what kind of relationship you have, you won't get the sale if you can't solve a problem for the client.

*Can you give me an example of a big sale you made that incorporated the two elements of the sales process?*

In the auto industry, car doors are made of stamped metal. The outside shell of the bottom of the door is wrapped up and around the inside shell, and the two pieces are welded together at the bottom. Welding has several key problems. First, even the best robots are inconsistent. Second, every weld spot is a point that is susceptible to corrosion. Finally, you can't weld aluminum or composite materials, which companies are using to reduce the weight in their vehicles. We approached one of the big three U.S. auto companies to try to get them excited about using adhesives as a replacement for the welds on car doors. It took several years of study, trial runs, data analysis, and persuasion to convince them to spend thousands and thousands of dollars on robots, safety equipment, and health measures for employees. Today, our adhesives are all this manufacturer uses for its hem-flange bonds. Now, the other two car companies have begun using the same approach. That was a $6- or $7-million-a-year sale for our company.

*What's one of the largest problems young people encounter when they are learning to sell?*

A lot of young people never ask for the order. They get all the way to the end, they're feeling good, and they say, "I'll call you in a week." When they do call back, the prospect says, "We started using a competitor's product." Instead, the salesperson needs to ask, "When do we start shipping the product?" Salespeople must remember to get a commitment and to follow up.

## *Audience Analysis for Sales Presentations*

Conrad Levinson, author of the internationally acclaimed book *Guerrilla Marketing,* advises salespeople to "Identify a need your prospect has and be certain you can fill it."[5] Michele Marchetti, writing for *Sales & Marketing Management,* says that the preparation to understand audience concerns will undoubtedly take more time than the actual presentation. Failing to analyze the prospect for particular needs can result in presentations that are ill suited for the client.

> That was a mistake that Joan Mariani Andrew, vice president of sales and marketing for Chicago-based Bell & Howell Document Management Product Company, made for the first time and last time. Her first presentation—a "data dump" of everything she learned in sales school—consisted of samples, detailed flip charts, and an elaborate speech about the quality of the product. Although the prospects thanked her for a thorough sales presentation, she lost the sale because they could not see how the product fit the company's individual needs.[6]

A study of face-to-face selling in the construction industry indicates that salespeople who were able to adapt their presentations to the three client types served by this industry—government agencies, large private developers, and small one-time buyers—were more successful than salespeople who did not change their proposals for each client segment. The authors conclude that

> there appears no substitute for salespeople with adaptability skills. Adaptable salespeople are sensitive to different buying situations. They pick up cues from buyers and adjust their selling behavior. Less adaptable salespeople do not possess this sensitivity.[7]

The ability to analyze and adapt to audience needs is a vital component in sales presentations. In this section we present two means of assessing audience concerns for sales presentations: asking questions and using metaphors. Used together, these methods provide powerful insight into the needs and interests of the audience.

## Asking Questions

As we learned in Chapter 6 on audience feedback, asking questions is an effective means of understanding and adapting to your audience. The direct approach helps salespeople in two ways. First, direct questions help salespeople find **qualified prospects**—potential clients who have the need, interest, and financial resources to purchase their product or service.[8] Although making calls on unqualified prospects is not necessarily a waste of time (altered business circumstances may change a prospect's needs), qualified prospects are the source of most sales. Figure 11.1 provides a partial list of questions for screening prospects. If, by asking these questions, the salesperson learns that the prospect company is unaware of his or her product, then the persuasive task is to introduce it as a solution to a particular problem. If, on the other hand, the organization needs the product but can choose from several competing brands, the salesperson's task is to distinguish his or her product from the competition.

Audience analysis does not end after prospects are screened. Sales presenters must analyze the situational features and listener predispositions toward the product. Use the Audience Analysis Checklist in Figure 6.4 (p. 114) to fit the presentation to audience needs.

## Listening for Metaphors

Whereas asking questions requires overt interaction with potential clients, **listening for metaphors** is a more subtle means of gaining insight into a prospect's thinking. **Metaphors** suggest that some object or event is to be understood as if it were another object or event; for example, "American Airlines is the on-time *machine.*" Although neither the people nor the physical, mechanical, and informational resources of American Airlines are a machine, the metaphor encourages us to think of the airline as if it were. Through the metaphor, the company wants us to associate American with the reliability and predictability of a machine. Metaphors structure how people perceive themselves and their surroundings.

**Similes** are very much like metaphors but include "like" or "as" in the phrasing "American Airlines is like an on-time *machine.*"[9]

According to marketing professors Robert W. Boozer, David C. Wyld, and James Grant, some business metaphors reflect the perceptions of competitiveness in that business or industry. For example, an industry can be thought of as war (we need to *capture* market share and gain

**FIGURE 11.1**    *Questions for Qualifying Sales Prospects*

1. What are your needs or problems?
2. Is your organization considering the kind of product or service we offer?
3. Why are you considering or not considering this kind of product or service?
4. What criteria does the product or service have to meet?
5. What performance standards are required of this product or service?
6. What criteria tend to be most influential for decision makers?
7. Has anything changed since the last time we talked?

back *lost territory*), a game (we need to get out of this *inning without losing* any more market share), a machine (a *breakdown* caused that delivery problem), an organism (we need to *grow* our marketing department), or a conduit (information *flow* is not sufficient in sales).[10] A second category of metaphors reflects one's personal experience working in the organization (we are a *family* here; this place *grinds* careers to chopped liver).

Listening for metaphors provides a basis for "talking the customer's language."[11] If the customer is at war, then your product or service is a weapon. If the organization is an organism, then your product or service is nitrogen that is vital for growth. If the organization is a machine, then you can fix broken or damaged parts. By skillfully employing direct questions and paying attention to metaphors, salespeople can learn to qualify potential customers, learn about their needs and interests, and understand the perceptions under which they operate. Adapting to these needs and perceptions is the core of effective selling.

## *Visual Aids for Sales Presentations*

The past few years have seen enormous growth in visual aid technology for presentations, some of which was detailed in Chapter 8. Nowhere has the growth of this technology been more evident than in sales presentations, where the use of high-tech visuals is almost mandatory. Without repeating what was covered in Chapter 8, we highlight several technologies commonly used in face-to-face or group sales presentations.

A **sales videotape/DVD** can demonstrate a product in a controlled manner that communicates precisely what the company wants to communicate.[12] The downside however, is that watching a screen is a passive rather than an active experience. A video/DVD may also interfere with the dialogue the salesperson tries to establish with the client. As a result, sales videos/DVDs should be less than five minutes in length. Because they can be easily adapted to the needs of each client, they are best used as a "leave-behind" for clients to examine at their leisure.[13]

Computerized multimedia sales presentations take the basic PowerPoint program covered in Chapter 8 a step further by adding text, audio, graphics, video footage, and spreadsheets. The computer presentation can be used in a face-to-face presentation, with the salesperson sitting beside the client, or in larger presentations with the computer linked to an LCD projector.

Organizations now customize their PowerPoint presentation to include background information about the product, competitive data, price lists, delivery schedules, product specifications, research statistics, spreadsheet performance data, and even video testimonials from satisfied customers.

Like any technological innovation, computers have produced problems for some salesforces. Many companies give only minimal control of the content to the salesperson, preferring instead to have their own or an outside graphic arts department create the presentation. If the salesperson can't adapt the program to individual clients, the presentation becomes less effective. Other critics believe salespeople rely too heavily on the new technology, losing some of their important persuasive skills in the process. Betsy Wiesendanger, senior associate editor at *Sales & Marketing Management,* says that electronic presentations have in some cases

> become a cloak that hides poor selling skills or a straitjacket that constricts spontaneity. A whole new generation of salespeople is cropping up for which learning to fine-tune the video monitor is as important a skill as asking probing questions or overcoming objections. . . . It means you need to stop thinking about your presentation as a series of visuals and start thinking about what you can say or do to meet a particular client's needs.[14]

**FIGURE 11.2**    *Criteria for Testing the Usefulness of Sales Visual Aids*

1. Does the visual aid broaden experience by demonstrating a process or object that can't be demonstrated in any other way?
2. Does the visual aid improve client information retention?
3. Does the visual aid simplify complicated information?

Computer-generated visual aids and video demonstrations are no substitute for a solid relationship with the client, persuasive content, and the ability to respond to audience objections.

Jack Falvey, a contributing editor at *Sales & Marketing Management,* recommends that salespeople ask themselves the following question before adding any visual aid to their presentation: "Does the visual contribute to (and not interfere with) the selling process?"[15] Once you have decided to include visual aids in your presentation, check each slide or visual against the three criteria in Figure 11.2. If an individual slide or visual cannot meet all three criteria, it should be removed from the list. Use visual aids carefully for the greatest persuasive effect in sales presentations.

## Content Considerations for Sales Presentations

Image is *not* everything! The content of a sales presentation is vital. Because selling is simply a specific kind of persuasion, the techniques covered in Chapter 10 are applicable to most sales presentations.

In this section, we explore some techniques for developing customer trust (an element of the salesperson's credibility), and discuss argument methods specific to selling.

Michelle Nichols, writing for *BusinessWeek,* says, "When salespeople lament that they didn't win the big sale they thought they deserved, the reason is often because the customer had more trust in another vendor."[16] Nichols's five methods of building customer trust are summarized in Figure 11.3.

**FIGURE 11.3**    *Methods to Build Customer Trust*

| Method | How to Make It Work |
|---|---|
| Build trust in your company | Keep paper or digital copies of certificates, licenses, or awards your organization has achieved and make the client aware of these by including them in the presentation. |
| Build trust in your products and services | Fold testimonial letters or videos into your sales presentation that describe how problems were solved or sales increased because of your product or service. |
| Build trust in you | Be on time to all meetings. Meet all communication and delivery deadlines. Provide the products or services you promised. Quickly and efficiency solve problems. Apologize for problems that are your fault (see Chapter 13). |
| Build trust in your marketing | Don't exaggerate advantages or short-sell problems in any of your sales and marketing materials. |
| Build trust in your industry | Watch for articles in respected media that tout the progress or benefits of your industry. Fold these into your sales presentation. |

Developing a clear, specific purpose statement is vital for sales presentations. As you recall from Chapter 7, a specific purpose statement is not the subject of your presentation, it is what you want your listeners to remember or do as a result of the presentation. Many salespeople fail because they begin presentations with elaborate detail about company history or product development. James E. Lukaszewski, an organizational consultant, encourages people to "Always put your communications objective or message first. Then support the objective with an appropriate amount of additional information and detail."[17]

The meat of any sales presentation is in its arguments. Josh Gordon, president of Gordon & Associates, a publisher's representative firm in New York, says the sales pitches that succeed are the ones that offer proof for their claims.[18] Proof, of course, involves solid inductive and deductive arguments as described in Chapter 10.

Lukaszewski recommends that deductive arguments avoid merely listing features of the product or service. **Features,** he argues, are things that the salesperson or company that made the product care about. Arguments should be made about the **benefits** the product or service provides the customer.[19] Focusing on benefits helps the salesperson select deductive arguments appropriate for the prospective customer.

There are three different kinds of continuing requirement purchases that companies or government agencies make, and each suggests different benefits. As we stated earlier,

*Trust is vital for effective sales presentations.*
Credit: IndexOpen

a **commodity purchase** is a product that is essentially undifferentiated from one supplier to the next. Because all the suppliers produce essentially the same thing, the only benefit the salesperson can highlight is low price. Unfortunately, commodity prices are in a deflationary race to the bottom. Every company is cutting its process to the bone and reducing its prices to customers. Manufacturing and selling commodities is one of the most challenging jobs in modern business.

**Specialty products** are technically different from competitors' products. These are often easier to sell because the salesperson can talk about various benefits (price, quality, technical superiority) that differentiate his or her product from the competitors'. If these features are important, the client may be willing to pay more for the product. To sell specialty products, the salesperson must match the key benefits of the product to the client's needs.

Finally, **systems products** require the organization to spend money not only for the product, but also for special machinery or equipment needed to use the product properly. For example, in the interview in this chapter, Lord Corporation was able to sell one of the big three auto manufacturers on its adhesives, but to apply them properly, the manufacturer needed to make additional investments in robots, safety equipment, and employee health measures. To sell systems, the salesperson must be able to show that her product and its accompanying equipment will create a measurable improvement in the buyer's process.

Examples are valuable inductive reasoning tools for selling. Relevant examples drawn from industries similar to the prospective client's are useful because they force the salesperson to talk in terms of benefits to the customer.[20] **Stories** are a valuable form of example in sales presentations. The psychological process of being caught up in a story resembles becoming engaged in a film or novel. The narrator includes good characters who arouse sympathy, who are pitted against bad characters or circumstances that must be defeated. The conflict creates suspense because the outcome is in doubt.[21] To create an intense response, stories should be nontechnical and focus on the actions and emotions of people.

A Roadway Express ad in the *Wall Street Journal* describes a furniture warehouse manager who had to move an entire order to a trade show in Kansas City at the same time he needed an emergency appendectomy. In this case, time and the manager's health are portrayed as the enemy eventually conquered by Roadway's efficient customer service staff. A picture of the warehouse manager and the Roadway staff member are also included to create greater identification with the "good guys." In oral presentations, stories engage an audience and provide an opportunity for the salesperson's personality to shine through.

Metaphors can help communicate the intangible qualities of a product or service.[22] For example, the Roadway Express ad begins with the metaphor "Once again, Roadway beats the clock" and pictures a semi truck in front of a stopwatch. The reader is encouraged to think of business as a race or sprint in which time is the sole measure of success. Roadway is fast enough to "beat the clock" and help customers win the race. To be successful, metaphors must communicate pleasing and attractive associations to the customer.

Finally, multimedia allow salespeople to tailor engineering, cost, and performance statistics for each customer. Spreadsheets allow customers to examine various operating scenarios and the results of each in productivity, power costs, energy savings, and pollution reductions. The adaptable nature of these tools is what makes them so persuasive.

Despite misconceptions suggesting that businesspeople are rational decision makers, emotion is a powerful and persuasive force in sales communication. Almost all organizational decisions involve a host of emotions—from exhilaration, pride, satisfaction, and excitement to anxiety, worry, dread, and escape.

According to Joel D. Whalen at DePaul University, the effective salesperson must diminish three common fears before the customer will purchase a product or service. People fear that they will not get what they were promised, they fear that they will pay too much, and they fear that other people in the organization will criticize them for buying your product or service.[23] Building a strong personal relationship with the client can reduce fears of being "taken." Relating objective performance data or a list of satisfied customers can also build faith in your company. The refutation tactics in Chapter 10 can be used to ease a client's fear of paying too much for the product or service. To counter the fear of criticism, Whalen suggests "inoculating" the client against the arguments of others by stating counterarguments (objections) that the client is likely to hear and refuting these arguments. The client will then have a series of arguments to make if criticized. As you can see, advances in sales technology have not lessened the need for strong content in the sales presentation.

## *Delivering the Sales Presentation*

**Enthusiastic delivery** is vital for effective sales presentations. In Chapter 7 we emphasized that great delivery depends on an attitude of respect for your listeners and enthusiasm for the topic. Dynamic delivery also contributes to audience perceptions of dynamism, which improves perceptions of credibility. There are several delivery issues that relate directly to sales presentations. Our delivery tips for sales presentations are listed in Figure 11.4. Good delivery means being **extemporaneous.** Working from notes rather than a script allows the presenter to immediately adapt to audience concerns. Extemporaneous delivery produces an informal quality that is difficult to duplicate with a script. No matter how many times the presentation is delivered, it must look as if it is being presented for the first time. A scripted performance will lead others to assume they are hearing a canned presentation. **Spontaneity** is more easily generated from an outline than from a script.

Also remove all vocalized pauses from your speech patterns, such as "um," "ahhh," and the like. Vocalized pauses are annoying to listen to and indicate hesitation and a lack of confidence. Practice removing vocalized pauses from daily conversation, which usually translates into similar reductions during formal presentations.

Finally, don't hide your intention to sell a product or service; make it clear what you want at the beginning and the end of the speech. Ask for the order when you close a sales presentation.

**FIGURE 11.4** *Delivery Tips for Sales Presentations*

1. Use extemporaneous delivery from notes rather than reading from a manuscript.
2. Create a sense of spontaneity, so that clients believe this is the first time you are giving the presentation.
3. Pace yourself appropriately and speak every sentence with its appropriate meaning.
4. Eliminate vocalized pauses from your speech.
5. Cite common experiences to establish common ground with the audience.
6. Be direct; don't hide your persuasive intent.

# *Structuring the Sales Presentation*

Many consultants argue that the most persuasive sales presentations first arouse awareness of a problem, describe a need, or present an unsatisfactory situation, followed by a step that (through the use of the salesperson's product or service) resolves the problem, satisfies a need, or corrects an unsatisfactory situation. As you recall, this two-step process of creating and fulfilling a need is the basis of several patterns including the problem solution structure and Monroe's motivated sequence. As such, these are ideal structures for many sales presentations. Of course, other structures can be equally useful. The N-A-R structure works by providing an engaging narrative at the beginning of the presentation and the refutations to inoculate clients against objections. The balance structure is useful for audiences who know the full history of the problem.

Another structure developed by one of your authors is the Make-a-Claim-and-Prove-It pattern. As the label suggests, each main idea in the sales presentation is a claim about the benefits of the product, and inductive and deductive reasoning support the claim. For example,

    **I.** Vuarnet sunglasses protect your eyes from the sun's radiation better than any other pair of glasses on the market.
        **A.** The sun emits large amounts of short wavelength or ultraviolet radiation.
        **B.** Ultraviolet rays damage the eyes faster than any other kind of light.
            **1.** Exposure to ultraviolet light can cause temporary loss of vision, cataracts, and blindness.
            **2.** According to Richard Young, professor of anatomy at the University of California Medical School, we should "choose glasses with the most ultraviolet protection."
            **3.** To protect our eyes against ultraviolet rays, the lenses of our sunglasses should cut off 380 nanometers of ultraviolet rays.
        **C.** Vuarnet sunglasses ranked higher than any other glasses in the amount of ultraviolet rays eliminated from the eyes.
            **1.** Researchers found that the Vuarnet eliminated up to 470 nanometers of ultraviolet light.
            **2.** This was 60 nanometers higher than the second best pair of glasses.
    (*Internal Summary:* As these independent assessments verify, Vuarnet glasses protect your eyes far better than any other pair of glasses on the market.)

Notice how the main point of this example makes a bold statement about the product's superiority. The subpoints then demonstrate that superiority through extensive reasoning. The complete body of the Make-a-Claim-and-Prove-It structure could look like this:

### *Introduction*

### *Body*
    **I.** First assertion about the product
        **A.** Support
        **B.** Support
    **II.** Second assertion about the product
        **A.** Support
        **B.** Support

   **III.** Third assertion about the product
       **A.** Support
       **B.** Support

*Conclusion*

To conclude, structure is a vital part of any sales presentation. Good structure is equated with the ability to lead an audience to the conclusion you desire.

# Summary

Sales presentations are vital for many businesses and government agencies. Sales situations come in two varieties: one-time buys and continuing requirement purchases. Questions can be used to qualify prospects. Metaphors are a less overt means of adapting to prospects' needs. Multimedia aids are also common and may include background information on the product, competitive data, price lists, delivery schedules, product specifications, research statistics, spreadsheet data, and "live" testimonials from satisfied clients. Good visual aids do not lessen the need for strong content.

Presentations should focus on the benefits of the product or service to the customer. The only benefit a commodity seller can point to is price. Specialty products and systems purchases are easier to sell because the salesperson can talk about various benefits. Testimony from satisfied customers adds impact to a presentation. Stories are dramatic examples that arouse interest and sympathy in the audience. Metaphors can help the salesperson communicate the intangible elements of a product or service and software can tailor statistical data for each customer. Salespeople need to reduce three common fears among clients: the fear that they will not get what they were promised, the fear that they will pay too much, and the fear that others will criticize them for buying the product. Good delivery is spontaneous in that it sounds as if the presentation is being given for the first time. The Make-a-Claim-and-Prove-It structure makes a series of claims and supports each with persuasive reasoning.

# Questions and Exercises

1. Whether it was an appeal to buy a car, take home a new washer and dryer, purchase the latest pair of Nikes, or buy something over the phone, everyone has heard sales presentations. Discuss with your class some of the sales pitches you have heard recently. Did you purchase or refuse to purchase the product or service? What was the source of this purchasing decision? Were the visual aids and the delivery appropriate and persuasive? Did the salesperson effectively employ appeals to logic, credibility, and emotion? What would you have done to make the sales presentation stronger?

2. Think of the last time you heard a sales presentation and refused to buy the product or service.

Could anything the salesperson said have induced you to buy this product or service? Were you a qualified candidate? Describe the specific things that make a prospect qualified. When is it best to cease sales attempts to unqualified prospects?

3. Think of a product or service that could be sold to members of your class. As a group, develop several objections to purchasing this product or service. Brainstorm possible refutation strategies to each of the objections. Which strategies will be the strongest for each objection? Why?

## *Notes*

1. Jeter, J., "Indianapolis May Have Found a Way to Turn Lead into Gold," *Washington Post,* 29 September 1997, National Weekly Edition.

2. Yarbrough, J. F., "Toughing It Out," *Sales & Marketing Management,* June 1996, 81–84.

3. Tate, T., "Cold Calls: Don't Dread This Effective Sales Tool," *Sound and Video Contractor*, May 2004, 26–27.

4. DiSanza, R. A., telephone conversation with first author, 3 September 2001.

5. Levinson, J. C., "Show Time: Creating Presentations That Pay Off," *Entrepreneur,* February 1997, 90.

6. Marchetti, M., "That's the Craziest Thing I Ever Heard," *Sales & Marketing Management,* November 1995, 77–78.

7. Withey, J. J., and E. Panitz, "Face-to-Face Selling: Making It More Effective," *Industrial Marketing Management* 24 (1995): 245.

8. Kennedy, D., "Screen Test," *Entrepreneur,* August 1996, 84–87.

9. Boozer, R. W., D. C. Wyld, and J. Grant, "Using Metaphor to Create More Effective Sales Messages," *Journal of Consumer Marketing* 8 (1991): 59–67.

10. Koch, S., and S. Deetz, "Metaphor Analysis of Social Reality in Organizations," *Journal of Applied Communication Research* 9 (1981): 1–13.

11. Boozer, Wyld, and Grant, 62.

12. King, A., and K. Fischer, "Sales Videos Put You in Control," *Business Marketing,* August 1991, T10–T11.

13. Falvey, J., "Does Your Company Need First Aid for Its Visual Aids?" *Sales & Marketing Management,* July 1990, 97–99.

14. Wiesendanger, B. "Are Your Salespeople A-V Junkies?" *Sales & Marketing Management,* August 1991, 58.

15. Falvey, 99.

16. Nichols, M., "Five Ways to Build Customer Trust," *BusinessWeek Online,* 2006, Academic Search Premier (http://search.ebscohost.com)

17. Lukaszewski, J. E., "Bridging the Communication Gap," *Sales & Marketing Management,* August 1991, 62.

18. Gordon, J., "Making a Sales Presentation Work," *Sales & Marketing Management,* March 1992, 91–93.

19. Lukaszewski.

20. Ibid.

21. Bormann, E. G., "Symbolic Convergence: Organizational Communication and Culture," in *Communication and Organizations: An Interpretive Approach,* ed. L. L. Putnam and M. E. Pacanowsky (Beverly Hills, CA: Sage, 1983), 99–122.

22. Boozer, Wyld, and Grant.

23. Whalen, J. D., *I See What You Mean: Persuasive Business Communication* (Beverly Hills, CA: Sage, 1996).

# 12

# *Risk Communication*

According to William D. Ruckelshaus, former head of the U.S. Environmental Protection Agency, the American public and its elected representatives must eventually "abandon the impossible goal of perfect security and accept the responsibility for making difficult and painful choices."[1] Eating meat, sitting in front of a computer screen, living near a large manufacturing operation, rock climbing, driving, smoking, eating fish from polluted lakes, nuclear power, and pollution, all entail a certain degree of risk.

In a society filled with risks, the science of risk assessment has developed to quantify the various tradeoffs people consider. **Risk communication** is any communication about uncertain physical or environmental hazards.[2] The field of risk communication has developed as a relatively new communication specialty in the larger fields of communication, public relations, and public administration. As such, risk communication is practiced by people employed in large business firms, by regulators such as the Environmental Protection Agency (EPA), and by government agencies at all levels. For example, in a southeastern Minnesota city, the development of a waste-to-energy incinerator was preceded by an extensive risk communication program.[3] In Los Angeles, the construction of an aeration tower to strip contaminates from the groundwater entailed public involvement to explain the risks and benefits of the proposal.[4]

Risk communication is a burgeoning new field, with many opportunities for people skilled in presenting complex technical information and in effectively leading small groups. This chapter provides an important foundation for future learning and practice. The best way to learn about risk communication is to participate as an interested member of the public. We therefore encourage you to involve yourself in risk communication in your community.

This chapter opens with an overview of the importance of risk communication in business and government. We then briefly explain the process of risk analysis, with an emphasis on its benefits and weaknesses. Third, we examine what leads audiences to fear some risks and ignore others. The fourth section covers the many credibility challenges that risk communicators must overcome during a risk campaign. Finally, we close with a discussion on specific strategies for successful informative and persuasive risk communication.

## The Significance of Risk Communication in Business and Government

According to M. Granger Morgan at Carnegie Mellon University, "Americans live longer and healthier lives today than at any time in their history. Yet they seem preoccupied with risks to health, safety, and the environment."[5] Many industry and elected representatives believe the public suffers from a poor sense of perspective, forcing industry and government to spend billions to reduce minuscule hazards. We believe quite the opposite: that most people's concerns about risks are legitimate.

First, many of the diseases we face are more frightening than ever. Dying from cancer is neither painless nor pretty, and few have been able to avoid losing a family member or friend to the disease. Previously unknown diseases, including SARS, West Nile virus, mad cow disease, and avian flu-H5N1, crop up with alarming frequency. Even worse, medical science is often unaware of the exact cause of many diseases. Did a cancer death in your family stem from smoking, poor diet, pollution, radon gas, or a genetic predisposition to the disease? Not knowing precise causes only increases our fear.

Second, our fear of a hazard is amplified by the interconnection we all share as residents of this planet. Interdependence means that the actions taken in one time and place can have consequences to others at distant times and places. During the spring of 2003, an outbreak of SARS that originated in China spread to Toronto, resulting in hospital quarantines and serious harm to the tourist industry. Thus, our risks often increase or decrease without us ever knowing about or having a voice in the decision, and this increases our concern.

Finally, the complex nature of technology isolates decision making among a small group of technically proficient people, closing the lay public out of choices that affect their lives. We fear that which we do not understand and resent technical elites who make decisions without our consent. All these factors, and many more, legitimately increase our fears.

The federal government recognizes these concerns and has tried to make itself more accountable to the public. For example, the "Community Right to Know" provision of Title III of the Superfund Amendments and Reauthorization Act of 1986 mandates increased communication among all parties affected by environmental risks.[6] The Emergency Planning and Community Right-to-Know Act, also part of Superfund, dictates that the public be provided with information about hazardous chemicals in the community and establishes emergency planning and notification procedures to protect the public from the release of those chemicals.

Finally, Executive Order 12898, Environmental Justice in Minority Populations, mandates that the government carefully consider and report environmental and human health risks to minority or low-income populations posed by an agency's activities or policies.[7]

Three factors make any communication about uncertain physical or environmental hazards very complicated. First, despite its foundation in the scientific discipline of risk assessment, risk communication is inherently value laden. A sophisticated risk analysis may be able to provide accurate estimates about the chances of a nuclear reactor meltdown, but no scientific risk analysis can answer the next question: Is the need for electrical power great enough and our concern about pollution and global warming from coal-fired plants severe enough to justify building more nuclear power plants? Although the scientific analysis of risk involves **questions of fact** (exactly how much risk does an activity present?), the act of deciding on which risks to embrace and which to avoid are **questions of value.** As we learned in Chapter 4, people debate values in political forums in order to work out solutions to complex problems.

Second, because it deals with values, risk communication is filled with **conflict.** People who do not share the same values will not agree on the risks to be approached or avoided. Although secure employment is, for example, more important to some than the pollution exposure they and their family suffer from a manufacturing facility, others reject that risk out of hand. In fact, it is entirely possible that risk communication campaigns will increase rather than decrease conflict as community members state their divergent beliefs.

Finally, despite its tendency to create conflict, an open process of risk communication is still the most effective means of making complicated risk decisions. To remain democratic, our society must find ways to put technical information into the service of public choice. According to Marjorie G. Shovlin and Sandra S. Tanaka, employees of the Metropolitan Water District of Southern California, "Public participation is the key to community acceptance of projects and positions. In order for people to support a project or position on an issue, they must be satisfied with the process by which the decision is made. This usually requires that the affected community have a voice in the decision-making process."[8] This does not, however, mean merely informing the public about a decision that has already been made. According to Peter Sandman, a noted expert in risk communication, community participation must come before the research stage, before the experts have assessed the risks, and certainly before any preferred solutions have been discussed. "This sort of genuine public participation is the moral right of the citizenry. It is also sound policy."[9] When the public is involved, individuals show a surprising ability to master technical details and work their way through appropriate solutions. The next section explains the science of risk analysis.

## The Scientific Process of Risk Analysis

**Risk analysis** is a relatively new science designed to provide quantitative estimates of the health and environmental risks posed by various hazardous substances and processes. In this section we explain the goal of risk analysis and then review the uncertainties always present in this science.

### The Goals of Risk Analysis

Although it is beyond the scope of this chapter to explain the many intricacies of risk analysis, it's important that students of risk communication understand how risk scientists attempt to quantitatively measure the risk posed by a particular hazard or measure the costs or benefits of a specific risk.

Many risk studies assign a single number to the exposure level to a particular hazard and map the linear relationship between that exposure level and its consequences. For example, to describe the increased risk of cancer due to cigarette smoking, a scientist might set an exposure level of ten cigarettes a day and, after extensive study, conclude that this level of exposure increases the smoker's chances of contracting lung cancer by a factor of tewnty-five. A twenty-cigarette-a-day exposure level increases the chances of lung cancer by a factor of 50.2.[10]

Other studies analyze aggregate risks across large populations. The basic formula for calculating risk for a specific population is

Potency of a particular hazard × the number of people in the affected population = risk

The EPA has concluded that if the nation could meet a stricter PM-2.5 standard of 15 micrograms per cubic meter of air (a 50-percent reduction from the current standard), it would produce the following results: 4,000 to 17,000 fewer premature deaths and 63,000 fewer cases of chronic bronchitis.[11]

Finally, other forms of risk analysis examine the costs of reducing a risk. For example, while critiquing the EPA's proposed standards on ozone, the Center for the Study of American Business calculated that every dollar of benefit derived from ozone reduction provisions in the 1990 Clean Air Act costs consumers and taxpayers $3.30 to $5.10 in increased charges and regulatory expense.[12]

Based on risk assessment studies, Figure 12.1 explains and assesses the actual risks of five commonly encountered hazards. Each hazard is explained and the specific risks it poses are cited. In the final column, the relative risk is assessed with a judgment (low, medium, or high) about the **likelihood** that individuals will be exposed to the hazard, and the population-wide **consequences**—in terms of both severity and number of victims—of the risk. The assessments presented in Figure 12.1 may surprise you.

Most of our information about risk comes from three major risk sciences. The first of these is toxicology, which studies the effects of poisons on human health. Because toxicologists cannot test poisons on humans, animal tests are used as substitutes. Epidemiology, the second science, studies what is currently going on in the population and tries to make sense of which hazards and exposure levels might be associated with various negative consequences. For example, epidemiological studies have examined air-pollution records and hospital-admissions data in various communities and found that admissions for respiratory ailments increase for several days following the pollution increase. This finding leads them to conclude that the pollution *probably* caused the respiratory problems. This example also illustrates one of the primary limitations of epidemiology; it can only provide associations rather than absolute cause-and-effect proof that exposure to a hazard leads to a particular result. Finally, statistical analyses cull existing data sets for risk information. For example, auto accident data kept by the government can offer rich details about how many people are injured or killed in motor vehicle accidents, which might lead to risk calculations for the relative risks of death in autos versus SUVs. However, because government and industry statistics are general, they suffer from imprecision, which makes clear conclusions difficult to draw.[13]

## Risk Analysis as an Inexact Science

Although risk analysis has improved enormously in the past twenty years, it remains an inexact science. The sources of imperfect knowledge in risk analysis are numerous. To begin with, toxicity studies have not yet been done on a majority of industrial chemicals now in use in the United States. The financial resources do not exist to conduct all the studies that are needed.

**FIGURE 12.1** *Explanation and Assessment of Common Hazards*

| Hazard | Explanation | Risk | Assessment |
|---|---|---|---|
| Genetically modified foods (sometimes referred to as Frankenfoods) | Genes for particular traits from one species are inserted into another, different species to produce a particular result. Examples: a gene from a flounder is inserted into a strawberry to improve its resistance to cold. Genes for pest resistance in one plant are inserted into corn to reduce the need for pesticides. | The inserted gene could produce new allergens, toxins, or proteins that might cause human health problems. | In the United States, exposure to genetically modified foods is ubiquitous. No hard data on human health effects are available, but animal tests suggest few concerns. Likelihood: Low Consequences: Low |
| Mad cow disease (bovine spongiform encephalopathy, BSE) | A neurological disease in cows whose symptoms include unexplained aggression and abnormal posture. The infections agent, a prion, or misshapen protein, is passed to cows through their feed, which was supplemented with meat and bone meal from slaughtered, infected cattle. | The prion can be passed along to humans who consume the beef of infected cows. Cooking the beef does not eliminate the problem. The injested prion creates a variant of Creutzfeldt-Jakob disease, which destroys normal brain function and is always fatal. | Large numbers of cattle in 18 European nations (mainly the United Kingdom) were infected in 2000 and 2001. Although a few animals in Canada and the United States have been diagnosed with the disease, the U.S. government has banned feeding leftover parts from slaughtered animals to cows, breaking the spread of the disease. Likelihood: Very low Consequence: Very low |
| Solar radiation | Short-wave, ultraviolet radiation from the sun causes three kinds of skin cancer: basal cell carcinoma (the least aggressive); squamous cell carcinoma, which can spread to lymph glands and internal organs; and melanoma, the most lethal form because it spreads to other body parts. | The depletion of the ozone layer, combined with the North American and European preference for tanned bodies, makes this an especially dangerous risk. | Solar radiation produces 1.3 million cases of skin cancer each year. Melanoma kills about 7,800 in the United States each year. Likelihood: High Consequences: Medium |

(continued)

**FIGURE 12.1** *Continued*

| Hazard | Explanation | Risk | Assessment |
|---|---|---|---|
| Obesity | A simple, yet imprecise way of knowing if you are overweight is to measure your waistline. A high-risk waistline is more than 35 inches for women and 40 inches for men. Environment plays a role in obesity, mainly the amount of physical activity the person is engaged in. Weight is not only an issue of habits, however; people can have a genetic predisposition to obesity. Also, the body's normal resting metabolism can be low or high, contributing to obesity in the former. | Being overweight increases the risk of premature death from all causes by 50 to 100 percent. Obesity increases the risk of heart disease and doubles the risk of Type 2 diabetes. Obesity increases the risk for several cancers, as well as diabetes, and increases the likelihood of infertility in women. | Obesity is one of the leading killers in the United States. Obesity is associated with approximately 300,000 deaths a year from various forms of cancer, heart disease, stroke, and Type 2 diabetes. Roughly 1 in 6 Americans, 44,500,000 people, are overweight by 30 pounds or more. About 14 percent of children aged 6–19 were overweight in 1999. Likelihood: Medium Consequences: High |
| Water pollution | The surface or subsurface water supply can be polluted by a variety of sources. Pesticides and fertilizers can migrate from fields, and chemicals can leak from factories or underground tanks. Storm water runoff from roads carries contaminants. Landfills can leak a host of solvents and household chemicals. | Polluted water poses two basic risks: biological and chemical. Biological risks come from pathogenic bacteria, viruses, and parasites that can cause acute and immediate effects, though usually nonfatal and short-lived. Chemical pollutants pose longer-term risks such as cancer or birth defects. | The average American uses 53,500 gallons of water a year, and thanks to extensive public health monitoring and water treatment, health problems are rare. Likelihood: Low Consequences: Low |
| Motor vehicle accidents | Most crashes involve multiple vehicles, collisions with fixed objects, or pedestrian deaths. | Alcohol, youth, and speed contribute significantly to the chance of injury or death in a motor vehicle accident. | Motor vehicles are the eighth leading cause of death in the United States. In 2000, crashes killed nearly 42,000 people and injured more than 3 million. On average, one U.S. resident dies in a motor vehicle accident every 13 minutes. Likelihood: High Consequences: Medium |

*Source:* Adapted from Ropeik, D., and G. Gray, *Risk: A Practical Guide for Deciding What's Really Safe and What's Really Dangerous in the World Around You* (Boston: Houghton Mifflin, 2002).

Second, once a study is initiated on a particular toxin, estimating exposure levels can be difficult. Although measuring exposure in a laboratory is simple, exposure in the real world comes after toxins are diffused through the air, water, soil, and food chain. The toxin comes into contact with other chemical compounds, where it may undergo physical and chemical transformations that may dilute the substance to unimportant proportions, make it inert, or combine to make the substance more dangerous. Additionally, once they enter the body, hazardous substances are altered by a series of chemical reactions that make a substance sometimes more dangerous and sometimes less dangerous. As a result, inferring exposure requires numerous assumptions on the part of the risk analyst.[14]

Third, estimating the probability of harm in a particular substance can be difficult. It is not easy to attribute a group of deaths or disease to a single cause. To make matters worse, many of today's hazards show up as ill effects only many years after exposure, which makes tracking extremely complicated. Finally, any estimates are complicated by the fact that toxic substances cannot be tested on humans. Scientists must rely instead on animals and computer models for their tests. Although there are various methods for making extrapolations from animal and computer data to inferences about human harm, each method includes a variety of assumptions, with various advantages and disadvantages.[15]

As a result of the problems just discussed, all risk assessments are characterized by substantial uncertainties. For example, "A study by the U.S. Nuclear Regulatory Commission estimated that the risk of a core meltdown at a nuclear power plant ranged between 1 chance in 10,000 and 1 chance in 1,000,000, depending on the assumptions that were made."[16]

The limitations of risk analysis pose an ethical dilemma for risk communicators. Should a speaker focus on the bottom-line conclusions of a risk study and omit a necessarily complicated discussion of limitations, or should the speaker cover a study's limitations even at the risk of confusing the audience and distracting them from important conclusions? The Ethics Brief in this section addresses this dilemma.

Finally, no matter how accurate a scientific analysis is, it cannot address the inevitable value and policy questions. Although scientists may conclude that it will cost the nation $23 billion to reduce particulate emissions to a level at which 2,000 lives are saved, it is up to government leaders, industry, and the public to weigh the costs and benefits of the choice. In the next section we examine how audiences perceive various hazards.

## Audience Perceptions of Risk

Risk managers and government officials often take a skeptical view of the public. The public, they say, is concerned about hazards that, according to mortality (death) and morbidity (disease) statistics, pose little real threat. On the other hand, the public ignores hazards that pose major risks. For example, *Consumer Reports* notes that people want the government to regulate pesticide residues on fruits and vegetables, which pose a minimal health risk, but most Americans haven't been persuaded to check for radon gas in their basement, a hazard estimated to kill 14,000 people a year.[17]

However, when people are asked to rank hazards by the number of people killed each year, they do so with remarkable accuracy, demonstrating good sense of the magnitude of risk implied by various hazards. When the question of managing risks comes up, however, a series of value choices serve to expand concerns beyond the number of illnesses and deaths that result. In this section we explain the perceptual issues that drive our level of concern about hazards.

## BOX 12.1 • *Ethics Brief*

As we described early in this chapter, risk analysis is an inexact science. Even the best study with the smallest margin of error and the most certain conclusions rests on a series of assumptions that are open to criticism. The temptation for many people in government or industry is to focus on the bottom line, omitting discussion of both how risk studies are conducted and the limitations of the scientific data. Many fear that such details will only confuse audiences, distracting them from bottom-line conclusions. Research indicates that succumbing to these temptations is both unethical and ineffective.

It's unethical to gloss over the technical complexities of risk assessments and their limitations. Democracy is based on helping people make informed choices, and risk communication is a field devoted to putting technology in the service of democracy. The alternative is unattractive—technologically sophisticated people making judgments for others about the kinds of risks they will live with, the hazards they must accept or reject, and the technologies that will govern their lives. How would you like to be told that you are going to live near a potentially risky manufacturing operation, that you will have no say in the decision, but that experts (who, by the way, don't live near the facility) have deemed it safe and tell you your concerns are not supported by the data? When risk communicators gloss over the details and limitations of risk analysis, they are, in effect, taking decision authority away from an affected audience and reserving it for themselves. Risk communication should provide all the information audiences need to make informed decisions. It is unethical to tell people what risks they have to live with. It is equally unethical to appear to be giving people a choice but covertly making a decision for them by withholding information.

In addition to being unethical, closed risk communication is less effective than open and complete risk communication. Most risk communication is conducted in an environment of competing interests and conflicting messages. If a communicator fails to cite the limitations of a study, it won't take long for a competing interest to hire its own scientists and make the omissions public. When uncertainties are exposed, the offending company or agency will lose credibility because it will appear as if it was covering up flaws in the study. Future messages won't be accepted, and the success of the effort will be jeopardized.

A county in Minnesota learned this lesson the hard way. The plan for a waste-to-power incinerator passed all the appropriate permitting processes mandated by the state, and the county engaged in an extensive risk communication campaign with the public. However, that campaign did not discuss the minimal risks associated with the facility. When opposition to the incinerator did eventually arise, it focused on the project's potential risks. Because people hadn't heard about these risks, they concluded the county had acted deceptively, and this initiated strong resistance. Mary Anne Renz, who conducted a case study of the Minnesota incinerator incident writes,

> If the county had made the point from the beginning that the incinerator carried some degree of risk, the county could have had the upper hand. Not only would the issue have been debated on their ground, then, but also the element of openness implicit in an admission of risk would have added a perception of trustworthiness, creating a long-term gain in credibility.[*]

Although there is a temptation to gloss over scientific details and minor risks, this is an unethical and ineffective practice. Risk communicators should take pains to communicate the limitations of, and be open about, all the findings of risk studies.

[*]Renz, M. A., "Communicating About Environmental Risk: An Examination of a Minnesota County's Communication on Incineration," *Journal of Applied Communication Research,* 20 (1992): 9.

**FIGURE 12.2** *Perceptual Factors Leading to Different Degrees of Concern About Hazards*

| Less Concern | More Concern |
| --- | --- |
| Voluntary | Involuntary |
| Control | No control |
| Natural | Unnatural |
| Familiar | Unfamiliar |
| Not memorable | Memorable |
| No dread | Dread |
| Fair | Unfair |

Researchers have discovered over 20 different factors that influence people's perception of risk.[18] Several of these factors are listed in Figure 12.2. If the hazard is perceived to involve factors on the left side of the figure, it will raise less concern than if it involves factors on the right side of the figure.

First, whether a hazard is **voluntarily** or **involuntarily** undertaken affects people's level of concern. We view even very hazardous activities such as mountain climbing, tanning, and smoking as less risky because they are done voluntarily, but we react with more concern to genetically modified foods because we did not knowingly ingest them. The next perceptual factor is the degree of **control** over the activity. "People who hate to fly know perfectly well that it's among the safest forms of travel. The lack of control over the plane's mechanical upkeep and operation makes the small risk from flying feel intolerable to them."[19] However, people will happily accept a far higher risk of death or injury from automobiles, because they have control over the vehicle's operation. Less control increases our concern about risk.

Referring again to Figure 12.2, **nature's** hazards are considered less risky than those created by humans. For example, although we want the government to control the use of industrially created pesticides on food, we ignore the far greater risks that natural toxins create in foods. In a similar vein, **familiar** hazards are of far less concern than the **unfamiliar.** The effluent from an obscure manufacturing process seems far more dangerous to us than the more concentrated exposure we get using household pesticides and herbicides.

A **memorable** accident—for example, the one at Three Mile Island—makes a hazard more vivid and easier to imagine than an event that is **not memorable,** such as obesity or daily automobile crashes. **Dreaded** events create greater concern than events that imply **no dread.** The public's concern about ebola outbreaks rests mainly on the grotesque way the virus kills (massive internal hemorrhaging and external bleeding from every orifice), not on the number of people the disease kills. Such diseases as tuberculosis and flu kill far more people (by many orders of magnitude) than ebola.

Finally, **fairness** influences the degree of concern we feel. Do the people who bear the risks receive any of the benefit? If members of a community believe they bear the brunt of risks while a polluting company makes a large profit, concern over the pollution will increase. The converse is also true and explains why small towns that benefit from a single plant for their livelihood are generally less concerned about pollution than would occur with the same plant in a city with many employers.

It's important to remember that the factors in Figure 12.2 are not irrationalities. The public's concerns are motivated by values greater than simple mortality statistics, and in a democratic society the public has a right to inject these values in decisions. Whatever the goals of a risk campaign, they are easier to accomplish if the communicator understands the degree and source of audience concerns.

## Credibility and The Process of Risk Communication

Credibility is important because the goal of a risk campaign cannot be accomplished if the public doesn't trust the source. Several factors special to risk communication make credibility even more important than in mundane persuasive contexts.

Because the science of risk analysis is difficult to understand, the public will ignore details and make decisions based on source credibility. According to the National Research Council, "The reputation of the source, in terms of past record with regard to accuracy of content and legitimacy of the process by which it is developed, will be an important influence on the way recipients view particular messages."[20]

Although credibility is vital for risk communication, it is very difficult to achieve, for a variety of reasons. First, trust in major institutions—including the office of the president, Congress, labor unions, large corporations, the legal profession, the media, the armed forces, universities, churches, and the medical profession—declined from the mid-1960s to the mid-1980s.[21]

Although the September 11 terrorist attacks and the subsequent victory in Afghanistan increased the public's confidence in the government and the military, federal, state, and local government's response to Hurricane Katrina and the war in Iraq have again diminished confidence in our government. Even immediately after 9/11, trust in the government was about half what it was in 1966.

The scandals of the late 1990s (Martha Stewart, Enron, Global Crossing) severely depressed the public's confidence in business organizations.[22] Following the trend for other

*The public expects organizations to protect employees, the commnunity, and the surrounding environment.*

Credit: Bill Burke

institutions, trust in science and technology has also declined, although not as precipitously. Thus, the would-be risk communicator faces a credibility deficit. He or she probably represents a government or private institution that has less credibility than it did thirty years ago, and the science on which risk analysis is based is confusing, and may be distrusted.

A second credibility problem is created by the conflicting messages that may be put forward by the various involved parties (e.g., industry, federal regulators, state and local authorities), each of whom may have something to gain by slanting information.[23] In these circumstances, it's difficult for the public to identify reliable sources and everyone's credibility becomes stained.

In this section we discuss ways to create and maintain individual, process, and institutional credibility.

### Individual Credibility

The source of a message is an important context for building and maintaining credibility with an audience. As described in Chapter 10, individual credibility refers to an audience's perception of a speaker's competence, trustworthiness, and dynamism. Competence refers to the audience's assessment of the speaker's knowledge and expertise on the topic. Trustworthiness refers to the audience's estimate of the source's honesty, objectivity, fairness, and concern for the audience. **Dynamism** is the audience's perception of the speaker's energy, confidence, and enthusiasm. Figure 12.3 shows the factors that contribute to or detract from individual credibility.

If audiences detect hidden persuasive appeals, they will perceive the source as both untrustworthy and lacking in good will. Risk communicators should make their persuasive intentions clear to the audience from the beginning.[24] Of course, a source that is thought to be **objective** will be viewed as more trustworthy than a **biased** source. Slanting information to support organizational

**FIGURE 12.3    *Factors Leading to Positive or Negative Attributions of Individual Credibility***

| Positive | Negative |
|---|---|
| Persuasive intent (if any) stated | Persuasive intent hidden |
| Objective content | Biased content |
| Fairness to opposition viewpoints | Unfairness to opposition viewpoints |
| Uncertainty admitted | The absolute truth maintained |
| Audience familiar with the source's education and experience | Audience unfamiliar with the source's education and experience |
| Liked | Not liked |
| Perceived similarity | Perceived differences |
| Sources cited | Vague or no sources cited |
| Clear and concise | Overly technical |
| Organized | Disorganized |
| Metaphors and similes used | Literal presentation |
| Humor used | Lacking humor |

interests always hurts credibility and should be avoided. The next factor in Figure 12.3, **fairness,** can compensate for bias. "Even if people are aware that the communicator has a vested interest in the issue and that s/he argues from a specific viewpoint, they may trust the message or develop confidence in the speaker provided that the information presented appears to be fair to potential counter-arguments and that it is presented with technical authority."[25] Credibility can be enhanced by addressing objections to the preferred position rather than making one-sided presentations. Thus risk messages that use the N-A-R structure or the balance structure are likely to improve the audience's perceptions of source trustworthiness and goodwill.

**Admitting uncertainties** in the risk analysis increases audience perceptions of source credibility. A speaker who adopts an attitude of informing the ignorant, correcting misinformation, and presenting the **absolute truth** diminishes credibility perceptions. Steven D. Perry, an environmental scientist based in Syracuse, New York, tells a story about attempts to site a low-level radioactive waste disposal facility in a community strongly opposed to the plan. At a meeting attended by several thousand citizens, a respected nuclear medicine researcher was scheduled to speak and "announced in a loud confrontational tone that he was there to tell the 'real truth' about LLRW risks. The audience responded with a roar of disapproval and disbelief, at which point the speaker shouted, 'If you don't want to hear the truth, then I won't say anything at all!' and stormed off the platform to the accompaniment of jeers and insults."[27] The audience was appalled by the speaker's display of arrogance. Years later, Perry reports, the state still has no site for storing low-level waste. Admitting uncertainty increases the audience's perception of source trustworthiness.

As mentioned in Chapter 10, when an audience believes that a source has **relevant education, credentials, and experience** with the topic at hand, this tends to increase perceptions of source competence. The source's credentials must be carefully presented so that they do not create psychological distance between the "all-knowing expert" and the "lowly, uneducated" audience members. This can be done by stating credentials matter-of-factly, with a sprinkling of humanizing information about the source's life, work, and family.

Looking again at Figure 12.3, research shows that **being liked** by an audience contributes to audience perceptions of trustworthiness.[26] Being liked involves being friendly, nice, and outwardly pleasant to others during meetings and presentations. The figure suggests that displaying **similarity** with the audience increases perceptions of source trustworthiness if the similarities are clearly related to the risk at hand. Unrelated similarities (we both like to go boating) contribute little or nothing to perceptions of trustworthiness. For example, a statement such as "I know that the fact that this change is being forced on you is of grave concern to many and I share that concern" helps point out areas of similarity and improve credibility.

In terms of the content, **citing sources** increases the audience's perceptions of competence and trustworthiness, and specific citations increase credibility more than vague ones (e.g., many people argue that . . .).[27] In addition, messages that are **clear and concise** rather than complicated and technical improve audience perceptions of competence. **Organized** messages lead to greater perceptions of competence than **disorganized** messages. Use structures suggested in Chapters 7 and 10 to arrange written or oral presentations. Because **metaphors and similes** help listeners understand complicated risk data, their use improves perceptions of competence and trustworthiness over more **literal presentations.**[28] Follow the instructions for the use of metaphors and similes in the chapter on technical presentations. Finally, the use of **humor,** if appropriate and not excessive, can lead to a small increase in audience belief about individual trustworthiness and dynamism.

## *Process Credibility*

The risk communication process is itself a source of increased or decreased credibility. Unlike source factors, however, **process credibility** factors are rarely in the hands of a single communicator; most risk campaigns are run by large institutions or government agencies that control the process. Nevertheless, if the process is to be considered credible, it must be open and treat the public as an equal member of the decision-making team.

As you can see in Figure 12.4, there are three primary factors that influence the audience's perception of process credibility. Traditional risk communication uses the decide-announce-defend practice, wherein public input is not sought during the stages of problem definition, risk analysis, and decision making. The public becomes involved only after the solution is selected and then only to gather public reaction. According to Judy A. Shaw and Jeanne Herb, employees in the New Jersey Department of Environmental Protection, "A commitment to opening the decision-making process is vital. Although from a governmental agency's perspective this may appear to have the potential for making unsound decisions, case studies indicate that this is not necessarily true."[29] In fact, agencies have learned that **opening** the process pays off down the line in less public outrage and blocking.

Agencies have recognized that even minor lapses in openness and inclusion can be disastrous. In Los Angeles, the Department of Water and Power decided to install air-stripping towers to remove TCE (trichlorethylene) that was contaminating about 50 percent of its wells. Risk assessments revealed that, in the worst environmental conditions, the cancer risk from the TCE off-gassing near the towers would be less than one in a million, assuming an uninterrupted 70-year exposure—a very minimal risk. However, the community located near the site was not informed, and residents first learned of the project from a local newspaper article claiming that the project would spread toxins throughout the area. To minimize public concerns, the department installed scrubbers on the towers, increasing the project's cost by over 50 percent.[30] Citizens will be satisfied only if the avenues for public input provide open and meaningful forums for discussion.[31]

Second, the process will be seen as credible only if **conflict is allowed** rather than suppressed. As we mentioned in the introduction to this chapter, risk communication is a process that increases rather than decreases conflict, at least in the short run. Attempting to stifle conflict by limiting access or suppressing opposition will backfire and cause the audience to question the process.

Finally, the process will seem more fair to people if they are allowed to talk in a language to which they are accustomed. For many people, this is the **language of emotion** rather than science. Risk communicators should not deny or rule out emotional expressions. Such statements as "We are only here to talk about the scientific facts of the matter" serve to limit the public's ability to participate and reinforce the notion that individuals do not have a voice in the process unless they are scientists. The goal is to turn personally directed emotional responses into clear positions on the issue at hand.

**FIGURE 12.4** *Factors Leading to Positive or Negative Evaluations of Process Credibility*

| Positive | Negative |
| --- | --- |
| Early and consistent openness | Closed (decide-announce-defend) |
| Open to conflict | Conflict stifled |
| Emotional expressions allowed | Emotional expressions stifled |

**FIGURE 12.5**   *Factors Leading to Positive or Negative Evaluations of Institutional Credibility*

| Positive | Negative |
| --- | --- |
| Sound environmental policy | Unsound environmental policy |
| Consistent messages across time | Contradictory messages across time |
| Messages consistent with actions | Messages inconsistent with actions |
| Positive press or public relations | Negative press or public relations |

## Institutional Credibility

Finally, audiences will be more or less likely to accept risk messages based on the level of credibility they ascribe to the institutional source. The halo effect means that risk communicators fortunate enough to be working for a credible institution (in the eyes of the affected public) will see some of that credibility cover them and their messages. Of course, the opposite is also possible. The factors that contribute to **institutional credibility** are depicted in Figure 12.5.

The most important factor influencing institutional credibility is the audience's perception of the organization's policies. According to Peter Sandman, "Over the past several decades our society has reached a near-consensus that pollution is morally wrong—not just harmful or dangerous, not just worth preventing where practical, but *wrong* [emphasis in original]."[32] A solid record of **proenvironmental attitudes and actions** will go a long way toward building credibility in the eyes of an affected public.

**Consistent messages** from the organization also contribute to credibility. Changing or **contradictory messages** decrease audience perceptions of competence or trustworthiness. Referring again to Figure 12.5, messages need to be **consistent with actions**. Organizations must be ready to act on statements about both environmental cleanup and risk reduction with rapid and appropriate action.

High credibility in these three contexts is likely to lead to greater acceptance of risk messages than will low credibility.

# Creating Risk Messages

With an understanding of audience concerns and the various credibility factors, it is now possible to examine the goals of risk campaigns and learn ways to achieve these goals communicatively. Risk communicators must be perfectly clear about whether they are seeking private or public action. Asking for input about a new landfill or a waste incinerator, for example, involves **public debate and action.** On the other hand, attempts by a local health department to have people check their homes for radon gas or to get their children vaccinated are examples of **private action.** Whereas vigorous conflict and inconsistent messages from multiple sources are significant problems in public risk communication, overcoming apathy is a significant obstacle in private contexts.

Be it public or private, risk communicators may have one or more **outcome goals** during a risk communication campaign. Figure 12.6 portrays these options on a continuum.

In many cases, risk communication aims to **decrease public or private concern** about a risk; communicators explain the minimal extent of risks and calm fears. For example, a city's water department may wish to ease concerns about TCE contamination that is well within EPA

**FIGURE 12.6**    *Three Outcome Goals for Risk Communication*

| Decrease concern | Neutral information | Increase concern |
| --- | --- | --- |

limits. In the middle of the continuum a communicator presents the results of risk analysis studies **neutrally,** leaving the decisions to individual or public discretion. For example, a state regulatory agency contemplating stronger auto emission standards can clarify the benefits and costs of the new regulation but leave the decision to citizens, voters, or elected officials. Finally, in some cases, risk communicators want to **increase public or private concern** about various risks. For example, to increase the infant vaccination rate, the local health agency may try to raise concerns about the return of such diseases as polio, measles, or diphtheria that can strike children. In this case, increasing concern may motivate private action. Although providing neutral information is an **informative goal,** increasing or decreasing concern is a **persuasive goal.** Let's examine the various methods of achieving both informative and persuasive goals in risk communication.

*ex: H1N1*

Katherine Rowan at Purdue University has created an excellent taxonomy of various goals, obstacles, and strategies for risk communication (see Figure 12.7). Whereas goals 1 and 2 in Rowan's taxonomy are informative, 3 and 4 are persuasive.

## Informative Risk Communication

*2 goals*

Informative risk communication provides neutral information for its own sake or as a precursor to decreasing or increasing concern about a particular hazard. According to Rowan, two primary informative goals include **creating awareness** and **creating a deeper understanding** of risk (see Figure 12.7). Creating awareness alerts people to the existence of a potential hazard, which involves making messages detectable and decodable.

**Detectable** messages are **vivid or concrete** and have some **surprise or startling elements** to them. For example, vividness is enhanced by demonstrating the information's effect on the receiver's life. Newspaper and television news reporters are skilled at finding ways to portray events vividly. For example, Idaho has one of the lowest childhood immunization rates in the country. A television news story portrayed a couple whose child came down with whooping cough and almost died. At the end of the story, the father implored the audience to have their children immunized or share the same near-death experience they faced. This story vividly demonstrated the risks involved in not immunizing children. Other ways to create a vivid message involve highlighting the surprising nature of the risk or finding startling statistics or stories to support the risk. Alerting people to risk also requires **brief** messages.

Creating awareness also requires **decodability**—meaning that a literate person is able to paraphrase the message easily.[33] Rowan recommends that, when referring to a hazardous substance by its technical name, a speaker should also relate that substance to the audience by **stating familiar products** made with the substance. For example, "Liquefied phosphorus is a highly dangerous substance that ignites on contact with air. However, when processed into phosphoric acid, it makes an excellent detergent additive and is also used in soda pop." Rowan also recommends using **simple, familiar language** for easy decoding.

Whereas awareness of risk is fine, if the public is to participate in decision making, a deeper understanding of risk is needed. Goal 2 in Figure 12.7 suggests two obstacles to comprehending complicated risk information: difficult concepts, and difficult structures and processes. Follow guidelines in Figure 12.7 when communicating technical information.

**FIGURE 12.7   *A Summary of Goals, Obstacles, and Strategies in Risk Communication***

Goal 1: Creating Awareness of Risk Information

*Obstacle 1:* Difficulties in Detecting a Message

*Strategy 1:* Make information psychologically vivid by emphasizing its effects on individuals, concretizing abstractions, giving many specifics about the nature and consequences of harms and benefits.

*Strategy 2:* Keep messages brief; highlight key elements.

*Obstacle 2:* Difficulties in Decoding a Technical Message

*Strategy 1:* In naming technical phenomena, also describe familiar products they are associated with.

*Strategy 2:* Use simple, familiar language; keep sentences, words brief.

Goal 2: Creating or Deepening Understanding of Risk

*Obstacle 1:* Difficulty in Understanding a Word

*Strategy 1:* Define a word by its critical (always present) attributes.

*Strategy 2:* Give a range of examples and nonexamples (instances that people might think are examples but are not).

*Strategy 3:* Explain why examples and nonexamples have their respective statuses.

*Obstacle 2:* Difficulty in Envisioning a Structure or Process

*Strategy 1:* Use diagrams.

*Strategy 2:* Use organizing analogies.

Goal 3: Gaining Agreement

*Obstacle 1:* Disagreement About the Existence of a Condition

*Strategy 1:* Identify multiple signs of the condition's existence.

*Strategy 2:* Identify analogous situations in which similar signs lead to the same outcome.

*Obstacle 2:* Disagreement About the Condition's Likelihood or Severity

*Strategy 1:* Identify multiple signs of likelihood or severity or the lack of either.

*Strategy 2:* Describe ways in which these signs are already observable or question whether these signs are traceable to their supposed causes.

*Strategy 3:* Heighten perception of a condition's severity by emphasizing the risk's nature as involuntary, poorly understood, or having capacity for irreparable damage.

*Strategy 4:* Minimize perception of risk's severity by emphasizing the risk's nature as voluntary, well understood, and having capacity for minimal damage only.

*Strategy 5:* If both risks and benefits exist, acknowledge both to avoid losing credibility.

*Obstacle 3:* Disagreement About the Best Solution

*Strategy 1:* Argue that problem is of a certain type and that all problems of this type require a certain solution.

*Strategy 2:* Argue that the solution allows the best balance of risks and benefits.

*Strategy 3:* Argue that the best solution meets certain criteria and that a given solution most fully meets these criteria.

*Goal 4: Motivating Action to Volunteer or Overcome Habit*

*Obstacle 1:* Steps to Action Seem Unclear

   *Strategy 1:* Urge a specific act, not a broad goal.

*Obstacle 2:* Action Seems Too Difficult, Expensive, Time-Consuming

   *Strategy 1:* Make first step easy, not time-consuming, not expensive.

*Obstacle 3:* Doubt That One Person's Efforts Will Make a Difference

   *Strategy 1:* Describe similar situations in which small acts of many individuals resulted in great success.

*Source:* Adapted from Rowan, K. E., "Goals, Obstacles, and Strategies in Risk Communication: A Problem-Solving Approach to Improving Communication About Risks," *Journal of Applied Communication Research* 19 (1991): 300–329.

## *Persuasive Risk Communication*

Persuasive risk communication is difficult to achieve. As previously mentioned, risk communicators from any institution have difficulty establishing credibility, and campaigns are further jeopardized by divergent interests and competing messages. Despite formidable obstacles, persuasion plays a vital role in risk communication. In Figure 12.7, persuasive communication involves goal 3, **gaining agreement** about the existence and severity of a hazard and agreement about solutions to reduce the risk, and goal 4, **motivating people to take action** to reduce a risk.

    Under gaining agreement, three obstacles exist. First, parties to a risk campaign may disagree about the existence of a risk. Rowan suggests that risk communicators **identify multiple signs of the condition's existence** (argument from sign) and **identify analogous situations** (arguing from analogy) in which similar signs lead to the predicted outcome (see Figure 12.7). In towns where local health officials want people to test their homes for radon, they should point to the large number of homes that have tested positive for the hazardous gas. In the second strategy, the risk communicator identifies similar radon exposures that have led to cancer.

    If reducing concern is the goal, the communicator identifies multiple signs that a hazard poses no significant risk and identifies analogous situations in which similar hazards produced no significant increase in disease or mortality. Electric companies, for example, can use studies that show no increase in leukemia for children living near high-voltage power lines as a sign that the lines are safe.

    The second obstacle described by Rowan is a disagreement about a condition's likelihood or its severity. To overcome this disagreement, identify multiple signs of the likelihood or severity of the risk or the lack thereof. A community that wants to construct a waste-to-power incinerator should identify multiple examples of communities that have successfully installed this technology. In strategy 2, audience concerns can be increased by describing **signs that a risk is already causing problems** in the community or by **denying that problems are caused by the risk** in question. This, of course, requires excellent causal reasoning, as described in Chapter 10.

    In strategies 3 and 4, likelihood and severity can also be heightened or reduced by **emphasizing the perceptual factors** of the hazard identified in Figure 12.2. A communicator can, for example, heighten concern for the risk of radon by emphasizing its nature as involuntary, poorly understood, and having the capacity for dread diseases. Of course, communicators can also reduce concerns by educating people so the hazard is more familiar, by providing input into the process so they have more control, and so forth. In the case of a hazardous waste facility in North Carolina, the company's vice president made extensive efforts to involve the local community and continuously explained the nature of the hazards involved. This tended to increase the community's feeling of control, made the risks more familiar, reduced dread, and was more fair than if the company had made unilateral decisions.[34] These efforts reduced the community's concern about the site. Finally, in strategy 5, a speaker should **acknowledge both risks and benefits** to build credibility.

Another persuasive goal in risk communication is to **acquire agreement about the best solution.** In Figure 12.7 you can see three strategies to reach agreement. In the first strategy, the communicator argues that the problem is of a certain kind, and **all problems of this type require a particular solution.** This form of reasoning represents the syllogism discussed in Chapter 10. The categorical syllogism uses a major premise to create a general category, the minor premise places the particular risk into that category, and the conclusion states that what is true of the major premise is true of the minor premise. For example, if TCE contamination levels exceed EPA standards, then the wells should be shut down. TCE contamination in three wells now exceeds EPA limits. The obvious conclusion is that the three wells should be closed down. The persuasive challenge is explaining the major premise to the group and then convincing them that the risk in question fits into that general category.

In the second strategy, a communicator **identifies and compares the risks and benefits of several solutions,** and the group selects the options with the greatest risk-to-benefit ratio. This is a conflict-prone form of risk persuasion because it is based on differing values over which costs and benefits to bear, who bears them, and so forth. Finally, **setting criteria for the best decision** means using the reflective thinking sequence discussed in Chapter 3. In this process, leaders and citizens devise a series of criteria for the best solution and select the solution that meets most or all of the criteria. This, too, is difficult because multiple criteria will be debated, and it's likely that no single solution will meet all the criteria. Nevertheless, these are viable forms of persuasive risk communication.

**Motivating action** to volunteer or overcome a habit is a second form of persuasive risk communication. Rowen notes that such persuasion should **urge a specific action** rather than a general goal. For example, in the Great American Smoke Out, participants are encouraged to take a specific action (stop for a day) rather than a broad general goal, such as quitting altogether.[35] In addition, risk communicators need to do whatever is necessary to make action seem **easy, not time-consuming,** and **inexpensive,** and to **describe similar situations** in which the efforts of individuals acting alone have helped.

As you can see by the information in this section, risk communication messages, be they informative or persuasive, involve a complicated and conflict-prone process. It is doubtful one can enter a career in government, nonprofit advocacy, or business without needing to communicate with some group about risks.

## *Formatting Risk Communication Messages*

Risk messages come in a variety of forms, including oral presentations, newsletters, pamphlets and fact sheets, posters and displays, and advertising. However, Regina Lundgren and Andrea McMakin, risk communication consultants and trainers, say that whatever the format, the same basic information should be included.[36]

1. The goals and content of the information material.
2. The nature of the risk.
3. Alternatives to the action causing the risk and any risks associated with these alternatives.

4. Uncertainties in the risk assessment.
5. How the risk will be managed.
6. Benefits of the risk.
7. Actions the audience can take to mitigate or manage exposure to the risk.
8. Contact information.

Lundgren and McMakin recommend that any materials over two pages long should, first, summarize the goals and content of the informational material. The summary allows the audience to quickly decide whether the message will fit their needs, and provides a useful way to sort through and organize various risk documents.

Second, risk messages should describe the central elements of the risk, including the likelihood of exposure to the risk and the severity, either in numbers of victims or in consequences, of the risk if people are exposed.[37]

Third, communicators should discuss alternatives to the actions producing the risk and any other risks associated with those alternatives. For example, a community may decide to remove solvent contamination from its groundwater by building air-stripping towers. Unfortunately, this technology does not make the contaminants go away, and some of them are released into the air near the tower, creating a hazard, albeit a small one, for nearby residents.

Fourth, risk messages must briefly review the uncertainties of risk assessment studies.

Fifth, the agency or organization should discuss what they are doing to manage the risk. What steps are being taken to reduce the risk of exposure, who is supervising the work, and how will the risk mitigation be evaluated are all things that might be included in a risk message. After a discussion of risk management, risk communicators should discuss whether there are benefits to be gained by accepting this risk. Risk communicators should avoid making promises that can't be kept; such promises only alienate citizens and create ill will, which most organizations can't afford.

Sixth, if private action on the part of citizens can help reduce the likelihood or severity of a hazard, citizens should be told what to do and how to do it.

Finally, all risk information should include contact information, be it a phone number or Web site, where people can go for more information.

## Summary

Risk communication is a means of exchanging information so that the public is involved in decision making about the hazards they face. The science of risk analysis provides quantitative estimates of the health and environmental risks posed by various hazards. Despite the advances made in risk analysis over the past twenty years, the results of this science are always inexact.

Credibility is vital in risk communication campaigns. Source credibility is the audience's perception of a speaker's competence, trustworthiness, and dynamism. A credible process is created when the public is involved in the early rather than late stages of a project, when conflict is allowed rather than suppressed, and when the audience is allowed to express relevant emotions. Institutional credibility can be enhanced through sound environmental policies, consistent messages and actions across time, and positive press and public relations messages.

Risk communicators should decide whether they seek private behavior change or public debate. Communicators must also decide if they want to increase concerns, decrease concerns, or provide neutral information. Two primary informative goals include creating awareness of risk and deepening understanding about that risk. Persuasive risk communication attempts to increase or decrease concern about a hazard. As such, it focuses on gaining agreement and motivating action. Risk messages come in a variety of forms, including presentations, newsletters, pamphlets and fact sheets, posters, and advertising.

## Questions and Exercises

1. What are the major risks in your community? What organizations or agencies communicate these risks to the public? Are messages aimed at changing private behavior or creating public dialogue? Are the messages primarily informative or persuasive? Are the persuasive messages trying to increase or decrease concern about the risk?

2. Think again about some of the important risks in your community. What agencies, organizations, or individuals communicate these risks to the public? Use the credibility factors introduced in this chapter to analyze the relative credibility of the individuals, processes, and institutions involved in public communication. Are the risk messages in your community credible? Why or why not?

3. Throughout the chapter we emphasized that risk decisions always involve questions of value. The ongoing debate about automobile safety provides a case in point. According to scientific risk estimates, automobile travel is extremely risky, calculated as a 1 in 4,000 chance of dying annually. What to do about this problem, however, is a question of value.

   - Although seatbelts were available in cars for years, few people buckled up.
   - Many states were then coerced into enacting seatbelt laws by the federal government's threat to withhold federal highway dollars from those states that refused.

   - State laws mandating seatbelt usage and expensive seatbelt campaigns eventually increased seatbelt usage in most states.
   - The introduction of airbags made cars safer but increased the cost of a new car.
   - Airbags have saved the lives of approximately 3,000 people but have been found to be dangerous to small adults and are estimated to have killed approximately 30 children.

   The position you take regarding each of the above statements implies a series of sometimes-conflicting values. For example, the first statement implies that people who refused to wear seatbelts value freedom of choice over safety. Discuss the values implied by each of the above statements or by your beliefs about them. Are these values consistent, or are they contradictory? Which values should take priority? Why? Do your classmates agree with your prioritization?

4. In the section on persuasive risk messages, we noted that audience concern factors (voluntary, memorable, dread) can be used to increase or decrease concern about a risk. Imagine that your university or college is creating a campaign to encourage use of condoms. This requires increasing the audience's concerns about unprotected sex. Develop a brief list of arguments that use the audience concern factors to increase both concern about unprotected sex and condom use.

## Notes

1. Ruckelshaus, W. D., "Risk, Science, and Democracy," *Science and Technology* 1 (1985): 31.
2. Renz, M. A., "Communicating About Environmental Risk: An Examination of a Minnesota County's Communication on Incineration," *Journal of Applied Communication Research* 20 (1992): 1–18.
3. Ibid.
4. Shovlin, M. G., and S. S. Tanaka, "Risk Communication in Los Angeles: A Case Study," *Journal of the American Water Works Association,* November 1990, 40–44.
5. Morgan, M. G., "Risk Analysis and Management," *Scientific American,* July 1993, 32.
6. "Facing Our Fears," *Consumer Reports,* December 1996, 50–53.
7. Lundgren, R., and A. McMakin, *Risk Communication: A Handbook for Communicating Environmental, Safety, and Health Risks* (Columbus, OH: Battelle Press, 1998).
8. Shovlin and Tanaka, 42.
9. Sandman, P. M., "Explaining Environmental Risk," Environmental Protection Agency, Document #0789, 20.
10. Morgan.
11. Hopkins, T. D., "Proof? Who Needs Proof? We're the EPA!" *Wall Street Journal,* 21 May 1997, A14.

12. Chilton, K. W., and S. Huebner, *Has the Battle Against Urban Smog Become "Mission Impossible"?* (Washington University in St. Louis: Center for the Study of American Business, Policy Study Number 136, November 1996).

13. Ropeik, D., and G. Gray, *Risk: A Practical Guide for Deciding What's Really Safe and What's Really Dangerous in the World Around You* (Boston: Houghton Mifflin, 2002).

14. National Research Council, *Improving Risk Communication* (Washington, DC: National Academy Press, 1989).

15. Ibid.

16. Covello, V. T., "Risk Comparisons and Risk Communication: Issues and Problems in Comparing Health and Environmental Risks," in *Communicating Risks to the Public,* ed. R. E. Kasperson and P. J. M. Stallen (Boston: Kluwer Academic, 1991), 107.

17. "Facing Our Fears."

18. Sandman, P., presentation to the Los Angeles Dept. of Water and Power (February 1989). Quoted in M. G. Shovlin and S. S. Tanaka, "Risk Communication in Los Angeles: A Case Study," *Journal of the American Water Works Association,* November 1990, 40–44.

19. "Facing Our Fears," 51.

20. National Research Council, 119.

21. Renn, O., and D. Levine, "Credibility and Trust in Risk Communication," in *Communicating Risks to the Public,* ed. R. E. Kasperson and P. J. M. Stallen (Boston: Kluwer Academic, 1991), 175–218.

22. Purdy, J., "Suspicious Minds," *Atlantic Monthly,* January/February 2003, 82–84.

23. National Research Council.

24. Renn and Levine.

25. Ibid., 126.

26. O'Keefe, D. J., *Persuasion: Theory and Research* (Newbury Park, CA: Sage, 1990).

27. O'Keefe.

28. Renn and Levine.

29. Shaw, J. A., and J. Herb, "Risk Communication: An Avenue for Public Involvement," *Journal of the American Water Works Association,* October 1988, 44.

30. Shovlin and Tanaka.

31. McComas, K. A., "Citizen Satisfaction with Public Meetings Used for Risk Communication," *Journal of Applied Communication Research* 31 (2003): 164–184.

32. Sandman, P. M., "Explaining Environmental Risk," 16.

33. Rowan, K. E., "Goals, Obstacles, and Strategies in Risk Communication: A Problem-Solving Approach to Improving Communication About Risks," *Journal of Applied Communication Research* 19 (1991): 300–329.

34. National Research Council.

35. Rowan.

36. Lundgren and McMakin.

37. Ropeik and Gray.

# 13

# Crisis Communication

Any organization—be it an international conglomerate, medium-sized manufacturing firm, local government, government agency, or family business—is subject to crisis. The list of potential crises is daunting and includes terrorism, food poisoning, fraud, product recalls, hostile takeovers, employee injuries or deaths, environmental pollution, shootings at a plant, product liability lawsuits, and many others. Laurence Barton, a professor of management, defines an **organizational crisis** as "a major, unpredictable event that has potentially negative results. The event and its aftermath may significantly damage an organization and its employees, products, services, financial condition, and reputation."[1] Because the impacts of crisis are significant and the possibility of crisis is high in today's complex, interconnected world, this chapter covers communication strategies for organizational crises. We do so by explaining the significance of crisis communication in modern organizations, describing the components of crisis communication, and outlining the process of precrisis planning. We define communication responses to organizational crisis, review ways these strategies can be employed for greatest effect, and close with a discussion of structures for crisis communication.

Although the focus of this chapter is large—organization-threatening crises—the analysis methods and communication strategies we cover are also useful in less serious incidents, referred to as "problems" rather than "crises." Problems could include minor accidents, employee injuries, small chemical spills, product liability complaints, and so forth that do not threaten the organization's future but still require effective responses. In addition, the methods and strategies described in this section are useful for managers who need to restore their image inside the organization after a personal or team crisis or problem. In sum, although you may never plan for or manage a crisis in your organization, the material in this chapter is useful in a variety of other situations.

Before we begin, it is important to discuss the fundamental assumptions we hold about organizational crises. First, when crisis occurs, managers are responsible for two interdependent processes: crisis management and crisis communication. **Crisis management** focuses on solving the technical or human problems that precipitated the crisis. For a chemical company, a spill of several thousand gallons of ammonia would force managers to stop the leak, contain the spill, and clean up the affected site. Because crisis management techniques differ for every industry, this chapter cannot provide specific crisis management advice. Instead, we offer suggestions for developing individualized plans for the most predictable crises.

**Crisis communication,** on the other hand, involves what the organization says to its employees, the media, the community, customers, suppliers, stockholders, and creditors during and after the crisis. Crisis communication has two primary goals: to protect affected publics and to restore the organization's image. Thus, crisis communication includes the things the chemical company says to protect its employees, as well as how and when it notifies local, state, and federal emergency management agencies and the local community. Crisis communication also includes the things the organization says to explain the accident, and managers must do this in such a way that the organization's image is maintained or improved. These two goals are interdependent. If an organization does little to protect the public, the environment, and so forth, there is little that it can later do to restore its image.

A second assumption is that crisis communication depends on the audience. Although, from an organization's point of view, a minor chemical release may not represent a crisis, if an important audience (the community, local media, stockholders, consumers) sees a crisis, then a crisis exists. Intel learned this in 1994 when problems cropped up in the Pentium microprocessor. A college professor (we're all troublemakers) discovered that the chip made errors when performing complex mathematical calculations, and he reported this to the company. "So confident was the company in its product that it reportedly gave the professor a polite brush-off. Turning to the Internet to see if others could confirm the problem he had encountered, he triggered an avalanche of some 10,000 messages."[2] The media jumped into the fray, and the result was a devastating flood of complaints to Intel. Although the error occurred only in extremely complicated calculations beyond the need of most users, and only 3 percent of affected consumers actually returned their chips, Intel made the mistake of assuming that a crisis is determined by objective measures of impact.

## *The Significance of Crisis Communication in Business and the Professions*

Because organizational crises have a severe effect on employees, products, services, and the financial condition of the organization, all managers should spend time preparing for crises. Although threats vary from one organization to another, Figure 13.1 depicts a list of possible threats.[3]

According to W. Timothy Coombs, a researcher at Clemson University, most of the crises listed in Figure 13.1 can be grouped into one of nine larger crisis types depicted in Figure 13.2.[4]

Organizational crises seem, from our point of view, both more frequent and more severe than they were thirty years ago. We believe this is true for several reasons. The increasing globalization of markets has forced business into more complex manufacturing, transportation, and financing arrangements than in the past. The increased complexity means that management errors or systemic breakdowns that could have been checked and limited to a single site or a small area can now reverberate throughout entire organizations and communities. For example, the simple filtering error at Perrier caused the firm to recall 70 million bottles of water in the United States. The recall cost 40 million in lost sales, and Perrier's stock on the French market tumbled.[5]

Not only do complex manufacturing and global distribution processes increase the likelihood of crisis, the web of communication technology that now encircles the globe ensures that any major crisis will be widely reported. In the Intel case, the Internet served as a convenient rallying point for thousands of upset customers. In addition, Bloggers connected through the Internet can immediately communicate crisis information to interested publics. Television and digital media sites such as YouTube can add vivid pictures to any depiction of organization crisis. Look at Figure 13.3, which displays a selection of major organizational crises since 1982.

In addition to greater interdependence, two public movements have made it next to impossible for organizations to hide disastrous events: governmental regulation and the environmental movement.

**FIGURE 13.1**   *Possible Threats*

| | |
|---|---|
| Accidents | Infection/disease |
| Allergic reactions | Information loss/IT failure |
| Armed intrusion or holdup | Kidnap/ransom |
| Bankruptcy | Lawsuits |
| Berserk employee | Layoffs |
| Bomb damage | Loss of market |
| Boycott | Loss of shareholder value |
| Business scandal | Malicious damage/vandalism |
| Chemical spill | Murder |
| Class action | Pollution |
| Collapse of building/structure | Product tampering |
| Death (of customer or employee) | Riots, strikes, civil commotion |
| Demonstrations | Sabotage |
| Explosion | Sexual harassment |
| Extortion | Spills |
| Fire | Suicide |
| Government investigation | Terrorism |
| Hostile takeover | Theft |

**FIGURE 13.2    *A Typology of Crises***

Natural Disasters: When an organization is damaged by an "act of God."

Example: On January 17, 1994, a magnitude-6.8 earthquake struck Southern California, virtually destroying much of the California State University–Northridge campus.

Malevolence: When some outside actor or opponent employs extreme tactics to express anger toward the organization or force it to change.

Example: The 1982 and 1986 cyanide poisoning of Tylenol capsules.

Technical Breakdowns: When the technology used or supplied by the organization fails.

Example: In 1990, a failure of its filtering system introduced trace amounts of benzene to Perrier's bottled-water product.

Human Breakdowns: When human error causes disruptions.

Example: In 1989, human error caused the grounding of the Exxon *Valdez*, which released a massive oil spill in Prince William Sound, Alaska.

Challenges: When the organization is confronted by discontented stakeholders who believe the organization is operating in an inappropriate manner.

Example: Throughout the 1990s, Nike corporation was the subject of repeated challenges and boycotts from stakeholders who criticized labor practices at its overseas manufacturing plants.

Megadamage: When an accident creates significant environmental damage.

Example: In 1988, the National Park Service was accused of bad policies that led to the massive fires in Yellowstone National Park.

Organizational Misdeeds: When management takes actions it knows will harm or place stakeholders at risk for harm without adequate precautions.

Example: The leaders and employees of Enron, hell-bent on making a killing in the energy futures market, engaged in enormously risky, illegal, and unethical practices that cost the public millions and eventually destroyed the company.

Workplace Violence: When an employee or former employee commits violence against other employees on organizational grounds.

Example: The U.S. Postal Service experienced repeated examples of violence between 1983 and 1993.

Rumors: When false information is spread about an organization or its products.

Example: In 1990, a Snapps restaurant in Florida was the victim of a rumor that claimed the manager contaminated meat with his own AIDS-infected blood.

---

In the 1970s, the public took an active interest in regulating organizations. Ralph Nader, among others, organized a consumer movement that demanded higher quality and safer, more thoroughly tested products from American business. As a result, the public began to influence the regulatory and reporting environment of U.S. business. The laws increased the reporting obligation for all organizations, meaning that any problematic situations or crises that occur must now be reported to local, state, and federal regulatory agencies.

The environmental movement, which also began in the late sixties and early seventies, is one of the most significant public movements of this century. Responding to years of hideous

**FIGURE 13.3**    *Major Organizational Crises From 1982–2007*

1. Beech-Nut is fined $2 million for mislabeling baby juice concentrate as 100 percent pure fruit juice (1982).
2. Tylenol pills are poisoned, resulting in seven deaths (1982).
3. Brinks is robbed of 3.5 tons of gold bullion at Heathrow Airport (1983).
4. Union Carbide disaster in Bhopal, India, kills over 2,000 (1984).
5. Bank of America unexpectedly closes 132 branches employing 2,200 people in 90 California communities (1984).
6. During a strike by Hormel workers, razorblades were found in some of the company's products (1985).
7. A. H. Robins files Chapter 11 amidst claims that its Dalkon IUD causes miscarriages and deaths (1985).
8. Eleven adults and children perish in a fire that started through an attempt to evict members of the radical group MOVE from its Philadelphia headquarters (1985).
9. Tampon makers Johnson & Johnson, Kimberly-Clark, Procter & Gamble, and others face a problem when the product is linked to toxic shock syndrome (1985).
10. Rumors spread that Procter & Gamble's logo reflects Satan-worshiping management (1986).
11. Morton Thiokol struggles to explain its role in NASA's *Challenger* explosion (1986).
12. For a second time, Tylenol pills are poisoned, resulting in more deaths (1986).
13. Audi vehicles accelerate without explanation (1987).
14. The Park Service is accused of bad policies during the massive Yellowstone Park fires (1988).
15. Dean Witter stockbroker charged with bilking investors of $2.6 million (1989).
16. Massive oil spill from the Exxon *Valdez* along the coast of Alaska (1989).
17. Veryfine Products and other apple juice manufacturers face public scrutiny when the safety of using apples treated with Alar is questioned (1989).
18. Perrier's benzine incident leads to a massive product recall (1990).
19. Walkout of 6,300 Greyhound bus drivers inconveniences thousands of travelers (1990).
20. Florida Snapps restaurants work to contain a rumor that an AIDS-infected manager regularly contaminated hamburger meat with the disease (1990).
21. Sudafed capsules are tainted with cyanide, causing two deaths (1991).
22. Newspapers report that the United Way's CEO earns more than $400,000 a year in salary and spent more than $100,000 a year for first-class air travel and Super Bowl tickets (1991).
23. An interruption of long-distance telephone service blocks more than 5 million AT&T calls into and out of the New York City area (1991).
24. Sears Auto Centers in California are accused of defrauding customers by performing unnecessary repairs (1991).
25. Dow Corning targeted in FDA breast implant probe (1992).
26. NBC News is accused of ethical impropriety when it rigged a GM truck to blow up for footage on its *Dateline* story (1993).
27. Jack-in-the-Box restaurants are linked to more than 600 cases of food poisoning throughout the Pacific Northwest that eventually killed several children (1993).
28. Syringes are found in cans and bottles of Pepsi Cola (1993).
29. CBS News is accused of violating journalistic ethics when Connie Chung interviews Newt Gingrich's mother (1995).
30. The army is rocked by scandal when five drill instructors in Maryland are charged with rape, forcible sodomy, and improper relations with female recruits (1996).

**FIGURE 13.3   Continued**

31. Texaco is accused of racism when audiotapes reveal upper management using derogatory language about African-American employees (1996).
32. *Consumer Reports* rates the Isuzu Trooper sports utility vehicle "not acceptable" because of its tendency to roll over (1996).
33. Hudson Foods, Inc., in Columbus, Nebraska, is accused of causing an outbreak of *E. coli* bacteria that kills several people (1997).
34. The Targhee National Forest is the subject of a *National Geographic* article that depicts vivid images of clear-cutting practices (1997).
35. The Salt Lake City Olympic Organizing Committee is accused of paying bribes to International Olympic Committee members to secure votes for the games (1998).
36. Over 249 people across Belgium and France become sick after drinking Coke (1999).
37. SabreTech, a maintenance contractor to ValuJet airlines, is convicted of criminal charges in connection with the 1996 plane crash over the Everglades (1999).
38. Burger King recalls its Pokemon toy/ball giveaway after one child dies and another is injured (1999).
39. Eleven Texas A&M students are killed and 27 injured when a giant bonfire structure collapses (1999).
40. A federal judge determines that Microsoft Corporation engaged in unfair, monopolistic business practices against competitors (2000).
41. An explosion rocks the Phillips petroleum plant near the Houston ship channel. The complex was the site of a 1989 explosion and fire that killed 23 and injured 130 (2000).
42. Employees sign a letter criticizing Alaska Airlines for poor maintenance procedures following a crash off of California (2000).
43. Both Firestone Tires and Ford Motor Co. are accused of negligence for a series of vehicle rollovers that involve Firestone Wilderness tires and Ford Explorers (2000).
44. Most U.S. airlines are devastated by financial losses following the September 11th terrorist attacks on the World Trade Center and the Pentagon (September–December 2001).
45. Facing charges of fraudulent bookkeeping and deceptive business practices, Enron declares bankruptcy, wiping out the retirement savings of many of its employees (January 2002).
46. The accounting firm Arthur Andersen struggles to survive after it is charged with ignoring Enron's shoddy business practices (January 2002).
47. Martha Stewart is charged with insider trading; the controversy threatens her home decor empire (2003).
48. Major League Baseball's long-drawn steroids scandal is renewed when Rafael Palmeiro admits to taking performance-enhancing drugs (August 2005).
49. Federal, state, and local governments come under heavy criticism for various failures during the Hurricane Katrina aftermath in New Orleans (September 2005).
50. The bagged vegetable business suffers enormous losses when spinach from California suppliers is found to contain *E-coli* bacteria, a potentially lethal pathogen (September 2006).
51. JetBlue Airlines receives sharp criticism when passengers on dozens of planes are stranded on the tarmac at a New York airport for up to 11 hours (February 2007).
52. Menu Foods is forced to recall 60 million cans and pouches of dog and cat food tainted with a poison used to kill rats in some countries (March 2007).
53. Toy-making giant Mattel is forced to recall more than nine million toys that contained magnets or lead paint that could be swallowed (August, 2007).

pollution from manufacturers, the environmental movement pressed organizations to consider the health of local populations, the local environment, and the long-term survivability of the planet in their manufacturing operations. As a result, even small organizational problems may become public knowledge and precipitate a crisis. Organizations must plan and prepare for crisis situations, and know what to say to affected publics in such situations.

Significant crises have severely tested managers at different organizations. Following are several examples of major organizational crises; some of these were handled well by management; others were not. We will refer to several of these examples throughout the rest of the chapter.

On September 29, 1982, seven people in the Chicago area died when they ingested cyanide-laced Extra-Strength Tylenol capsules. Apparently, someone was able to remove bottles from store shelves, take apart the capsules, insert a lethal dose of cyanide, and replace the bottles without the knowledge of store employees. Within two weeks of the tragedy, 99 percent of the public became aware of the poisonings through the media.[6] As a result, Tylenol's position in the market fell from 37 percent to 12 percent, and experts were predicting the company's demise. Four years later, in 1986, a second poisoning incident took place in Yonkers, New York, when a 23-year-old woman was killed. No arrests have ever been made.

As soon as they were notified of the tainted capsules, the company suspended all Tylenol advertising and recalled 93,000 bottles from across the country. They established numerous communication ties with consumers through 800 numbers, as well as print and electronic media.[7] Johnson & Johnson executives appeared on a variety of television shows, from *Nightline* to *Today*. In response to the tampering, the company announced new triple-safety-seal packaging for Tylenol capsules and made free coupon offers. McNeil officials argued that a disgruntled employee could not have tampered with the product because the poisoned bottles came from plants in both Puerto Rico and Pennsylvania. In addition, it was very unlikely that, had poison been inserted at the two plants, those bottles would have ended up in several stores in one Chicago suburb. The location suggested that someone tampered with the product after it

*Global communications and marketing, combined with high-tech manufacturing processes, have left organizations more vulnerable to crisis than ever before.*

Credit: IndexOpen

was on store shelves. Thus, the company blamed the incident on a "madman" intent on randomly killing innocent people. The FDA agreed with this reasoning. Soon after the incident, Tylenol regained an amazing 93 percent of its original market share.[8]

In the second Tylenol poisoning incident, the killer was able to defeat the three safety seals added to the Tylenol bottle. Subsequently, Johnson and Johnson decided to drop the manufacture of Extra-Strength Tylenol capsules in favor of caplets—solid, white pills that cannot be separated and would discolor if coated with a foreign substance.

For another model of crisis management and communication, we turn to the Exxon *Valdez* oil spill, which occurred on March 24, 1989. The spill was caused when the *Valdez* struck a reef in Prince William Sound, Alaska, releasing 240,000 barrels (11 million gallons) of crude oil into the water, creating a slick the size of Rhode Island that threatened more than 600 miles of coastline.[9] Later, the public learned that the ship's captain, Joseph Hazelwood, was drunk at the time, ordered the ship put on autopilot, set a risky course, and left the bridge in the hands of a relatively inexperienced third mate. Scientists and the media reported that Exxon was poorly prepared to handle the disaster. Supplies of dispersants were inadequate to the task, and equipment that was supposed to be available for such emergencies was missing. These revelations suggested that Exxon's crisis management plan was inefficient and lethargic.[10] In addition, Exxon sent a succession of lower-rank executives to Alaska to handle the problem. The company's CEO, L. G. Rawl, did not make his first comments about the incident until six days after the spill.[11] To sum up, Exxon failed to exercise visible, high-level leadership in managing the crisis.

Exxon attempted to shift the blame for the incident by scapegoating the captain. Later, however, it was reported that Exxon knew the captain had gone through an alcohol rehabilitation program but still put him in command of the *Valdez*. Exxon also blamed state and Coast Guard officials for not giving immediate authorization for cleanup operations to commence.[12] Finally, Exxon made unrealistic pledges to restore the fouled beaches of the sound. When it became apparent that this would not be possible, the company was chastised for backing away from its promises. Rather than helping to restore its image, these responses further hurt Exxon in the eyes of the public. Stockholders criticized Exxon's handling of the situation, consumers boycotted the company, and Exxon became the butt of jokes among the public.

In yet another major incident, on September 17, 1991, AT&T experienced an interruption of long-distance service that blocked more than five million calls into and out of the greater New York City area. This was worse than an inconvenience. Because air traffic control depends on phone lines, all air service into and out of the New York metro area was halted. The shutdown occurred because AT&T had agreed to supply power for its New York City long-distance switching plant from its own generators to relieve peak demand on Consolidated Edison. When generators malfunctioned, the plant automatically switched over to battery power, which provided energy for about six hours. Alarms that notify workers that the plant was on battery support went unnoticed, and the system collapsed for want of power.[13] The shutdown affected airports as far west as Chicago and produced numerous problems in the eastern hubs of Boston, Philadelphia, and Washington, DC. The breakdown also diminished the margin of safety for planes flying through the region. Rival phone services MCI and Sprint took out advertisements suggesting that AT&T was unreliable.[14]

Initially, AT&T blamed its employees and lower-level union workers at one of its plants for not noticing the battery alarms. However, the Communication Workers of America Union quickly refuted this attempt to move the blame. They said that the audio alarms did not go off because they were not working properly, and visual alarms were hidden behind recently installed equipment. They also blamed the problem on staff reductions that left the plant with fewer trained workers, while experienced workers were at a mandatory training session, ironically, to learn about a new computerized alarm system. After hearing this response, AT&T changed strategies. In full-page newspaper advertisements in the *New York Times* and the *Wall Street Journal*, AT&T apologized for the error, promised to fix the problem, and announced a comprehensive review of all facilities, policies, and maintenance measures.[15] This effort (see Figure 13.4) worked.

The late 1990s and the new millennium brought new organizational crises. In June 1999, more than 100 people in Belgium, most of them schoolchildren, became ill after consuming

# "Apologies are not enough."

"I am deeply disturbed that AT&T was responsible for a disruption in communications service that not only affected our customers but also stranded and inconvenienced thousands of airline passengers. I apologize to all of you who were affected, directly or indirectly.

Apologies, of course, are not enough. We have identified the cause as a combination of mechanical and human failures. And, most regrettably, management practices were not followed that would have prevented the problem from affecting the public.

We have already taken corrective and preventive action at the affected facility. But the issue is a broader one. That's why I have directed a thorough examination of all of our facilities and practices, from the ground up. Perfect service continuity is our goal.

Through billions of dollars of investment and the skilled work of AT&T people, we have designed and built our systems to the world's highest standards. No communications systems have more backup or alternate routing. And we plan to spend billions more over the next few years to make them even more reliable.

I am also committed to working closely with government officials to satisfy concerns about the need for communications backup in situations that affect the public's welfare. This is not a simple issue, though, because the depth of our technology and the breadth of our capabilities can't be backed up by anyone else in the marketplace. Ultimately, we have to be able to provide the certainty of service that is its own safety net. And we will.

We feel a deep sense of obligation not only to our customers, but to the public at large. The recent disruption underscored a fundamental truth: our services have a crucial impact across the economy, across society. They affect people's work and personal lives, in the most critical ways.

We built our business, in a far simpler day, on an unyielding ethic of service. With the incredible volume of communications handled by today's systems and with people so deeply dependent on communications, we know that service ethic is more important than ever.

I have great confidence in AT&T people. They have always set us apart from the competition and been the cornerstone of our customers' trust in us. You can count on our people's commitment to service to drive the management of this business more than ever in the years ahead."

*R.E. Allen*

Robert E. Allen, Chairman

**FIGURE 13.4** *Sample Image Restoration Advertisement from AT&T*
Courtesy: AT&T

Coca-Cola. The Belgian government ordered all Coke products removed from the shelves. A day later, the scare spread to France, where more than 80 people reported similar symptoms. The governments of Luxembourg and France imposed a partial ban on Coke sales. After an investigation, Coke officials said the problem stemmed from bad carbon dioxide in drinks made in Antwerp and from the odor of a fungicide (used on shipping pallets) that coated the cans. Coke claimed there were no serious health concerns related to the bad taste and odor, and quickly pressed the three governments to lift the restrictions. Badly underestimating how much explanation government officials would demand, Coke was rebuffed in its attempt to return to business as usual. Douglas Ivester, Coke's new CEO, took a week to apologize for the incident.[16] Ivester resigned his position less than six months later, partly in response to the criticism he received about the episode.[17]

In January 2000, an Alaska Airlines jetliner plunged into the Pacific killing all 88 people aboard. The airline long possessed a reputation for safe operations and strong customer service. However, within four months the FAA began an investigation of the firm's maintenance procedures. In mid-March, 64 mechanics signed a letter to Alaska's top management, saying they felt "pressured, threatened, and intimidated" by a supervisor to move planes from maintenance back into service too quickly. *USA Today* accused the airline of foot-dragging and shifting the blame.[18] The airline eventually made a series of expensive maintenance and managerial improvements to prevent future tragedy.[19]

One of the most spectacular crises in recent years was a joint problem for both the Ford Motor Company and the Firestone Tire Company. The tread on the Firestone tires was prone to separation, throwing the vehicle out of control and producing rollover accidents. In August 2000, Ford issued one of the largest recalls in American automotive history when it decided to replace the 15-inch Firestone Wilderness ATX and ATXII tires on all Explorer vehicles nationwide. The recall was so large that it was expected to take until spring to complete. As of August, 62 deaths were linked to tread separation.[20] By February 2001, the death toll had climbed to 174.[21] Ford estimated the costs of the recall at $500 million, and Firestone estimated its costs would come to $750 million.

In one of the highest profiles, most hotly debated white-collar crime cases of the new century, Martha Stewart was accused of illegal insider trading during the winter of 2002 when she sold 3,928 shares of ImClone Systems, Inc., a biotechnology company. After being convicted on lesser charges of lying to federal investigators and sentenced to five months in prison, Stewart issued several statements and made several television appearances during July and August 2004. Several of these comments are quoted in Figure 13.5.

Finally, in February 2007, the low-cost airline JetBlue suffered an enormous service breakdown during an ice storm that hit the eastern United States. JetBlue, believing that the weather would break, kept passengers on planes on the tarmac at John F. Kennedy International Airport for up to 11 hours before finally deplaning them. The massive cancellations, combined with JetBlue's minimal operational staff and small reservations system, created a cascade of continuing cancellations for several more days, as the airline struggled to contact its employees and move them into the proper positions to resume normal service. JetBlue's founder and CEO David G. Neeleman said he was "humiliated and mortified" by the problems and promised to compensate stranded passengers.[22] He eventually issued a Customer Bill of Rights that outlined various compensation plans for delays and overbookings, and promised vouchers and specific services for passengers who experience onboard ground delays. JetBlue's reputation did not appear to suffer significant long-term damage from the crisis.[23]

**FIGURE 13.5    *Martha Stewart's Post-Sentencing Comments***

---

Prior to sentencing, Stewart asked the judge to "remember all the good that I have done, all the contributions I have made," as she pleaded for a minimal sentence.

After sentencing Stewart said, "Today is a shameful day. It is shameful for me, for my family, and for my beloved company and all of its employees and partners. What was a small personal matter became over the last two and a half years an almost fatal circus event of unprecedented proportions spreading like oil over a vast landscape, even around the world. I have been choked and almost suffocated to death."

In a public letter on the Internet Stewart said, "Remember, please, that this was a personal matter that, because of the power of the press and the persistence of the government, spilled over onto an uninvolved company, harming all the people who labor so very hard, doing such admirable work."

---

*Source:* Masters, B. A., "Martha Stewart Sentenced to 5 Months in Prison," *Washington Post*, 16 July 2004 (online: www.washingtonpost.com/ac2/wp-dyn/A54591-2004July16?).

## *The Components of Crisis Communication*

Effective crisis communication involves several components. First, a crisis management team must be formed within the organization. Its job is to engage in precrisis planning to create a crisis management plan for the organization. In the next section we explain how to form an effective crisis management team and discuss the precrisis planning process.

In the major section in this chapter, titled Communication Responses to Organizational Crisis, we cover a typology of image restoration strategies that organizations may use to restore their credibility during a crisis. Finally, we provide a series of guidelines for effective crisis communication, and we help you format a crisis briefing presentation.

## *Forming a Crisis Management Team and Precrisis Planning*

Forming a crisis management team and precrisis planning involve several important steps and processes. Because this chapter focuses on crisis communication, our discussion of precrisis planning will be brief, focusing on three processes: forming a crisis team, reviewing and rehearsing crisis responses in advance, and formalizing these into a written implementation plan.

A **crisis team** is the group responsible for both precrisis planning and crisis management and communication during an actual emergency. In a large or midsized firm, the crisis team should include several senior administrators, such as the CEO, the chief financial officer, or various directors or upper-level managers. This is necessary so that the appropriate information and authority will be included in the plan. In addition, operations managers should be included, because these people understand the manufacturing and technical aspects of the organization. The crisis team should include public and/or government relations employees who can anticipate and respond to the media, the public, and government agencies. In addition, the crisis team should include any individuals responsible for environmental, health, or safety engineering. People responsible for sales and investor relations can also provide valuable input to crisis planning and management. Finally, the crisis team should include legal counsel.[24] The individuals who form the crisis team and engage in crisis planning should also be the central management team during an actual crisis.

Once formed, the team must create a **crisis management plan (CMP).** The CMP is a written document that (1) anticipates the most predictable crises that could afflict the organization and (2) plots management and communication responses. Developing the CMP involves two primary steps. First, the team should brainstorm a list of potential crises that could affect the organization. However, because an organization cannot prepare for all fathomable crises on their brainstormed list, the team must focus on those that are more likely to occur and eliminate from the list the less likely crises.[25]

After the list has been narrowed, the crisis management team develops a written plan of crisis management and crisis communication for each disaster on the short list. This written document can be organized in a number of ways, but Barton suggests that the following information be included: The CMP should include the names, phone numbers, fax numbers, and Internet addresses for all members of the crisis team. This section should also include the names of the people who are in charge during different crises and clarify who has authority in each situation. In another section, the team should include information about the appropriate community leaders, media outlets, and government agencies that need to be contacted in emergencies. This section should include updated phone, fax, and Internet information and the like for immediate use by employees in a crisis.

Barton suggests that the next section include crisis assessment, wherein the various crises on the team's short list are discussed. For each type of crisis, a series of crisis management and communication action plans should be detailed. For example, if an industrial accident involves employee injuries or fatalities, the crisis plan should specify how and when employee families are notified. Suggestions for how information will be communicated to the public can also be included in this section of the CMP.

Next, a media relations contact sheet must be included that has updated contact information for relevant media outlets. This section should also detail who handles the media and the preferred communication outlets for each crisis. Press releases, press kits, and news conferences are three typical ways of dealing with the media. A press release is a printed statement, faxed or e-mailed to media organizations, that details the nature of the crisis and the organization's responses. Press kits are packets of important background information about the company that may be sent along with a press release or prepared for the press when they attend a news conference. These may include fact sheets on key executives and the organization, data on the corporation and its history, and names and phone numbers for press contacts. "The preparation time involved in the generation of a press kit can be considerable, so many leading companies keep a 'boilerplate' press kit with essential corporate data that is already packaged and ready in boxes for distribution in case of emergency."[26] News conferences ensure that representatives of the media get timely information from an appointed company spokesperson. The Demonstration Crisis Briefing in this chapter simulates a news conference wherein students act as organizational representatives responding to a crisis.

Finally, Timothy Coombs, a crisis communication expert, says that the financial and legal ramifications and options for specific crises must be included in the CMP.[27] Therefore, experts on the crisis team should have information on how to reach consumers, how to temporarily suspend trading of a firm's stock, and how to address stockholders quickly, or how to address the various liabilities the organizations has for each particular crisis.

## *Communication Responses to Organizational Crisis*

This section discusses the importance of maintaining a favorable image during a crisis and then lists and exemplifies William Benoit's typology of image restoration strategies.

Let's start our discussion by reviewing the importance of credibility to any communication event, either individual or organizational. In Chapter 10 we emphasized the importance of favorable credibility to a communicator's persuasive efforts. Credibility is also important for organizations. Organizations must have credibility in the eyes of various publics, such as the local community, investors, customers, and stockholders. A tarnished image imperils an organization's ability to influence the surrounding environment. Thus organizations spend millions on public relations campaigns for various audiences. For all the reasons we mentioned in the introduction to this chapter, organizations are prone to problems and crises that leave them open to attack. Because image is important, most organizations are compelled to respond to attacks.

**Crisis communication strategies** are messages that help restore an organization's tarnished image. The strategies we discuss fall into the five general categories depicted in Figure 13.6: denial, evading responsibility, reducing offensiveness, corrective action, and mortification.

**FIGURE 13.6**   *A Typology of Crisis Communication Strategies*

---

*Denial:* Denies performing an act that precipitated the crisis or denies that a crisis occurred.

   *Simple Denial:* Denies that a crisis happened or denies that the organization is responsible.

   *Shifting the Blame:* Provides a different target for the audience by applying blame to another party.

*Evading Responsibility:* Evading or minimizing the organization's responsibility for the crisis.

   *Provocation:* A crisis-precipitating act was performed in response to another wrongful act.

   *Defeasibility:* The organization lacked information about or control over factors that precipitated the crisis.

   *Accident:* Reducing the organization's responsibility for the crisis by appealing to factors that can't be controlled.

   *Good Intentions:* Claim that the crisis was precipitated by actions that were done with good intent.

*Reducing Offensiveness:* Reducing the degree of ill or harm that various audiences experience because of the crisis.

   *Bolstering:* Relating positive attributes of the organization that might mitigate the negative consequences of the crisis.

   *Minimization:* Reminding an audience that the effects of the crisis are not as harmful or widespread as they might appear.

   *Differentiation:* Distinguishing some acts from other similar, but less desirable acts.

   *Transcendence:* Placing the crisis in a different context that directs attention to higher, more important values.

   *Attack the Accuser:* Reducing the credibility of the source of an accusation.

   *Compensation:* Remuneration to crisis victims to counterbalance the negative effects of the crisis.

*Corrective Action:* Vow to restore the situation to the state it was before the crisis or to prevent recurrence of the crisis.

*Mortification:* Admit responsibility for the crisis and ask forgiveness.

---

*Source:* From *Accounts, Excuses, and Apologies: A Theory of Image Restoration Strategies* by William L. Benoit. 1995, State University of New York Press.

The crisis communication strategies in Figure 13.6 should be applied with two primary goals in mind. The first and most important goal for managers is to do whatever is necessary to alleviate the human suffering or environmental harm caused by the crisis. If the organization is focused on managerial interests to the exclusion of the affected publics, then it deserves all the derision that can (and probably will) be heaped on it. If for no other reason than self-interest, organizations should accept their responsibility to the public and act accordingly. Second, as the organization succeeds in the first goal, it can then look to its own survival, which involves restoring its credibility in the eyes of various publics. Look at the Ethics Brief in this chapter for more information on the ethical responsibilities of organizations in crisis.

## *Denial*

When using **denial,** the organization does not acknowledge a wrongful act or denies that a wrongful act occurred. For example, in 1991 Sears auto repair shops were accused of performing unnecessary repairs. After a rise in customer complaints, the California Department of Consumer Affairs conducted an investigation in which undercover agents took older cars to Sears centers with a specific problem, but no other mechanical difficulties. The department found that Sears consistently replaced additional components that were not worn or damaged. The department charged that by slashing hourly wages in favor of sales commissions, setting sales quotas, and sponsoring sales contests, Sears had encouraged managers to sell parts whether they were needed or not. Sears's early image restoration efforts focused on denial. In various statements, Sears said that all employees involved in the controversial repairs were interviewed and the company was satisfied that there was no wrongdoing.[28] Denial strategies may take one of two forms: simple denial or shifting the blame.

In **simple denial,** the organization issues statements indicating either that no crisis has taken place or that the organization is not responsible for the crisis. In the early stages of the breast implant crisis (see Figure 13.3), Dow Corning released documents demonstrating that implants do not increase the risk of breast cancer.[29]

A second form of denial is **shifting the blame.** This strategy not only claims that the organization is not responsible, but also shifts the blame to another target. For this move to be ethical, the target must be legitimately responsible for the crisis. Like simple denial, this claim may also be accompanied by various forms of reasoning and evidence. If the audience accepts the evidence, the organization's image should improve, because someone or something else is responsible. Early during its oil spill crisis, Exxon shifted blame for the accident to Captain Hazelwood, the *Valdez* skipper. Later, when accused of a slow response to the spill, Exxon attempted to move the blame to the state of Alaska and the Coast Guard for not immediately authorizing Exxon to begin cleanup efforts. Neither of these moves was accepted by the public, however. During the SUV debacle of 2000, both Ford and Firestone shifted the blame to the other firm.

As with all image strategies, there is nothing inherently unethical about denial if indeed no real crisis exists or the organization is truly not responsible. However, denial strategies will be both ineffective and unethical if not supported by the facts and strengthened with reasoning and evidence (see Chapter 10). For example, during the 1982 Tylenol poisoning, Johnson & Johnson claimed that neither it nor any of its employees could have introduced cyanide into the capsules. It provided evidence that the bottles came from two different plants and argued that it was unlikely the poisoned bottles from the two plants would end up in the same Chicago suburb. The company supported this logical appeal with testimony from the Food and Drug

**BOX 13.1 • *Ethics Brief***

Crisis communication is a special form of persuasive communication. As we stated earlier in this chapter, the two primary goals of crisis communication involve protecting the health and well-being of affected publics and restoring the image of the organization. It is important to consider both ethics and effectiveness issues when involved in any form of persuasive communication. This is especially true in crisis communication.

What constitutes ethical crisis communication? Crisis communication strategies must meet several goals to be considered ethical. First, ethical crisis communication protects the health and well-being of affected publics. To fail at this is to fail at one's responsibility as an employer and member of your community. After that, ethical crisis communication persuades using evidence and logic, rather than appeals to ignorance or emotion. Finally, ethical communication is true to the facts as organizational members know them. It is unethical, for example, to try to blame others for a crisis that is your fault or to inappropriately minimize the harm of a very serious crisis. Thus, ethical crisis communication helps others affected by the crisis and makes an honest attempt to explain the crisis to the public.

What is effective crisis communication? Simply put, effective communication improves the organization's image during or after the crisis. This may be done to a greater or lesser degree, depending on the severity of the crisis. In most cases, ethical and effective crisis communication strategies are closely linked. By this we mean that the most ethical strategies are also the most effective strategies for improving the organization's image. Unethical strategies that do not protect the public and do not argue from the truth pose a double danger to the organization. If and when such things are exposed, the organization suffers not only for having precipitated the crisis, but also for lying or distorting information. The reason for the close connection between ethical and effective strategies is that, in most crises, the media, government regulatory agencies, and the public are watching the organization closely. Therefore, if the organization fails to protect affected publics or if its communication strategies are based on half-truths and distortions, it is likely that the public

will be made aware of these indiscretions. Once that occurs, the organization's attempts at image restoration will have suffered a serious, if not fatal, blow. Thus, the scrutiny that organizations receive during a crisis means that ethical communication strategies are also the most effective communication strategies.

Unfortunately, many examples in this chapter illustrate that the simple connection between ethical and effective communication eludes many managers in a crisis. For reasons that involve both personal embarrassment and legal liability for the organization, managers are reluctant to admit responsibility for a crisis and have engaged in numerous unethical approaches that later backfire. Perhaps it is human nature that encourages us to diminish, cover up, and distort the facts surrounding a crisis in order to minimize blame. Issues of legal liability are also involved. An open admission of guilt and an expression of remorse can lead to huge lawsuits. Perhaps managers are hoping that, by using less than ethical strategies, they can avoid short-term pain and, if the strategy is effective, accrue long-term benefits as well. Such rationalizations may be common in the heat of crisis.

Because there seems to be a lot of pressure on managers to try to have it both ways during a crisis, we suggest the following ethical guidelines. First, if you find yourself managing an organization's response to a crisis, you must avoid being trapped by the belief that unethical practices will produce a gain. Remind yourself of the inherent connection between ethical and effective communication during a crisis. Second, because the connection between ethical and effective communication in a crisis might elude other members of your crisis team, you must constantly remind people that the best, the safest, the most effective (for the organization) responses to a crisis are also the most ethical strategies. Third, if the situation calls for an admission of guilt and an apology to restore the company's image, but legal liabilities are too high, consider making an ambiguous apology. And, fourth, whether you decide to apologize or not, avoid attempts to distort information and cover blame. Although an ethical strategy may produce short-term pain, it is probably the most effective strategy for the organization over the long haul.

Administration (presumably perceived as an unbiased authority), confirming that the tampering could not have occurred in the plants.[30] Johnson & Johnson moved the blame to a "madman" who removed bottles from the shelves in order to randomly poison unsuspecting customers. This effort was persuasive because it was supported by the evidence. On the other hand, Sears's attempts to restore its image were less effective than Johnson & Johnson's. The denials had to overcome very convincing evidence of overcharges by officials in the California Department of Public Affairs. Because Sears offered little convincing evidence or reasoning, its image restoration strategies were ineffective.[31] Based on these case studies, we believe denial strategies will be effective only if the organization can offer convincing proof.

In addition, crisis managers should think carefully before attempting to shift the blame to employees. Benoit states that shifting the blame is effective only when it is to someone clearly disassociated from the organization and plausibly responsible for the action.[32] Shifting the blame inside the organization does not meet these criteria. For example, in the *Valdez* oil spill, Exxon began by shifting the blame to Captain Hazelwood, who was reported to have been drunk at the time of the accident. In this instance, blaming an employee only casts doubt on Exxon's ability to hire, train, and supervise its workforce.

## *Evading Responsibility*

The second set of strategies for restoring an image during crisis is **evading responsibility.** In this category, the organization attempts to avoid or diminish responsibility for the crisis. Strategies for evading responsibility take four specific forms: provocation, defensibility, accidents, and good intentions.

**Provocation** responses claim that the act was performed in response to another wrongful act. Self-defense is the classic provocation defense. "I had to kill the person because he provoked a fight and threatened my life." It is unlikely that a provocation response would help restore a company's image during a crisis. Imagine your response to this reasoning: "We minimized our

*Organizations are complex, which makes crises more likely than in the past.*
Credit: Bill Burke

spending on safety equipment because our employees went on strike last month." We can think of no instances in which provocation would prove useful to an organization in crisis.

More useful in organizational crises are appeals to **defeasibility.** Defeasibility is the claim that the organization lacked information about or control over important factors and thus shouldn't be held fully responsible for the crisis. When AT&T blamed employees for the long-distance failure, the union responded with several defeasibility arguments. They said that audio alarms were not working and the visual alarms were hidden behind newly installed equipment. The employees didn't know the alarms sounded and shouldn't be blamed for the failure. Apparently, these arguments were effective because AT&T recanted. When criticized for not moving earlier to recall tires for its SUVs, Ford said it was not aware of any problems until the summer of 2000.[33]

Like denial, defeasibility is effective only if information was truly unavailable or situational factors were truly out of the organization's control. For example, rather than blaming the Coast Guard and state officials for withholding permission to commence cleanup (a charge that doesn't sound reasonable), Exxon could have blamed water conditions that were too calm and cold for oil-dispersing chemicals to work effectively. Even if Exxon personnel could have been there earlier, the effect of the oil dispersants would have been negligible.[34] For defeasibility to work, conditions must truly be out of the organization's control, and the case must be strongly made with solid evidence and reasoning.

An appeal to **accidents** helps reduce the organization's responsibility by appealing to factors that cannot be controlled. For example, part of NASA's early strategy for repairing their image following the *Challenger* accident was to remind audiences of the complexity of space travel, claiming that some accidents are inevitable and uncontrollable. However, this strategy was undercut when it was reported that Morton Thiokol engineers advised that the cold weather launch might result in catastrophe. As such, the "accident" was preventable. If an appeal to accidents is to be effective, the crisis must be an unpredictable event that cannot be controlled or foreseen.

Sometimes organizations can reduce responsibility for an event by citing their **good intentions.** If the act was done with good intentions, audiences may be willing to reduce the organization's responsibility for the crisis. In late 1992, NBC News was accused of irresponsible journalism on its *Dateline NBC* program about C/K pickup trucks manufactured by General Motors. The trucks have a tendency to catch fire in high-speed side collisions because their gas tanks are mounted on the outside of the truck frames, rather than the inside. The *Dateline* story claimed that 300 people had died in these accidents and included a 57-second sequence showing a GM truck bursting into flames after a side collision. GM hired detectives who accused *Dateline* of attaching miniature rocket motors to the gas tank to produce the explosion. In addition to apologizing, NBC could have responded by saying that they made the errors while dramatizing the real dangers the C/K pickup trucks presented to the public. Sometimes audiences will forgive errors in pursuit of a noble goal. Rather than trying to reduce responsibility, the next category of responses attempts to reduce the offensiveness of the crisis.

## Reducing Offensiveness

If the organization can reduce the degree of ill or harm experienced by the affected public it may succeed in **reducing offensiveness** of the crisis. In this way, the organization's image may be restored. This strategy takes six specific forms: bolstering, minimization, differentiation, transcendence, attacking the accuser, or compensation.

**Bolstering** involves relating positive attributes of the organization or actions it performed in the past that might mitigate the negative consequences of the crisis. Although the guilt for the crisis remains, increased positive feelings about the organization may offset negative feelings about the crisis. For example, when AT&T created a long-distance service interruption, its newspaper advertisements used bolstering to restore its image. AT&T chair Allen cited the billions AT&T had spent on customer service and the billions it planned to spend improving its system. If the audience perceives the comments to be sincere, it may reduce the offensiveness of the crisis.

To be effective, bolstering should be directly related to the charges made against the organization. For example, when accused of overcharging customers, Sears tried to bolster its case by referring to the thorough technical training that Sears's mechanics receive. However, even if true, the claim is not very effective because technical training does not make a mechanic ethical.[35]

**Minimization** is an attempt to reduce the amount of negative affect associated with the crisis or to convince the public that the crisis isn't as bad as it might appear. After the illnesses in Europe, Coke claimed that there were no long-term health consequences and no one was at risk. After her sentencing, Martha Stewart told audiences that the accusations against her were based on a "personal matter" that had been blown out of proportion.

*not that bad*

The effectiveness of minimization depends on the magnitude of the crisis. Organizations should avoid trying to minimize large crises that are well publicized in the media. For example, Exxon tried to minimize the effects of the spill by claiming that the company did not expect major environmental damage, and it talked of record salmon catches in Alaska, not mentioning that these statistics were not from the spill area.[36] This strategy was especially ineffective given the nightly television pictures showing oil-soaked beaches, fouled habitat, and dead birds and marine life.

**Differentiation** distinguishes an act performed from other similar, but less desirable actions. In comparison, the action that precipitated the crisis seems less offensive. For example, in responding to charges of unnecessary repairs, Sears characterized its "sales quotas" as "sales goals" or guidelines based on surveys of the public's needs.[37] Sears hoped that goals or guidelines would be perceived as less offensive than "sales quotas."

*"that was different..."*

*terrorism*

**Transcendence** places the crisis or actions related to the crisis in a different context that directs attention to higher values. The higher values justify the act and explain the crisis. When Martin Luther King was asked how he dealt with the contradiction that he wanted people to follow civil rights laws, but that he purposely refused to obey laws of segregation, he referred to a higher law. He said, "A just law is a man-made code that squares with the moral law of God. An unjust law is a code that is out of harmony with the moral law. Any law that uplifts human personality is just. Any law that degrades human personality is unjust. All segregation statutes are unjust, because segregation distorts the soul and damages the personality."[38] Violating unjust laws is not wrong, it is the responsibility of every moral person. Of course, the ethics of transcendence depend on the existing evidence and on moral judgments supporting the value of the strategy.

Transcendence was used by Volvo when it responded to charges of false advertising in 1989–1990. Volvo ran a TV commercial claiming its vehicles could survive being run over by a monster truck, but that other vehicles would be crushed. In reality, the Volvo used in the ad was reinforced with a steel roll cage, making it stronger than the other cars depicted. The Texas attorney general sued Volvo for deceptive advertising. In its response, Volvo attempted to reduce the offensiveness of the act through transcendence. An advertisement in *USA Today* made the following claim: "On October 30 Volvo management learned for the first time that the film production team had apparently made modifications of two of the vehicles [referring to the steel support cages]. There were two reasons for the modifications: first, to enable the filming to be done without threatening the safety of the production crew, and second, to allow the demonstration Volvo to withstand the number of runs of the 'Monster Truck' required for filming."?[39] In this response, Volvo explains the charge by saying the steel roll cages were installed to protect the film crew, an appeal to the importance of safety.

During one Christmas holiday season, American Airlines was in the midst of a long contract negotiation with its pilots. Many pilots called in sick as part of the protest, and American was forced to cancel over 10 percent of its flights. In newspaper advertisements American apologized to its customers and attempted to reduce the offensiveness of the event through transcendence. The company said it would continue to negotiate with the Allied Pilots Association but would not accede to demands that would create high costs. The airline cited its duties to reasonable fares for customers and reasonable profits for stockholders.

In some crises, if the credibility of the source of the accusations can be reduced, the damage to one's image from the accusations may be diminished. Thus, **attacking the accuser** may divert attention away from the undesirable act. When Dow Corning was accused of selling silicon breast implants that caused cancer, the company attempted to reduce the offensiveness of the safety issue by attacking the Food and Drug Administration, the agency investigating the implants.[40] If one can show that the accuser is trying to create a crisis for personal gain, then attacking the accuser becomes a viable strategy.

When offering **compensation,** the organization remunerates the victim to offset the negative effects of the crisis. The redress can be made in valued goods and services or a monetary reward. In effect, compensation represents a "bribe" to lessen the effects of the crisis.[41] Of course, the degree to which the organization follows through on such claims is an important determinant of the success of this strategy. JetBlue offered to compensate passengers who were stranded on its planes in February 2007.

To conclude, none of the six strategies just covered denies that the organization committed the bad action or diminishes the organization's responsibility for the crisis. Instead, they attempt to reduce unfavorable feelings by increasing audience esteem for the company or decreasing the audience's negative feelings.

## Corrective Action

**Corrective action** entails a vow to correct problems created by the crisis. This can work in two ways. The organization can vow to restore (**restoration**) the situation to the conditions that existed before the crisis, or the organization can make changes in its operation to prevent (**prevention**) recurrence of the crisis. Benoit helps clarify the difference between this strategy and compensation. Whereas compensation consists of a gift designed to counterbalance, rather than correct, the source of the crisis, corrective action addresses the source of the crisis (rectifying damage or preventing future crises).

For example, Exxon promised to clean up the oil and restore Prince William Sound to its original state. When AT&T's long-distance service failed, the company said it had already corrected the problems to prevent similar incidents in the future. Ford promised to replace all of the Wilderness ATX and ATXII tires on all Explorers nationwide. JetBlue created its Customer Bill of Rights to correct its treatment of passengers. Whether corrective action helps restore the organization's image depends on the degree to which promises are kept and supported by action.

## *Mortification*

**Mortification** means that the organization admits responsibility for the crisis and asks forgiveness. If the audience sees the apology as sincere, it may forgive the organization for its role in the crisis. Mortification is one of the strongest image restoration strategies available. However, many companies avoid this strategy, especially early in a crisis. This avoidance may be based on two things: lack of information and legal liability.

First, most organizational crises are characterized by a lack of information, and managers may not know what precipitated a particular event. Thus, it is wise to wait before apologizing until more information is available and clear attributions of responsibility are possible. Unfortunately, although temporarily withholding mortification may be prudent, many organizations make the mistake of opening with denials that must later be recanted after the facts are known. A belated apology often follows. Mitsubishi initially denied charges that female employees were subject to sexual harassment on its assembly lines, but later recanted and settled a large lawsuit brought by the government. Although sometimes effective, belated mortification can do more harm than good for an organization's image. When the first strategy, be it denial, shifting the blame, attacking the accuser, or whatever, is refuted, the organization looks as if it tried to cover up the facts. Mortification looks like it was forced on the organization by circumstances rather than being a sincere request for forgiveness. If you must delay mortification because of a lack of information or legal concerns, don't compound the problem by issuing denials or blaming others based on inaccurate information.

Legal liability is the second reason organizations avoid mortification. Mortification is not a problem in less severe crises in which no one is killed, injuries are minor, and the damage to the environment is contained and relatively easy to clean up. However, in severe crises, managers are torn between the demands of two audiences. Although the public insists on a sincere apology, managers also have an obligation to consider the damage that liability lawsuits will produce for employees, stockholders, and creditors. Admitting an error implies guilt, inviting lawsuits and providing ammunition to plaintiffs in court. After all, if the organization isn't guilty, why did its executives apologize? In severe crises, corporate managers are trapped because—much as they might like to apologize to meet the demands of the public—they cannot apologize without violating their fiduciary responsibility to stockholders.[42] Lisa Tyler, a professor at Sinclair Community College, suggests that ambiguous apologies are one solution to this problem.

As you may recall from Chapter 1, ambiguity occurs when there is low correspondence between the intention of the sender and the interpretation of the receiver. Ambiguous mortification omits important details and asks the audience to infer that an apology has been made without a clear admission of guilt. There are several methods of making an ambiguous apology. First, Exxon's response to the *Valdez* grounding admitted that the spill was the company's responsibility but continued to refer to the incident as an "accident," thus suggesting it was an "unavoidable act of God rather than a preventable result of human error."[43] The apology is ambiguous because it makes contradictory claims: that Exxon is both responsible and not responsible for the spill. Another method of ambiguous mortification is to express regret for the crisis without admitting guilt. Avoiding admission of guilt provides legal protection, whereas regret puts a human face on the corporation. According to Coombs, organizations must express compassion for victims. The compassion of an organization indicates that it is trustworthy—the organization is concerned about its stakeholders; and trustworthiness is a central component of organizational credibility.[44] Finally, a third method is to focus on prevention measures without admitting any responsibility for the event. As such, the company promises to correct whatever it is that it hasn't admitted doing.[45] Thus clear mortification is more ethically pure and preferable from the standpoint of the organization's image. However, when legal liability is high, ambiguity may be the only way to mediate the conflicting demands of various audiences.

## *Responding to Questions*

When the organization has finished presenting its case, the media and other interested parties must be given time to ask questions, and the organization's spokesperson must be able to respond to these questions in an appropriate manner. Timothy Coombs, makes the following suggestions for responding to questions. First, crisis managers must be able to answer questions clearly and concisely. Answers must be free of organizational jargon, which may lead people outside the organization to assume you aren't telling the truth. Explain technical information in such a way that it is understandable to nontechnical audiences.

Second, if you get a question you don't know the answer to, admit it and promise to deliver the information as soon as possible. Telling people you don't know an answer or don't have information is far superior to the "no comment" response. According to Coombs, 65 percent of stakeholders that hear "no comment" equate it with the organization saying it is guilty. The "no comment" is also a form of silence that gives other actors and stakeholders free reign to interpret the crisis in any manner they desire.[46] Remember from Chapter 1 that events don't carry particular meanings; they are given whatever meaning they hold by people through communication. Silence, as represented in the "no comment" response, gives opponents the chance to create their own interpretation of events, which is probably not the interpretation you are trying to maintain. Those who are ill informed or misinformed or who hold a grudge against the organization will fill in for your silence, presenting their own interpretation of events.

Third, crisis communicators must be able to handle several types of difficult questions, including long or complicated questions, multiple questions, questions that are based on erroneous information, and multiple-choice questions that present unacceptable options.[47] To handle long or complicated questions, ask the questioner to restate the inquiry. This gives them a chance to improve the clarity of the question and gives you time to compose a response. When responding to multipart questions, you have the freedom to choose which part of the question you are going to answer. Select the part or parts of the question that best fit the interpretation you are trying to create with your crisis message. And, if you need to respond to all parts of a multipart question, number each part of the answer so your response is clear.

Questions based on erroneous information must be challenged and corrected. The spokesperson must clearly explain why the information is in error and present the organization's understanding of the crisis in clear and concise terms. Finally, for multiple-choice questions you must determine whether the response options presented are fair. You shouldn't feel constrained to remain within the limits of the question if the only choices being offered are that you are being (a) stupid or (b) uncaring. You should explain why the limited options presented are unfair and develop your own option that better fits the interpretation you are trying to create.

Any organizational spokesperson acting in a crisis is going to feel tremendous pressure when handling questions from the media and other interested stakeholders. As part of their crisis management plan, many organizations spend time once or twice a year rehearsing questions and answers for particular crises with their designated media spokespersons. Such rehearsals can help prepare crisis managers and spokespersons to better handle the pressure that inevitably comes with their role.

# Effectively Employing Crisis Communication Strategies

In this section, we present general guidelines for the effective use of organizational image restoration strategies. Of course, no set of rules can guarantee successful image restoration. Instead, these guidelines provide signposts for reasoned choices when communicating to various audiences.

## Use Multiple Strategies in Concert with One Another

Rarely will an organization focus its image restoration campaign on a single strategy. Rather, the best campaigns use multiple strategies in concert with one another. AT&T used mortification, corrective action, and bolstering to rebuild its credibility.[48] However, it is vital that the strategies not contradict one another or contradict vivid and accurate media accounts. Unfortunately, these two prescriptions are often violated.

For example, Sears's image restoration strategy went through contradictory phases. The company started by attacking the accuser, the California Department of Consumer Affairs, but later dropped these attacks and promised corrective action. In addition, Sears opened with sharp denials and then backed off, saying there had been incidents of unneeded repairs.[49] Rather than improving the company's image, contradictory strategies make the problem worse by creating a second problem of confidence and trustworthiness. Although it is wise to use multiple strategies, they should be consistent with one another.

In addition, multiple strategies should not contradict vivid and accurate media portrayals of the crisis. Such portrayals are more likely to be seen and believed by the audience than the organization's PR efforts and will make the organization look disingenuous.

## Support All Strategies with Strong Reasoning and Evidence

All image strategies must be supported with strong reasoning and evidence. A crisis means that something negative has happened and at least some audiences see the organization as responsible. The organization will begin management efforts from a credibility deficit. Crisis communication is, by definition, a "come-from-behind" game. The organization must marshal all the evidence and reasoning it can to support its positions and make this information available to the public repeatedly through the media.

How does an organization do this? It is best to think of the image restoration strategies as claims that require support if they are to be believed. As we mentioned in Chapter 10, a claim is a statement that the organization believes is true or a simple statement that concludes an argument. However, claims by themselves are rarely convincing. They require inductive and deductive reasoning, appeals to credibility, and emotion to persuade. Thus it is not enough to say, "This was an unavoidable accident" or "We had good intentions" or "The crisis is not as bad as it seems" or "Corrective action will be taken." These claims must be backed up by appropriate appeals to logic, credibility, and emotion.

## Exercise Visible Leadership from the Highest Executives

Effective image restoration requires that the highest executives handle the crisis in a visible manner. This means that owners or managers should go to the scene as soon after the crisis as possible. They should personally speak with the press on a regular basis, and they should be forthcoming at all times. Sending lower-rank employees to the scene suggests that management isn't concerned about the crisis. Exxon was criticized, for example, for sending lower-rank managers to the scene in Alaska. This failed to show the company taking control of the situation in a visible, forceful way.[50] In addition, higher-rank employees should communicate with the press, and the same members should communicate throughout the crisis.

According to Ross Campbell, a consultant in crisis management and planning, there are five key issues that corporate executives should highlight in any media interview or press conference. First, the corporate spokesperson should express concern for human life or environmental protection. This means reassuring the audience that lives are safe and there is no threat to the environment or that the company is doing everything possible to protect both.[51] As we mentioned earlier, protecting the public is the primary goal of crisis communication, and concern for the public must be expressed first in any media event. The second goal in a media interview is explaining the current situation. The company spokesperson should answer all questions and bring the media up-to-date. Third, the spokesperson should build individual and organizational credibility by expressing concern for what has happened. The fourth step is explaining the organization's interpretation of events, supported by all the evidence that is available. If the spokesperson is not sure about elements of the current situation, he or she should say so. Finally, the interview should close by emphasizing what the organization is doing about the problem. Campbell emphasizes that no spokesperson should conduct long interviews. Keep interviews or press conferences short, precise, and limited to key information. There's always time to call another interview later should more information become available.

## Identify the Target Audience and Select Strategies Accordingly

As we mentioned at the beginning of this chapter, it is the audience's perception of the crisis that counts. As you may recall from Chapter 1, effective strategic communication requires an understanding of the audience. The strategies you select depend on the specific audience's perception of two important factors: the organization's responsibility and the severity of the crisis. Placing these two perceptions together creates a two-by-two matrix that depicts four different kinds of audiences for organizational crisis communication (see Figure 13.7). Each category in the matrix represents a different kind of audience, and each audience requires different strategies for effective image restoration.

Category A represents what we refer to as an **animated audience,** who believes the crisis is severe but that the organization's responsibility is minimal. These audience members pay attention to news reports and experience emotional feelings of concern and regret for victims. However, for whatever reason, they do not believe the organization is primarily responsible for the tragedy. As such, they are concerned for the victims or for their own interests if they are affected.

Denial and shifting the blame are unnecessary for the animated audience, because they don't hold the organization responsible for the crisis. It may be useful on occasion to remind the audience that the organization is not responsible, but this is all that is necessary for the animated audience. On the other hand, strategies that reduce the offensiveness of the event (bolstering or compensation) may have a positive effect on animated audience

**FIGURE 13.7** *The Different Audiences for Crisis Communication*

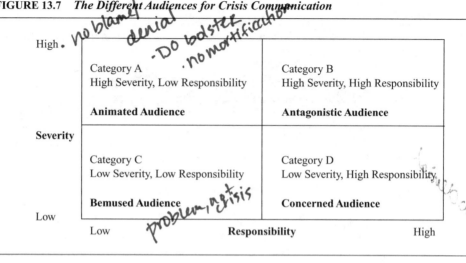

*[handwritten: no blame, denial -Do bolster, no mortification]*

| | |
|---|---|
| **Category A**<br>High Severity, Low Responsibility<br><br>**Animated Audience** | **Category B**<br>High Severity, High Responsibility<br><br>**Antagonistic Audience** |
| **Category C**<br>Low Severity, Low Responsibility<br><br>**Bemused Audience** | **Category D**<br>Low Severity, High Responsibility<br><br>**Concerned Audience** |

**Severity** — High / Low

Responsibility — Low / High

*[handwritten: problem, not crisis]*

perceptions. The organization is likely to appear humane because it is trying to solve a problem it did not create.

Early in the Tylenol crisis, Johnson & Johnson effectively employed denial strategies to demonstrate that tampering couldn't have taken place in its factories. It shifted the blame to a madman who tampered with the product after it was on the shelves. Once this was accepted, the public became an animated audience. Further attempts to deny or reduce responsibility for the crisis were unnecessary. Johnson & Johnson then focused on corrective action by pioneering the safety seal security system that is now found on many consumer products. During the second poisoning, Johnson & Johnson ended the production of capsules in favor of caplets, because caplets cannot be separated or opened. The corporation took corrective action despite the fact that few blamed them.

Mortification should be avoided for such a reactive audience. An organization that is not responsible for the crisis should not apologize. However, there is no problem in reminding the audience that everyone is sorry the event occurred and expressing concern for the victims is both expected and appropriate.

Category C represents a **bemused audience,** one that perceives both the severity of the crisis and the organization's responsibility as minimal. Bemused audiences look at the situation as a problem rather than a crisis. Despite the inconsequential nature of events, the bemused audience can become more concerned or antagonistic if the media or competitors attempt to publicize the problem. In 1991, for instance, Earth's Best Baby Food, of Middlebury, Vermont, accused Beech-Nut Nutrition Corporation of deceiving customers with its new line of organic baby food. Whereas Earth's Best used foodstuffs from farms that have not used synthetic fertilizers or pesticides for three years, Beech-Nut used the California Organic Food Act of 1990, which requires that farms be free of synthetic chemicals for only one year. Beech-Nut maintained that it was doing nothing deceitful or against the law.[52] Although committed environmentalists might be concerned about Beech-Nut's interpretation of "organic" foods, we suspect the average audience member doesn't see the incident as a crisis. If such situations merit a response, denial, shifting the blame, attacking the accuser, and minimization may be effective strategies. In addition, taking time to respond to the problem can provide an opportunity for extensive bolstering, which amounts to public relations for the organization.

Referring back to Figure 13.7, you can see that low-impact, high-responsibility perceptions create a **concerned audience,** category D. Although the audience believes that the harm to people or the environment is minimal, individuals are concerned because a weakness in the organization has been revealed that could cause a more serious crisis later. Such an incident occurred in 1987 when Beech-Nut paid a $2 million fine to the federal government for selling "apple juice" that was nothing more than sweetened water, chemicals, and preservatives. Although the incident was not a threat to public safety, the company was fully responsible.[53] In this case, although no one was physically harmed, the public's belief in the company's competence and trustworthiness was diminished. These concerns must be addressed if the company is to weather the storm.

The concerned audience is difficult to convince with denial. The audience already believes the organization is responsible, and attempts to change this perception must be well documented and based on the truth. The same is true of responsibility-reducing strategies. For the concerned audience, the combination of minimization, bolstering, and some form of corrective action is likely to be effective. Minimization reminds the audience that the severity of the event is low. Bolstering reinforces the credibility of the organization, and corrective action reassures the audience that the problem is unlikely to recur. Mortification is also effective for the concerned audience and poses small legal liability because the severity of the crisis is minimal.

Finally, the **antagonistic audience,** category B, believes the organization is mainly responsible for a very severe crisis. In such a crisis, denial strategies are unlikely to be effective unless supported by overwhelming evidence. Also, avoid knee-jerk denials that must later be recanted. Responsibility-reducing strategies can be effective for the antagonistic audience if the action is well supported and constantly repeated in the media and through advertisements. Appeals to defeasibility, accidents, and good intentions may also work to help reduce the organization's responsibility for the crisis. Because the impact of the crisis is perceived as severe, responsibility-reducing strategies should be combined with offensiveness-reducing strategies. To be effective, all strategies must be well supported with evidence and reasoning.

Finally, two of the most important image restoration strategies for the antagonistic audience are corrective action and mortification. Corrective action helps reassure the public that the situation will be restored or, at the very least, the organization will prevent its recurrence. Mortification can also be vital in these circumstances. As we discussed previously, there may be legal reasons that prevent an organization from offering mortification. However, refusing to offer an apology, even after the organization has been firmly and convincingly blamed for the crisis, makes the organization look both guilty and unrepentant. Ambiguous mortification may be required to minimize legal liability.

Our suggestions provide reasonable guidelines for selecting image restoration strategies during a crisis. However, each audience is different, including many shades and hues of opinion that can't be categorized by a single descriptive label. These differences may necessitate altering or violating any or all of the guidelines. They are meant as a starting place for analysis, not a concluding summary of what is correct in all circumstances. Crisis communication is an art rather than a science; messages must be adapted to particular circumstances.

### Recognize the Limits of Persuasive Communication

William Benoit emphasizes that the power of persuasive communication is limited.[54] When organizations are responsible for egregious errors, overlook standard procedures, or make inept decisions, there may be little that communication itself can do to help. Although damage can be mitigated, the best solution to this problem is to avoid the crisis in the first place. This is why risk management, following government regulations, and paying attention to in-house health and safety experts is a good idea. Vigilant crisis prevention is always the best form of image protection.

## Structuring Organizational Crisis Communication

Finding an appropriate structure for organizational crisis communication is a difficult task. Most communication research is devoted to content rather than structure. Most of the written image restoration advertisements that we have seen and the ones included in this chapter follow the topical structure discussed in Chapter 7. The topical pattern moves through a series of image restoration claims and associated evidence in a point-by-point manner. Although this pattern is acceptable, it may not be very persuasive. There is nothing in the content of the image restoration strategies that prevents the use of other organizing structures.

Despite the fact that almost any pattern can be used for crisis communication, we believe the N-A-R structure has special utility. The narrative section allows the speaker to review details of the crisis in a way that is beneficial to the organization. The arguments section allows the organization to deploy and support image restoration claims. Finally, the refutation allows the organization to correct inaccurate information that affected audiences, regulatory agencies, or the media might have. For example, the Demonstration Crisis Briefing in this chapter works from the point of view of Michael Gartner, then president of NBC News, who needed to justify the *Dateline NBC* story on GM pickup trucks. This briefing was never presented by NBC; rather, your authors created it as a demonstration of what NBC could have said to restore its image. We structured this briefing using the N-A-R pattern:

> Introduction
> Narrative (tells story that uses minimization, moving the blame, and apology)
> Refutation (denies and minimizes certain claims made by GM)
> Arguments (explains NBC's good intentions, apologizes, attacks the accuser)
> Conclusion

As you can see, we modified the structure slightly by reversing the refutation and arguments sections. We felt that this was necessary in order to first deny inaccurate claims before making arguments that include good intentions, apologies, and attacking the accuser. This reversal is perfectly acceptable if it makes a stronger case for the organization. It is possible that network lawyers would omit our attacks on GM (because NBC was so clearly negligent, lawyers would counsel against further antagonizing GM). However, we believe that the public for this event represented a concerned audience that would be persuaded by reminders of GM's responsibility to the public. The exercise was a useful one for us in learning how to structure and support image restoration speeches.

## BOX 13.2 • *Demonstration Crisis Briefing*

*Background*

I am playing the role of Michael Gartner, president of NBC News, and I am under pressure to explain and justify the handling of a story on General Motors's trucks by my division's *Dateline NBC* program. The program was broadcast on November 17, 1992, and dealt with the controversy surrounding the design of General Motors's C/K pickup trucks. Six million of these trucks were produced between 1973 and 1987 and have demonstrated a tendency to catch fire in high-speed side collisions because of their "sidesaddle" gas tanks—tanks that are mounted on the outside, rather than the inside, of the truck's frame rails. Between 300 and 600 people have died in these crashes, prompting more than 100 product liability lawsuits.

In a recent press conference (mid-February 1993), GM accused NBC of irresponsible journalism and presented evidence to refute almost every major point made in the *Dateline* story—especially a 57-second sequence showing a GM truck bursting into flames after a side collision. GM revealed that it hired detectives who learned that the crash sequence was rigged. GM charged that *Dateline* had said incorrectly that the truck's gas tank had ruptured when it hadn't and, more serious, had used explosive miniature rockets to make sure the truck would burst into flames—two important facts NBC's viewers were not told.

I am holding this press conference in mid-February 1993 for members of the media who will disseminate information to the general public.

**Crisis Briefing**

> *Specific Purpose:*  To explain the errors NBC News made and to work to restore the image of the news division.
> *Strategic Summary:*  Minimization and apology followed by attacking the accuser.

*Introduction*

  I. To a journalist, nothing is more important than credibility. If the audience doesn't believe in the facts of our reports, we have no reason to exist.
  II. People rely on the media to report both the actions of our government and unsafe business practices. Because of problems in a *Dateline NBC* story in November, we have damaged our credibility, and this concerns us here at NBC News.
  (Trans: Let me open by providing some background information on the events in question.)

*Narrative*

Many of you already know the story. In November of 1992, while trying to alert people to an important danger to public safety on our highways, the staff at *Dateline NBC* made a mistake. *Dateline*'s November 17 show featured 14 minutes of balanced debate capped by our mistake—57 seconds of crash footage that showed how the gas tanks of certain GM trucks could catch fire in side-on collisions.

Despite my previous comments defending the segment, the crash footage, conducted by the Indiana-based Institute for Injury Reduction, now appears to have been a mistake. Ultimately, I am troubled by two primary problems. First, our story reported that the gas tank had ruptured when it had not, and second, we did not fully disclose the nature of the crash test to *Dateline NBC* viewers.

(Trans: Let me explain these two errors through reference to claims GM has made against us.)

*Refutation*

  I. First, according to GM, our segment claimed that the gas tank ruptured when no such damage occurred, and that the fire was caused by an ill-fitting gas cap that was not original equipment. These claims are partially true.

**A.** It is true that we made an error in falsely reporting the gas tank rupture, and for this we are chagrined and embarrassed.

**B.** In addition, GM is correct in its claim that the gas cap was not original equipment (Henry, 1993).

    **1.** However, it was an after-market replacement cap similar to those found on many vehicles on the road today.

    **2.** The fire was not, as GM claimed, caused by an ill-fitting gas cap.

        **a.** Instead, the force of the collision blew the cap off the filler tube, and gas was ejected from the crushed tank.

        **b.** It was the ejected gas that caught fire and caused the explosion.

(Trans: In addition to criticizing our report on the gas tank rupture, GM has made another claim against NBC.)

**II.** GM also claims that *Dateline NBC* purposely used incendiary devices to ignite the 1977 Chevy pickup used in the crash test; again, this claim is partly true.

**A.** Although incendiary devices were wired to the truck, these would cause a fire only if fuel was spilled from the tank (Henry, 1993).

**B.** In addition, our investigations reveal that the cause of the fire in the test crash was a spark from a broken headlamp, not the incendiary devices (Henry, 1993).

    **1.** Nevertheless, it is the responsibility of reporters to explain all the relevant details behind video demonstrations like this.

    **2.** We did not tell the public about the presence of the incendiary devices, as we should have.

(Trans: Having explained the background of the events in regard to GM's claims, I would now like to make three additional points.)

*Arguments*

**I.** First, although we acknowledge serious errors in creating this story, we began the investigation with good intentions.

**A.** Our nation's founders intended the media to serve as a check on the actions of government, and in this century, this watchdog function has been extended to big business.

**B.** The safety of GM trucks is exactly the kind of issue that a popular news program such as *Dateline NBC* should address (Henry, 1993).

**C.** Any product whose design injures or kills a significant number of people is worthy of investigation.

    **1.** Estimates suggest that 600 people have died in side-impact crashes in GM trucks, and many lawsuits have been filed against GM (Multinational Monitor, 1994).

    **2.** As a result, these trucks deserve the scrutiny of news programs like ours, and such scrutiny is necessary to protect public safety.

    **3.** I firmly believe that in this matter our intentions were honorable and in keeping with journalistic traditions.

(Trans: Our good intentions aside, we did commit significant errors that I have discussed above, and we would like to apologize for these.)

**II.** As I stated above, we made two major errors in judgment, and for these we wish to apologize.

**A.** First, we were in error reporting that the tank ruptured when it did not, and we were in error when we failed to report the presence of the after-market gas cap.

    **1.** There is no excuse for these omissions in a network news organization.

    **2.** We wish to offer our sincere apology to our viewers.

*(continued)*

## DEMONSTRATION CRISIS BRIEFING    Continued

    **B.** Second, we were also negligent in failing to report the full details of the crash test, including the presence of the incendiary devices on the gas tank.

        **1.** NBC News presents 225,000 minutes of news each year.

            a. We don't wish to be defined by the errors in this 57-second crash test (Henry, 1993).

            b. We ask the public's forgiveness for these errors.

        **2.** To prevent such errors in the future, we have created the following policy:

            a. In the future, no unscientific demonstrations will be used in hard news stories.

            b. In the future, no simulations of real events will be produced (Byron, 1993).

            c. In the future, we will report all relevant details about how scientific demonstrations are produced and edited.

            d. We believe that strict adherence to these guidelines will prevent the errors we made for the GM segment and hope this will help restore the public's faith in NBC News.

(Trans: Finally, although we apologize for our errors, we regret the use of these errors to divert attention from an important public safety issue.)

**III.** It is unfortunate that our errors have allowed GM to divert attention from the central issue, that there may be a fundamental flaw in the safety of C/K pickup trucks (Diamond, 1993).

    **A.** Automotive research clearly demonstrates the safest location for fuel storage tanks.

        **1.** According to Richard Alexander, of the San Jose-based Alexander Law Firm, auto industry researchers have known for years that placing the tank between the frame rails, rather than outside the rails, and forward of the rear axle is the safest location (Alexander, 1998).

        **2.** That fuel tanks should never be put in the crush zone, for example, outside the frame rails, was well understood when the 1973 GM pickups were in their design stage (Alexander, 1998).

        **3.** According to Department of Transportation Secretary Federico Pena, "The record clearly shows that there is an increased risk associated with GM C/K series pickups and leads me to conclude at this point that the risk is unreasonable. This case involves not only serious injuries, but a significant number of fatalities, in crashes that were otherwise survivable" (Multinational Monitor, 1994, p. 7).

    **B.** Some people claim that the flaw in the C/K truck designs has led to unacceptable injuries and deaths.

        **1.** Clarence Ditlow, director of the Center for Auto Safety, estimates that more than 600 persons have been burned to death in GM pickup fire crashes, and thousands more have been injured (Multinational Monitor, 1994).

        **2.** This past week in Atlanta a jury awarded a $105.2 million judgment against GM for a Georgia teen who died when his truck was struck from the side, the fuel tanks ruptured, and the vehicle exploded in flames (Henry, 1993).

        **3.** "Joe McCray, a San Francisco-based trial lawyer who has handled 19 GM pickup truck injury and death cases, estimates that about 300 such cases have been brought against GM" (Multinational Monitor, 1994, p. 8).

    **C.** Finally, evidence exists that GM has known about the dangers of the C/K pickups since the late 1970s.

        **1.** According to Secretary Pena, "Of critical importance in this matter is the evidence that GM was aware, possibly as early as the mid-1970s, but certainly by the 1980s, that this design made these trucks more vulnerable and that fatalities from side-impact fires were occurring. . . . However, GM chose not to alter the design for 15 years" (Multinational Monitor, 1994).

2. It is possible that GM has violated provisions of the National Traffic and Motor Vehicle Safety Act.
   a. The act states that, if a company becomes aware that its vehicles are dangerous, it must notify the government and consumers, and repair the defect.
   b. If GM was aware of the problems with its "sidesaddle" tanks since 1978, it has also been in violation of the law.
   c. Did we make errors in our November 17 story? Without question.
   d. But GM has arguably made errors with its C/K pickup trucks as well.

(Trans: Having made my arguments and apologies, let me conclude this briefing.)

*Conclusion*
I. Today I have explained the circumstances behind our errors and again wish to acknowledge these errors and apologize for them.
A. For a news organization, credibility is vital.
B. We hope that by admitting our errors and creating a policy to prevent future incidents we can move toward restoring our credibility with viewers.
II. However, we don't want our errors to obscure other issues.
A. You can't put a price on safety.
B. We at NBC News will continue to pursue product safety stories in the belief that this is one of the most important services a news organization can provide.

*References*
Alexander, R. (1998, June 19). "Gas Tank Fires." The Consumer Law Page: Articles [On-line]. Available: http://consumerlawpage.com/article/gm-exploding-tank.shtml
Byron, C. (1993, February 22). "Crash and Burn." *New York*, 26, 19–20.
Diamond, E. (1993, March 15). "Auto-Destruct." *New York*, 26, 18–19.
Henry, W. A., III. (1993, February 22). "Where NBC Went Wrong." *Time*, 141, 59.
Multinational Monitor (1994). "10 Worst Corporations of 1994." [Online]. Available: www.ratical .com/corporations/mm10worst94.html

## Summary

Organizational crisis is defined as a major, unpredictable event that has potentially negative consequences. When a crisis occurs, managers are responsible for crisis management (solving the problems that precipitate the crisis) and crisis communication (interacting with various audiences to protect affected groups and restore the organization's image).

To manage crises, organizations should form a crisis team and develop a crisis management plan. The team should brainstorm a list of potential crises and narrow that list to cover the most likely scenarios. The crisis team should select an individual or a few individuals to handle media contacts during various crises.

A variety of image restoration strategies are available to organizations during a crisis. In denial strategies (simple denial and shifting the blame), the organization denies performing acts that caused the crisis. Responsibility-reducing strategies diminish or avoid responsibility for the crisis. This category includes provocation, defeasibility, accident, and good intentions. A third category of image restoration is reducing the offensiveness of the event. This includes bolstering, minimization, differentiation, transcendence, attacking the accuser, and compensation. Corrective action is a strategy that vows to restore the situation to its state before the crisis or to make changes that prevent recurrence of the crisis. Mortification is a strategy that admits responsibility for the crisis and asks forgiveness. Ambiguous mortification may be necessary when legal liability is high.

Multiple strategies can and should be used as long as they do not contradict one another. The organization should exercise visible leadership from the highest executives. It should be sure to identify the nature of the target audience and adapt image restoration strategies to them. Audiences may be animated, bemused, concerned, or antagonistic. Finally, managers should remember that prevention is the best image insurance.

## *Questions and Exercises*

1. Examine the list of possible threats in Figure 13.1. Take each of the individual threats and fit it into the typology of crises in Figure 13.2. How readily do the threats fit into the typology? Does the typology cover all the threats listed in Figure 13.1, or are more categories needed? Can you think of any threats that do not fit into the typology?

2. Examine again the advertisement from AT&T in this chapter (Figure 13.4). Label the specific image restoration strategies used in the ad. What combination of strategies are used in the ad? Discuss which strategies are effective and which are ineffective. Why do you feel this way? What do you think about the ethical implications of the advertisement? Are there some strategies that strike you as especially ethical or unethical? Why?

3. Examine the Demonstration Crisis Briefing for NBC News near the end of this chapter. Label each of the image restoration strategies throughout the speech. What, if any, strategies seem most effective? Why? What strategies seem ineffective? Why? What legal ramifications do you think the briefing might create? What ethical issues does the briefing raise? Does the briefing help restore your image of NBC News? Why or why not?

4. Our belief that ethical image strategies are also the most successful strategies may be controversial. Can you think of examples in which an individual or organization used unethical image restoration strategies that nevertheless succeeded? What made these strategies unethical? Why did these succeed rather than fail? What role, if any, did the media play in the crisis? Can you think of more ethical strategies that would have accomplished the same goal?

5. On the night of September 20, 1995, in the small town of Lava Hot Springs, Idaho, 19 hungry African lions were shot to death by county sheriffs after escaping from Ligertown, a ramshackle, squalid game farm less than a mile east of the city.

The incident attracted national news attention. The game farm, owned by a recluse couple from Oregon, had been an eyesore to Lava citizens for years, but little was done because there were no county or state laws against keeping exotic pets. When a neighboring farmer saw one of the animals loose, he killed the lion and called the sheriff. By 2 A.M. a perimeter was set up around the compound, and wandering lions that had managed to escape their pens were shot to death before they could move into the town itself. After the incident, the sheriff's department was attacked in several editorials and phone calls for killing the lions rather than tranquilizing them. The "Guest Opinion" of Sheriff Bill Lynn (Figure 13.8) is a response to the accusations made during the crisis. Read the response from Sheriff Lynn and label the image restoration strategies used in the response. What is the primary image restoration strategy employed? Was it effective? Why?

6. In the Ligertown crisis just described, Lava Hot Springs also came under attack from animal rights activists who claimed the town had not done enough to close down the Ligertown operation. They cited articles in the newspaper demonstrating that many of the 27 surviving lions and 40 wolf hybrids were suffering from disease and malnutrition. The town, the accusations said, should have done more to prevent the animals' suffering. By failing to act, the critics claimed the city of Lava Hot Springs was partly responsible for the escape and the deaths of 19 lions. The second "Guest Opinion" (Figure 13.9) is from the mayor of Lava Hot Springs, Newt Lowe, who responds to the criticism the town received. Read the response from Newt Lowe and label the image restoration strategies that he uses. How effective was the mayor's attempt to restore Lava's image? Why? Compare this opinion with the sheriff's above. Which was the most effective? What characteristics account for the relative effectiveness or ineffectiveness of each article?

# Sheriff credits officers with heroic action at Ligertown

**By Bill Lynn**
Bannock County Sheriff

Please allow me the opportunity to express some feelings on the events which have taken place at Ligertown. Much has been written in the Journal, and much more has been presented by the national and international media. It is easy to see that the stories involving animals are popular, and I think on the whole, the news of the incident has been reported very responsibly, and I thank you for your balance and understanding.

I do not want to dwell on the negative, but feel obliged to use the Journal to explain to those who may not understand why we did not "dart" the animals escaping from the compound instead of euthanizing them.

The darting of animals is a very precise talent which requires specific skills and very specific equipment. Even the Fish and Game Department usually only has one person per district who is fully trained in the practice, and the equipment is scarce. I suspect many people assumed that any rifle could be used and you would just put in a drug dart and shoot.

In actuality, the darter must use very exact amounts of numerous compounds, and each dart must be made up individually. Beyond the one dart per shot problem, the type and gender of the animal, the weight of the animal, and many other factors would determine the serums used in each darting.

Beyond the above problems, the darter must get to within about 10–20 feet of the animal to be darted, and then the animals, if they are lions, take from 15 minutes to 1 1/2 hours to knock down. During this 15-minute to 1 1/2-hour time frame, the lions would have the ability to injure or kill the darter, other officers, or wander downstream to Lava Hot Springs which was less than one mile away. While the lions begin to get lethargic, they are still very aggressive and capable of inflicting injury or death.

At the worst time, about 2 A.M., even if we had had a darter with a dart ready, little could have been done, as we had at that time as many as 14 lions on the loose. And we had them on all four sides of the compound.

The fact that we were able to put down the lions without them escaping to town or injuring anyone was a miracle in itself, which we are grateful for. While we wish that darting would have been an option, it simply was not, and the Humane Society of the United States as well as the lion experts from California both confirmed that we did all that we could do, and praised us for our response and for maintaining the public well-being.

As for the officers who responded to Ligertown that Wednesday night and Thursday morning, let me make comment. During the worst time, we had many brave men and women, from numerous agencies, putting their very lives on the line for the public well-being.

As for those who would say that it is their job to put their lives on the line, I would say you are right to a point, but no responsible set of individuals, no community, or no person can expect its law enforcement officers to have to deal with an escaping pride of lions, and consider it anything but heroic.

It is hard to express to you, the public, as well as to the officers themselves, how very proud I am of them. I have tried by private letter, but anything I say falls short.

All of you must know the bravery of those who were in harm's ways, but further you must know that few groups of people in the world could have pulled off this situation with so much class, so much calm, and so much courage.

Many officers have said before that they would follow each other across the threshold of Hell, and indeed, that is exactly what they have done for each other. I not only count them as friends. I count them among the heroes I have known.

I believe that in life we find heroes very seldom, but when we do, we find them in the most unlikely places. I found so many that night in Lava Hot Springs, and I am honored to count them as friends, but even more honored to walk by their side. Perhaps as their leader, that makes me the luckiest man in the world, and that is exactly how I feel!

**FIGURE 13.8**

*Source:* Reprinted by permission of the *Idaho State Journal*

# Recovering from Ligertown

**By Newt Lowe**
Mayor of Lava Hot Springs

As a lifelong resident of Idaho, a resident of Lava since 1950, and Mayor for the last 10 years, I am compelled to respond to the spate of unfavorable publicity that the Ligertown situation has forced upon us.

Since the Ligertown owners first arrived, it has been apparent that they did not aspire to "good citizen status." Soon after their arrival in 1986, they presented the City with a spurious claim for damages and threatened a law suit. Things went down hill from that point. It was soon apparent to anyone with a sense of smell and an eye for beauty that Ligertown was rapidly deteriorating into a blight, a cancerous growth that needed excision.

The various government agencies that control such problems were duly alerted, each in turn fulfilled their legal responsibility to a point. All agreed that a problem existed but that until something additional— i.e. some further violation occurred, their hands were tied. A classic case of "bureaucratic shuffle."

This is not an attempt to place blame on any agency. There is enough for all to share, including the City of Lava. I'm suggesting that a situation such as this should not have gotten to this deplorable state. Hindsight is wonderful, isn't it?

Ligertown has been a "Sword of Damocles" hanging over us. The Sheriff's Department and the City of Lava have been aware of the problem. It didn't come as a surprise.

Kudos to the Sheriff's Department and all others for the professional way in which the recent catastrophe was handled. The circumstances precluded the use of tranquilizers and in protection of the public they acted appropriately.

In our society, everyone is entitled to an opinion. The aftermath has brought the kooks and bleeding hearts crawling out of the woodwork. The hate mail to Lava City is astounding, but easily dismissed. The Ligertown owners now claim that their "rights" have been violated and threaten all sorts of litigation against anyone involved. They have

forgotten the judicial admonition that "You have the right to swing your fist until it collides with your neighbor's nose." Don't get downwind from the compound or your nose will be violated.

I'm sure that there is an aspiring Kunstler out there, who for the publicity or on a contigency will take the people of Bannock county to court for a multitude of alleged damages. Count on it. An oxymoron for sure.

There is no defense for the maltreatment of animals or the endangerment of the public that Ligertown has posed. The drama has almost played out. Thanks, that no innocent person has yet been injured. Now that the cancer has been defined, let's hope that it can be controlled. If it takes legislative action, so be it. Let's back that approach. Idaho could use a "Fieber" law, along with Oregon.

It is my sincere hope that the authorities do not let this matter slip "under the rug." Now is the opportune time to make Lava a better place.

Think of the money that has been and will be spent in rectifying this problem. Who pays? We do.

Whose rights have been violated?

**FIGURE 13.9**
*Source:* Reprinted by permission of the *Idaho State Journal.*

## Notes

1. Barton, L., *Crisis in Organizations: Managing and Communicating in the Heat of Chaos* (Cincinnati, OH: South-Western, 1993), 2.

2. Augustine, N. R., "Managing the Crisis You Tried to Prevent," *Harvard Business Review*, November–December 1995, 152.

3. Campbell, R., *Crisis Control: Preventing & Managing Corporate Crises* (Maryborough, Australia: Prentice Hall Australia, 1999).

4. Coombs, W. T., *Ongoing Crisis Communication: Planning, Managing, and Responding* (Thousand Oaks, CA: Sage, 2007).

5. Barton.

6. Clare, D. R., "The Tylenol Story: From Crisis to Comeback," *Cross Currents* 12 (1983): 38–43.

7. Benoit, W. L., and J. J. Lindsey, "Argument Strategies: Antidote to Tylenol's Poisoned Image,"

*Journal of the American Forensic Association* 23 (1987): 136–146.

8. "Company Turnarounds: Johnson and Johnson Reincarnates a Brand," *Sales & Marketing Management*, 16 January 1984, 63.

9. "Oil Slick Spreads Toward Coast: FBI Begins Probe," *Los Angeles Times*, 2 April 1989, Part I, 1, 24.

10. Benoit, W. L., *Accounts, Excuses, and Apologies: A Theory of Image Restoration* (Albany: State University of New York Press, 1995).

11. Tyler, L., "Ecological Disaster and Rhetorical Response: Exxon's Communications in the Wake of the Valdez Spill," *Journal of Business and Technical Communication* 6 (1992): 149–171.

12. Benoit, *Accounts, Excuses, and Apologies.*

13. Benoit, W. L., and S. L. Brinson, "AT&T: 'Apologies Are Not Enough,' " *Communication Quarterly* 42 (1994): 75–88.

14. Ibid.

15. Ibid.

16. Hagerty, J. R., and A. Barrett, "France, Belgium Reject Pleas to Lift Ban," *Wall Street Journal*, 18 June 1999, B1.

17. McKay, B., and N. Deogun, "After Short, Stormy Tenure, Coke's Ivester to Retire," *Wall Street Journal*, 7 December 1999, B1.

18. "Evidence of Irresponsibility Mounts," *USA Today*, 5 June 2000 (online: http://www.usatoday.com/news/comment/nceditf.htm).

19. Carey, S., "Alaska Air Aims to Restore Credibility After Plane Crash," *Wall Street Journal*, 28 April 2000, B4.

20. Kiley, D., "Nasser Calls Spring Goal 'Unacceptable,'" *USA Today*, 17 August 2000 (online: http://www.usatoday.com/money/consumer/autos/mauto764.htm).

21. Healey, J. R., "Death Toll Linked to Firestone Climbs to 174," *USA Today*, 7 February 2001 (online: http://www.usatoday.com/news/nation/2001-02-06-tire.htm).

22. Bailey, J., "JetBlue's C.E.O. is 'Mortified' After Flyers Are Stranded," *New York Times*, 19 February 2007 (online: http://www.nytimes.com/2007/02/19/business/19jetblue.html?ex=1329541200&en=a9dbe269ede6bf58&ei=5088&partner=rssnyt&emc=rss).

23. "JetBlue Flyers Stranded on Plane for 8 Hours," *CNNMoney.com*, 15 February 2007 (online: http://money.cnn.com/2007/02/15/news/companies/jetblue/index.htm).

24. Barton.

25. Barton.

26. Barton, 129.

27. Coomb.

28. Gellene, D., "New State Probe of Sears Could Lead to Suit," *Los Angeles Times*, 12 June 1992, D4.

29. "Breast-Implant Maker Releasing Data to Back Safety Claim," *New York Times*, 18 July 1991, A16.

30. Benoit and Lindsey.

31. Benoit, "Sears' Repair of Its Auto Service Image: Image Restoration Discourse in the Corporate Sector," *Communication Studies* 46 (1995): 89–105.

32. Benoit, *Accounts, Excuses, and Apologies.*

33. Kiley, D., and Healey, J. R., "Ford CEO Handles Tire Recall," *USA Today*, 17 August 2000 (online: http://www.usatoday.com/money/consumer/autos/mauto765.htm).

34. Benoit, *Accounts, Excuses, and Apologies.*

35. Benoit, "Sears' Repair of Its Auto Service Image."

36. Benoit, *Accounts, Excuses, and Apologies.*

37. Benoit, "Sears' Repair of Its Auto Service Image."

38. King, Martin Luther, Jr., *Why We Can't Wait* (New York: Harper & Row, 1963), 77–100.

39. Volvo advertisement, *USA Today*, 6 November 1990, 2B.

40. Brinson, S. L., and W. L. Benoit, "Dow Corning's Image Repair Strategies in the Breast Implant Crisis," *Communication Quarterly* 44 (1996): 29–41.

41. Benoit, *Accounts, Excuses, and Apologies.*

42. Tyler, L., "Liability Means Never Being Able to Say You're Sorry: Corporate Guilt, Legal Constraints, and Defensiveness in Corporate Communication," *Management Communication Quarterly* 11 (1997): 51–73.

43. Ibid, 61.

44. Coombs.

45. Rothchild, J., "How to Say You're Sorry," *Time*, 20 June 1994, 51.

46. Coombs.

47. Ibid.

48. Benoit and Brinson.

49. Benoit, "Sears' Repair of Its Auto Service Image."

50. Tyler, "Ecological Disaster and Rhetorical Response."

51. Campbell.

52. Miller, C., "Competitor Rips Beech-Nut Organic Line," *Marketing News*, 10 June 1991, 1, 12.

53. Henriques, D. B., "10% of Fruit Juice Sold in U.S. Is Not All Juice, Regulators Say," *New York Times*, 31 October 1993, A1, A24.

54. Benoit, *Accounts, Excuses, and Apologies.*

# Index

Page numbers followed by italicized *f* and *t* refer to figures and tables respectively.

# *Photo Credits*